Cremation in Modern Scotland

Cremation in Modern Scotland

History, Architecture and the Law

Peter C. Jupp,
Douglas J. Davies,
Hilary J. Grainger,
Gordon D. Raeburn and
Stephen R. G. White

published in association with
The Cremation Society of Great Britain

First published in Great Britain in 2017 by
John Donald, an imprint of Birlinn Ltd

West Newington House
10 Newington Road
Edinburgh
EH9 1QS

www.birlinn.co.uk

ISBN: 978 1 906566 79 1

Copyright © Peter C. Jupp, Douglas J. Davies, Hilary J. Grainger,
Gordon D. Raeburn and Stephen R. G. White 2017

The right of Peter C. Jupp, Douglas J. Davies, Hilary J. Grainger,
Gordon D. Raeburn and Stephen R. G. White to be identified
as the authors of this work has been asserted by them in accordance
with the Copyright, Designs and Patents Act, 1988

All rights reserved. No part of this publication may
be reproduced, stored, or transmitted in any form, or
by any means, electronic, mechanical or photocopying,
recording or otherwise, without the express written
permission of the publisher.

The publishers gratefully acknowledge the support of
The Cremation Society of Great Britain,
Edinburgh Crematorium Ltd and
The Scottish Cremation Society
towards the publication of this book.

The law is as stated on 1 September 2016. Most of the Burial and
Cremation (Scotland) Act (p. 243) has yet to be brought into force.

British Library Cataloguing-in-Publication Data
A catalogue record for this book is available on request from the British Library.

Typeset by Initial Typesetting Services, Edinburgh
Printed and bound in Britain by T. J. International, Padstow, Cornwall

Contents

List of Illustrations	vii
Notes on Contributing Authors	xi
Foreword by Sir Kenneth Calman, KCB MD FRSE	xiii
Acknowledgements	xv
List of Acronyms	xvii
Map of Scotland's Crematoria	xix

	Introduction	1
1	History, Law, Architecture	9
2	Issues in Burial Arrangements in Scotland, 1830–1886	33
3	The Scottish Burial Reform and Cremation Society and Maryhill Crematorium, 1888–1895	59
4	Cremation in Scotland: The Early Years, 1895–1918	81
5	Cremation in the Depression: Failure and Success, 1918–1939	109
6	The Second World War and the Aberdeen Scandal, 1939–1952	139
7	Glasgow and the West, 1945–1967: The National Context of Post-war Planning	161
8	Edinburgh and the East, 1945–1967	187
9	Cremation: Social and Cultural Change, 1967–2016	214
10	Scotland's Setting of Cremation	247

Bibliography	273
Index of Names	313
General Index	317

List of Illustrations

Dates in brackets indicate date of crematoria opening.

Black and white plates

1. 'A Scheme of Cremation Suited to the Requirements of Glasgow', upper level
2. 'A Scheme of Cremation Suited to the Requirements of Glasgow', ground floor plan
3. Woking Crematorium (1889)
4. Maryhill Crematorium, Glasgow (1895)
5. Maryhill Crematorium, Glasgow (1895–1963)
6. Maryhill Crematorium, Glasgow (1895)
7. Maryhill Crematorium, Glasgow (1985)
8. Unpublished drawing for a proposed Edinburgh crematorium (1913)
9. The opening of Warriston Crematorium, Edinburgh, 3 October 1929
10. Golders Green Crematorium, London (1902)
11. Warriston Crematorium, Edinburgh (1929), exterior
12. Warriston Crematorium, Edinburgh (1929), interior
13. Warriston Crematorium, Edinburgh (1929), interior
14. Warriston Crematorium, Edinburgh (1929), cloisters 1958
15. Warriston Crematorium, Edinburgh (1929), later entrance porch
16. Dundee Crematorium, Angus (1936), exterior
17. Dundee Crematorium, Angus (1936), interior
18. Aberdeen, Kaimhill Crematorium, Aberdeenshire (1938)
19. Aberdeen, Kaimhill Crematorium, Aberdeenshire (1938)
20. Paisley Woodside Crematorium, Renfrewshire (1938)
21. Paisley Woodside Crematorium, Renfrewshire (1938)
22. Seafield Crematorium, Leith, Edinburgh (1939)

Colour plates 1

1. Daldowie Crematorium, Glasgow (1955)
2. Site plan of Daldowie Crematorium, Glasgow (1955)
3. Daldowie Crematorium, Glasgow (1955), pergola
4. Daldowie Crematorium, Glasgow (1955), entrance to the East Chapel
5. Daldowie Crematorium, Glasgow (1955), interior of the East Chapel
6. Daldowie Crematorium, Glasgow (1955), interior of the Chapel of Remembrance
7. Craigton Crematorium, Glasgow (1957)
8. Greenock Crematorium, Inverclyde (1959)
9. Greenock Crematorium, Inverclyde (1959), entrance hall
10. Greenock Crematorium, Inverclyde (1959), chapel interior
11. Greenock Crematorium, Inverclyde (1959), side window of chapel
12. Cardross Crematorium, Argyll and Bute (1960)
13. Cardross Crematorium, Argyll and Bute (1960)
14. View across the Clyde and surrounding Argyll hills from Cardross Crematorium
15. *All Embracing Truth*, sculpture by Hew Lorimer, Cardross Crematorium, Argyll and Bute
16. The Linn Crematorium, Glasgow (1962)
17. Blackley Crematorium, Manchester (1957)
18. The Linn Crematorium, Glasgow (1962)
19. The Linn Crematorium, Glasgow (1962)
20. The Linn Crematorium, Glasgow (1962), interior of St Mungo Chapel
21. The Linn Crematorium, Glasgow (1962), interior of the Room of Remembrance
22. Ayr Crematorium, South Ayrshire (1966), exterior
23. Ayr Crematorium, South Ayrshire (1966), interior
24. Ayr Crematorium, South Ayrshire (1966), chapel windows
25. Dalnottar Crematorium, Clydebank, West Dunbartonshire (1967)
26. Dalnottar Crematorium, Clydebank, West Dunbartonshire (1967)
27. Dalnottar Crematorium, Clydebank, West Dunbartonshire (1967), interior of chapel
28. Kirkcaldy Crematorium, Fife (1959)
29. Prize winning entry for the Kirkcaldy Crematorium Competition held in 1953–54

List of Illustrations

30 Oldham Crematorium, Greater Manchester (1953), chapel interior
31 Kirkcaldy Crematorium, Fife (1959), chapel interior
32 Kirkcaldy Crematorium, Fife (1959), chapel interior
33 Falkirk Crematorium, Falkirk (1962)
34 Falkirk Crematorium, Falkirk (1962)
35 Falkirk Crematorium, Falkirk (1962), interior showing side windows
36 Falkirk Crematorium, Falkirk (1962), chapel windows
37 Perth Crematorium, Perth & Kinross (1962)
38 Perth Crematorium, Perth & Kinross (1962), interior of chapel
39 Perth Crematorium, Perth & Kinross (1962), Hall of Remembrance, stained glass window

Colour plates 2

40 Mortonhall Crematorium, Edinburgh (1967), entrance to the main chapel
41 Mortonhall Crematorium, Edinburgh (1967), Chapel of Remembrance
42 Mortonhall Crematorium, Edinburgh (1967), stained glass in the main chapel
43 Mortonhall Crematorium, Edinburgh (1967), Calvary Cross view toward the crematorium
44 Dunfermline Crematorium, Fife (1973)
45 Dunfermline Crematorium, Fife (1973), interior of chapel
46 Dunfermline Crematorium, Fife (1973), chapel windows
47 Hazelhead Crematorium, Aberdeen (1975)
48 Hazelhead Crematorium, Aberdeen, extension dating from 2010
49 Hazelhead Crematorium, Aberdeen (1975)
50 Hazelhead Crematorium, Aberdeen (1975), entrance canopy
51 Hazelhead Crematorium, Aberdeen, extension 2010
52 Parkgrove Crematorium, Friockheim (1993)
53 Parkgrove Crematorium, Friockheim (1993), view from the porte-cochère
54 Parkgrove Crematorium, Friockheim (1993), chapel interior
55 Parkgrove Crematorium, Friockheim (1993), porte-cochère
56 Inverness Crematorium (1995)
57 Inverness Crematorium (1995), Tower Chapel
58 Holmfirth Bridge Crematorium, Irvine, North Ayrshire (1997)

59 Holmfirth Bridge Crematorium, Irvine, North Ayrshire (1997)
60 Holmfirth Bridge Crematorium, Irvine, North Ayrshire (1997)
61 Holmfirth Bridge Crematorium, Irvine, North Ayrshire (1997), chapel interior
62 Holytown Crematorium, North Lanarkshire (2004)
63 Holytown Crematorium, North Lanarkshire (2004)
64 Holytown Crematorium, North Lanarkshire (2004)
65 Roucan Loch Crematorium, Dumfries (2005)
66 Roucan Loch Crematorium, Dumfries (2005)
67 South Lanarkshire Crematorium, Blantyre (2006)
68 South Lanarkshire Crematorium, Blantyre (2006)
69 West Lothian Crematorium, Livingston (2010)
70 West Lothian Crematorium, Livingston (2010)
71 West Lothian Crematorium, Livingston (2010)
72 West Lothian Crematorium, Livingston (2010)
73 Borders Crematorium, Melrose (2011)
74 Borders Crematorium, Melrose (2011), entrance
75 Borders Crematorium, Melrose (2011), porte-cochère
76 Borders Crematorium, Melrose (2011), Wairds Cemetery in the foreground
77 Houndwood Crematorium, Scottish Borders (2015)

Graphs

1 Annual numbers of cremations at each of Scotland's first six crematoria, 1918–39
2 Annual numbers of cremations at each of Scotland's first seven crematoria, 1939–56
3 Growth in cremation numbers for the nine sites in south-west Scotland, 1955–77
4 Growth of cremation in south-west Scotland, 1992–2015

Notes on Contributing Authors

Douglas Davies is Professor in the Study of Religion, Department of Theology and Religion at Durham University and Director of the University's Centre for Death and Life Studies. He is an Oxford D Litt and has an Honorary Doctorate in Theology from Uppsala University. His many publications include *Mors Britannica* (2015), *Natural Burial* (with Hannah Rumble, 2012), *Emotion, Identity and Religion* (2011), *A Theology of Death* (2007) and *The Encyclopedia of Cremation* (with Lewis H. Mates, 2005).

Hilary J. Grainger is Dean and Professor of Architectural History at University of the Arts London. She is the leading authority on both the late Victorian architect Sir Ernest George and the architecture of British crematoria. With Douglas Davies she was Principal Co-Investigator in the Leverhulme Trust-funded team based at Durham University, researching the history of cremation in modern Scotland. She is a Council member of the Cremation Society of Great Britain and chair of the Victorian Society.

Peter C. Jupp is an Honorary Fellow in the School of Divinity, Edinburgh University, and a former Chair of the Cremation Society of Great Britain. Co-founder of the journal *Mortality* and of the International Conference on Death, Dying and Disposal, his edited books include *Death in England: an Illustrated History* (with Clare Gittings, 1999) and *Death Our Future* (2008). He published *From Dust to Ashes: Cremation and the British Way of Death* in 2006.

Gordon Raeburn completed his PhD at the University of Durham UK in 2013. His thesis, 'The Long Reformation of the Dead in Scotland', investigated the changing nature of Scottish burial practices between 1542 and 1856. He is a historian of early modern Scotland and currently a postdoctoral fellow with the Australian Research Council Centre of Excellence for the History of Emotions at the University of Melbourne and is working on emotional responses to Early Modern Scottish disasters and how these emotional responses shaped personal, emotional and national identities.

Stephen White has held teaching and research positions in departments of law, social science, history and theology at Cardiff, Durham, Oxford and Southampton universities, the Australian National University, the Victoria University of Wellington and the London School of Economics. He has been a member of the Council of the Cremation Society since 1997 and is the author of *What Queen Victoria Saw: Roderick Maclean and the Trial of Lunatics Act 1883* (2000).

Foreword

Cremation might seem to be a slightly negative subject, and not something to write about and discuss. Yet this book opens up the issue to uncover a wide range of ways in which cremation is important. It is also about Scotland. John Buchan in his book *The Kirk in Scotland* (Dunbar: Labarum Publication, 1985) makes a relevant point: 'Without some understanding of the Church there can be no true understanding of Scottish history or the nature of the Scottish people.'

The same might be said about cremation. This book records in some detail the introduction of cremation into Scotland and the social and religious implications it brought with it. The names associated with its introduction in the nineteenth and early twentieth centuries make a formidable line-up. They include not only the church leaders from many denominations, but also legal luminaries and medical experts. Key legal and ethical topics such as the disposal of body parts, certification of death, public health consequences of outbreaks of infectious disease on the burial process, cremation of children and assisted dying are all examined, and all have been controversial.

The growing significance of crematoria in Scottish culture, their architectural language and the exploitation of the power of their landscape setting reflect changing attitudes to death and frame the emotional experience of mourners. Such architectural dimensions highlight the range of topics raised in this book. In addition, there is a reference to a new, more environmentally friendly process which might be the next way forward, beyond cremation: resomation, to whose development Scotland has been the United Kingdom's main contributor.

I read this book with great interest, as it raised so many current debates in Scottish society and beyond. It tells a series of complex stories and interactions about what to do with a body or parts of a body at the time of death, and about the introduction of cremation into a land with particular beliefs on the place of the body after death. These are stories worth telling. They also set a base for further discussion and debate especially at a time when the Scottish Parliament has just passed an Act which completely revamps the statutory law of burial and cremation. For those wishing to know the developments that shaped parts of the Act relating to cremation the publication of this book could not be more timely.

Sir Kenneth Calman, KCB MD FRSE
Chancellor of Glasgow University
Formerly Vice-Chancellor and Warden of Durham University

Acknowledgements

Without considerable financial support from others we could not have written this book. Our first thanks must, therefore, go to those who provided it. The Golders Green Foundation funded preliminary exploratory research in 2007–8, which led to an application to the Leverhulme Trust. The Trust made a very generous grant to cover the expenses of research from 2008 to 2011, upon which this book is based. It also provided the salaries of Peter Jupp and Stephen White, as Research Fellows at the Department of Theology and Religion at the University of Durham, and awarded Gordon Raeburn a Postgraduate Studentship, to write their parts of the text. The University of Durham and the London College of Fashion, University of the Arts London, permitted Douglas Davies and Hilary Grainger, respectively, to participate as Principal Investigators in the project as part of their normal academic duties. We submitted our report to the Leverhulme Trust in December 2011.

The Cremation Society of Great Britain (CSGB), the Scottish Cremation Society and Edinburgh Crematorium Ltd have made generous contributions to the cost of publication of the book.

To all these benefactors we give our heartfelt thanks.

We have benefited from the support and assistance of members of the Council of the CSGB and of the past and current Secretaries of the Society, Roger N. Arber and Miriam L. Deacon. The managers and staff of many cemeteries and crematoria in Scotland, and participants in the annual Cremation and Burial Communication and Education (CBCE) conferences have shared their professional insights with us. We thank the individuals in Scotland who gave us interviews. Hilary Grainger has photographed the sites and buildings of all 28 Scottish crematoria and thanks all the managers and staff for their unfailing hospitality and expertise.

Many Libraries and Archives have opened their catalogues for us and provided ready and frequent personal help. These include, first, the archives of the CSGB (formerly housed at the Society's office in Maidstone but now part of Durham University Library's Special Collections), the archives of Edinburgh Crematorium Ltd at Seafield Crematorium, Leith; and the archives of the Scottish Cremation Society in Glasgow where we especially thank clerical administrator Janet Hill. We thank the Cremation Society of Great Britain and the Federation of Burial and Cremation Authorities for the statistical information in the four diagrams.

In Aberdeen we have had recourse to the Central and University Libraries, and the City Archives at the Town House and Old Aberdeen House; in Edinburgh to the University and Central Libraries, the General Register Office, the National Records (previously Archives) of Scotland, the National Library of Scotland, and the libraries of New College, and the Royal College of Physicians of Scotland; in Glasgow to the University and Mitchell Libraries; and in Inverness to the City Library and the Highland Archive Centre.

In London we have used several of the libraries of London University, namely those of the Institute of Advanced Legal Studies, the Institute of Historical Research, King's College, the London School of Economics, the Senate House, and University College. Also in London we have worked in the British Library and Dr Williams' Library, The National Archives, and the libraries of the British Medical Association; the Institute of Cemetery and Crematorium Management; the Reform Club; the Royal College of Surgeons, Royal Institute of British Architects and the Wellcome Institute.

During the years that our research was based at Durham we were fortunate to have the advice of four consultants: Professors David Brown (St Andrew's University), Stewart Jay Brown (Edinburgh University) and Steve Bruce (Aberdeen University), and Dr Ronnie Scott of Glasgow. We are grateful for the advice of Ms Rachel K. Clark of the University's Legal Department.

We thank Hilary Grainger for generously providing the selection of her own photographs from her archive of crematoria. We thank Stephen White for accepting responsibility for the painstaking task of organising the bibliography.

Peter Jupp thanks Professor Stewart Jay Brown, Dr Susan Buckham, Dr Glenys Caswell, Dr Paul Laxton, Professor Elaine McFarland, Dr Brian Parsons, Dr Ronnie Scott and Dr Michael Smith for their support and advice. He has been particularly helped by two friends: Katherine Riley, who has provided secretarial assistance, and Katherine Walker Brodie, whose professional editorial experience has helped him edit much raw material into a coherent narrative. Their patience and labours have been vital. Stephen White thanks Robert Shiels for advice about Scottish law.

Several individuals have offered hospitality along the way: Peter Jupp thanks John and Dr Christine Steele (Durham), Ed Jupp and Samantha Garnett, Professor David and Judge Tanya Parker (Edinburgh), the Revd Dr Peter and Jane Howson (Inverness) and the Warden of Launde Abbey. Stephen White thanks Gail Joughin and Ian Smith (Edinburgh). Hilary Grainger thanks Professor Frances Corner OBE, Head of London College of Fashion, Pro-Vice Chancellor of University of the Arts London for her continued support, Susan De La Rosa for her invaluable expertise in preparing the images for publication, Dr Alexandra C. Viner, Simon Green and library staff at Historical Environment Scotland (formerly RCAHMS), staff at the Fife County Archives, Ruth Jardine, and Geoff Brandwood.

The rest of us thank Peter Jupp for his efforts in doing most of the administrative work in coordinating our researches and in finding a publisher for this book and the funds to support its publication. We all have to thank Dr Elizabeth Cumming for introducing Peter to Birlinn where academic managing editor Mairi Sutherland has been a model of patience and courteous efficiency; Nicola Wood has been an exemplary copy-editor. Birlinn has proved a thorough and friendly publisher.

From the outset this project was intended to be inter-disciplinary and each of us is extremely grateful to the others for what we have learned from our hugely enjoyable collaboration.

Finally, the home front: completion of this book would have been far more difficult but for the support and indulgence of friends and family, especially of wives and husbands throughout its nine years gestation. For their encouragement, excitement at our progress, forbearance, and rousing cheer on completion, Hilary thanks Colin Viner; Peter, Elisabeth Jupp; Gordon, Emily Ball; and Stephen, Jan White.

List of Acronyms

Acronyms for legislation are in the Bibliography alongside the legislation to which they refer.

ACC	Aberdeen City Council
BATNEEC	Best Available Techniques not Entailing Excessive Costs
BMA	British Medical Association
CAMEO	Crematoria Abatement of Mercury Emissions Organisation
CCGB	Cremation Council of Great Britain
CS	Cremation Society of England (after 1930 of Great Britain)
CSA	Cremation Society Archives, University of Durham
DHS	Department of Health for Scotland
ECL	Edinburgh Crematorium Ltd
ECS	Edinburgh Cremation Society
FBCA	Federation of British Cremation Authorities (after 2006 Federation of Burial and Cremation Authorities)
FPCS	Free Presbyterian Church of Scotland
GRO	General Registry Office
HAC	Cabinet Home Affairs Committee
HO	Home Office
IBCA	Institute of Burial and Cremation Administration (until 2003)
ICCM	Institute of Cemetery and Crematorium Management (after 2003)
LGB	Local Government Board
LGBS	Local Government Board for Scotland
MH	Ministry of Health
MHLG	Ministry of Housing and Local Government
MOH	Medical Officer of Health
MOW	Ministry of Works

NACCS	National Association of Cemetery and Crematorium Superintendents
NAFD	National Association of Funeral Directors
NHS	National Health Service
PA	Parliamentary Archives
PCA	Proprietary Crematoria Association
RCAHMS	Royal Commission on the Ancient and Historical Monuments of Scotland (after 2015 Historic Environment Scotland)
SBC	Scottish Borders Council
SBH	Scottish Board of Health
SBRCS	Scottish Burial Reform and Cremation Society
SHD	Scottish Home Department
SO	Scottish Office
TNA	The National Archives, Kew
TPO	Town Planning Officer

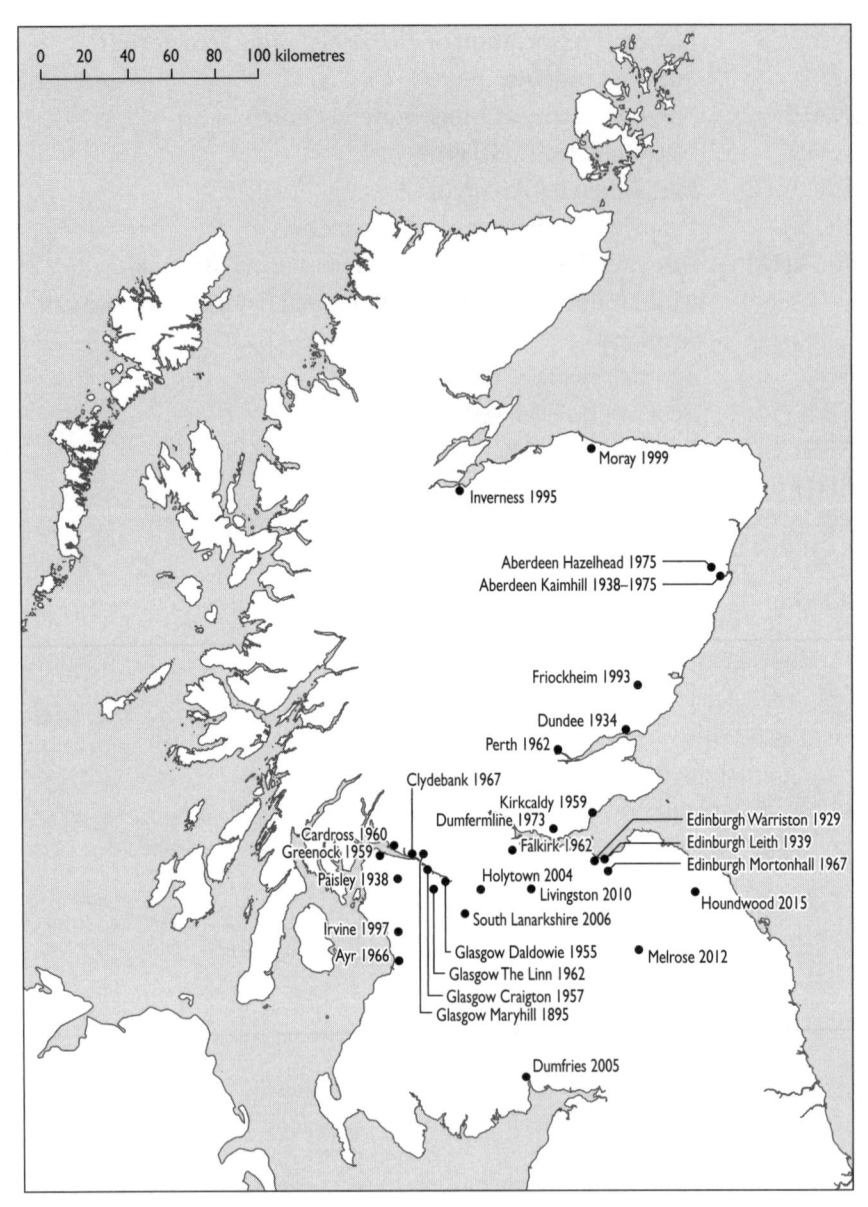

Scotland's crematoria, 1895–2016, showing location and dates of opening.

Introduction:
Cremation in Modern Scotland

This book is about cremation in Scotland. How did it come about? Who argued for it and against it? What about the scandals over coffins and cremated remains that hampered the efforts of socially-minded Scots to establish this new method of dealing with the dead? And what about the choice of architects who might create appropriate buildings and design landscapes able to help bereaved people as they mourned their dead? Was there any sense of competition between cities, and what about the religious beliefs that, at various points, held many back from any whole-hearted support of this way of dealing with dead bodies? Legal issues surrounding cremation as well as burial have been deeply significant, especially bearing in mind Scotland's own legal system. How might its deliberations align or not with what had been happening in England and Wales and their late nineteenth- and early twentieth-century progress in this area? In terms of history, there was Scotland's very distinctive Protestant Reformation, as well as its cultural creativity in the country's philosophical and ethical enlightenment. As the twentieth century progressed new kinds of issues of secular life-styles also emerged that would impact on funeral rites and, inevitably, on cremation.

In its own way, then, cremation posed distinctive questions concerning life, death and memory that raised religious, philosophical, legal, ethical and secular issues and opened new windows onto Scottish life. These were challenges that prompted the authors of this volume to get together as a group of people with diverse academic/intellectual interests but with a shared focus on cremation as a form of funeral that opens up deep questions about a people's way of life, attitude to the past, present and future, and even to a sense of destiny.

Scotland emerged as the central topic of this study when the rising tide of the later 1980s witnessed the emergence of what came to be called 'death studies', a field of interest that had cremation deeply embedded within it. Much of this was signalled in the 2005 publication of *The Encyclopedia of Cremation*, itself a task of some seven years' work (Davies and Mates 2005). The absence of Scotland even from its quite full Index prompted Peter Jupp to ask Douglas Davies, who had edited that *Encyclopedia* – which benefited from much support of the Cremation Society of Great Britain and enormous assistance from modern historian Dr Lewis Mates – why Scotland was absent from it. At the same time Jupp was completing his history of cremation in England, to be entitled 'From Dust to Ashes: cremation and the English way of death'. His publishers Macmillan directed a change in the sub-title, to read 'Cremation and the British way of death', the book appearing in 2006. Given this new title, the omission of Scotland, Wales and Northern Ireland from the book's contents prompted both surprise – in cemetery historian James Stevens Curl's subsequent review in the journal *Mortality* – and the research question enquiry about Scotland's real role in the shift from burial to cremation in Britain. Jupp began his own research on Scottish data, supported by a starter grant from the Golders Green Foundation Trust.

After discussion Davies and Jupp engaged with architectural historian Hilary Grainger and academic lawyer Stephen White, resulting in Davies, as director of Durham University's Centre of Death and Life Studies, itself set within Durham's well-known Department of Theology and Religion, making a successful application to The Leverhulme Trust. The ensuing Scottish Cremation Research Project forged by these four scholars was enhanced by a fifth when Gordon Raeburn was appointed to a post-graduate studentship. In due course Raeburn successfully completed his doctorate at Durham University on post-Reformation funeral rites in Scotland, 'The Long Reformation of the Dead in Scotland'. This charted hitherto virtually unexplored territory in the Scottish history of death between 1542 and 1856.

This five-strong team, now drawing from their disciplinary bases in social, Church and architectural histories, anthropology, law, sociology and theology, set about mapping factors and forces driving developments in funerary life in modern Scotland, with the main focus on the emergence and significance of modern cremation. The team already possessed a wide international frame of funerary reference and with particularly extensive knowledge of cremation in England and Wales. (Our individual publications have been listed in Authors' Information.) Together, we have sought a workable interdisciplinarity in planning, executing and writing up our findings on selected crucial dimensions of Scottish life relating to burial and cremation. While the majority of the ensuing chapters include interwoven contributions from two or more team members, they have also involved constant team discussion from the outset.

The Task

Funeral rites frequently serve as windows upon the culture of their societies. The core values and beliefs that inform and drive a people's social world become visible through their behaviours and beliefs surrounding dying, death, the treatment of the corpse and the management of the identity of its previous 'self'. Moreover, the strong emotions bonding the relationships that sustain our lives as social animals assume a distinctive intensity when illness and dying make their presence felt, when funerals are organised to cope with the dead, and when both formal and intimately private memories of and hopes for our dead arise.

Carrier-institutions

While funerals often carry cultural ideas in ways that allow a local community to unite around bereaved members, they also have the capacity to express shifts in people's feelings and outlooks on life. Funeral rites are what we might call 'carrier-institutions' for, despite often involving simple ways of preparing and disposing of the corpse, they are open to a great range of significance and interpretation. This 'carrier' capacity means that funerary rites are highly significant during periods of personal, communal or national change, especially when people in positions of authority can use them as means of expressing their own version of 'reality' (Davies 2015). We shall return to these issues more fully as this book proceeds but, even at this stage, it is worth noting how the ordinary carrier-capacity of a funeral involves social status and religious or ideological identity, however high or lowly – 'Rattle his bones over the stones: he's only a pauper whom nobody owns.' By contrast, even John Knox broke his own 'silent funeral' rule when he preached in Edinburgh at the funeral of Regent Moray in the crisis of 1571. In further contrast the cultural credit vested in heroic deaths takes on a different social force when the form of the rite is changed, as from cremation to burial in early Christianity or from burial to cremation, as in the similarly grand cultural shifts of nineteenth- and twentieth-century Europe.

Ritual-symbolic capacities

So, the power of funerary rites as ritual-symbolic processes lies not only in their capacity to carry a particular significance but also as a relatively ready means by which to alter that significance. Moreover, as part of their complexity, funerary rites frequently possess a multi-vocality that may not only give predominance to one set of ideas but may also allow individuals or groups to take from a single rite a variety of meanings (V. Turner 1969). So, for example, Freemasonry in nineteenth-century Europe sought to undermine the authority of the Catholic Church by proposing the secularisation of certain institutions, including funerals. So much so that in Italy, for example, Freemasons constructed 'cremation temples' for the disposing of the dead, not that these gained extensive popular support from a largely Catholic population (Novarino 2005). It has intrigued the team that when the pioneering Scottish Burial Reform and Cremation Society was formed in 1888, this was only two years after the Vatican's ban on cremation (Newton 2005; Salice 2005). Thus Catholics were excluded until 1964, when the Roman Catholic attitude to cremation changed, from Scotland's first major impetus for funeral reform.

Traditional Cremation

Cremation had, of course, been long performed in the Indian subcontinent where the practice easily expressed the dissolution of the corpse and the freeing of its life-force, now subject to the consequences of karma in its transmigrating destiny (Parry 1994; Firth 1997). Modern cremation can also serve that transformation and rerouting of post-mortem identities as it does, for example, for millions of Europeans of Indian ancestry. So too for those Christians in the later nineteenth century whose preference emphasised the on-going existence of the soul after the demise of the body rather than on its future transformational resurrection. Cremation is distinctive in its symbolic capacity to express both the ongoing flight of the soul and the utter demise of the self as its body decays: it can satisfy religious believer and unbeliever alike. Inhumation, by contrast, more easily symbolises the 'burial' and resurrection of Jesus and, accordingly, the potential resurrection of the believer (Davies 1990). Others, who see this human existence as the sole arena of existence, can also find the practical symbolism of the burning of the corpse a fitting expression of their belief in the cessation of active identity, with death as the end of life. For those, cremated remains can amply accommodate their memory of the dead. In quite different cultural deployments of cremation, the twentieth-century world has witnessed cremation as a deliberate replacement for burial in, for example, in the Communist regime of the former USSR with its desire to replace Orthodox Christianity's foundational preference for burial (Merridale 1999). Something similar occurred in the People's Republic of China with its governmental directives to replace traditional patterns of burial and commemoration with cremation (Jinlong et al. 2005: 121–22). While we will return to similar themes of the expression of diverse and even contradictory ideas through the medium of cremation in chapter ten, these briefest of references hint at cremation as opening its own perspective upon Scotland. In this, of course, cremation does not stand alone but is ranged alongside the historical and contemporary influence of burial (M. Smith 2014).

Ideas, values, and beliefs

Here the nature of ritual-symbolism becomes significant not only in terms of the affinity between the emotion-pervaded outlook of a group and its funerary rites, but also in the link between theological doctrines and the preferred emotions aligned with liturgical practice. Given that participation in grave-side rites by Church of Scotland clergy was not restored until 1897, on the understanding that people, and the minister as their 'voice', could do nothing for the dead, there is an assumption that such Protestant burial wished to disassociate 'emotion' between the living and the dead precisely because there was no theological basis for framing emotion. It is, in practice, hard for human relationships not to carry significance and be framed by some narrative of 'the dead', their status, identity and destiny. The Presbyterian tradition as espoused in Scotland from the Reformation was that 'we can do nothing for the dead': in particular, we cannot pray for them. This established a ritual silence at the grave, perhaps at odds with the mourners' suppressed and unarticulated hopes that, despite the official doctrine, their beloved dead would be chosen for Heaven with God. This formal silence was, in part, broken through elements of Scottish folklore (M. Bennett 2004) and, later by Spiritualism (Kollar 2000; McCorristine 2010).

Hope is intrinsic to much of human life and to encounter a theological stance that renders it inappropriate is extremely unusual. In this Protestant context of silent funerals, as in liturgically expansive rites of Anglican or Catholic traditions, we are ever engaged in an analysis of emotions and their influence on human identity and a person's surrounding relationships. One simple theoretical way of approaching this topic is to say that when an idea is pervaded by an emotion it becomes a value; that when a value helps constitute a person's identity it becomes a belief; and that if a belief helps frame a person's destiny it is a religious belief (Davies 2011). To this scheme of thought we will return in chapter 10; for the moment it suffices to suggest that the removal of emotional ties with a corpse (Laqueur 2016) – if that is in fact possible – would, on this reckoning, reduce a person to being more like a thing or an idea devoid of emotional attachment. It is quite possible that some theologically-driven individuals might school themselves through a doctrine of predestination to be so utterly subject to the divine will that they could espouse such a position, but it is equally possible to understand why some others would find that less easily accomplished.

Thinking more strictly in terms of theological issues we know that over time certain values can lose their emotional appeal and leave their nuclear 'ideas' as bare ideas. At other times an idea does attract emotional attachment to become a value or indeed a belief or even a religious belief. This may well be the case with the demise of firm predestination belief to allow for words at funerals or, indeed, for a shift towards Humanist funerals at the start of the new millennium in Scotland. Or, yet again, it looks as though the alignment of some emotional ties with 'nature' and the earth itself has begun to speak in favour of woodland burials. So that, for example, the bare idea of 'woodland burial' gains an emotional investment and not only becomes its own 'value' but also a form of 'belief' insofar as it comes to frame a sense of identity for a person as he or she imagines themselves when buried at a particular site.

In this study it will be convenient to set shifts of perspective, whether religious, secular or, indeed, 'spiritual' as forms of world-view (Droogers and van Hartskamp 2014). A 'world-views' approach, though it will not predominate or be made to intrude into our on-going account of Scotland's funeral rites, will allow us to be equal handed. This is, perhaps, wise at a time when some scholars find those categories of 'religion', or indeed 'spirituality' and the secular difficult to handle, and when the rather negative form of words like 'atheist' or 'non-religious' seem to define folk by what they are not rather than by what they are.

Cross-mapping Worldviews

Such complexity challenges any scholar, and not a few have risen to it to produce detailed accounts of one or another dimension of death in Scotland. Death studies, as such, is relatively new in Scotland, especially in the inter-disciplinary context, though its themes are never far from research in medicine, archaeology and anthropology. The three inter-disciplinary conferences on 'Death in Scotland' hosted by New College, Edinburgh, have drawn old and new scholars to share their work. The first conference's collection *Death in Modern Scotland, 1855–1955: Beliefs, Attitudes and Practices* (Buckham, Jupp and Rugg (eds), Peter Lang: Oxford and Bern) was published in June 2016. The authors are particularly inspired by individual scholars over recent years: Anne Gordon's studies of *Death is for the Living* (1984) and *Candie for the Foundling* (1992) presented detailed studies of Scottish death and funerary rites; Rory Williams' *A Protestant Legacy* (1990) showed how Reformed cultures still permeated ageing and dying in 1980s Aberdeen; Sarah Tarlow's *Bereavement and Commemoration* (1999) charted how the memory of the dead mutated in twentieth-century Orkney; Margaret Bennett in *Scottish Customs from the Cradle to the Grave* (1992) described the landscape of folkloric beliefs lying parallel to orthodox religious beliefs. Margaret Crowther, Anne Cameron and Gayle Davies investigated the development of Scottish registration procedures for births, marriages and deaths in their project 'The Scottish Way of Birth and Death' (University of Glasgow, 2003–8). Elaine McFarland (2005, 2008, 2010) has published studies of funeral directing, war memorials and contemporary funeral rites and a number of successful PhD theses have brought out a new generation including: Ronnie Scott on the origin of the Glasgow Necropolis (Scott 2006); Glenys Caswell comparing contemporary death beliefs and practices in Edinburgh, Inverness and on the Isle of Lewis (Caswell 2009); and Michael Smith's study of death in Victorian Edinburgh which has been published as *The Secularization of Death in Scotland, 1815–1900* (M. Smith 2014).

This present volume, which also has the excitement of research as its driver, will engage with some of these and other studies as each chapter proceeds. Our major concern has been to document and interpret the fascinating ways in which Scotland's particular Reformation history generated significant consequences for resetting a funerary worldview that has eventually contributed to today's mixed funerary economy. This book is, certainly, not intended as a history of burial in nineteenth- and twentieth-century Scotland – that book has not yet been written – but it does give prominence to the rise and practice of cremation and to the crematoria in which it takes place. At this point it remains to say that the authors of this volume were pleased to work as a team of 'death studies' scholars on this Cremation in Scotland Project funded by The Leverhulme Trust through Durham University's Centre for Death and Life Studies, and in the interdisciplinary way already highlighted. Moreover, at the very outset of our work we benefited from advice and encouragement from a Project Reference Group constituted by eminent individuals from the scholarly world, viz., Professors David Brown, Jay Brown, Steve Bruce and Dr Ronnie Scott.

CHAPTER ONE

History, Law, Architecture

The Reformation of Burial in Early Modern Scotland

Prior to the Reformation of 1560 Scotland was a Catholic nation, and as such Scottish burial practices did not differ greatly from those seen throughout the rest of the Catholic world, although slight differences did occur. All of this changed when in August 1560 a session of the Scottish Parliament officially decreed Scotland to be a Protestant nation, thereby signalling the success of one of the last Reformations in Europe.

The Scottish Reformation was a decidedly Calvinist movement. Considering the similarities in their theologies, it is no surprise that Knox (Dawson 2015: ch. 12), the largely self-anointed leader of the Scottish Reformation, shared with Calvin and Zwingli certain beliefs as to the ideal Christian burial, uncorrupted by 'various falsifications' (Calvin 1960: 995). One aspect of pre-Reformation burial that Knox was particularly keen to reform was the performance of intercessory acts on behalf of the dead. Knox believed that the removal of any belief in purgatory had proven the inefficacy of these intercessory acts, acts that were therefore deemed 'superstitious'.[1] In Geneva in 1556 Knox had produced *The forme of prayers and the ministration of the Sacraments* for the use of the Scottish and English congregations there. The work contained a brief section concerning the new and correct method of the disposal of the dead:

> The corps is reuerently brought to the graue, accompagnied with the congregatio[n]; with owte any further ceremonies, which

1. See further Raeburn 2016.

beyng buriede, the minister goeth to the churche, if it be not farre of, and maketh some comfortable exhortacion to the people, towchyng deathe, and resurrection. (Maxwell 1931: 161)

This passage, though very brief, makes it very clear that for Knox there should be no ceremonies, such as intercessory actions, on the occasion of a death or at a burial. Subsequently, in 1560, *The First Book of Discipline* was produced by a group of unnamed Scottish ministers, although Knox was probably among them (J.K. Cameron 1972: 3–4). The work, although not having as wide a dissemination as the *forme of prayers*, did attempt to expand further upon the Reformed Protestant position on burial practice. It explicitly forbade 'superstitious' practices such as Mass and prayers for the dead (J.K. Cameron 1972: 199–201). *The First Book of Discipline* was also clear as to the ideal location for burials:

> we think it neither seemly that the Kirk appointed to preaching and ministration of the Sacraments shall be made a place of burial, but that some other secret and convenient place, lying in the most free aire, be appointed for that use, which place ought to be walled and fenced about, and kept for that use onely. (J.K. Cameron 1972: 201)

Another important aspect of the removal of burial locations from the kirks in the towns and cities was that these new spaces should not be consecrated, or considered as 'sacred'. Indeed, as Houston has noted, the law in post-Reformation Scotland refused to recognise any burial space as *res religiosa* (Houston 2010: 216). Knox, at the Reformation, had attempted to make burials civic events, and to make burial locations civil sites. The extent to which he was successful in this undertaking will be seen in more detail below.

Although *The First Book of Discipline* is undoubtedly an important text concerning the reform of burial practices in Scotland, its impact should not be overstated as it was, as stated above, far from being a widely disseminated text. It is, however, in combination with the *forme of prayers*, a very important one in giving a better understanding of the early Scottish reformers' attitudes to the correct form of Christian burial in the first years after the Scottish Reformation.

The Practicalities of Burial Reform

Not everyone in early modern Scotland immediately adopted the new methods of burial. Intra-mural burial in particular, the practice by which individuals were buried within the fabric of the kirk, endured, with many continuing to adhere to the pre-Reformation belief that one's location in death could have an effect upon one's journey towards ultimate salvation.[2] Unsurprisingly, it was often the upper classes who could flout the new burial regulations, paying nominal fines for intra-mural burial, but many common men and women also persisted with intra-mural burial. Indeed, continuing adherence to intra-mural burial was so pervasive that a solution had to be sought. It was found in the development of burial aisles and their classification as extra-mural – a tenuous distinction, but nevertheless a distinction that was to prove popular with those who could afford such a luxury (Spicer 2000: 168). Burial aisles were essentially annexes built onto the side of pre-existing kirk buildings, often also serving as accommodation during services for the family of the laird who had it built, and as a display of their position in the local society (Spicer 2007: 66–7). William Birnie, minister for Lanark, defended the use of burial aisles in 1606, describing them as 'adjacent and incontiguous', and stating that 'this kynde may content our most honourable' (Birnie 1606: sig. C4^r). Clearly, whilst suitable for the higher classes, burial aisles were not to be universally appropriate or practical.

Another issue that was to prove continuously problematic for the early reformers was the display of the deceased's social status in life on the occasion of their funeral. *The First Book of Discipline* had stated that:

> For seeing that before God there is no respect of persons, and that their Ministrie appertaineth to all alike, whatsoever they doe to the rich in respect of their Ministrie, the same they are bound to doe to the poorest under their charge (J.K. Cameron 1972: 201).

The reformers clearly intended that there should be no distinction of status at burials. This, however, was to prove unpopular with those who believed they deserved such distinction. Some members of the aristocracy appear to have accepted the ban on intra-mural burial, but were less willing to abandon displays of wealth and power. Indeed, the desire to display one's social status in death was to remain strong throughout the seventeenth and eighteenth centuries. For example, at the burial of the Earl of Mar in Alloa in 1689 there were four ushers in mourning garb, the coffin was adorned with small escutcheons, a mortcloth, cyphers, and a helmet and coronet, and the footmen were also garbed in mourning (NRS GD124/15/192). Yet these

---

2. See further Spicer 2000 and Fitch 2009.

funerals were not just for the family of the deceased. An individual's peers were also watching, and judgements would be passed if a funeral were seen to be inadequate. In a letter to the Earl of Arran, dated 28 April 1695, the Duke of Hamilton wrote of the funeral of the Duke of Queensberry that Queensberry was carried by an 'ugly common closs [closed] hearse and hackney horses' in very bad order, and that there was a very small company present. Despite the poor show, £1,000 was rumoured to have been spent on the funeral and an additional £1,000 on a tomb (NRS GD406/1/4006). It was clearly important that one be viewed by one's peers as deserving of respect.

As with the development of burial aisles the position on signs of status at funerals would ultimately yield to the wishes of the Scottish higher classes. In 1645 *A Directory for the Publike Worship of God*, also known as the *Westminster Directory*, was approved by Parliament. It came in the wake of an attempted imposition of an Episcopalian form of church operation upon Scotland, and in many ways was a reaction to that. The work included a section on burial which, although largely following on logically from the preceding works, also included the statement 'That this shall not extend to deny any civill respects or differences at the buriall, suitable to the ranke and condition of the party deceased whiles he was living' (*Directory* 1645: 58). Burials were once again permitted to reflect the social status of the deceased. In 1690 Presbyterianism was finally established within the Kirk and whilst other disputed practices such as funeral sermons ultimately faded away, the same cannot be said of this feature. Burials from this point on would continue to allow for the differences in social status of the deceased.

The Rise of the Cemeteries

After over a century of vacillating between Presbyterianism and Episcopalianism, Scotland finally saw Presbyterianism established throughout the country at the end of the seventeenth century. Although Catholics and Episcopalians continued to have a presence in Scotland almost all of the kirk buildings, and as such the kirk-yards, were controlled by members of the Church of Scotland.[3] In times of persecution and acrimony they sought to regulate the provision and use of burial grounds under spurious claims of right or veneers of legality. So in the 1670s the walls round the Quakers'

---

3. See further M. Smith 2009. Strictly speaking, it is not correct to say that the kirk-yards were owned by the Church (J.M. Duncan 1864: 221; Innes 1867: 324).

new burial ground in Aberdeen were repeatedly demolished and the bodies buried therein repeatedly removed by order of the magistrates, who decreed that all who died in the burgh should be buried in the parish churchyard and nowhere else (DesBrisay 1996: 156; Burnet and Marwick 1952: 103). And, in the aftermath of the Disruption in 1843, members of the newly formed secessionist Free Church of Scotland were interdicted by the sheriff from using land they had provided for burials because it was attached to a church of the Establishment. To add insult to injury the first two persons buried in it were influential members of the Kirk who had been instrumental in obtaining the interdict. This was not an isolated incident, as a similar record from Argyllshire shows; and indeed in one case an elderly gentleman, whilst looking upon the graves of some of his children in the Kirk-owned burial ground, was told that, unless he left the Free Church, he 'shall never lie beside those below' (T. Brown 1878: 161).

The correct legal position had been laid down by the Court of Session in a series of cases in the early 1830s when the Kirk attempted to secure a monopoly in the supply of burial space and mortcloths but without success (Swan v Halyburton 1830; Kirk-Session of Duddingston v Halyburton 1832; Kirk-Session and Heritors of Leith v Friendly Society of Restalrig 1831; Heritors and Kirk-Session of South Leith v Scott 1832; Michael Smith 2014: 44–9, 2009: 111; Duncan and Johnston 1903: 218; Houston 2010: 221). Had it been otherwise, the private cemeteries established around the time of the Disruption would not have been permitted except by Act of Parliament, which was most opportune for the Free Church and non-Presbyterians.[4]

The first planned Scottish cemetery was the Necropolis in Glasgow,[5] opened in 1833, and designed from the start to be multi-denominational (Curl 1983: 139), with sections for Catholics, Lutherans, Episcopalians, Jews and Presbyterians.[6] Shortly afterwards other cemeteries were opened, such as the Southern Necropolis in Glasgow in 1840 and in Edinburgh at Warriston in 1842, Dean in 1845, and both Grange and Dalry in 1846 (Gifford

---

4. The existence of separate burial grounds belonging to Jews and Quakers was recognised by the Burial Grounds (Scotland) Act 1855, about which see below. See too NRS CH10/1/43 for Jewish grounds in the early nineteenth century and NRS CH10/1/50 for Quakers' in the mid- to late eighteenth.
5. The Old Calton burial ground in Edinburgh, opened in 1718, was intended for the specific use of the village of Calton, and was not initially multi-denominational.
6. See ch. 2.

et al. 1984). Through a combination of increasing religious tolerance and the massive overcrowding of the city kirk-yards the private cemeteries quickly became popular with many people across Scottish society.

Of course, the development of the private cemeteries did not counter all of the social problems of the time overnight, or for several decades. It was a very real fact of life then that, if an individual or the family of the deceased could not afford to bury them they would likely go to the common graves, graves designed to take multiple bodies. These common graves were particularly unhealthy, as they were frequently over-filled and rarely dug sufficiently deep. The private cemeteries did not remedy this immediately, as they could not provide an individual grave for every dead body: it was simply unfeasible. As a result, the private cemeteries still required areas for common graves, but such areas were planned from the start, and some steps were taken to ensure that they were healthy, and not unsightly (Loudon 1843: 41; Laxton and Rodger 2014).

For the Free Church and other dissenting groups the new cemeteries were clearly an opportunity too good to be missed. Indeed, founding members of the Free Church, such as Thomas Chalmers (1780–1847), Hugh Miller (1802–1856) and, later, Thomas Guthrie (1803–1873) were among the first burials to take place in the Grange, and that of Chalmers was to set a precedent for Free Church burials. Chalmers was the first moderator of the Free Church of Scotland, and died from suspected heart disease on 31 May 1847 (*Bristol Mercury*, 12 June 1847). His funeral took place on Friday, 4 June 1847. He was buried in the Grange cemetery, apparently at his own request, and the procession to the cemetery was of a scale infrequently seen in the capital. 'The funeral was the longest that perhaps ever took place in Edinburgh or in Scotland, all classes and denominations vieing [sic] with each other in paying the last tribute of respect to this venerated divine' (*The Express*, 7 June 1847). Following a devotional exercise the General Assembly of the Free Church began their march to Chalmers' house, stopping along the way to allow other groups to join the procession. Upon reaching the approach to the house the procession stopped, and the members of the Free Church present entered the house to attend further devotional exercises. These exercises were brief, and the procession began its journey to the cemetery once the coffin had been placed in the hearse. Hugh Miller stated:

> On entering the cemetery, the procession was arranged along the different walks leading to the grave. None of the carriages were

admitted to the cemetery grounds, and the coffin was removed from the hearse at the gate, and carried to the grave shoulder-high by six men. On the approach of the coffin the procession defiled to the side, leaving space in the centre for the mourning train to pass through. The coffin was then lowered into the grave by the immediate relatives of the deceased, and in a few minutes the clods were heard rattling upon the coffin which contained all that was earthly of one of Scotland's best and greatest men. (*The Witness*, 5 June 1847; Wolffe 2000: 118)

The Consolidation of Burial Reform

One of the stated goals of the Scottish reformers following 1560 was the reformation of burial practices in Scotland, in order to remove all perceived Catholic superstitious and intercessory acts. However, burial practices in Scotland were continually changing and evolving, and would continue to do so for several centuries. So at what point, if any, can it be said that the reformers had succeeded in their goal? At the Reformation it was determined that burials should take place with no ceremony, no intercessory acts, no superstition, and in an unconsecrated location that was set aside for that sole purpose. Ceremonies, intercessory acts and superstitious practices were gradually reformed over the decades and even centuries that followed the Reformation, but it was not until the opening of the private cemeteries in the mid-nineteenth century that the location of burial had finally met the standards set by the reformers. The new cemeteries were, in many ways, ideal for Presbyterian burial. They were used for no other function than burial, and they were walled off and separate from the cities. And, importantly, those sections reserved for Presbyterians were not consecrated. The opening of the private cemeteries was, for the Free Church in particular, an opportunity to establish its own burial ground and its own burial traditions, and as a result, to cement its own new identity.[7] That the new cemeteries were shared with other denominations and other faiths did not matter. What mattered was, from the very beginnings of the Free Church, it could establish its new burial traditions in the private cemeteries. No longer did it have to struggle with the Kirk over where to bury its dead.

Chalmers' funeral fits rather neatly with the ideal Protestant funeral as laid out by the early Scottish reformers. He was laid to rest in a dedicated,

---

7. See further Davies 1997: 93–110.

unconsecrated cemetery which, at the time, was outside of the city bounds, and despite the unspecified 'devotional exercises' there appear to have been no perceived 'superstitious' elements. It could perhaps be argued that the numbers of those attending attested to his social status, which would not have agreed with the earliest prescriptions for Scottish Protestant funerals, but, as explained above, this was an aspect of funeral practice that was exceptionally difficult to reform. Additionally, Chalmers' burial in the Grange kick-started a desire amongst the members of the Free Church to be buried in private cemeteries rather than kirk-yards, which in turn enhanced the rise of the private cemetery movement within Scotland, as those belonging to the Free Church aimed to establish and cement their new identity in part through their chosen burial location. It could be suggested, therefore, that for a brief period of time, approximately two and a half centuries after the Scottish Reformation, one Protestant faction adhered as closely to the early reformers' desired form of burial as would ever be the case. This situation, however, was not to last. As the Free Church became more established it obtained the ownership of more and more Kirk buildings, and inevitably members of the Free Church once again desired burial in the kirk-yards. By this stage, however, the private cemeteries had been established, and accepted, throughout Scotland.

It is interesting to note that it was the effective expulsion of the Free Church from the Kirk-owned burial grounds that ultimately allowed for the final success of the reformation of burial. However, whilst the 1847 burial of Thomas Chalmers in the Grange perhaps marked the final success of the reformation of burial, it can also be suggested that it came too late. The practices that the Free Church had adopted, simple burials with no perceived 'superstitious' qualities, were not spread to the other denominations and faiths within Scotland, and with the tolerance of these other groups there was no need for them to adopt the form of burial used by the Free Church. The reformation of burial that had been attempted in 1560, therefore, can only be said to have been a success in that at least one Presbyterian faction adopted, at last, in the 1840s, the burial order as laid down at the Reformation.

By the time Scottish burial practices truly began to reflect the desires of the early reformers, however, Scotland had become a very different place. Old prejudices were themselves being eroded, and other faiths and denominations were beginning to be tolerated. Additionally, the Kirk had begun to lose its control over Scottish burial (see ch. 2 below and Smith 2014). As a result of these changes each group was allocated its own burial locations within the private cemeteries, and the form of burial service that each group practised was different. As such there were areas of the private cemeteries, those given over to Catholics and Episcopalians, that had been consecrated, and in which graveside prayers would take place, practices of which the reformers definitely would have disapproved.

In the later mid-century, changing attitudes to liturgy within the Church of Scotland included seeking General Assembly approval for clergy to conduct Christian rituals at gravesides, finally achieved in 1897. (This was two years after the first crematorium opened in Glasgow.)

The fact that both Kirk and Free Church clergy were forbidden from participation in burial rites, meant that they had been in no strong position to reform burial practice in churchyards or cemeteries they neither owned nor managed. Post-Reformation burial grounds in Scotland did not provide cemetery chapels as the 1850s legislation had permitted in England and Wales. So when cremation emerged as an alternative to burial in the 1880s, Presbyterians had, firstly, little experience or authority as would-be burial reformers, and secondly, once the liturgical revival had begun, were unlikely to switch to cremation from a burial tradition in which they were now increasingly investing liturgical and pastoral energies. Clerical reorientation towards cremation had to await the 1930s. Presbyterian clergy may well have acquiesced in rather than led their parishioners' persistence in burial or their new choice for cremation. Only an in-depth study of Presbyterian pastoral and liturgical ministry at funerals between 1897 and 1939 will reveal which were the persuasive forces and which the deterrent in this era.

Legal Considerations

When 'modern' cremation was first advocated the United Kingdom had a single parliament. Its legislation sometimes applied to one constituent part and sometimes to more. Acts that applied to England applied almost invariably to Wales but not Scotland. England and Wales had one system of courts and common law: Scotland had its own system of courts and common law. The law of Scotland was quite distinct from that of England and Wales, though appeals in civil cases in both jurisdictions could be taken to the House of Lords, where judges from all three countries sat. The final court of appeal in Scottish criminal cases was the High Court of Justiciary in Scotland.

The salient features of the Scottish legal landscape into which cremation would have to fit were: the statutory law about the registration of deaths and burials; the law, part statutory and part common, about the provision of burial grounds in Scotland; and the law about means of dealing with dead bodies, which, the Anatomy Acts apart, was almost entirely common.

Death Registration

Before 1854 Scotland had no system of registering deaths. Burials were recorded by Kirk Sessions and might be recorded by the non-established churches; and their details might be entered not in special registers but in accounts and other papers of the churches. The records were incomplete, far from uniform and only rarely showed a cause of death (Seton 1854; Sinclair 2000; A. Cameron 2008). In 1854 a system of compulsory death registration was enacted (A. Cameron 2007). The Registration of Births, Deaths and Marriages (Scotland) Act applied only to Scotland, England and Wales having acquired a Registration Act eighteen years previously. It was tinkered with by Acts of 1855 and 1860 (Seton 1860).

This system required details of every death to be recorded in special registers by district registrars (usually parish clerks) who had to 'learn' them from 'informants' identified either by familial or social relationships to the deceased. If the deceased had a doctor, the doctor had to certify a cause of death.

The inadequacy of systems of death registration was an obstacle to the adoption of cremation. Although the Scottish legislation was slightly differently worded from the English and Welsh, requiring a certificate from a doctor who had 'been in attendance during the [deceased's] last illness [...] until the death', it is unlikely that this was understood to require the doctor to have witnessed the death. In neither jurisdiction did the doctor have to verify by examination that the deceased was dead before issuing a certificate (Crowther 2006).

The proportion of deaths whose cause was not medically certified – and the absence of proper post-mortem examinations in cases where it was – was constantly criticised by cremationists (Glaister 1884–5, 1893; C. Cameron 1887: 32–6). They were very largely responsible for the establishment of the House of Commons Select Committee on Death Registration in 1893 (see ch. 4). Drs Charles Cameron and Robert Farquharson, the MPs for Glasgow College and West Aberdeenshire respectively and founder members of the Scottish Burial Reform and Cremation Society (SBRCS), were the only members of the Committee to attend all its sessions. The Committee recommended that before a person's corpse could be disposed of the cause of their death should be medically certified after inspection of their body; and that the precautions taken by the Cremation Society of England (CS) before carrying out cremations should be made compulsory (House of Commons, 1893).

Burial Ground Provision

Scottish legislation to permit the compulsory closure of insalubrious graveyards followed more quickly upon English and Welsh legislation than legislation for the registration of deaths. If the ill-fated experiment of burial ground monopoly under the Public Health Act 1848 (Finer 1952: bk 9; Lewis 1952: ch. 11; Rugg 2013: 45) is overlooked, the first legislation in England and Wales consisted of the Burial Acts of 1852 and 1853. The Burial Grounds (Scotland) Act followed in 1855. It permitted the presentation of a petition to a sheriff alleging that a ground was 'dangerous to health or offensive or contrary to decency'. If he found any of the petition's allegations true he had to embody his findings in an interlocutor and send a copy to the Home Secretary. The Home Secretary[8] could then apply to the Privy Council for an Order prohibiting burials within specified limits and/or banning the opening of new burial grounds within specified limits without ministerial approval.[9]

The Act also required parochial boards (in urban areas town councils) to provide burial grounds to replace ones closed by Orders in Council and introduced a mechanism whereby they could be required to provide suitable grounds even in areas where burials had not been prohibited. A ground provided under the Act could be designated a parish burial ground. Thus began a process of transferring responsibility for providing public ground for burial from 'heritors' (landowners in a parish) to local authorities, a process advanced to completion by the Local Government (Scotland) Act

8. Any Principal Secretary of State could discharge this function but the Home Secretary undertook it until the establishment of the Scottish Office in 1885, when the Secretary for Scotland took it over.
9. The National Archives (TNA) HO 45/6677 has papers relating to the first request for a burial to be permitted within a burial ground closed under the Act. It also has a printed version of the petition to have it closed and a full report of the sheriff's consequent enquiry in January 1856. This was probably the second ground closed by Order in Council (*Edinburgh Gazette* for 2/11/1855, p. 1335, 11/12/1855, p. 1537 and 5/2/1856, p. 129 [Markinch]; and 29/1/1856, p. 111, 27/6/1856, p. 569 and 24/10/1856, p. 929 [Dumbarton]).

1894 s. 30(6), the Church of Scotland (Property and Endowments) Act 1925 ss 32–4, the Local Government (Scotland) Act 1929 ss 1–2 and the Church of Scotland (Property and Endowments) Amendment Act 1933 s. 2 (Slevin 1956). Section 18 of the 1855 Act empowered parochial boards to sell exclusive rights of burial in grounds provided under it but in no more than half the area of the ground. Acts of 1881 and 1886 removed the restriction. Section 12 also allowed a board, instead of acquiring ground for burial itself, to contract with the owners of cemeteries for the burial of those entitled to burial in its parish.

From 1867 there was another, simpler, procedure for closing burial grounds available to a local authority by having it declared a nuisance under the Public Health Act. Unlike a ground closed by Order in Council under the 1855 Act, one closed under the 1867 Act did not have to be replaced.

One provision of the Burial Acts, copied into the Cremation Act 1902, restrained the development of cremation in Scotland and caused controversy at the end of the period of this study – the 'radius' clause (below chs 5 and 9). Sections 10 and 11 of the 1855 Act prohibited land being used for burials without the written consent of the owner, lessee and occupier of a house within 100 yards of the ground. The restriction applied only to burial grounds provided under the Act[10] and not to private burial grounds (Bain v Seafield 1884) or to cemetery companies unless they had incorporated clause 10 of the Cemeteries Clauses Consolidation Act 1847 into their founding instruments. This set the distance at 200 yards.

Documentation of Burials

The Registration Act required registrars to give a certificate that a death had been registered to the informant of the death. The certificate's form was prescribed by Schedule I to the Act and came to be referred to simply as a Schedule I. It was for the use of the 'undertaker or other person having charge of the funeral', who had to give it, before burial, to the 'person having the charge of the churchyard, cemetery, church, chapel, aisle, vault or other place of interment […] in which the body is to be buried'; and then within three days of the burial deliver to the registrar a certificate of interment. This certificate's form was prescribed by Schedule H and was referred to as

10. But once proceedings were set in motion under the Act to provide a new ground, its provision had to comply with the Act (Fulton v Dunlop 1862 and *Edinburgh Gazette* 20/1/1860, p. 80, 16/4/1861, p. 508, 30/4/1861, p. 570 and 7/2/1862, p. 223).

a Schedule H. Failure to produce a Schedule I to the person in charge of the churchyard etc. before burial was punishable, but the person in charge of the churchyard etc. who permitted a burial in the absence of a Schedule I was not, if within three days they informed the registrar of the burial by means of a Schedule H. The undertaker also had to send a Schedule H to the registrar in such a case.

The 1855 Act required registers to be kept of all burials in grounds provided under the Act, but neither this Act nor the Registration Act imposed any obligation on the person in charge of the ground to inform the registrar of all burials or on a registrar who did not receive such information to inquire what had become of the body. Schedule B to the 1854 Act, which prescribed the details of a death to be recorded, included a column headed 'Burial Place. Undertaker by whom certified'. A year later, exercising powers given him by s. 54 of the Act, the Registrar General amended this heading to 'Burial Place. Undertaker or other Person by whom certified'. In 1860 he removed the column completely.

The question that would arise if cremation were determined or accepted to be lawful was whether these provisions applied to it and the disposal of cremated remains (below ch. 4). In England and Wales statutes that referred to 'burial' were taken to apply only to the burial of uncremated bodies. Probably because of this precedent Charles Renshaw, the MP for Renfrewshire, and Cameron took advantage of the consolidation of public health legislation in 1897 to secure an amendment to the Public Health (Scotland) Act to the effect that 'burial includes cremation', thus, presumably, allowing local authorities with responsibility for dealing with infectious corpses to 'cremate' them instead of 'burying' them (below ch. 4).

Administration of Acts of Parliament

The day-to-day oversight of the operation of Acts of Parliament was parcelled out among Government Departments. This involved, among other things, collating proposals for the Acts' amendment, repeal or replacement, and responding to enquiries about their interpretation. To these the almost invariable response was that the Department or its Minister had no authority to interpret Acts of Parliament. Less frequently a Department might proffer a favoured interpretation while warning that it could not be taken as authoritative.

As society became more complex, urban and industrialised, Acts increasingly empowered Ministers or subordinate agencies, such as, for example, town councils, to make regulations, rules and bye-laws. Such was the case with the Cremation Act of 1902. The Act applied to England and Wales, and Scotland, but not to Ireland. It required the sites and plans of crematoria to be approved by the Local Government Board (LGB) in England and the Local Government Board for Scotland (LGBS) in Scotland and it required a Secretary of State in England and Wales (but in fact the Home Secretary) and the Secretary for Scotland in Scotland to make regulations about the carrying out of cremations. In Scotland these responsibilities were later transferred to other Departments, that for approving sites and plans to the Scottish Board of Health (SBH) in 1919, the Department of Health for Scotland (DHS) in 1928, and the Secretary of State for Scotland in 1939 until 1980 when the need for this was removed (below ch. 9). Responsibility for making the regulations passed to the Secretary of State for Scotland in 1926 and to Scottish Ministers in 1999.

Thus, although there was a single Act applying to England and Wales, and Scotland, the regulations for the two jurisdictions were made by different subordinate legislators and could be (and were) different. Devolution has added a further twist to this. Since 1998 the Scottish Parliament has been able to amend or replace the Cremation Acts so far as they apply to Scotland (SA 1998) and it has done so (CDSA 2011 s. 30 and Schedule 2 and BCSA 2016) (below ch. 9). Since 2011 the Welsh Assembly has had a similar power (GWA 2006 s. 108 and Schedule 7, Part I, Subject 6), but it has yet to be exercised.

The position is somewhat similar with respect to legislation controlling emissions from processes, among them cremation, to atmosphere. Crematoria in Scotland, and England and Wales are subject to the same Pollution Prevention and Control Act 1999 but to separate regulations, guidance and directions made under it.

'Subordinate legislation' has force as if enacted in the primary Act under which it is made. There is this difference, however: the scope for courts to impugn primary Acts is very limited. Subordinate legislation, however, can be declared void by a court if it is beyond the subordinate legislator's power to make it (e.g. McCreadie v McBroom 1860). The most recent 'scandal' to have affected cremation in Scotland, namely the disposal of ashes from the cremations of the stillborn and non-viable foetuses (below ch. 9), can be used to illustrate this.

Regulations 16 and 17 of the current Scottish Cremation Regulations are very little changed from the first Scottish Regulations (1927) and the first

English and Welsh ones (1903). Regulation 16 lays down the circumstances in which a stillborn child can be cremated. Regulation 17 prescribes how the ashes from the cremation of a 'deceased person' are to be treated. It is not clear that regulation 17 applies to the ashes of a stillborn child, which, arguably, was never a 'person' who lived and died. The Regulations were made in exercise of the power given by section 7 of the Cremation Act 1902 to make provision prescribing 'in what cases and under what conditions the burning of any human remains may take place, and directing the disposition or interment of the ashes'. Are stillborn children 'human remains'? Those who drafted the first regulations must have thought so else they would not have penned regulation 16; but when Scottish lawyers first had to ponder the question some doubted it (below ch. 5). If a stillborn child is not 'human remains' regulation 17 should not be interpreted as applying to its ashes and regulation 16 should declared void, even though Parliament has (in theory at least)[11] approved the regulation.

The foregoing discussion suggests a further conundrum. Cultural attitudes to the stillborn and the products of miscarriages have undoubtedly changed over the past century. Could what is meant by 'human remains' have changed since 1902 so as to render it lawful now to make regulations about stillborn children which, if made in 1902, would have been void? If 'human remains' in an Act passed in 1902 must be taken to mean what the parliamentarians of the time meant by it, the answer might be 'No'. On the other hand, some statutory terms are taken to be 'always speaking' and these can be given their contemporary rather than their historic meaning. If 'human remains' is such a term the answer might be 'Yes'. Those who drafted the most recent Cremation Regulations for England and Wales apparently thought that 'human remains' can encompass parts taken from a living person – though they cannot be cremated under the Regulations until the person has died (CEWR 2008 reg. 2(1); Marlow 2008).

Means of Dealing with the Dead

The common law of Scotland has been more influenced than that of England and Wales by the civilian tradition. It did not treat burial grounds as beyond the bounds of commerce to the extent that Roman law did (Duncan 1864:

11. The Regulations, like much subordinate legislation, had to be presented to Parliament, which could acquiesce in or reject them. Parliament could not, as with a Bill, amend or even debate them.

220, 207) but resort to Roman law has enabled Scotland to provide redress to those close to a deceased person for the distress caused by an unauthorised interference with the corpse (Whitty 2005) beyond that as yet available in England and Wales.

As to the legality of cremation, the common law of Scotland was the same as that of England and Wales. In 1884 an English judge ruled that in itself cremation was not unlawful (S. White 2002a). The prosecutor's line had been that the common law required a person having or undertaking the responsibility of dealing with a dead body to bury it: no other method was allowed. This was a conclusion which might have been drawn from litigation a few years earlier when the friend of a deceased unsuccessfully sued his executors for her expenses in arranging his cremation as he had wished. Turning a blind eye to this precedent the judge ruled that in the absence of a distinct rule that burial was required or that cremation was prohibited it would be possible to carry out cremations lawfully (ch. 2).

That this was also the position in Scotland was not doubted (Chisholm 1896: 265; 1909: 385); and in so far as cultural attitudes play a part in forming judicial decisions, the Calvinist cast of mind would be likely to make judges in Scotland, should they have to adjudicate upon it, less concerned about whether a dead body was buried or burned than their counterparts down south.[12]

Architectural Principles

Until comparatively recently, Scotland's twenty-eight crematoria, together with the other 248 operating across the remainder of the UK and Republic of Ireland, have been almost entirely absent from architectural histories.[13] In many ways and for many people they remain the 'invisible' buildings of the twentieth century. But given that (from provisional figures supplied by the Cremation Society) in 2015 76.32% of deaths in the UK and 66.71% of deaths in Scotland resulted in cremation, the crematorium represents a significant element in contemporary life, an architectural form that reflects the values and social being of a modern, increasingly socially and geographically mobile society. Crematoria offer a paradigm of modernity. They represent a new building type, firmly located in the twentieth century. Reliant on innovative and complex technology their location, planning and design are

---

12. Striking examples of such attitudes are discussed by Hiram 2010.
13. The first full-length study is Grainger 2005.

predicated on motor transport. Crematoria not only gave rise to new types of ancillary buildings – columbaria and Halls and Chapels of Remembrance – but their Gardens of Rest and Remembrance also created a new landscape for collective mourning, replacing the overcrowded and sentimentalised Victorian cemetery, with its often ostentatious memorialisation. Crematoria demonstrate the highly significant role that architecture plays, not only by providing meaningful ritual spaces for the disposal of the dead, but also as an agency for the promotion of cremation. For these reasons, crematoria and their surroundings form an important, but neglected element of our cultural heritage (Grainger 2000).

As cremation slowly gained acceptance in Scotland, its progress was reflected in the design of its crematoria and surroundings. Each stands as 'a symbol of social change' (Davies 1995:1) expressive of a constantly evolving social and cultural order. Scotland's crematoria tell us a great deal not only about the complex, changing and distinctive nature of Scottish attitudes to death and disposal between 1895 and 2016, but also reflect in microcosm the progress of architectural thinking in a period when the relationship between traditionalism and modernism and the continued search for a 'Scottish architecture' occupied many architects. An understanding of the characteristics of, and challenges common to, all UK crematoria is important if we are to identify and evaluate Scotland's distinctive contribution to the architectural expression of cremation.

The Cultural Context

Forty years ago the English and Welsh crematorium was principally a place for cremation only, designed to accommodate a brief committal ceremony on the assumption that this would be preceded by a local church service. During the late twentieth century, however, the crematorium increasingly replaced the Church as the main focus for the important function of saying farewell to loved ones, this shift in purpose resulting from changing patterns in belief and attendant funeral practices. Scotland's burial tradition was singular, with a linear journey from the home to the burial place. However, after 1948 not only did NHS hospitals steadily replace the home as the location of death but funeral directors' premises (with enhanced refrigeration techniques) introduced an intervening point on the journey before reaching the crematorium or cemetery.

Increasingly, crematoria find themselves accommodating the functions of disposal, ritual and remembrance. This is an onerous responsibility for buildings that were never designed for that purpose, given that three-fifths of crematoria in England and Wales, and just under half in Scotland, date from between 1950 and 1970. It is no wonder that such buildings have at best been ignored or at worst vilified as being soulless, 'non-places' of transition with little significance to the individual.

Paradoxically, despite the growing popularity of cremation, those using crematoria often find them unsatisfactory, both emotionally and aesthetically, their design banal and uninspiring. Converted cemetery chapels are often the worst offenders. Their popularity in England and Wales in the 1950s resulted from their relatively low cost and the ease with which they obtained planning permission in the austerity of the post-war years. However, there were no cemetery chapels in Scotland, sparing the country this often less than satisfactory option.

Aside from the quality of the buildings, many feel that the Church has lost its hold on the great ceremony of death and has been replaced in their view by diminished rites enacted in a mundane crematorium with its depleted landscape, characterised by playwright and actor Alan Bennett as being

> Set in country that is not quite country it [the crematorium] looks like the reception area of a tasteful factory or the departure lounge of a small provincial airport confined to domestic flights. The style is contemporary but not eye-catchingly so; this is decorum-led architecture which does not draw attention even to its merits [...] Related places might be the waiting area of a motor showroom, the foyer of a small private hospital or a section of a department store selling modern furniture of inoffensive design: dead places. This is the architecture of reluctance, the furnishings of the functionally ill at ease, decor for a place you do not want to be [...] The whole function of the place, after all, is to do with tidying something away. (Bennett 2005:121)

Crematorium architecture nevertheless has an enormous responsibility to provide significant ritual spaces capable of resonating with both belief and non-belief (Grainger 2008). The relationship between the configuration of space and inner condition is paramount. But the challenges must not be underestimated. As architectural historian Alan Crawford argues,

> Christian burial is a hard act to follow. And in a sense it makes the design of a successful crematorium impossible. How, without

a framework of belief and shared meanings, can the design of a building reach out to the hearts of mourners, the people who have lost someone in death? It is hard enough for a person to do this, but a building?[14]

The Architectural Challenge

From the outset the crematorium presented the architect with one of the most demanding commissions imaginable. It was a building with no architectural precedent, in many ways analogous to the nineteenth-century railway station, where form and function also sought resolution. At once utilitarian and symbolic, religious and secular, the lack of a shared and clear expectation of what is required from a crematorium explains the cultural ambivalence lying at the heart of many designs (Grainger 2011). Is this building a sacred, secular or industrial space? Complex human and cultural issues are at play when a large cross-section of religious, secular and ideological needs have to find resolution in a single building. For many people a cremation is a religious act but the design of a crematorium as a religious space, deriving directly from liturgical imperatives – the accepted norm in ecclesiastical architecture – is problematic because there is no agreed order of service for cremation. It is instead a somewhat uneasy adaptation of the traditional burial service. For theologian Geoffrey Rowell 'the character of crematoria, both architecturally and symbolically' has been determined outside a Christian frame of reference. These are 'churches which are not churches, often having altars which are never used as Christian altars'.[15] For those for whom cremation is a secular act, the building must nevertheless provide a fulfilling sense of place, one in which they are prepared to make an emotional investment.

Cost and planning permission emerge as perennial constraints. Crematoria have to conform to the Cremation Act 1902 – they must be 200 yards from the nearest dwelling whose owner did not consent, and fifty yards from any public highway. It was this radius clause that accounted for the thirty-four year delay in finding a suitable site for Edinburgh's first crematorium. New crematoria require a disproportionately large site, which explains their often being confined to the margins of towns and cities, served

14. Crawford 2005 in Preface, Grainger 2005: 12.
15. Rowell 1977: 113.

by the dual carriageways necessitated in the new town planning for an age of mass car ownership.

A crematorium requires two very distinct spaces: the functional and the symbolic, linked by a transitional space through which the coffin passes from the chapel or meeting hall to the cremator. John Moore, architect of Telford Crematorium (2000), argues that the crematorium does not pose major design problems, as the brief is relatively straightforward. After all, certain practical elements are common to all: a porte-cochère, a waiting room or vestibule, toilet facilities, a vestry, chapel or meeting hall, condolence area, cloistered wreath court, crematory, service areas, administrative offices and, from the 1930s, vehicular access and car parking facilities. One of the principal requirements is to provide circulatory routes for both pedestrians and cars, arranged to keep groups of mourners apart. Not the least challenge facing architects has been the inescapable chimney. Historically this did not sit happily either with Greek temples, Renaissance domes or Gothic chapels. In most early examples it was concealed within a bell-tower – a course hardly to be recommended on the grounds of truth. As James Stevens Curl remarked, 'The louvres that should have emitted joyful peals often belched smoke' (Curl 2002: 310). Modern crematorium chimneys need to avoid industrial connotations and the Environmental Protection Act (EPA) 1990 has required some modification of their height and design.

While the utilitarian purpose, that of reducing a dead body at high temperature to vapour and ashes, remains unequivocal, the search for symbolic architectural forms imbued with associative and psychological value has proved highly problematical from the outset. Moore argues 'to create something special, appropriate to its purpose and with a sense of place over and above the ordinary. That's the challenge'.[16] Unsurprisingly, architectural responses have often been ambiguous and evasive. Hugh Thomas, architect of Sittingbourne (2003) summed it up when he asked

> Where do I start? Unlike housing, factories, schools etc. there are not many crematorium projects to provide an everyday vocabulary of design, and one has virtually to start from scratch. Not necessarily a bad thing?[17]

16. J. Moore. Correspondence with author, May 2005.
17. H. Thomas. Correspondence with author, June 2005.

The Emotional Challenge

The crematorium is an unfamiliar place for many. Uncertainty of purpose is most clearly felt in crematorium chapels. The term 'chapel' has come to be applied gingerly as changing patterns of religious belief and unbelief unfolded during the twentieth century. It comes as a surprise to many, however, that crematoria are not consecrated buildings, although often dedicated by a wide range of faith groups. This lack of religious allegiance is often revealed in the decoration, which can only ever hint at denomination. Early crematoria followed broadly the design of churches, but this changed in 1953 when Sanger and Rothwell converted a cemetery chapel in Oldham, Lancashire, removing an entire wall on one side to open up the space to offer a view of a garden. When in 1954, Fife Council selected the Lancashire firm as winners of the competition to build a new crematorium in Kirkcaldy incorporating this innovation, the distinction between a crematorium chapel and a church was established at a stroke.

A further telling issue is the indecision surrounding the positioning of the catafalque in relation to the altar, if indeed an altar has been provided. Defined in general terms as a temporary structure, representing a tomb or cenotaph, the catafalque has a specific meaning in the context of crematoria being not only the structure upon which the coffin rests, but also often the means by which it is removed. What happens to the coffin at the point of committal has varied from the outset. There are generally three ways in which it is moved (Davies 1995). First, the coffin resting on the catafalque is passed mechanically and slowly through an aperture in the wall to the committal chamber. Second, the coffin, again resting on the catafalque, slowly descends to a lower level, or the coffin resting on the 'paving' of the chancel descends similarly. All six Scottish crematoria built before 1939 chose this method, probably because it was closest to burial. Third, the coffin resting on the catafalque or draped trolley is placed in a recess and either a curtain or gates are slowly drawn across at the point of committal and the coffin is removed after the mourners have left; alternatively, the coffin remains *in situ* until mourners leave the chapel.

The positioning of the catafalque is also a significant decision on the part of the architect and varies across the UK. Many think that it ought to be placed centrally, raised and lit from above or from the side, to make it the focus of attention in accordance with traditional funeral services. Significantly, in Scotland twenty-five out of twenty-eight catafalques follow this arrangement.

It can, however, be positioned to the side allowing mourners to focus their attention elsewhere, often on a view of a garden or wider landscape.

The point of committal, which ought to be the emotional climax of cremation, the moment of departure and final separation, is often one at which the greatest uncertainty arises. Mourners watch from some distance as the coffin is removed and remain passive observers rather than active participants. While there may be something theatrical about the event, there is occasionally, more disturbingly, something mechanical and possibly even comical about it, owing to an uncertainty on the part of some mourners resulting from unfamiliar surroundings and practices. The curtains are often closed by *remote* control. It is at this point that the lack of ceremony becomes most marked leaving many mourners feeling uncertain and dissatisfied. Moreover, there is evasion. While mourners acknowledge tacitly the departure of the coffin for cremation, there still remains a great deal of ignorance about the ensuing process. The most certain way of facing finality is to witness the cremation. Although it is a legal right to view the event, very few choose to other than Hindus and Sikhs, although those numbers are rising because of the changing demography of the UK.

The ultimate point of separation, the entry of the coffin into the cremator, is therefore distanced, both physically and emotionally, from those assembled in a space where they would expect some participatory ending to a funeral held in a church. This would be signalled traditionally by the carrying out of the coffin, followed by the procession of mourners who leave 'the ritual arena of the church' by the same door through which they entered, in accordance with the important social and religious rituals of baptisms, weddings and ordinary church services (Davies 1996: 85). But in the vast majority of newly designed crematoria, indeed in all but Glasgow, Maryhill (1895), Edinburgh, Warriston (1929), Moray (1999) and Houndwood (2015) mourners enter through one door and leave by another, which combined with the association with the 'twenty minute' slot,[18] serves to magnify the impression of mourners themselves being part of a production line (Davies 1995: 22). In summary, for many the fragmentation, banality and depersonalisation compound to impede the important act of mourning leaving them feeling 'cheated' emotionally. The architect must seek ways of mitigating this.

---

18. Today, the length of service may vary on request.

The Pattern of Building in Scotland

Crematorium building and patronage in Scotland occurred in three distinct phases, the first between 1895 and 1939 where the six crematoria opened were all privately owned (Grainger 2016): Glasgow, Maryhill (1895), Edinburgh, Warriston (1929); Dundee (1936); Aberdeen, Kaimhill (1938); Paisley (1938) and Edinburgh, Seafield (1939). In keeping with the governing agenda of 'Improvement', which prompted the harnessing of 'material betterment to secular utopian ideals' (Glendinning and MacKechnie 2004: 195), the second phase between 1955 and 1975 witnessed the 'heroic age' of local authority building. Scotland built eleven crematoria, Daldowie (1955); Craigton (1957); Greenock (1959); Kirkcaldy (1959); Cardross (1960); Falkirk (1962); Perth (1962); The Linn, Glasgow (1962); Ayr (1966); Clydebank (1967); Edinburgh, Mortonhall (1967); Dunfermline (1973) and Aberdeen, Hazelhead (1975). Only one of these, Craigton, was private.

An eighteen-year interregnum followed, building being halted during the 1970s along with large-scale reconstruction projects in Scotland, including urban motorways and city centre developments, as the building boom came to an end. The country's stock of hospitals, schools and other social buildings was thought to be more or less complete, as, presumably, was the number of crematoria. The slow-down in Scottish crematorium building reflected the pattern elsewhere in the UK, where the surge of building had taken place between 1950 and 1970, with 149 crematoria opening in the 1960s, dropping to sixteen in the 1970s and a mere seven during the 1980s. By 1970 the heyday of local authority crematorium building in England, Wales and Scotland was over, with the *Architects' Journal* reporting in 1982 'the completion of a crematorium in the UK is a rare occurrence' (Hellman 1982: 47).

Scotland's third phase of building, beginning in 1993, was dominated by privately-owned crematoria and the need for cremation to be cost effective. It was clear that commercial and environmental factors would bring about significant changes. The move towards private ownership was inextricably linked with arguably one of the most influential of social changes, that of society's reassessment of its relationship with nature. Environmental issues surfaced when Government research and publications began to draw attention to the increase in atmospheric dioxins attributed to emissions from the combustion of man-made materials. These environmental concerns had a direct impact on existing crematoria, which had to be modified to comply with the EU requirements via the EPA 1990 (Jupp 2006a: 173–6). By 1998, most had done so. However, sometime later, concern was expressed about the level of emissions released from mercury dental fillings. The EPA demanded far greater investment infiltration technology by crematoria, encouraging first national, and then international commercial companies to compete for sites in areas less well served by existing urban provision. Crematoria were now too expensive for local authorities to finance. Significantly, of the nine crematoria built – Friockheim (1993); Inverness (1995); Irvine (1997); Moray (1999); Holytown (2004); Roucan Loch, Dumfries (2005); South Lanarkshire (2006); Livingstone (2010), Melrose (2011) and Houndwood (2015) – all but two, Inverness and South Lanarkshire, are privately owned, the pattern of patronage and density of building at any given time matching that in England and Wales. It therefore fell to the private sector to determine the aesthetics of the spaces required to address an increasingly wide range of social, economic and psychological needs.

The forthcoming chapters will reveal that while the architectural expression of cremation corresponds broadly with that in England and Wales, in many ways following their lead, Scotland's crematoria are distinctive in five important ways: first, in the swiftness of rejection of ecclesiastical style in favour of modernism and a contemporary style; second, in their design by the best architects possible; third, their employment of high quality, local materials; fourth, their not being cemetery chapel conversions; and fifth, and perhaps most significantly, in their recognition and exploitation of the relationship of a crematorium to the wider landscape. However, in view of the increasing importance of the role of crematoria in society, the challenge for architects remains as taxing as ever. As Alan Crawford points out,

> In another sense, and mercifully, it is not necessary for the design of a crematorium to carry all this heavy burden of relieving pain, or giving meaning. It is the mourners who do the work, who bring such meaning as they can muster with them. Seen in this way, the design of the building is on the same footing as the undertaker's lowered tones, the well-kept lawns, the transitory flowers, friends in unfamiliar outfits, the hint of suburbia in the background: all nothing in themselves, hopeless in the face of what has happened, but ready to be invested with meaning by the mourners.[19]

---

19. Crawford, in Grainger 2005: 12.

CHAPTER TWO

Issues in Burial Arrangements in Scotland, 1830–1886

The years 1831–86 were particularly important for shaping the characteristics of Scottish funerals of the early twentieth century, lessening the power of the Church, advancing private enterprise and widening class differences. These characteristics account for the persistence, indeed tenacity, of the burial tradition in Scotland and, compared with England, for its prolonged resistance to the arguments for cremation.

Burial reform and public health

The rapid growth of Scotland's major cities in the nineteenth century, especially Glasgow and Edinburgh, meant that their long-established burial grounds were becoming over-used – unsightly, ill-kept and their nauseating conditions a health risk. Cholera was not the only mass epidemic – typhus claimed more victims – but being sudden, fatal and no respecter of class, it was the stimulant to an accelerated concern for better public health in Britain. In the early nineteenth century, the two rival explanations for poor public health focused on miasmas (from inhalation) and contagion.

More widely, rapid urbanisation, with immigration from the Highland and rural areas as well as Ireland, brought to the fore a number of issues whose consequences – personal, financial and social – affected the way in which people and institutions sought to confront them: in health, medical practice and the causes of disease; in poverty, housing and social class; in religious belief and the interpretation of disease; and national and local government, including Poor Law legislation. Urbanisation and population growth put huge strains on existing traditional institutions, including the religious. Death was transformed during this century, largely due to the unprecedented demographic switch in so short a time.

Nations north and south of the border followed different courses in burial reform. Britain's key civil servant, Edwin Chadwick, was a miasmatist. Based in London, he began in Poor Law administration then progressed to sanitary reform.[1] In 1843 his *Interment Report* (Chadwick 1843), following on from Walker's *Gatherings from Graveyards* (Walker 1839) and MacKinnon (*Report* 1842), brought increased public scrutiny of the abject state of English burial grounds and their management. Thus, through Chadwick there was formed in England and Wales a direct link between the reform of public health and of burial grounds. The second cholera epidemic of 1848–9 was the stimulus for a series of Burial Acts in the early 1850s and helped strengthen Chadwick's stinging criticisms of burial and undertaking practices. With Chadwick holding the miasmic position, intermural churchyards had become obvious candidates for closure. As the old urban church- and chapel-yards and burial grounds were being closed, public cemeteries funded by local rates took their place, particularly in towns.[2]

In Scotland the situation was very different and no full comparison has yet been made. It is notable, first, that the Scottish sanitary movement was led not by civil servants but by medical professionals. Second, some of the medical leaders (like W.P. Allison) dismissed the miasmic hypothesis and believed in contagion. These Scottish reformers were concerned to reduce the mortality rate by tackling poverty. Their focus of attention was the gross facts of death and disease in the cities like Glasgow and Edinburgh. In this era – forty years before the establishment of the Scottish Office – Scots were governed by the Home Office (HO) in London. Burial conditions in Scotland were not subject to the same civil service critique in the early 1840s as in England and Wales; Chadwick's 1842 Sanitary Report on Scotland had paid very little attention to burial conditions (Chadwick 1842; Lewis 1952).

From 1820 private cemetery companies had sprung up in England and Wales, partly the inspiration of Nonconformist families enriched by the Industrial Revolution, and challenging the Church of England's virtual monopoly of provision (Rugg 1999, 2013). Inter-denominational antagonism over burial grounds was far less in Scotland, for since the Reformation

1. Chadwick 1842. For Chadwick, see Lewis 1952.
2. See further, Rugg 2013.

280 years before, burial grounds had been provided and often owned by Burgh Councils or local lay heritors, although parish elders played a part in their management. The churches in Scotland had little proprietary interest in burial grounds. While the private cemetery movement in England and Wales peaked in the 1840s, in Scotland it was only just beginning and, unaffected by subsequent English and Welsh legislation, grew steadily. Until the 1930s, Scottish local government left burial ground provision to private cemeteries and did not develop many public ones until the twentieth century.

England had established an early lead in public health legislation and the introduction of Medical Officers of Health (MOHs). Scotland's first MOHs were appointed in the 1860s. The Burial Grounds (Scotland) Act 1855, though only five years after the first burial Act for London, only weakly encouraged local government to provide their own cemeteries. The new breed of MOHs had to fight their local authorities and private entrepreneurs as they tried to secure the public health reforms they sought. The first cremationists faced the resistance of both.

Resurrection Men, the Anatomy Act and Cholera

Resurrection Men

The first thirty years of the nineteenth century saw a sharp increase in a sinister aspect of burial: body-snatching (Richardson 1987, 2008; Gorman 2010). From the seventeenth century the medical universities of Scotland had each received four corpses a year – two male, two female – for public dissection. The inadequacy of this supply was solved by criminality: 'Resurrection Men' would disinter recently buried corpses from kirk-yards and sell them at anatomy schools in Glasgow (McDonald 2011), Edinburgh, Dundee and Aberdeen.

Gorman described the range of deterrents with which relatives and parishioners defended their dead. Mort-stones could be placed upon the graves and metal mort-safes could encase the individual grave or vault, to be removed when the body was estimated to have decomposed beyond anatomical use. Local volunteers organised rotas to watch for an agreed season after a funeral. Mort-houses, for the temporary custody of the dead, acted as shelters for the volunteers. The many surviving structures in Gorman's survey reveal how widespread the fear of body-snatching was. Beyond the connection between dissection and capital punishment, there were other reasons why protecting the recently dead now became strong in the Scottish psyche: attitudes towards the integrity of the corpse in relation to Judgement Day; morality and mores related to the naked body being viewed by strangers; and the general relationship between the corpse and the numinous (Richardson 1987; Metcalfe and Huntingdon 1991).

The activities of grave-robbers in the 1820s came to a dramatic peak with the arrest and trial of Burke and Hare (Edwards 1980; Richardson 1987). Burke and Hare were not, strictly speaking, resurrectionists: they were arrested for killing fourteen people whose corpses they then sold to Dr Robert Knox – though many other surgeons had also bought corpses. The mob showed its feelings by attacking Knox's house and burning his body in effigy.

The Anatomy Act 1832

'Burkophobia' undoubtedly provided ammunition for the Anatomy Bill campaign, led by MP William Warburton. The Act was intended to undermine the threat of the resurrectionists by increasing the legal supply of corpses for anatomy. Practical anatomy was a core element of medical training; at this time no-one would donate their body to medicine, not even 'enlightened' surgeons.

Formerly, the legal supply of corpses for dissection had come principally from workhouses, prisons and prison hulks. Now, unclaimed bodies could be dispatched to an anatomist. The Inspector of Anatomy for Scotland, Dr Craigie, had to persuade local parishes to organise the supply of unclaimed corpses and ensure a fair distribution to the competing anatomy schools (Richardson 1987: 242). Some anatomists evaded the Inspector by arranging a monopoly of supplies from specific parishes. Fears of dissection magnified the terrible stigma of the Scottish pauper's funeral (Strange 2015).

This precipitated new fears for people who could not rely on relatives or neighbours to claim their body and organise a funeral. People took a range of precautions to secure a 'decent' burial. '[T]he desire to secure respectful interment of themselves and their relations is perhaps the strongest and most widely diffused feeling [...] among the labouring classes' (House of Lords 1842: 54). Smith argues that the Anatomy Act, coupled with increasing parsimony in poor relief, combined to fuel the death economy (M. Smith 2014). The working classes were forced to take private measures, and their purchase of (relatively) showy funerals reflected their diligence and care. Friendly Societies – for sickness and burial expenses – had flourished for decades (Gosden 1961: 29). These catered for the regularly-employed but, after the Anatomy Act, for those in seasonal, casual or low-paid work a new range of burial clubs and societies sprang up. They relied upon weekly contributions and were often organised by publicans. The risks for subscribers were considerable: a period of unemployment might lead to unpaid subscriptions and forfeiture of the whole account. Companies could provoke lapses deliberately by withdrawing their collectors. The post-1832 system became known as Industrial Assurance. It survived successive investigations until the Fabian Society's Report (1944) helped precipitate its end.

Cholera

Cholera came to Scotland in four epidemics: 1831, 1848–9, 1853–4 and 1866 (Lewis 1952; Longmate 1966; Morris 1976). Neither the Civil Service nor the medical profession had any sound explanation either for its character or its spread. Government policy, caught in the crossfire between contagion and miasmatic hypotheses, faced two alternatives: contagion implied quarantine, with a consequent loss of trade and the disruption of civic and family life, whilst miasmas required sanitary measures, funding and Poor Relief on a massive scale. The Privy Council had the responsibility for dealing with the cholera and in June 1831 set up a Central Board of Health (CBH) to advise it about cholera prevention. As there was no Scottish Office until 1886, the country was administered from London. The CBH organised local Boards of Health, which were to detect cholera victims, purify their accommodation, isolate victims in temporary hospital space and bury the dead in the hospital grounds or close by.

Cholera challenged traditional customs and forms of mourning and burial, especially among the poorer classes. Some churchyards refused to bury cholera victims (M. Smith 2014: 65); some parishes refused to allow their mort-cloth to be used during a cholera funeral; both denials offended families affected. Cholera funerals were particularly horrid, with shrouds dipped in coal tar, coffins containing lime, and rushed and lonely burials. All these measures, hasty and impersonal, were an affront to traditional domestic life. They provoked hostility to the medical profession and to public health administrators. The initiatives of local Boards of Health met with uproar and riots in Edinburgh's Fountainbridge, Glasgow's Gorbals and in Paisley (Morris 1976: 108–14). The Boards acknowledged the violence they did to 'ordinary feelings' but held their course.

Glasgow's 1832 epidemic was Britain's worst. Just over 3,000 people died, with over 1,000 deaths in August alone. Its particular effect was to widen awareness of the need for better public health. The epidemics also probably helped encourage the middle classes to transfer their funerals from the (public) kirk-yards to safer (private) cemeteries after 1840.

The Private Cemetery Movement

The private cemetery movement (Rugg 1992) was introduced into Scotland by the opening of the Glasgow Necropolis in 1833 (Scott 2006). In 1828 Dean of Guild James Ewing persuaded the Merchants House – the old Merchant Guild – to develop a cemetery on their Fir Park, the hill east of Glasgow Cathedral. Ewing's proposal was for a garden cemetery, based on the best European models, particularly Père Lachaise in Paris (1804) to which British tourists had flocked after the defeat of Napoleon (but see Rugg 1997).

The City Chamberlain, John Strang, wrote *Necropolis Glasguensis* (1831) emphasising the public health benefits of the project. He recommended the cemetery have wide graves, be open to all denominations but with memorials approved by the Merchants House. Such conditions all ensured the success of the venture with the wealthy and middle classes. Only the wealthiest could afford the plots on the hilltop. The poor were buried in unmarked graves, following the centuries-old tradition in the city's churchyards. Scott wrote, 'Within the Necropolis the internal arrangements can be seen to mirror the social or class distinctions of the city.'

Todd, analysing Presbyterian burial customs, comments that the Kirk struggled to impose its puritanical ambitions: it could not prevent churchyard burial and therefore never entirely eradicated the associations between church land and the sacred in death (Todd 2002). Smith sees the private cemetery movement as a challenge to the Kirk's authority at death and at funerals (M. Smith 2014). Unlike the Anglican Church, the Church of Scotland had, since John Knox, no liturgy for funerals. The Kirk's controls over death were 'imposed' by the proximity of the kirk-yard to the kirk and by a theology that the churchyard was the custodian of the dead until God decreed the Day of Resurrection and the consequent Judgement (Raeburn 2012).

The traditional Presbyterian funeral involved common elements (Gordon 1984, 1992; M. Bennett 2004). These included the wake at home, the walking funeral along the road (the 'coffin road') and the burial in the allotted communal ground. The journey did not include the church. All these elements were hallowed by the associations learned from generations of funerals. They embedded in the public consciousness the symbolism of the transition of dead people from one state of existence to another, a new existence whose quality, however, the survivors were unable to influence by any human initiatives considered legitimate in a Scottish Presbyterian culture.

By providing new locations for burial, subject to company directors and shareholders rather than heritors and kirk-sessions, and offering gravesites as a consumer choice, the private cemetery movement established an alternative to traditional authority and practice. By its promotional references to 'non-denominational' sites, 'public health', 'decency' and the security of the bodies buried within cemetery walls, it allowed funerals to be used to enhance social class divisions to the benefits of the upwardly mobile middle classes. The dominance of the private cemetery movement in nineteenth-century Scotland would retard the adoption of cremation until the 1930s.

Undertaking from the 1840s

The history of undertaking in Scotland has only recently received analysis (M. Smith 2009, 2014; Parsons 2013). Smith has investigated the emergence of Edinburgh undertaking from part-time speculative entrepreneurship (as an adjunct to carpentry or carriage mastery) to a full-time specialism. Even by 1900, it could still be an ad-hoc industry. Yet the undertaker was an essential component in the high-mortality urban environment (whilst the minister was still restricted in the consolation he could offer).

For Smith, this development of undertaking in Edinburgh drew upon the city's tradition of service professions, among whose influential middle-classes undertakers emerged in the middle nineteenth century. A second characteristic lies in two parallel events: the decline of the Kirk's involvement in funerals and the growth of the private cemeteries (Raeburn 2012; above, ch. 1). The Kirk's role was severely reduced by the latter following the Disruption of 1843. The burial of Thomas Chalmers in the Grange Cemetery in 1847 helped establish a precedent for Free Church members which offered private cemetery companies a new clientele.

Smith has analysed the growth of undertaking in Edinburgh through listings in Post Office Directories. The first recorded business appeared in 1804, rising to ten undertakers listed in 1824, with twenty-eight in 1836. The number of specialist funeral directors rose to fifty-one in 1897. Their success depended on the opening up of client choice between church-managed and privately-owned burial grounds, with the social divide between rich and poor increasingly visible. The key stakeholders in funeral arrangements, especially after 1843, were the funeral directors.

Glasgow: Attempts at Burial Reform[3]

Councillor Salmon's initiative

When the Burial Grounds (Scotland) Act 1855 gave powers to close old burial grounds and permitted Councils to provide for new ones, Glasgow took no practical steps to close the old until, in 1862, a Councillor Salmon successfully proposed the Council consider 'the whole question of Intramural Interment in the city and suburbs' (Hutt 1996). Salmon was made chairman of a committee with power to 'obtain the consent of the lair-holders [...] to [the grounds'] early suppression as places of interment'. His initiative did not proceed far. Lair-holders' behaviour was conservative by nature and lair ownership too good an investment.

In 1863 Glasgow appointed W.T. Gairdner as its first Medical Officer of Health (MOH). In 1866 he and City Architect John Carrick persuaded the Town Council to survey the condition of eleven of its burial grounds (Carrick and Gairdner 1870). Carrick and Gairdner were determined to use the 1855 Act to effect closures. Their report recommended that all the burial grounds surveyed be suppressed at the earliest date; that they be laid out as parks, for whose maintenance the Corporation would pay; and that proprietary lair-holders be given lairs elsewhere. Closure of selected old sites should be accompanied by the provision of new, provided and funded from the public purse.

In October 1869 the Town Council responded to the Carrick–Gairdner report with discouragement. They estimated the cost of providing new (i.e. public) cemeteries at £60,000. This would require permissive powers of taxation at a halfpenny in the pound for ten years. However, the Council agreed to close the 'obnoxious' grounds in the poorest parts of the city. The Police Board petitioned the Sheriff to have the grounds closed under the Public Health (Scotland) Act 1867. This action succeeded and in 1870 one crypt and eleven burial grounds were closed to new burials.[4]

3. For Glasgow cemeteries see Curl n.d., c.1975; Mitchell 1958, 1968; Scott 2006; Willing and Fairlie 1997, Willsher 1985; and Buckham 2016.
4. These included St David's/Ramshorn; The High Church; St Mary's Roman Catholic, Abercrombie Street; St Mark's, Cheapside; and the Gorbals.

The Carrick–Gairdner report acknowledged the opposition between burial reform and poverty: it seemed 'impossible to regulate intramural interments upon any principle of immediate application without [...] pecuniary distress [...] to those who could least afford it'. As Littlejohn discovered in Edinburgh, closures of old city-owned burial grounds drove poorer citizens to patronise the private cemeteries, incurring higher funeral costs in both grave fees and funeral transport.

At this time the new Royal Infirmary, built in 1861, faced a burial problem of its own. It had three large wards, two in a new building. Despite the antiseptic regime instigated by Joseph Lister, patients with open sores proved particularly liable to infection. Investigations revealed that the new building was sited where the hospital had buried cholera victims in 1850 (Lister 1870 a,b). The Infirmary scandal was significant for funeral reform, for the pioneers of cremation in Scotland, England and Wales drew upon the story to support their case that traditional burial was a danger to public health.

Whatever the successes of the burial ground closure lobby, it could not persuade Local Authorities to provide new publicly-funded cemeteries. The Act, indeed, may have helped strengthen the private cemetery movement. No cemeteries had been opened in Glasgow since 1851. From 1873 until 1889, eight private cemeteries (including one Catholic) were established. This would profit owners and shareholders but give little improvement for poorer families.

Dr J.B. Russell MOH

In 1872 Dr John Burn Russell (1837–1904) succeeded Gairdner as Glasgow's MOH (Russell 1905; E. Robertson 1998). His successes in improving public health were far-reaching. In 1876 he ordered a survey of the City's closed burial grounds by Sanitary Inspector K.M. MacLeod (MacLeod 1876). By then there were only four open burial grounds left in the city. In 1875, these four carried out 12,930 burials from the city's total of 13,283 deaths. MacLeod concentrated on reducing overcrowding. He recommended separate graves, with no more than two children in each: allowing for family lairs another 13 acres were needed immediately. He proposed new mortuaries and a new public cemetery, preferably adjacent to a railway station.

In 1878, Salmon's and his Additional Extramural Burial Grounds Committee (AEBGC) reported on the suitability of land near Blackhill, already council-owned, as a cemetery. In April 1879 the Finance Committee considered land at Dalmuir and authorised negotiations with the North

British Railway for a siding and station accommodation. Over the next three years first one then the other site was favoured. After October 1881 the AEBGC minutes contain no further reference to proposals for cemeteries either at Blackhill or Dalmuir.

Glasgow's closed burial grounds

On 17 June 1878 the Glasgow Public Parks Act 1878 empowered the Council to 'lay out and maintain closed burial grounds'. MacLeod pleaded in vain for maintenance to be done, reporting in 1880 that only six of the eleven closed churchyards were still in good order. In 1889 his successor Peter Fyfe reported on the closed burial grounds. St David's/Ramshorn was kept in good order, with a gate always open to the public. However, St Mark's Cheapside was now closed to the public. Of the Gorbals, Fyfe wrote, 'A considerable part of the walk has been dug up to kill the fungus. The public, in the winter time, do not take advantage of the opening hours.'

Thus, despite the efforts of its civil servants and certain Councillors, the Town Council did all it could to avoid maintaining old burial grounds or providing new ones. Only in the vastly changed context of the post-1945 era would Glasgow's first municipal cemetery finally open in 1961 at the Linn.

The Failure of Burial Reform in Edinburgh[5]

Edinburgh's Greyfriars Church was built in 1620 on the site of the Greyfriars Monastery which had been sacked by the mob. As the City boundary extended, it and six more parish churches came into the ownership of the City Council. Edinburgh's first post-Reformation graveyard thus foreshadows the typical Scottish urban situation where church buildings and graveyards are owned by the secular local authority. The constant burying and reburying over three centuries at Greyfriars presented a health hazard for mid-Victorian Edinburgh.

Despite the growth of the city, no new burial space (save at St John's Episcopal, 1840) was provided between 1820 and 1843, by which time at least 100,000 corpses had been buried in the 19 acres of the seven city churchyards. During the cholera epidemic of 1848, burial pits in the old churchyard of Canongate lay open to the sky with bodies uncovered until the pits were full enough to be closed.

5. See Laxton and Rodger 2014.

In 1862, the Town Council appointed its first MOH, Dr Henry Littlejohn. Littlejohn was a man for whom 'the disposing of the dead in cities was a life-long concern' (Laxton and Rodger 2014: 147). He soon turned his attention to Greyfriars and persuaded the Council that 'no new burials should be permitted, excepting persons possessing private tombs'. When the Council proved dilatory, Littlejohn commented that the full closure of Greyfriars churchyard would be 'a sanitary measure of no small importance' (Littlejohn 1865: 94).

Littlejohn pursued a two-stage policy: old burial grounds within the city should be closed while new grave space was to be provided by the Council in new cemeteries beyond the city boundary. For him, municipal ownership was vital so that the poor could afford to give their dead decent burial. He faced an uphill task. The Town Council, having closed two public cemeteries (Canongate and Greyfriars), repeatedly failed to close more.

In 1865, Littlejohn published his celebrated *Report on the Sanitary Condition of Edinburgh* with the chapter 'Intramural Interment' (Littlejohn 1865: 83–99). He now proposed that the City Parishes should 'combine to provide [...] a public Cemetery of large extent at some distance in the country, and of easy access [...] in which the rate of [i.e. fee for] interment could be made as reasonable as possible' (Littlejohn 1865: 99). In September 1866 Littlejohn again pressed his case. Finally the Council agreed with Edinburgh's six private cemeteries to bury cholera victims at a standard fee. As for providing a new cemetery, Littlejohn commented that the Council's response conveyed the impression that 'they were hearing the argument for the first time' (Laxton and Rodger 2014: 154).

Littlejohn was more successful in 1874 when complaints about the condition of St Cuthbert's Churchyard led to a successful appeal to the Sheriff Principal (Lord Provost of Edinburgh v Kirk Session of St Cuthbert's 1874).[6] As a result all nineteen city churchyards were closed by the Town Council. This effectively delivered a monopoly to the private cemeteries (Laxton and Rodger 2014: 220). Littlejohn turned his attention back to them in 1882, conducting test borings in the public sections of the private cemeteries. At Dalry he discovered eleven of the thirty graves tested were less than two feet from the surface. Littlejohn sought to convince the Council that the private cemeteries were not to be trusted with the treatment of poorer families. Nevertheless, the Council again refused to provide a municipal cemetery.

6. See ch. 1.

When Duncan formed his Scottish Burial Reform and Cremation Society in Glasgow five years later, Littlejohn gave his support and later served as a director.

The Kirk's Diminishing Role in Death

The national position of the Kirk had been allowed to erode in several ways since the later eighteenth century. 'The parish state' describes the leading role of the Kirk Session in local government except in the towns (Mitchison 1977; Devine 2012). Kirk Sessions had exercised control of moral conduct, education and (albeit limited) social welfare. In the eighteenth century the administration of relief had passed, in the larger towns, to Town Councils. With urban development, the parish state proved increasingly inadequate an instrument though the reorganisation of local government had to await the Reform Act 1832 (Daiches 1977; Maver 2000). Thereafter secular authorities steadily took over a widening set of social responsibilities: Police Acts and the public health movement were outwith the Kirk: 'The church was being bypassed as new elements of provision and control were being set up' (Mitchison 1977: 162).

The Disruption (the latest in the series of Scottish religious secessions) occurred not only as the debates on Poor Law reform moved towards their climax but as the private cemetery movement took off. The burial of the dead had long been a civic responsibility (though the matter of the legal ownership and management for responsibility of post-Reformation and especially post-1855 kirk-yards remains an important agenda for research). The years 1843–55 proved crucial in the severe reduction of the Kirk's roles in death, including the private cemetery movement; the transfer of Poor Law responsibilities; the consequences of the Anatomy Act; and the Burials and Registration Acts of 1855 (Smith 2014).

The end of the old Poor Law did not terminate all of the Kirk's traditional responsibilities for Poor Law reform: its regular church door collections for the poor, including their funerals, continued (MacLean 1953). Meanwhile, the old paternalistic attitudes that had characterised the Kirk's attitudes to the dying poor were challenged by the Anatomy Act (Smith 2014). In permitting anatomy schools to obtain unclaimed bodies, the Act lifted a financial burden from the Kirk. Yet 'the Church at times found itself in an awkward position regarding the Anatomy Act' (Smith 2014:73). Smith has demonstrated how the income generated from the sale of corpses helped to finance the burial of paupers in Edinburgh. During the second cholera

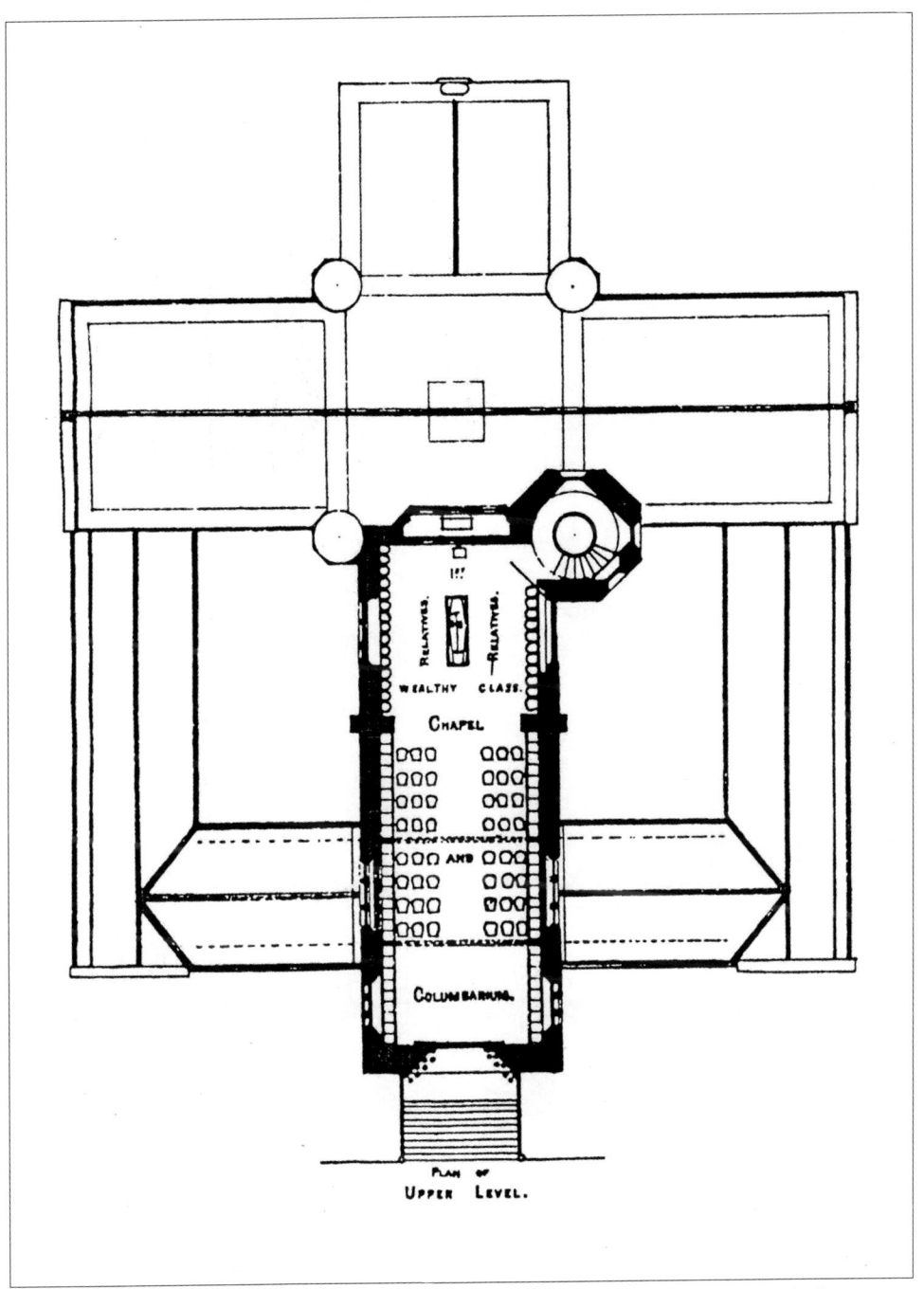

Plate 1. James Chalmers, 'A Scheme of Cremation Suited to the Requirements of Glasgow', upper level, showing the Chapel for 'the very rich'. (Drawing published in *Proceedings of the Royal Philosophical Society of Glasgow*, volume 20, 1888–89)

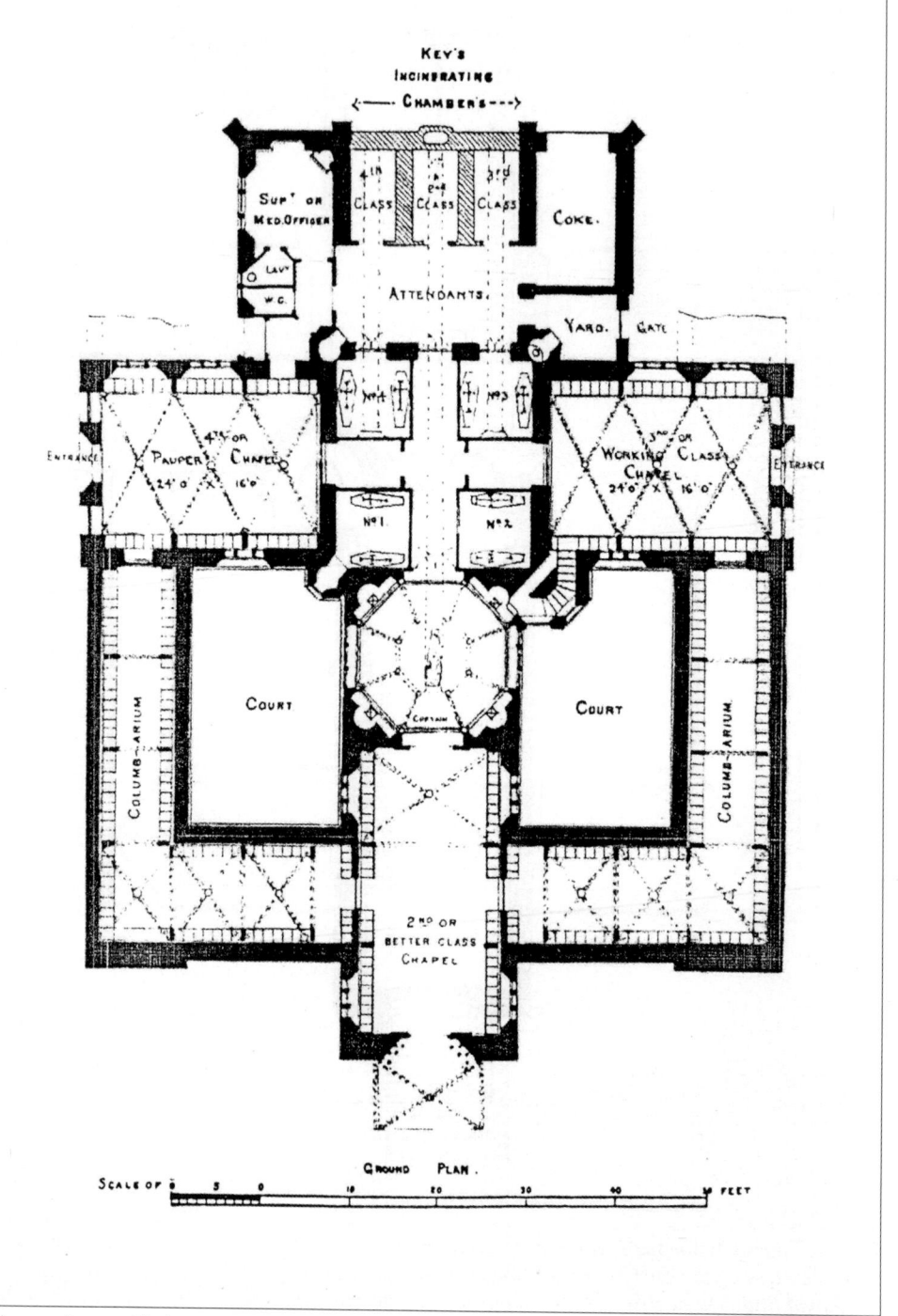

Plate 2. James Chalmers, 'A Scheme of Cremation Suited to the Requirements of Glasgow', ground floor plan (Drawing published in *Proceedings of the Royal Philosophical Society of Glasgow*, volume 20, 1888–89)

Plate 3. Woking Crematorium (1889), E.F.C. Clarke, Architect to the Cremation Society. (Drawing published in *Building News*, 21 September 1888)

Plate 4. Maryhill Crematorium, Glasgow (1895), James Chalmers. (Photograph published in *Cremation in Great Britain*, 1909, p.33)

Plate 5. Maryhill Crematorium, Glasgow (1895–1963), including the ground floor columbarium by James Chalmers (1926). The columbarium had an additional four floors added in 1939. The second chapel was opened in 1954 and further alterations made to the crematorium in 1963. (Photograph, Hilary J. Grainger)

Plate 6. Maryhill Crematorium, Glasgow (1895), James Chalmers. Interior of chapel showing the original arrangement with the catafalque placed centrally. (Photograph published in Herbert P. Jones (ed.), *Cremation in Great Britain*, Pharos Press, 1945)

Plate 7. (*left*) Maryhill Crematorium, Glasgow (1985), James Chalmers. Interior showing the current arrangement with the catafalque to the left. (Photograph, Hilary J. Grainger)

Plate 8. (*below*) Unpublished drawing for a proposed Edinburgh crematorium, Sydney Mitchell & Wilson (1913). (In the possession of Edinburgh Cremation Limited)

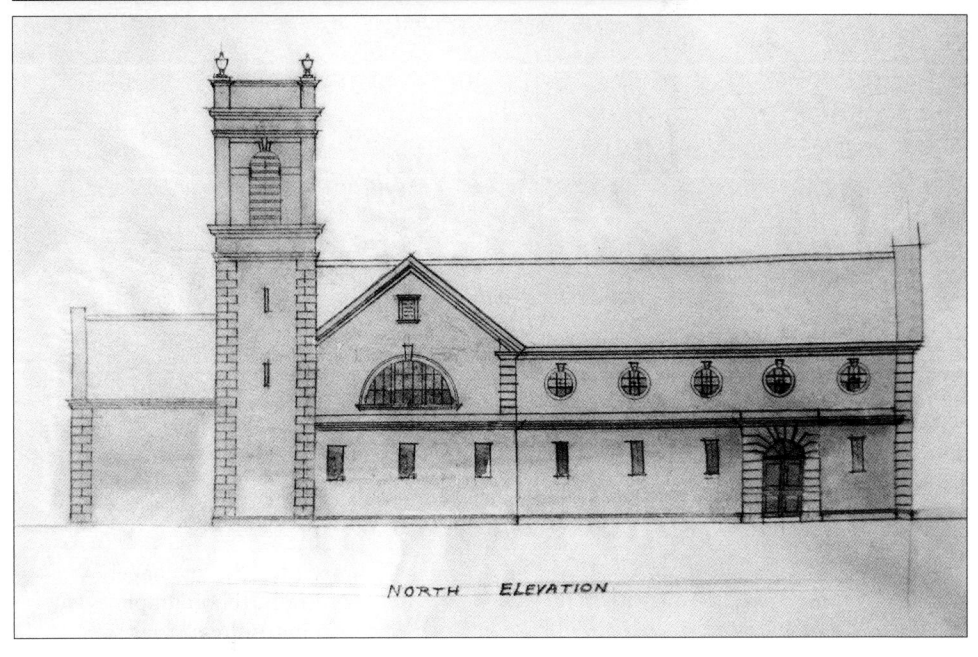

Plate 9. The opening of Warriston Crematorium, Edinburgh, 3 October 1929, showing Lord Salvesen in the centre. (Photograph, The Cremation Society of Great Britain)

Plate 10. Golders Green Crematorium, London (1902), Ernest George & Yeates, showing the West Chapel and porte-cochère. (Published in *The Architectural Review*)

Plate 11. (*above*) Warriston Crematorium, Edinburgh (1929), Sir Robert Lorimer & Matthew. The cloisters and second chapel were added in 1958. (Photograph, Geoff Brandwood)

Plate 12. (*left*) Warriston Crematorium, Edinburgh (1929), Sir Robert Lorimer & Matthew. Interior of Chapel. (Photograph published in Herbert P. Jones (ed.), *Cremation in Great Britain*, Pharos Press, 1945)

Plate 13. Warriston Crematorium, Edinburgh (1929), Sir Robert Lorimer & Matthew. Interior of chapel. (Photograph, Hilary J. Grainger)

Plate 14. Warriston Crematorium, Edinburgh (1929), Sir Robert Lorimer & Matthew. Cloisters 1958. (Photograph, Geoff Brandwood)

Plate 15. Warriston Crematorium, Edinburgh (1929), Sir Robert Lorimer & Matthew, showing the later entrance porch. (Photograph, Edinburgh Cremation Limited)

Plate 16. Dundee Crematorium (1936), T. Lindsay Gray. (Photograph, Hilary J. Grainger)

Plate 17. Dundee Crematorium (1936), T. Lindsay Gray.
(Photograph, Hilary J. Grainger)

Plate 18. Kaimhill Crematorium, Aberdeen (1938), R. Leslie Rollo & Hall.
(Photograph, Hilary J. Grainger)

Plate 19. Kaimhill Crematorium, Aberdeen (1938), R. Leslie Rollo & Hall.
(Photograph, Hilary J. Grainger)

Plate 20. Paisley Woodside Crematorium, Renfrewshire (1938), James Maitland Steel.
(Photograph, Hilary J. Grainger)

Plate 21. Paisley Woodside Crematorium, Renfrewshire (1938), James Maitland Steel. (Photograph, Hilary J. Grainger)

Plate 22. Seafield Crematorium, Leith, Edinburgh (1938), W.N. Thompson & Co. (Photograph published in Herbert P. Jones (ed.), *Cremation in Great Britain*, Pharos Press, 1945)

epidemic, when Kirk funds were straining to cope with burials of the poor, churches seem to have gone to great lengths to ensure a decent burial for as many as possible. Nevertheless, in Edinburgh in 1847–8, over 2,500 bodies were buried at the expense of the Kirk with an accompanying increase in bodies given up to the anatomy schools for dissection, as the Kirk sought to ease the pressure on its funds. Between 1857 and 1880 increased pressure was placed on the Kirk to supply subjects for dissection. When the Inspector for Anatomy pressed individual parishes to comply with the spirit of the Anatomy Act, it is not difficult to see why fewer poor people applied for burial from public funds. The poor became less and less inclined to expect assistance from the relevant authorities, hence their resort to insurance.

In the mid-1850s two successive Acts further diminished the Kirk's public responsibilities in death. The Burial Grounds (Scotland) Act 1855 authorised the closure of burial grounds for reasons of public health. The lack of parliamentary debates prevents our understanding what contrary arguments were advanced. Warner demonstrated from his USA study that cemeteries once closed to further burials hold different meanings and play different roles in the local community from those which remain open (Warner 1959). A study of the role of kirk-yards in Scots' culture, both before 1855 and beyond, awaits attention.

The Registration of Births, Deaths and Marriages (Scotland) Act 1854 (Gordon 1984; Sinclair 2000; A. Cameron 2007; above, ch. 1) had a more immediate effect upon the Kirk. In 1565 the General Assembly of the newly established Church of Scotland had been empowered to instruct every minister to register the burials of all who were buried within their parish. By the 1800s, massive overcrowding of city slums had overwhelmed the registration system. Growing medical concerns for public health had meanwhile revealed the lack of the very statistical information which might establish connections between health and social conditions. The Kirk system had a long-standing reputation for unreliability. This, given the fast increasing population, was unsuitable for the rational age that craved empirical data (Rugg 1997).

Beginning in 1810, ten successive attempts to achieve legislation failed. Although the English Registration Act of 1836 provided a working precedent, Scots could not agree on a civil registration system until 1854. The main objections included: first, its administrative complexity and expense; second, while the Bills required a registrar in each parish, was he to be paid out of the fees or from an additional parochial rate?; third, the public was hostile to any clause which imposed fees and penalties; fourth, attempts to incorporate marriage reforms within attempts to reform registration always proved controversial. Sinclair (2000) has shown how the Kirk resisted every attempt to wrest control of registration from its Sessions' control.

The 1854 Registration Bill successfully juggled most of the claims of the various vested interests. The Registration Office would be housed in the (existing) Register House in Edinburgh. Existing Sheriffs would be unpaid Superintendent Registrars. The Kirk was partly appeased by the proposal to appoint all currently officiating Session Clerks in office to be Registrars during their lifetime; their successors would be appointed by Parochial Boards. While a parochial rate was introduced for the payment of Registrars, the Bill sugared this pill by requiring fees only for marriages. It also prescribed penalties for failure to register births and deaths.

The vitally important consequence of this legislation was the element of compulsion. Scotland now had an administrative system backed by statute, for the collection and analysis of births and deaths for all its people and regions. Medical researchers and public health organisations could increasingly map Scotland's demography of death and prepare policies accordingly.

The Revival of Liturgy in the Church of Scotland from 1865[7]

As ch. 1 showed, funerals had been severely simplified by the Scottish Reformers, so as to prevent Presbyterian clergy from any liturgical acts regarded as Catholic 'superstitions'. The Disruption was a severe crisis for the Church of Scotland (S.J. Brown 1982; Brown and Fry 1993). When the Evangelical Party left the General Assembly, their new Free Church took 38% of the clergy and possibly 40% of its members. Thoughtful clergy and laity, surveying the wreckage, began to consider the future. They reckoned how much their service to God and their parishioners might be improved and the attractiveness of the Kirk enhanced. Improving the experience of worship was one way forward. Slowly, from 1865, reforming spirits reintroduced Easter Communion, Christmas Day services, Scripture reading in church and choral and instrumental music.

The liturgical reformers met opposition from the outset and were widely accused of bringing back Catholicism. Funerals played a part in their agenda. Since *The First Book of Discipline* (1560) there had been no religious service of any kind at burials. The reformers knew they would have to be especially

---

7. See Kerr 1909; A.K. Robertson 1956; S.J. Brown 1982, 2009, 2016; C.G. Brown 1987, 1997; Jupp 2009.

sensitive when bringing back the minister to play a formal and constructive part in burial rites. Several individuals promoted liturgical reform, but the role played by the Rev. George W. Sprott, minister of North Berwick (Church of Scotland) from 1867, is paramount.

Born in Nova Scotia, Canada, Sprott trained for the ministry at Glasgow. His pastoral work as chaplain of the Scots Kirk in Candy, Ceylon, alerted him to the bareness of Presbyterian worship, especially when compared with that of other British denominations active in the Empire (Kerr 1909: 47). For example, a letter from Turkey of 1857 to an Edinburgh minister complained of the minimal facilities for Christian worship, adding, 'How many of Scotland's sons have gone down to the narrow grave, and no minister to read a verse, or utter a word of prayer!' (qtd Bonar 1860: 53–5).

Kindred reformist spirits were considering an organisation to pursue liturgical reform within the Kirk. Sprott, as chair of the Editorial Committee, emerged as the Church Service Society's leading force. In 1882, Sprott itemised recent developments in funeral practice (Sprott 1882:166–7):

> Though an address at the grave was always legal, prayer and reading of Scripture, whether there or in the house, are [...] forbidden by the Directory, but the church has now virtually sanctioned them both [...] prayers in the house are now almost universal in this country, and they are becoming common also at the grave [...] Even the singing of Hymns at the grave has been introduced in some cases [...] and the General Assembly has gone the length of providing chants for the purpose.

Thus, two generations after the Disruption, certain Church of Scotland clergy were restoring liturgical initiatives at funerals, backed by a consensus forming in the General Assembly. Smith[8] has wondered to what extent was minister reform driven by lay demand for liturgical initiatives at funerals.[9] The Kirk's intellectual stance was also changing. The Free Church, which had originally proclaimed the innerancy of Scripture produced, after 1870, younger ministers with a sympathy for German theological developments; they were now accommodating biblical criticism, modern geology and evolutionary theory. It is not surprising that Sprott's graveside commendations make no reference to hell, damnation or predestination.

8. M. Smith, personal communication, October 2015.
9. MacLean 1953: 86–8.

In 1890 the results of Sprott's statistical enquiry, authorised by the General Assembly, revealed that 35% of ministers now took graveside services.[10] Sprott had thus demonstrated a solid basis of support from both ministers and congregations. His Committee was stood down in 1894 but in 1897 a new edition of the General Assembly's *Prayers and Devotions for Home and Abroad* provided forms of service for funerals, including prayers at the grave for the dead and the bereaved.

Given their enhanced role at the graveside, it was unlikely that most Presbyterian clergy would now seriously contemplate let alone endorse the new, radical alternative in disposal, made available at Maryhill from 1895. Cremation was resonant with European atheist and anti-establishment rhetoric and reputation. It also carried the implicit message that the body is finished and of no use, that the only hope beyond death was that of a surviving soul (Davies 1990: 33). The restoration of graveside ministry undoubtedly contributed to the persistence of burial into the first half of the twentieth century, effectively delaying the adoption of modern cremation.

The Background to the Cremation Movement[11]

From the Dark Ages until the nineteenth century human cremation in the West had been by funeral pyre, in the open air, associated with the dead gods of the Vikings and with the burning of witches and heretics. If cremation were to grip the modern Western imagination, then it needed a new mode of burning free from precisely those associations (Jupp 1990). Words like 'modern', 'progressive', 'mechanical', 'technological', 'sanitary', 'secular' and 'socialist' all spring to mind.

Effective responses to cholera had matured as rail and telegraphic communications linked the European medical profession. Several health conferences debated cremation as an alternative to the burial arrangements of the cholera years. Delegates at Florence (1869) and Rome (1871) voted to legalise cremation. Certain Masonic groups employed cremation as a way of undermining the Catholic Church. Engineers began to experiment with furnaces suitable for human cremation. The Crimean War and the realities of deaths in modern warfare had led Professor Edmund Parkes to suggest

---

10. New College, University of Edinburgh, Church of Scotland MS, CHU8.1–2, Committee on Public Worship and the Sacraments, 1890.
11. See further, Parsons 2005; Grainger 2005; Jupp 2006a.

cremation for soldiers killed on the battlefields (Parsons 2005: 24, 26; Jupp 1990). Voluntary societies were established to promote cremation (Irion 1976; Davies and Mates 2005).

The Founding of the English Cremation Society

In 1873 the Italian scientist Brunetti demonstrated his work on cremator technology at an international exhibition in Vienna. Among the English visitors was Sir Henry Thompson. Thompson was the son of a Congregationalist shopkeeper in Suffolk. He had risen to be surgeon to Queen Victoria by way of a successful bowel operation on King Leopold of the Belgians. His interest in cremation had been evolving for some years; it was the sight of Professor Ludovico Brunetti's cremating apparatus at Vienna that persuaded him that modern cremation was practically possible.

In January 1874 Thompson published a powerful argument for cremation (Thompson 1874a, b). He asked, 'how, given a dead body, to resolve it into carbonic acid, water and ammonia, and the mineral elements, rapidly, safely and not unpleasantly. The answer may be practically supplied in a properly constructed furnace'. Thompson tested the practicality for himself, experimenting with dead animals.

On 13 January 1874 Thompson invited to his house at 35 Wimpole Street a number of influential friends.[12] Shirley Brooks, the editor of *Punch*, drafted a declaration:

> We, the undersigned, disapprove the present custom of burying the dead, and we desire to substitute some mode which shall rapidly resolve the body into its component elements, by a process which cannot offend the living, and shall render the remains perfectly innocuous. Until some better method is devised we desire to adopt that usually known as Cremation.

The declaration was subscribed by the nine present, including Ernest Hart, the editor of the *British Medical Journal*, and later by seven others, including the noted ovariotomist and one-time editor of the *Medical Times and Gazette*, Thomas Spencer Wells, and John Millais, John Tenniel and Anthony Trollope. The declaration launched the Cremation Society (CS) which became the pressure group whose persistence was for seventy-five

---

12. White 1999, 2002c.

years the leading force behind the replacement of burial by cremation in England and Wales.[13]

Thompson misjudged public attitudes to the corpse and its funeral. The Protestant culture of England knew that funeral expenditure could not benefit the dead, but families invested in funerals to declare their affection and their status. Thompson drew immediate opposition from the Church, the Inspector of Burials and the funeral trades. Few believed his campaign would ever succeed. His journalist friends, however, helped keep cremation before the public consciousness.

The fear of premature burial, a subject regularly featured in *The Lancet*, was a late-Victorian fascination (Bourke 2005; Davies and Shaw 1995). The body had always been food for worms, but now that thought became poison for the imagination and raised new fears. Elias has described how the nineteenth-century bourgeoisie, in everything from table manners to speech, progressively 'refined' life by imposing controls upon the expression of the 'grosser' biological aspects of human activity. It seems the affront to decency was also at the forefront of opposition to the idea of cremation (Elias 1978; Leaney 1989).

The Cremation Society and the Trial of Dr William Price

One of the first actions of the CS was to obtain advice about the legality of cremation. Two barristers (CSA CRE/P/1/B1: 13/1/74, 19/3/74, 11/2/75), Frederick Meadows White and Thomas Hutchinson Tristram, were consulted. Whether they provided two opinions or one joint opinion is unclear. In 1879 the CS passed one, dated 1874 and signed by Meadows White, to the HO when seeking to counter the objections of Woking residents to the erection of a crematorium in their vicinity (TNA HO 45/9531/40582, f17). In a Lords debate on the matter the Earl of Onslow brandished an opinion which, he said, 'was signed by Dr Tristram and agreed to by Mr Meadows White' (*P. Debs*, ser. 3, vol. 244, col. 1407 [HL, 21 March 1879]).[14] The Society's Council had reported that the opinions were 'on the whole favourable [...] and such as to warrant the Council in concluding that [...] [cremation] was perfectly legal, provided that it involved no [...] nuisance' (TNA HO 45/9531/40582, f17). This was the best spin that could be put on Meadows White's opinion, which was that cremation was neither clearly

13. For a contrary view, see R. Williams 1992.
14. We have not found an opinion signed by Tristram.

legal nor clearly illegal and that the outcome of litigation might well depend on the personal predilections of judges; that it would be risky to put much money into its promotion; that one way of testing its legality would be to seek to register a company to promote it and to do so in connection with a cemetery; but that the safest course would be to secure legislation about it. The Law Officers' opinions were more favourable to cremation than this (TNA HO 45/9531/40582, ff5(2) and 17) and steps were taken to draft a Bill outlawing it. They were suspended on the CS Council's undertaking not to build a crematorium until it had drafted a Bill regulating cremation and introduced it into Parliament. The Council's plan was to ambush a Burials Bill.

Even after the 1880 Burial Laws (Amendment) Act, which permitted burials in Anglican burial grounds without Anglican rites (Fletcher 1974; Manning 1952), the introduction of a Burials Bill continued to be an annual feature of the parliamentary year. After 1880, however, ambushing a Burials Bill became slightly more difficult because in that year the single MP on the Society's Council, Watkin Williams, left the House of Commons to become a High Court Judge (and to die four years later in a brothel during a period presiding over the Assizes at Nottingham or 'between Nelly Blankey's thighs' as a memorial card circulating in Nottingham after his death had it (Bentley 1999; Morton 2003)). A list of members of the Council produced in 1874 but given to the HO in 1879 with what had by then become inaccuracies (S. White 1999) named a Scottish peer, the Earl of Mar. In the 1870s there was a long running dispute between two claimants to the title. One of these was a Scottish representative peer in 1876 and 1880, but probably the Society's Earl was the other. So after 1880, as far as one can tell, the Society had no MPs on its Council.

In 1882 a Captain Hanham of Sturminster Newton in Dorset asked to use the crematorium at Woking, built by the CS in 1878, to cremate his wife and mother who were lying in a specially built mausoleum. His request split the Society's Council and caused it to renew its efforts to get the HO to modify its opposition to non-statutorily regulated cremation. At the same time, in litigation about a cremation which had taken place abroad with the Society's assistance, Kay J refused the plaintiff's claim for her expenses against the deceased's executors. She was not an executor but a friend who had arranged the cremation as the deceased had wished (Williams v Williams 1882; TNA HO 45/9541/53096; S. White 2002a).

Although the Council had refused the use of its crematorium for the Hanham cremations, some members of the Council did assist the Captain.

William Robinson, the horticulturalist, helped him to build a small crematorium in which he cremated his wife and his mother in October 1882 (Robinson 1889: 113–30). A year later, Hanham himself was cremated there. His funeral was fully Masonic, attended by an MP among others, a protest against the impending change to the Freemasons' Book of Constitutions to put an end to Masonic rituals and displays at funerals. The Grand Lodge approved the change the next day (S. White 2002a).

No charges were brought against anyone involved in the Hanham cremations but when Elizabeth and Ann Stephenson were suspected of having murdered and incinerated the body of Elizabeth's month-old child near Scarborough and when William Price conspicuously attempted to cremate the body of his four-month-old son, Iesu Grist, near Cardiff on 13 and 14 January 1884 respectively, the Stephensons were prosecuted for cremating the body and preventing its burial, and Price was prosecuted, firstly, for attempting to cremate rather than bury his son (Powell 2012: 247–98).

The scene was at last set for a judge to determine whether cremation could be carried out lawfully, for the prosecutor at Price's trial, which came on first, contended that a person who was legally obliged to deal with a dead body had to bury it. Fortunately for the Society Fitzjames Stephen, who presided over the trial, was not unsympathetic to cremation, and was very sympathetic to Price. He rejected the prosecutor's submission and ruled that cremation would be unlawful only if it amounted to a public nuisance. The jury failed to agree on this first charge. A different jury was empanelled to try the second charge: attempting to dispose of a body with intent to prevent the holding of an inquest. The jury acquitted Price on this charge. When the trial resumed the next day to retry the first charge, the prosecutor offered no evidence, and Price was acquitted. The Society was now in possession of a full, learned, compellingly reasoned, and authoritative legal ruling that cremation was not necessarily unlawful (R v Price 1884; S. White 2002a; Powell 2012: 247–98). Moreover, given the provocative circumstances of the attempted cremation – an infant, the victim of suspected infanticide, in a barrel of petrol on a hillside in full view of chapel goers as they emerged from worship on a Sunday evening – and the commotion and local outrage it caused, the fact that the jury had failed to agree about whether this amounted to a public nuisance was telling indeed.

Charles Cameron's Disposal of the Dead Bill

A week before Price's discharge a Disposal of the Dead (Regulations) Bill had been given a First Reading in the House of Commons. It was exactly the measure the Society could have been expected to promote but, strikingly, its sponsors were all MPs for Scottish constituencies with no known connections with the CS. Charles Cameron and Robert Farquharson were two. The third was Lyon Playfair, the member for the Universities of Edinburgh and St Andrews. All were Liberals. The Society's Council had known of Cameron's intention to promote a Bill, since it had mandated Thompson, Spencer Wells and Hart to do all they could to further the Bill (CSA: CRE/P/1/B/I: 12/12/83), but there is no evidence of any previous contact between the Society and Cameron and no inkling of it in Cameron's account of the promotion of his Bill (C. Cameron 1887: 27). But Cameron must have known Thompson, Spencer Wells and Hart at least. During the debate on the Bill, Farquharson said that he accompanied Wells at the cremation of a horse, probably on 23 April 1884, and he exhibited the ashes of a cow said to have been cremated 'some time before'.[15]

After Price's discharge Henry Labouchere, the witty owner and editor of *Truth* and colleague of Charles Bradlaugh in the representation of Northampton, asked the Home Secretary whether he proposed to take action to impede cremation now that Stephen had declared it lawful. Harcourt replied that cremation's legality was not something he had any authority to determine but that he would do nothing to encourage cremation (*P. Debs*, ser. 3, vol. 285, cols 1356–7 [HC, 13 March 1884]). This led Cameron to ask whether Harcourt intended to 'interfere administratively with cremations conducted so as not to cause a public nuisance or provoke a breach of the peace in cases in which there is evidence that death has resulted from natural causes; and, if so, under what Law he claims the right to do so'. He was asking 'to prevent any misapprehension which may have arisen from your answer to Mr Labouchere [...] If you consider that you have the power to prevent cremations conducted as described in the question it might be necessary to raise the question of the legality of the practice in drafting the bill. If, as I understand, the authorities are agreed that the practice is not illegal, the necessity for its regulation is apparent'. Godfrey Lushington, an undersecretary at the HO, minuted 'If Cremation is legal, the S of S has no power to stop it. All that he could do would be to bring in a Bill to declare it illegal or to regulate its performance' (TNA HO 45/9531/40582, f37, 15 and 17/3/84).

15. The only cremation of a cow the Society had undertaken occurred on 1 April 1884 (Eassie 1884: 286).

In response to Cameron Harcourt went further than he had done previously. He expressed his personal repugnance regarding cremation and said he would use any power he had to discourage it. When Cameron asked whether he had that power Harcourt replied 'that is a subject on which I should not express an opinion; but if I have any such power I shall use it in the manner I have stated' (*P. Debs*, ser. 3, vol. 286, cols 37–8 [HC, 17 March 1884]).

The Bill applied to England and Wales, Scotland and Ireland equally. It dealt, first, with burial and, secondly, with all other modes of dealing with a dead body. English, Welsh and Scottish doctors had to issue medical certificates of the cause of the deaths of their patients (BDRA 1874 s. 20(2); RBDMSA 1854 s. 41 as amended by RBDMSA 1860 s. 4). In Scotland Registrars had to issue a certificate of registration of death on being informed of its occurrence even though not yet in receipt of the relevant medical certificates (RBDMSA 1854 s. 44). In England and Wales a Registrar could not register a death without receiving a medical certificate of the cause of death or information about the death from a coroner (BDRA 1874 ss 9, 14, 16 and 20).[16] On both sides of the border a body could be buried without the production of a certificate of registration of death or, in England and Wales, a coroner's order for burial, but, if so, the Registrar had to be informed within seven days in England and Wales and three in Scotland (BDRA 1874 s. 17 and RBDMSA 1854 s. 44).[17] In England and Wales all burials had to be registered (RBA 1864). The systems were not secure. As Cameron explained, 20,194 bodies, amounting to just over 4% of all deaths, had been buried in England and Wales without any certificate of the cause of death. In Scotland, he said, the situation was worse, the proportion being between 9% and 20% (*P. Debs*, ser. 3, vol. 287, col. 961 [HC, 30 April 1884]).

16. In England and Wales the medical certificate had to be given to the person who was obliged to inform the Registrar of the death. In Scotland the doctor had to 'transmit' it to the Registrar. The House of Commons Select Committee on Death Certification recommended that, in the interests of candour, doctors should send the certificates to Registrars otherwise than via the representatives of the deceased as an independent check on the occurrence of deaths (House of Commons 1893, xiv–xv, xxvi), and this was the course recommended by the Secretary to the General Registry Office (Seton 1860: 48).
17. Between 1854 and 1860 in Scotland Registrars had to be informed of all burials whether a certificate or registration of death was produced or not (RBDMSA 1854 s. 42 repealed by RBDMSA 1860 s. 1 and TNA RG 48/446, 28/9/27).

The Bill would have made it illegal to bury a body before a certificate of registration of the death had been issued; and Registrars were to be forbidden from issuing certificates until in receipt of a medical certificate of the cause of death (although they might register the death beforehand). If a medical certificate were not forthcoming from the deceased's doctor, the Registrar was to inform the local MOH who was to be able to supply an equivalent certificate. However, these provisions were to apply initially only in urban sanitary districts in England and burghs with a population of 5,000 or more in Scotland (DDRB 1884 cols 4–6).

These provisions were to apply also to methods of dealing with dead bodies other than burial, but with additional requirements drafted on the assumption that other methods could be lawful. The place in which the body was disposed of would have to be licensed by a Secretary of State and disposal would have to comply with regulations made by the Secretary of State. More rigorous certificates of the cause of death were to be required before disposal of a body in some way other than burial. The Bill specified two, one to be used after a post-mortem examination. Both required doctors to certify that 'there is no doubt in my mind that the death took place from natural causes, and that there is no reason whatever to suspect that it was caused or accelerated by any criminal act' (DDRB 1884 cols 7 and 8 and Schedule B).

On the day after Harcourt answered Labouchere, Price cremated the body of his son, albeit not in a barrel of petrol but on a grid above coals, without interference (Powell 2012: 310). So when the Bill came on for its Second Reading Cameron was able to bait Harcourt that 'his inaction must [...] be accepted as a practical endorsement of the statement of the law laid down by the Judge [i.e. Stephen], and a practical confession of his utter powerlessness to interfere in the matter' (*P. Debs*, ser. 3, vol. 287, col. 960 [HC, 30 April 1884]).[18] Apart from Farquharson and Playfair, one other Scottish voice contributed to the debate. Sir George Campbell, the MP for Kirkcaldy, supported the Bill but with reservations. Playfair too was not a completely wholehearted supporter. In his address as President of the Health

18. By the time the Stephensons came to trial on 15 May, the charge of cremating the body had been dropped, though they were convicted of disposing of a body with intent to prevent the holding of an inquest, a conviction which was unanimously upheld by the Court for Crown Cases Reserved which included Stephen J (R v Stephenson 1884).

Department of the National Association for the Promotion of Social Science in September 1874 he had spoken about cremation. He had approved of the aim of cremation but doubted whether cremation was the most practicable means of achieving it. Putting bodies in 'gas retorts heated white hot', which he had advocated 'many years since', would be more practicable. But 'as I get older I am inclined to think that the process of burial [...] is the wisest of all, provided it is done with honesty [...] allowing sufficient absorptive earth to secure the final result' (Playfair 1874: 84). Ten years later F.S. Haden's 'earth to earth' system of burial was available to produce this result (Parsons 2005: 204–20), and Playfair approved it as an ideal: on the virtues of this system he was not quite at one with Cameron. But he supported the Bill because he said burials did not take place under ideal conditions, and cremation was an efficient and harmless process, which should be permitted to those who wanted it. Even though some poisons, detectable after burial, might not be so after cremation, he judged the balance of advantage to be with cremation.

Against Cameron the Home Secretary and former Home Secretary presented a united front. Harcourt admitted that the law relating to the registration of deaths needed reform but denied that Cameron's Bill would supply it since the Bill did nothing to ensure that ordinary certificates of death would be completed accurately: it merely provided for a different certificate when an ordinary one was not forthcoming. Nor did Harcourt believe it would be possible, especially in rural areas, for all deaths to be medically certified even with the assistance of MOHs. The proposals about cremation he opposed generally on grounds of common sentiment and the development of civilisation, and because they would burden the Home Secretary with duties which he was quite incompetent to discharge, such as determining where crematoria were to be located and the conditions under which cremations were to take place. Harcourt was still reluctant to accept the authoritativeness of Stephen J's judgement. 'To allege that this judgment is a judgment inferentially in favour of cremation is as unfair a use of it as it would be to import it as a judgment in favour of cannibalism, or any other method of disposing of the human frame. All that it says is that the law is practically silent on the subject' (*P. Debs*, ser. 3, vol. 287, cols 977–8 [HC, 30 April 1884]). He was not to know that seven months later Baron Huddlestone was to tell a jury at the trial of sailors who, in extremis, had killed and eaten their cabin boy that there was indeed nothing illegal in cannibalism (R v Dudley and Stephens 1884–5, 31).

The motion for the Second Reading of the Bill was lost by a margin of seventy votes in a House of 228. The CS prepared to put its Woking crematorium to use and by the end of 1885 had carried out three cremations. The HO files in which any reactions to the first two might have been recorded have been destroyed. But Richard Cross, who had become Home Secretary again in June 1885, certainly did remark the third: 'What action did Sir W. Harcourt take? Should I or can I take any action? Is this practice thus to become usual and allowed by (inches?) [...] Consult L.Os'. (TNA HO 45/9531/40582, f44, 14/12/85).

The Law Officers advised that cremation was lawful and that legislation would be necessary to suppress it. Another election, however, had returned the Liberals to power and Cross left office minuting 'Must be brought before my successor' (TNA HO 45/9531/40582, f44, 27/1/86 and 30/1/86). Harcourt was now Chancellor of the Exchequer and Cross's successor was Hugh Childers. When asked whether he wished to do anything about cremation he replied 'Not this session. My individual opinion is in favour of legislation to regulate cremation but public opinion is not ripe for this' (TNA HO 45/9531/40582, f45).

The Vatican Forbids Cremation for Catholics

The character of cremation as a Protestant aberration was emphasised by the action of the Vatican in 1886 when the Roman Catholic Church paced a ban upon it.[19] The Catholic Church forbade Catholics to join societies promoting cremation, or to leave funeral instructions involving cremation. The ban lasted until 1963, its removal made public in May 1964.[20]

The background had been as much political as religious. The opposition to cremation was a by-product of the Catholic Church's response to threats from Italian nationalism, as well as from Modernist movements within the Church. The Papal States which girdled the very centre of the Italian peninsula were a major obstacle to Garibaldi's plans for the unification of Italy. The greater the defeats suffered (the loss of the Papal States in 1859; the loss of Rome outside the Vatican walls in 1870) the more intransigent Pope Pius IX became.

Articulate Masonic opposition to the Catholic Church had welcomed cremation as a weapon against Catholic theology and authority. When Pope Leo XIII reacted by banning cremation in 1886, the significant Catholic

---

19. Vaughan 1891.
20. See ch. 7 below and Jupp 1993, 2006a; McGinnell 2015.

minority populations, often poor, of certain cities in Scotland, principally Glasgow, found themselves confined to the meanest sections of cemeteries, private and public, where pit burial conditions were appalling.

The Vatican decision also made burial reform more difficult for the non-Catholic reformers. If they concentrated on how pit-burial conditions disadvantaged poor families, they ran the risk of being branded as Catholic sympathisers. This only made more rigid the Protestant–Catholic dividing line in funeral practice.[21] It was only when political and legal reforms in the early twentieth century effected greater equality of opportunity that Catholic–Protestant tensions began to lessen (McFarland 1990; Bruce, Glendinning and Rosie 2004).

---

21. Mr Sandy MacDonald, personal communication, 2011.

CHAPTER THREE

The Scottish Burial Reform and Cremation Society and Maryhill Crematorium, 1888–1895

Initiatives for Cremation in Scotland

The Scottish movement for cremation seems to have been a separate initiative from that in England. There had been cremation activists in mainland Europe and, from 1874, the Cremation Society of England (CS) had led an active publicity campaign (Parsons 2005; Grainger 2005; Jupp 2006a). Its arguments for burial reform and cremation were publicly available to Scottish readers for ten years. The Price verdict of 1884 established the legality of cremation. In 1885, the CS held the first cremation at its crematorium at Woking. Dr Cameron had made the first formal Scottish contribution to the debate with his 1884 Bill. Having started his professional medical career, he also inherited the editorship of one of Glasgow's leading newspapers, *The North British Daily Mail*. It is likely that he had turned his attention to cremation in association with his campaign for birth and death registration. However, his Bill seems not to have prompted any organised promotional activity in Scotland.

Dr Duncan's paper

On 27 April 1887 Dr Ebenezer Duncan gave a paper to the Philosophical Society of Glasgow on 'The Reform of our Present Methods of Disposal of the Dead: Earth-to-Earth versus Cremation' (Duncan 1887). It was the first public appeal for cremation in Scotland.

He reminded his listeners that the Burial Grounds (Scotland) Act 1855 gave local authorities in Scotland power to close or regulate all graveyards when 'dangerous to health, or offensive, or contrary to decency'. It also laid on Parochial Boards and Burgh Councils the onus of providing new cemeteries. The Act had one major flaw: it did not allow a Secretary of State to make regulations for private cemeteries as it did for public ones (section 31). With the private cemeteries' rapid success, said Duncan, local authorities had come to rely upon them, and to neglect their own responsibility for providing new burial grounds. Yet the very profitability of the private cemeteries was currently dependent on practices which did not follow the regulations made under the Act. Duncan claimed that the owners ignored proper sanitation and flouted public decency.

Duncan had already investigated three Glasgow cemeteries: the Southern Necropolis (Hutt 1996), Sandymount (both private) and Dalbeth (Catholic). The Southern Necropolis was 'owned by the lairholders and managed in their interest'. The interests of the poor were less considered: the common graves were dug sufficiently deep to accommodate sixteen adults and children, with the earth too thinly spread between the coffins to allow effective decomposition. Common graves were left open until they were filled. Coffins in Sandymount were laid on top of each other without an intervening layer of soil. When the grave was full, another pit was dug just one foot away. Dalbeth was nearer the river and its soil was damp clay. Each pit took up to sixty coffins of adults and of children. The smell was offensive. 'The [Catholic] funeral service is read over the edge of this mass of corruption, and priests, relatives, and friends alike are subjected to its unwholesome and dangerous effluvia.'

Duncan then connected inadequate burial grounds with the public health. Referring to the Glasgow Royal Infirmary case of 1867 (see ch. 2), he pressed home his moral, that, 'by this system of pit and common-grave burial, the soil beneath and the air above become tainted with the unwholesome and poisonous products of decomposition'. Such pollution also affected watercourses, both sewers and streams, claiming new victims.

Focusing his scorn on the private cemetery companies, Duncan asserted, 'These places are not graves, but pits of putridity and mines of profit to the shareholders.' The practice of reusing old graves after ten years meant that there would be no end to the pollution and no end to the desecration of the graves of the poor under the present regime. Duncan echoed the policy recommended by the Sanitary Commission of 1850, that the duty of supplying burial grounds should be taken away entirely from commercial companies and vested in the State.

Duncan then turned to the two alternatives that reformers had recently pressed: earth-to-earth burial and cremation. He discussed Haden's earth-to-earth proposals:[1] decomposable wickerwork coffins whose swifter decomposition would enable earlier reuse of the grave. He commended their advantages. But the disadvantage was that no soil was ever completely effective in eradicating disease. Duncan concluded, 'Cremation is the only practical method by which we can avoid the disgusting and dangerous products of putrefaction.' He discussed the mechanics of modern cremation, Gorini's model in Italy and at Woking (Gorini 1879), and Siemens' at Gotha.

As for the forensic concerns about poisoning (Leaney 1989: 118–35), and the concern that cremation would destroy evidence of foul play, Duncan commended the system of certification by two doctors of the cause of death, which Cameron and Farquharson had commended during the 1884 Commons debate and which had been adopted for cremations at Woking (operative since 1885). Duncan had himself tested which poisons might survive the cremation process. If cremation were preceded by dual certification in Scotland, it would make forensic investigation far more effective than after burial.

Duncan then invited the Philosophical Society to set up a Scottish Burial Reform Association in Glasgow. The society should have four objects:

> First, to call upon the local authorities at once to remove from among us the scandal of pit-burials, which leads strangers who come to Glasgow and see our methods of interment to say that we bury our poor like dogs. Second, to seek the necessary legislative amendment of the Burial Acts which will place private cemeteries under its regulations. Third, to advocate economy in funerals and the adoption of perishable coffins. Fourth, to secure the erection of crematories in our large cities, and their proper regulation.

He concluded the lecture by showing a working design for a cremator; and produced the ashes of a cremated sheep to demonstrate how pure, compact and portable they were.

Responses to Duncan's lecture

A first-hand account of Duncan's lecture and its reception was provided in 1952 by Sir John Mann, who in 1887 was a young accountant. Duncan, the

---

1. See Parsons 2005.

Manns' doctor (Mann 1952) had invited Mann's brother Harrington, an art student, to provide an illustration for the lecture, a decomposing body following normal burial. Mann attended the lecture, accompanying his father, who was Honorary Treasurer of the Philosophical Society. 'We were rather relieved to find that my brother's startling picture was not exhibited. It seemed that the Doctor had been persuaded that it would be too horrifying for a mixed non-medical audience.' In his memoirs, Mann continued:

> When he [Duncan] sat down, there was no applause, a most unusual thing, and the chairman threw the meeting open for discussion. At first there was frigid silence, then the storm broke. Speaker after speaker in anger and excitement rose in opposition, and protested at the subject being raised. I cannot remember, but I can imagine the adjectives which were used: 'Repellent and painful plan'; 'Distressing to the survivors'; 'Abominable and pagan idea'; 'Terrible'; 'Insufferable'; 'Odorous', and so on.

The Corporation Gas Manager, William Key, intervened. He offered to arrange for the cremation of another sheep to test Duncan's claim that the process was purifying, rapid and odourless. 'However, that did not halt the attack. Then an elderly, dignified man impressed the meeting with a plea for further examination and inquiry.' This was Sir Renny Watson, a leading engineer who specialised in making sugar machinery. He offered one of his own furnaces for the cremation of the sheep and challenged the objectors to come and satisfy themselves that there were no offensive fumes, with lunch to follow as a further incentive.

A fortnight later, Mann Jr with Duncan, Dr John Glaister (Professor of Forensic Medicine at Glasgow University) and others attended the demonstration. The furnace was a Siemens-Gorman design, and heated to about 2,000 degrees Fahrenheit. After the carcass had been inserted, Watson had Mann climb the ladder to the top of the chimney and satisfy himself that there was neither smoke nor smell.

So why the silent response to Duncan's address? The most plausible reason is his criticisms of burial. In attacking contemporary arrangements in Glasgow, Duncan had focused on two targets. The first was the Town Council for neglecting its duty to provide public burial grounds and relying on private cemeteries. This stance, in avoiding the burial laws, perpetuated stratagems of overcrowding and systematic reuse. The second target was far more sensitive: the private cemetery companies themselves.

Duncan's identification of overcrowding in the 'Commons' areas of private cemeteries as one cause of investors' high dividends was an explicit criticism of those members of his audience who held shares. It was an implicit criticism of his middle-class audience whose families had patronised private cemetery burial for nearly fifty years, enjoying these privileges at the cost of the many more numerous poor. He reminded Presbyterians present that they had paid for their graves to be kept inviolate until the Day of Resurrection, whereas the 'common graves' were much more likely to be disturbed by cemetery policies of reuse (Chadwick 1843). No wonder his audience was outraged.

Duncan was to suffer one more indignity. The Philosophical Society decided not to publish his lecture. It was then taken up by the *Philosophical Journal* for its September edition. By that time, however, the editor of *The Scottish Review* had commissioned Cameron to contribute an article on cremation for his July issue. (The Marquess of Bute, as the *Review*'s proprietor, had originally asked Playfair to write the article.)[2] Cameron's 'The Modern Cremation Movement' was thus the first published paper in Scotland to promote cremation (C. Cameron 1887).

Charles Cameron's restatement

Cameron first demonstrated how contemporary modern burial was disrespectful to the dead. He selected evidence from Edinburgh. St Cuthbert's Church had been the centre of a scandal in 1874, with a public investigation. It was estimated that 10,000 bodies had been buried in just 1.3 acres in the last fifteen years; the ground had been dug over three times, adult graves were reopened after seven years and children's after three-and-a-half. Even the lowest coffins in the deepest graves explored had not properly decomposed. A furnace house was in use, once a week in summer and twice a week in winter. Whilst he did not mention social class, Cameron was clearly speaking of St Cuthbert's common graves. The Kirk Session had sought to downplay the evidence, describing the practice as 'normal'.[3]

Cameron then turned to his home city. A Glasgow paper, perhaps *The North British Daily Mail*, had followed up Duncan's survey and investigated practices in the 'commonses', examining several acres in which pits contained sixty to seventy coffins, taking ten to twelve days to fill up. Cameron drew

2. Letter, Bute to Playfair, 8/2/1887, Lyon Playfair Papers.
3. For St Cuthbert's kirk-yard, see Anderson 1931: 37–45 and Smith 2008.

out the social class implications: 'People may say that such practices existed only in connection with the burial of the poor [...] but they compose the great mass of the population, and any violation of the laws of health incurred with their burial will impact on poor and rich alike.'

Cameron then offered a public health perspective. Over the previous fifteen years germ theory had developed (in succession to miasmatic theory). Louis Pasteur (to whom Cameron had earlier been an assistant) had connected anthrax with public danger and Frère in Brazil had demonstrated how cemeteries perpetuated the germs of yellow fever. In the face of such dangers, 'the practice of cremating bodies would suit completely'.

Cameron's Bill of 1884 had also been 'intended to provide for the more efficient verification of the cause of death in all cases, and dealing among other things with the subject of cremation'. Whilst the Bill had failed, the practice of cremation was now recognised as legal at common law. Yet, he emphasised, cremation was subject to no statutory regulations and was 'absolutely uncontrolled'. Burial was more conducive to crime than cremation, for 'the burial laws of the United Kingdom, as far as the question of their affording any protection against foul play is concerned, might almost as well not exist'. Like Duncan, he believed that 'a system of controlled cremation might be made infinitely more protective than that of burial' but, so far,

> the cremation movement has hardly reached that stage where its aid could prudently be invoked for the solution of the difficulty which arises in connection with the disposal of our dead poor. The practice, however, lends itself pre-eminently to such a purpose.

The initiative lay with the middling classes to set an example. Cremation only required to 'become familiarised to the public mind by its voluntary adoption among the wealthier and more intelligent classes' to spread down the social scale. If cremation became widespread, it would cost no more than a few shillings for fuel.

Cameron was convinced that cremation would increase as 'intelligent public opinion' was persuaded, and as the number of crematoria increased. He was astute enough to assume that private cemetery companies would have little incentive to provide facilities for cremation. He looked to 'local authorities [...] to substitute the prompt, innocuous and economical action of the crematorium for the noisome and revolting system at present resorted to for the disposal of the corpses of our poor'. He was to be proved too optimistic about human nature and too unrealistic about the priorities by which local governments would rank their policies.

Three comments are required. First, Cameron's difficulty was that the middle classes were the very people who patronised the private cemeteries. The 'privates' had a separate maintenance regime from the 'commonses' and their clients paid for it. It would be a brave family to choose such a radical, self-effacing and democratic precedent as cremation.

Second, given the Vatican's recent ban on cremation, Cameron was challenging Protestants to set an example in funeral reform of which only Protestants could take advantage. This hardened class boundaries and would alienate Catholic local councillors, for it underlined the irony of calling for an end to pit burial from the secure eminence of a different religion and class.[4] Around the turn of the century, Catholic councillors in Bute's Cardiff (Davies 1981; Hannah 2012), despite his favouring cremation (see below), prevented the Corporation's use of its recently acquired statutory power to build a crematorium.

Third, cremation was popularly understood to challenge traditional beliefs in the resurrection of the body, the theological restatement of which had hardly yet started. The public outcry about the Resurrection Men fifty years before had demonstrated the strong sentimental attachment to the integrity of the dead body. Even though Presbyterians believed that the future of the dead was entirely in God's hands, people could not yet accept the reasoning of such cremationists as Lord Shaftesbury that 'what God has once created, He could also re-create'. Neither burial nor cremation could impede what God chose to do for the dead. The common belief about the mode of burial and the hope of a Divine resurrection would last at least until 1914 (Jupp 2006b).

The founding of the Scottish Burial Reform and Cremation Society[5]

The most practical way to promote cremation was to build a cremator and to demonstrate its efficiency. Once the shock of his critical reception was over, Duncan took his next opportunity when the British Medical Association (BMA) advertised its Summer 1888 conference in Glasgow. *The British Medical Journal* (*BMJ*) was in favour of cremation; and its editor Ernest Hart was a leading cremationist.

---

4. For a similar situation in Cardiff see S. White 2003: 16–27.
5. See Lindsay 1999 for an earlier account of the SBRCS's origins.

With the conference imminent, Duncan called a private meeting for Monday 6 August 1888 of 'gentlemen favourable to the formation of a Scottish Burial Reform and Cremation Society'. The four present were Duncan, Glaister, sanitary engineer W.P. Buchan and architect James Chalmers. The meeting decided that Duncan would give a lecture promoting cremation on 10 August and they would invite members of the Philosophical Society. The four prepared an agenda for the Friday meeting, nominating proposers and seconders for a series of motions. They chose leading men from professional, cultural and business communities, intending that cremation should be supported by prominent and well-respected citizens.[6] The motions were:

1. 'That this meeting disapproves of the present methods of burial in Scotland both as regards the expense involved and as regards their dangerous effects upon the public health.'
2. 'That this Meeting desires to substitute less expensive and more sanitary methods of disposal of the dead and approves in particular of the method known as cremation.'
3. 'That this Meeting resolves that a Society be formed to carry out the objects aimed at in the foregoing resolutions under the style and title of the Scottish Burial Reform and Cremation Society.'
4. 'That a provisional committee be appointed to initiate the Society consisting of those present at Friday's meeting and others.'[7]

On 3 September the provisional committee[8] was appointed. It included Duncan and Glaister, Chalmers, Buchan and Key. They appointed a sub-committee to draft rules for the body that would either be a society or a company. The company's draft Memorandum and Articles were adopted at a meeting on 30 October.

6. This is evident from the names proposed at the public meeting on 10 August including W.P. Buchan, William Buchanan, Dr Charles Cameron MP, James Chalmers, Dr James Christie, Campbell Douglas, Dr Ebenezer Duncan, Dr Robert Farquharson MP, Peter Fyfe, Dr Glaister, D.G. Hoey, John Honeyman, Rev. John Hunter, Rev. Dr William Jeffrey, William Key, David N. Knox, Dr Henry Littlejohn, Dr Johnston Macfie, John Mann, Dr J.B. Russell and William Renny Watson.
7. Scottish Burial Reform and Cremation Society [hereafter SBRCS] Board minutes, vol.1.
8. SBRCS minutes, vol.1, p.3ff.

The provisional committee of 21 November grappled with the joint questions of identity and purpose, 'some members desiring to proceed at once with a Crematorium as the best means of ventilating the subject, while others [...] advocated delay until public opinion was more matured by the distribution of pamphlets. It was finally decided on the motion of the Chairman (Duncan) to re-appoint the sub-committee, adding the names of Campbell Douglas and DC Hoey with a remit to investigate the whole subject and to report to a future meeting of the provisional committee'. While no sub-committee minutes have been traced, it proposed a crematorium.

Planning Scotland's First Crematorium

The decision to establish a crematorium was not without precedent. In England, one had been operating at Woking since 1885 (Parsons 2005) and cremationists in Manchester were well advanced with proposals for a crematorium at Chorlton-cum-Hardy (eventually opened in 1892) (Makepeace 1990). The SBRCS had few allies outside Glasgow. Its isolation would be intensified by the prolonged wait for the launch of other local Scottish cremation societies. Unlike the CS in England, there was no national society to promote cremation and therefore little external stimulus or peer-group support. The SBRCS, according to the CS's minutes asked for the latter's patronage. The CS's difficulty was that burial reform was the SBRCS's first objective; this set it apart from the sister society. The CS declined the request on the grounds that the SBRCS recommended the 'earth to earth' system, a policy that the Scots could not be expected to drop. Given these handicaps, the role of specific individuals in Scotland became more important. Leading Glaswegians banded together to develop Scotland's first crematorium in circumstances of widespread apathy if not open hostility (cf. Grainger 2000).

Within six months of the SBRCS's founding meeting, a sub-committee began to prepare plans for building a crematorium. The committee included Douglas (Chairman), Chalmers, Brown, Buchan and Hoey. Chalmers had spent the winter months of 1889–90 working on his designs for the crematorium. The site would need two-thirds of an acre, and be within reasonable access of the city.

The not-for-profit decision

On 28 February 1889 the provisional SBRCS committee met for further consideration of the plans. It was unanimously agreed 'to take steps to form a limited company'. The meeting was significant for the future of the Society as the first Honorary Secretary resigned and John Mann Junior succeeded him, with J.T.T. Brown as Honorary Treasurer. Mann and Brown were charged with drawing up a prospectus for the Company. Mann was to play a prominent part in the Scottish cremation movement up to his retirement as Honorary Secretary in 1932.

There was no meeting of the Board for another nine months. It is likely that crematorium design, the formation of a limited company and the soliciting of support from friends and social networks occupied much of the time that Glasgow's enthusiasts could devote to the Board. The committee next met on 7 November 1889. Fund-raising was one issue and £5 guarantees were volunteered from seven committee members. Another issue concerned attracting Roman Catholic support. Spencer Wells (Shepherd 1965), then President of the Royal College of Surgeons, suggested in a letter to the SBRCS that the Marquess of Bute might accept the office of Honorary President. Mann was deputed to contact him.

Another seven months passed and when the committee met on 10 June 1890 some difficulty was reported in securing high-level patronage. Whilst precise details were not recorded in the Board's minutes, part of the difficulty seems to have been the Board's intention to form a limited company to build a crematorium. This policy would have had the twin advantages of financial economy and efficient fund-raising. But two of their supporters, Farquharson and Playfair, 'intimated that they could not accept office in any commercial undertaking'. Profitability was a sensitive issue for would-be funeral reformers.

Both Duncan and Cameron had criticised the profit-seeking of the private cemetery movement in 1887 and felt they could not change their stance. Littlejohn, as MOH for Edinburgh, had shown in his Edinburgh surveys of 1865 and 1883 that poorer people were disadvantaged not only by costs but by the allocation of grave space (Laxton and Rodger 2014). For Littlejohn to support a profit-making crematorium would have attracted the very opprobrium that he had himself directed at Edinburgh's private cemeteries.

Mann's sub-committee had recommended that a special licence be sought from the Board of Trade to drop the word 'Limited' from the title of the Company and also that 'the Company should be formed on the distinct basis that no dividend whatever should be paid' but that any surplus should be applied to the promotion of the Company's objects and a reduction of the charges for cremation. This was agreed and, in anticipation of the formation of the Company, a number of directors were appointed from leading Glaswegians representing medical, public health, legal, political and engineering interests. Following correspondence with the Board of Trade, the word 'Limited' was retained but a special clause in the *Memorandum of Association* prohibited any payment to the shareholders. The Scottish Burial Reform and Cremation Society Limited was incorporated on 22 December 1890.

The not-for-profit decision was to prove a heavy burden for the Glasgow Pioneers: the debt on the crematorium was not paid off until 1913.

The Marquess of Bute[9]

Meanwhile, sometime during 1890, the possibility of patronage had come from an unexpected source, described as 'a very wealthy Scottish Roman Catholic'.

Mann later recorded that the Marquess of Bute had invited representatives of the Society to confer privately with him at one of his country estates (Mann 1952). Mann and Brown had

> waited upon his lordship who while thoroughly in favour of the reforms urged by this Society, intimated that his Church had taken up rather a hostile position towards Cremation. As he [Bute] was not without hope that permission might be given for the practice of cremation in Scotland, he suggested that the Society should prepare a memorial to the Vatican on the subject [see ch. 2].

The Marquess 'virtually promised all the money we needed, provided that the objection of the Holy See could be overcome in some way'. Bute encouraged the Society to prepare suitable documents for submission to Rome via Archbishop Eyre in Glasgow along with a representation by himself.

> A Memorial was drafted, redrafted and finally approved by our potential supporter with the suggestion that it be translated into Latin. The first Latin draft was not considered sufficiently classical. With the help of friends in Oxford, we had a fresh translation made, extending to twelve quarto pages. This version was approved and we were told it would be transmitted to Rome, this was in May 1896, about six years after the subject was first raised, i.e. June 1890.

9. Hannah 2012, 2014.

Towards the end of 1896, Mann was invited to call on Bute at

> rather an inaccessible spot [...] involving a very long journey in mid-winter [...] What a contrast to my first meeting! No conveyance arranged at the railway station. My host a changed, depressed, and now cadaverous looking man. He told me coldly but still courteously that he was not *persona grata* at Rome, he regretted he was unable to give our Memorial his support and finance, that he did not wish his name mentioned in any way with cremation.

These discreet communications with the Marquess of Bute proved a preoccupation for the SBRCS's Board lasting six years. The delay does not seem to have affected the Society's material progress but the Bute connection will have been a sensitive issue for Presbyterians on the Board as Cameron was involved in the Disestablishment debate (Kellas 1964).

The search for a site

The Scottish Burial Reform and Cremation Society Ltd was incorporated on 22 December 1890. Following further correspondence with the Board of Trade, the word 'Limited' was to be retained but a special clause included in the *Memorandum and Articles* stating that 'The income and property of the Company, shall be applied solely towards the promotion and objects of the Company ... and no portion thereof shall be paid or transferred ... by way of profit to the Members of the Company.' By March 1891, it had allocated 266 shares and agreed that for every ten shares owned, one cremation free of charge should be offered, provided 'all the conditions set forth in the Forms about the cause of death had been fulfilled'. At this meeting Paul Rottenburg, a chemicals broker, was appointed a director. He was to prove an active and loyal supporter for over thirty years. The first ordinary meeting of shareholders was held in April 1891 by which time shares worth £572 had been allocated.

There were hopes that the Glasgow Necropolis might allow the Society space for its crematorium.[10] At the Society's second AGM on 13 May 1892, the Duke of Westminster was present; already President of the Manchester Crematorium Company, he now agreed to become the SBRCS's Honorary President. Mann asked the Merchants House if it would receive a delegation

10. Compare the CS's earlier attempt to work with the New Southgate Cemetery in 1875 (Parsons, 2005; Jupp 2006a: 54–5).

from the Board. The meeting took place at the Necropolis on 17 May 1892, and four days later the delegation signed a letter of application to the House.[11]

Negotiations continued during the summer. Mann recorded that the House had submitted the Society's application to its Annual Meeting 'as public sentiment was involved'. He learned afterwards that 'there was such an uproar at the [House's] annual meeting that the Dean of Guild had to give an assurance that the matter would be dropped' (Mann 1952). The seconder of the House's motion had declared that 'a Crematorium would destroy the Necropolis, injure the feelings of the lairholders and prevent further sale of ground'. The House rejected the application.

The Directors immediately wrote to other private cemetery companies. Board member G.L. Houston offered a site on his estate at Johnstone Castle. As with an earlier offer from Board member and banker T. Ripley Ker of Douglaston, the Directors decided not to consider this until other Glasgow sites had been explored. From now on, the pace of events accelerated.

One stimulus was caused by a family bereavement. Mann recorded in his 1952 memoirs that on a 'dark wet November afternoon' he had two visitors to his office, both 'distressed'. He described them only as two brothers, both wealthy clients, James and Henry. These were clearly the Allan brothers, shipping line directors. Henry demanded to know about progress with the crematorium project.

> We have just come straight from the burial in an ordinary grave of our dear Mother; all the mourners have been standing in the pouring rain without any protection; we are all most depressed [...] driving down from the cemetery, my brother and I have suddenly realised the great contrast under cremation, and I, at least, have been converted.

The sooner cremation could be introduced as an alternative to burial, the better. They were willing to provide whatever money was required to open a crematorium. Mann did not date the Allan brothers' visit but it is clear that, for him, it was a key moment in the young Society's life.[12]

11. Glasgow City Archives (GLA). Merchants House Necropolis Committee minute book no.4, p. 147 (17 May 1892) and pp. 148–9 (2 June 1892).
12. Mann 1952. The Allan brothers first attended a Board meeting in May 1892 suggesting that their visit to Mann was probably November 1891.

In December 1892, while a reply was still awaited from Sandymount, the Western and Cathcart cemetery companies had responded positively. Western was sited at Maryhill on the north-west side of the city and near a railway station. It seems to have been the only cemetery company not overly concerned at possible competition from a company providing less expensive funerals at a facility in its own grounds and, presumably, offering memorialisation in a columbarium similarly situated.

At any rate, Western was willing to discuss with the Society an annual rent of £50, reduced to £20 for each of the first five years, plus the net revenue from cremations up to £50 per annum. A superintendent as cleaner and caretaker could be provided for a maximum of £20 per week. Western was clearly profitable for it was willing for two of its Directors to be nominated by the Society; this would provide a subscription of between £500 and £1,000. Watson, Key and Mann then paid an inspection visit to Manchester Crematorium in March 1893.

On 16 March 1893 the Directors confirmed their negotiations with Western, so long as a columbarium was allowed. Progress quickened, the Board meeting three times in April 1893. On 11 April it was reported that Western had accepted the Society's offer and Chalmers undertook to prepare a block plan for the crematorium and chapel. Watson intimated that he would increase his subscription by a further £100. Rottenburg matched this on 25 April, just before the third ordinary meeting of shareholders.

A site on the east of Western Cemetery was now considered. Chalmers submitted plans for the buildings, estimating that those other than the furnace could be provided for between £2,150 and £2,300. The Board felt the company would not be justified in spending so much, preferring a more simple style at a maximum cost of £1,500 excluding the furnace. The plans were 'carefully discussed, and much admired'; however, Chalmers was 'asked to be good enough to prepare fresh plans of a more simple style'. The next month Chalmers produced new plans 'in Gothic style' at £1,450 excluding the furnace. Both design and cost must have been acceptable, for they were not referred to again until November. By that date the cost was estimated at £1,780 without the furnace. The Board may have been relieved to learn that subscriptions and shares had now reached £1,936 7s. The feu contract and agreement were engrossed on 6 November 1893.

Decisions on the furnace came next. Key undertook to provide a sketch for this. On 25 November 1893 the Board met at Watson's engineering works.

A 'box made of yellow pine weighing 10lb and containing 20lb of bone and 14lb of flesh was cremated in a modified Gorman furnace, taking 45 minutes; no offensive odour of any kind was felt'. As a result of this successful trial, Director R.A. Robertson offered to revise Key's furnace plan, for Chalmers to adjust. Robertson's plans were subsequently approved and the figure of £350–£400 was accepted for the furnace, including a steam boiler for heating the chapel. The available capital would cover the cost, which now stood at £2,003 9s 0d. In January 1894, building commenced.

The first cremation

The furnace was completed three days before Christmas 1894. Chalmers, Mann and Robertson undertook to ensure thorough testing. After a serious delay caused by a protracted frost, Chalmers resumed testing the furnace and reached the point at which one final experiment was required before it could be ready for use. Then, on Wednesday, 10 April 1895, Mann received a request for a cremation which the bereaved family had planned for Saturday, 13 April. A Mrs Elizabeth Haining Hendry, a fifty-nine-year-old widow, had died (on the Wednesday) and her family had supported her request for cremation.

A Board meeting was hurriedly called for Thursday, 11 April. The assembled Directors were both Allans, Douglas, Chalmers and Mann. They were not of one mind. Watson and Robertson had sent messages 'most strongly against the cremation being performed'. The Board agreed to reconvene at the crematorium at five o'clock the next day, when a further experiment would be carried out on the furnace. Present on Friday, 12 April were: Duncan, the Allans, Ripley Ker, Chalmers and Mann. On arrival, they learned that, due to a delay in lighting the furnace, it would be another two to three hours before the experiment could be completed. Mann brought a letter from Watson protesting against the cremation being carried out. 'Considerable discussion then ensued, and finally, as it transpired that the Representatives of the deceased had been led to understand that the cremation could take place and had made their arrangements accordingly, it was agreed to carry out the cremation, subject to Mr Chalmers and Mr Henry Allan being satisfied from personal observation that Friday's experiment was satisfactory.'[13]

13. Board minute, 12 April 1895, p. 90. The original minute read, 'It was remitted to Mr Chalmers and Mr Henry Allan to authorise the cremation to be carried out, if they were satisfied from personal observation that the present

Medical certificates of the cause of death were submitted on forms B and C.

The Board members probably did not sleep well that night. All had status – social, business or professional – in the city. If this first cremation were to fail, after seven years' work, the Directors might face embarrassing humiliation. Saturday's cremation proved a success.

The funeral of Mrs Hendry was the first and only cremation in Scotland that year.

Maryhill opened

Maryhill Crematorium, now the third crematorium in Great Britain, was officially opened on 27 November 1895. Three hundred people accepted invitations to the ceremony and a special train was laid on to Maryhill.[14] The opening was timed to coincide not only with the AGM but with the city's civic reception the previous day for Cameron who had lost his seat at the General Election earlier that year. Following a short service conducted by Dr Donald McLeod and Dr John Hunter, the Crematorium was declared open by Cameron. Maryhill may have been the only one of the UK's pre-1914 crematoria opened with a religious service. McLeod was the minister of Park Church, Glasgow and Moderator of the Kirk's General Assembly. Hunter was minister of Glasgow's Trinity Congregational Church. Whatever the churchmanship of the Directors, it seems that they were agreed that the opening should be marked by Christian ritual. The response of Scottish clergy to the new mode of disposal now remained to be tested.[15]

McLeod dedicated the building in prayer 'to the last services of the dead'. Hunter said that although the tradition of burial was associated in Christian doctrine with the resurrection of the body, 'a man of eighty years old might be said to have cast off two or three bodies, and death was only the casting off

    experiment was satisfactory.' The amended minute suggests that the decision was intended to be a formal decision of the Board, at its five o'clock meeting on 12 April at the crematorium.

14. *Glasgow Herald* 28/11/1895. A Mr Tarbolton is described as 'representing the Cremation Society of Edinburgh'.
15. Of the first nine cremations, six of the deceased had their religion recorded: Unitarian (1), Church of Scotland (1), Congregational (2), Episcopalian (1), Hindoo (1). Board minutes, 3/11/1896, p. 114.

of the last body',[16] hinting that the traditional doctrine was not challenged by the act of cremation. Sir Charles Cameron added that there was 'no longer heard the cries so vigorously made at first that cremation was nothing else than flying in the face of the Christian doctrine of resurrection'. Cameron and Littlejohn both spoke of the undignified and unhygienic character of contemporary burial and the requirement of the Society for dual medical certification to prevent the concealment of any crime.

An accompanying article in the *Glasgow Herald* commented that the rapid growth of cities and the overcrowding of burial grounds were 'nothing short of a menace to health'. Cremation's antiquity was the least of its commendations, 'it is cleanly, it is thorough, it exposes the living to no danger from the dead [...] and the more recent interpretation of the doctrine of resurrection, which regards the future life as solely spiritual, removes an objection to the practice which once had more weight than it can have today'[17] (see, further, Byrne 2010). Sentiment was the chief enemy of cremation but it was not well to dismiss or misunderstand it. While the city cemetery

> which is aggressively modern, and flaunts its ill-assorted and garish monuments in the face of the chance moralist who may turn to it for the soothing of spirit it is little capable of affording [yet] [...] when it has received our dead [it] becomes endeared to us and 'the kindly earth from which we have sprung' seems to have them in their keeping in a sense different from anything that can be urged in favour of the purifying fire [...] In the near future the crematorium will doubtless be hallowed by as many associations bound up with the dark hours of human life and experience as the cemetery now is.[18]

Glasgow's Maryhill was to be Scotland's only crematorium for thirty-four years. By 1910, it was not yet holding one funeral in each week. With such small numbers, it is not surprising that other Scottish cities did not follow Glasgow's lead. The new Maryhill Crematorium had provided very little competition to the cemetery.

---

16. *Glasgow Herald*, 28/11/1895.
17. 'Cremation v. Burial', *Glasgow Herald*, 28/11/1895.
18. Ibid. See Davies 1996 for a discussion on the sacred quality of a crematorium.

James Chalmers (1858–1927) and Maryhill

Chalmers' involvement with cremation appears to have been a direct result of his membership of the Glasgow Philosophical Society to which he was elected in 1884. A year later he became a council member of its Architecture Section, quite a meteoric rise for an architect whose early career remains somewhat obscure. He entered practice c.1882 and was in partnership with Andrew Robson from 1885 until 1889. By 1885 (and also of that year) his most well-known work was Pettigrew and Stephens Department Store warehouse in Glasgow. By 1886 it had become apparent that Chalmers had interests that strayed beyond architecture, since that year he addressed the Philosophical Society on 'Planning Sanitary Requirements of Farm Steadings'.[19] This perhaps explains why by 1887 he was serving both in the Architecture and the Sanitary and Social Economy Sections of the Society of which Duncan was President and Glaister and Christie Vice-Presidents. Chalmers would himself serve as President between 1892 and 1895. Somewhat unsurprisingly, therefore, given his interests, Chalmers became one of the four founding members of SBRCS in 1888. Members of the Philosophical Society had constituted a large proportion of those attending Duncan's lecture on cremation, amongst them prominent Glaswegian architects J.J. Burnet (1857–1938) and John Honeyman (1863–1945), Charles Rennie Mackintosh's master.

'A Scheme of Cremation' for Glasgow

In 1889, having clearly turned his attention to the crematorium project, Chalmers addressed the Society on 'A Scheme of Cremation Suited to the Requirements of Glasgow',[20] in which he proposed a design comprising four graded chapels and a series of columbaria grouped around two courtyards – the first arrangement of its type in the UK. It had a chapel for 'the very rich' on the upper level; a second for 'the better class' on the ground floor; a third for 'the working class' to the right; and a fourth for 'paupers' to the left of the receiving room or mortuary.[21] There were also incinerators designated for differing classes. The catafalque was placed centrally in a

---

19. J. Chalmers, *Proceedings of the Royal Philosophical Society of Glasgow*, 17 (1886), 404–39.
20. J. Chalmers, *Proceedings of the Royal Philosophical Society of Glasgow*, 20 (1889), 193–5; Grainger 2014.
21. J. Chalmers, *Proceedings of the Royal Philosophical Society of Glasgow*, 20 (1889), 194.

separate, octagonal space and on view only to the wealthy and better class of mourners. A curtain closed in the second chapel, while the coffin remained in situ in the principal chapel, flanked by seated relatives. Chalmers advocated 'the most beautiful form of architectural treatment', with the scope for the richest materials: marble, mosaic work, stained glass and statuary, adding, 'Possibly the most suitable form would be ecclesiastical architecture of the Norman or Early English periods, and the whole arrangement would be suggestive of extreme reverence for the dead',[22] all at an estimated cost of £3,600. Chalmers' paper also included a cremator designed by Key, who had pioneered air conditioning at Glasgow Royal Infirmary.

Maryhill Crematorium: Architecture and decoration

In appointing Chalmers, a relatively inexperienced architect but informed supporter of the movement, the Scottish Society followed the CS which had commissioned E.F.C. Clarke (1843–1904), a relatively low-profile church architect, to design England's first crematorium chapel at Woking in 1889. Chalmers, in common with Clarke, favoured an ecclesiastical idiom, presumably intended to offer reassurance to the sceptical and respectability to cremation through a visual connection with the Church and its tradition of burial (Grainger 2000, 2005). Chalmers had only two English examples to learn from: Woking (1889) and Manchester (1892), although he might have seen C.F.A. Voysey's design for a projected chapel and crematorium in Ayr (1886), designed in a collegiate style for John Hamilton (*Building News*, 5/11/1886). In March 1893, Duncan, Key and Mann[23] visited Manchester Crematorium which had been designed by local architects Edward Salomons and Alfred E. Steinthal and marked a change in architectural style, being loosely Lombard Romanesque, infused with a hint of Byzantine. In proposing a Norman Romanesque style Chalmers shared the view of his Manchester colleagues that an ecclesiastical idiom was required, but that Gothic might no longer necessarily provide the most suitable choice for a crematorium, given that by the end of the nineteenth century it was the orthodox style of choice not only for Anglicans, but also for Catholics and many Nonconformists.

In 1893, Chalmers once again addressed the Philosophical Society, this time as President of the Sanitary and Social Economy Section, on 'Some

22. Ibid., 195.
23. SBRCS Minutes Vol. 1, pp. 54–55.

Important Sanitary Problems'.[24] He revealed it was his belief that in view of the growing number of uncertified deaths 'the erection of a crematorium was a duty which fell to the Health Committee of the city, and that its administration should be placed under, and, in a sense, become the headquarters of, the Medical Officer of Health'. He argued that 'If this was done, the inquest room, or public mortuary, would form an important department of the official work,' but added 'In holding and expressing these views, I moved too fast.'[25] The authorities and the community as a whole were indifferent about uncertified deaths and coroners' inquests, 'while our civic authorities are not leading public opinion, but are waiting to be led either by it or us [...] The erection of a crematorium on these lines has, therefore, been rendered impracticable; but it is gratifying to know that, while those responsible for public health have done nothing to further the movement, sanitarians have combined with gentlemen interested in the decent burial of the poor to erect the necessary buildings'. Chalmers added, 'In this connection, I think that it cannot be too strongly stated that cremation, while it may be esteemed the luxury of the rich, is, in reality, identified with and essential to the respectability of the poor.'[26] Chalmers made the leap from theory into practice by producing sketch plans in 1893 at an estimated cost of £2,300, but the committee, anxious to keep cost down, requested 'fresh plans of a more simple design', thereby reducing the cost (without furnace) to £1,450. There was now only one lofty chapel, but tradition had prevailed as Chalmers had clearly been persuaded to adopt Free-style Gothic, rather than Norman. He nevertheless produced a commanding design, to be constructed in the characteristic red stone of the city, although additions have altered its appearance considerably over the years. The overall quality of the materials and decoration was high, with rare marble employed in the pillars and fine carvings, notably the bosses and dogtooth ornament.

Writing in 1927, Chalmers maintained that Maryhill was the only crematorium consisting of two floors; and it had four special features. First, the separation of 'the burial from the incinerating part', thus keeping the Chapel quiet and private. Second, it permitted burial as if in a new-made grave – for years the relatives were provided with the usual cords with which to lower

24. J. Chalmers, *Proceedings of the Royal Philosophical Society of Glasgow*, 25 (1893), 208–23.
25. Ibid., 222.
26. Ibid.

the coffin, although by 1927 there was a small hydraulic elevator by which the coffin was lowered silently. Third, the Superintendent was responsible to the Society for the carrying out of cremations and supervising of the undertakers. No workmen were required, thus keeping the funeral party select. Fourth, it was the only crematorium with an arrangement suitable for a Masonic funeral. As his later Episcopal Church designs attest, Chalmers was particularly concerned with symbolism and is recorded tellingly as saying, 'When the building was designed I was P.G.A. [Provincial Grand Architect] of Glasgow Province, and was satisfied that what appeared to make the best plan, lent itself admirably to members of the Masonic Order, when paying their last respects to their dead'.[27] This must surely account for the three steps and two pillars which recalled the steps of the Apprentice, Craft and Master, and Jachin and Boaz, the pillars of Solomon, so central to Masonic legend. In the wider context of cremation advocacy, the anti-clericalism of the Masons was particularly significant in Italy, Argentina, Austria, France, the Netherlands, Portugal, Spain and the USA. Freemasonry came to be associated with cremation and although it did not feature prominently in UK developments, some of the CS's Council were themselves Masons.

The catafalque at Maryhill was placed centrally and descended – the Directors clearly considered this less of a departure from earth burial, thereby causing least offence. Exclusive to Maryhill was the open-fronted stone table at the east end in front of a rear passage whereby the descent of the coffin and its removal onto an iron carriage for removal to the incinerating chamber could be viewed. By means of another opening, the attendant could be seen by relatives removing the ashes from the incinerator and depositing them in 'the selected urn', thereby satisfying themselves 'that the ashes delivered to them are those of the body given to the Society'.[28] The table could also serve as a temporary altar, and was 'either decorated with beautiful flowers or has a marble urn resting upon it, thus forming an appropriate finish to the chapel'.

Chalmers, a prominent lay preacher in the 1900s, proved to be a capable and inventive designer who went on to enjoy a varied and successful practice, encompassing commercial, domestic and ecclesiastical work in and around Glasgow. He continued his association with the Society, designing a new columbarium in 1926. This involved moving the catafalque and

27. Chalmers c. 1927:9.
28. Ibid., 10–11.

provided further opportunities for artistic embellishment in the form of two stained glass windows to Chalmers' designs and executed by Glasgow firm Messrs Guthrie and Wells, and marble work by Messrs Toffolo, Jackson and Co. and Galbraith and Winton Ltd. Chalmers was quick to pay testament to the Glasgow companies whose work in the crematorium endorsed his view that 'cremation, in permitting of the memorials being housed in suitable surroundings under cover, as in our Cathedrals and Art Galleries, provides scope for the finest of material and art – not possible in earth burial.'[29]

Chalmers also suggested that 'Those who have visited the Invalides in Paris will observe that in the opening in the Glasgow Columbarium between its two ground floors, I have followed much the same arrangement as in Paris; and looking over the fine pavonazza marble rail or descending the marble stair, one sees two full-sized angel figures in statuary marble, each represented as dropping flowers on to the urns at their feet.'[30]

In 1927, the year of his death, Chalmers reiterated his belief that 'cremation was bound up with the respectability of the poor; and I deem it a great honour to have designed for them and others an arrangement which in ordinary days and ways would be reserved for the very rich.'[31] He concluded,

> Does not the perfect day end with a perfect sunset? Does not the season end up with the glorious colours of autumn? If so, at the end of life man, instead of being consigned to darkness and decay, should enter the crematorium amid its rich colourings of marble – the colours of the celestial city like onyx – its richness of glittering stained glass, the apparent glory of our golden light, thence to pass into the sunlight of the incinerating chamber, and finally join those whose ashes *repose among the angels*.[32]

29. Ibid., 13.
30. Ibid., 11.
31. Ibid., 14.
32. Ibid., 15.

CHAPTER FOUR

Cremation in Scotland: The Early Years, 1895–1918

Managing Scotland's First Crematorium, 1895–1902

Following Maryhill's first cremation, the number of funerals rose frustratingly slowly. There were ten in 1896, twenty in 1900, thirty-five in 1905. The patience of the Scottish Burial Reform and Cremation Society (SBRCS) Directors was tested, especially in view of the progress in England where five more crematoria opened: at Liverpool (1896), Hull (1901), Leicester (1902), Golders Green (1902) and Birmingham (1903). Nevertheless, the twelve crematoria in England had just 569 cremations between them in 1905.

Finance was a continuing problem for Maryhill: the crematorium had cost £2,942 12s 4d, but only £1,899 of the bills had been paid. With leading professionals and businessmen among them, there is no doubt that in a sudden crisis the Directors could have rescued their project. Thanks to subscriptions, share purchases and loans, and a Clydesdale Bank overdraft, the deficit was held down. By the new century it stood at £342 0s 0d.

The Allan brothers' promise to Mann in 1891 to subscribe all the money needed to start on Maryhill appears not to have been fulfilled. The Board minutes do not record any exceptional sums from them. Mann received one modest amount from Kier Hardie who was particularly impressed by the Society's 'not-for-profit' principle. He gave a 'twenty-shilling Scotch bank note' for the Society's work, and promised to inform the miners' leader Bob Smillie of the project (Mann, September 1952).

Towards the end of 1899,[1] after fifty-five funerals, the Directors considered introducing an organ. This would have been a somewhat radical development as the introduction of organs to Scottish churches in 1858 had been controversial and many still did not use them. Moreover, Scottish burials went straight from the home to the burial ground, bypassing the church.[2] The provision of a crematorium organ would have given funeral congregations an advantage which burial could not provide (Parsons 2012). The Directors postponed a decision – there had after all been only twelve cremations in eighteen months.

Funeral services, however infrequent, still needed to be a model of decorum. When members of the congregation expressed concern about noise from the furnace-room below the chapel, the Board agreed to install a speaking-tube and to request the furnace operator to wear slippers. In December 1898 the Board recognised that a hydraulic lift between Chapel and furnace-room would be an advance on the 'perhaps noisy, certainly slow, manual operation'. The decision to proceed would eventually be taken in 1906, when Dr Russell donated a 'force-pump'.

One source of funds was the donation of memorial windows. When Director W.P. Buchan died in 1896, he was the second person to be cremated at Maryhill and 'several plumbers wanted to provide a stained-glass window in his memory'. The Board agreed that altar furnishings could be provided for Episcopalian funerals, provided that these were donated. A weighted purple pall was bought to cover the catafalque.

The care of the building and cremator proved difficult. In December 1895, Superintendent Tyler of Western Cemetery agreed to take responsibility for the working of the furnace and the state of the crematorium building. An agreement was made with the Cemetery Company and Tyler was paid 10% of every cremation fee for his services. This system seems to have worked satisfactorily until 1902 when two men were then employed: one on each floor during a cremation. A subsequent complaint by some Directors about the cleaning and caretaking then brought to the surface simmering tensions between the Directors of the crematorium and those of the cemetery.

If cremation was to grow as an alternative to burial, it would jeopardise the financial stability of the cemetery. Maryhill was the perfect site for a

1. See *UJ* 33(2) (February 1898), 24-26 for a description of Maryhill in 1898.
2. 'Mac', *UJ* 26(9) (September 1911), 249; McKim 1944: 8–9.

potential confrontation between rival methods of disposal and may well have influenced later decisions by private companies and municipal authorities in Scotland post-1945 to build their crematoria on land totally separate from burial grounds.

After negotiations by Chalmers and Mann, the Board offered £40 to terminate the cemetery Superintendent's work in the crematorium but the Cemetery Company declined. An alternative was more easily suggested than achieved, the Superintendent's immediate successor being suspended within six weeks. In September 1902 Mann reported that under threat of legal action he had advanced £57 5s 9d to pay off the Cemetery Company to date. It appears that cremations during the autumn had been carried out by workmen supplied by the Mirrlees Watson Company, but the latter had 'experienced great difficulty in inducing their men to work at the crematorium'. Another approach was made to the Cemetery Company to supply staff for cremations. In April 1904 the current Superintendent handed back his keys. The July minutes reported that much of the Superintendent's work was being performed by James Chalmers.

Recruiting Clergy, Salespersons and Directors

In 1895 Mann assembled a first list of clergy to preside at cremation services. In the first fifteen funerals ministers came from the Church of Scotland (three), the Free Church (three), the United Presbyterian Church (three), the Congregationalists (one), the Unitarians (one), and the Scottish Episcopal Church (four, including the Bishop of Galloway). The list suggests that the introduction of cremation in Glasgow was not perceived as the secular threat that it had been in Woking ten years before (Parsons 2005), despite the continuing opposition of some Presbyterian clergy to taking part in graveside rituals. By 1902 there were fifty-nine clergy listed as available, by 1904 sixty-eight and by 1910 eighty-one. In 1912, the Directors examined the print of a service used in some crematoria in England. They judged that 'such a printed form was not suitable for Scotland but authorised the Secretary to print a modified card of procedure at the service'. This preference for a better funeral liturgy indicates that lay Scottish Presbyterians had come some way since the Kirk's authorising graveside liturgies in 1897.

Another formidable task was securing men and women to attract subscriptions to the Society. Those employed never lasted many months in the work; canvassing must have been arduous. Even Mann Junior sought to resign as Honorary Secretary in June 1902 but was persuaded to continue.

Recruiting Directors was easier although there was a small and regular turnover. There were no more conversions as dramatic as that of the Allan brothers. Cameron and Farquharson were elected Vice-Presidents. The Duke of Argyll, the Earl of Home and Lord Balfour all declined to lend their authority to this radical alternative to burial. The attempt to secure the support of the Marquess of Bute has been described above (pp. 69–70). The Episcopal Bishop of Glasgow had declined an invitation to the 1903 AGM. The apology sent to the 1908 AGM by Professor George Adam Smith, the leading Old Testament scholar of his day, deserves quotation. 'I have your kind invitation [...] [for] 18 December at 1.30. Without knowing it, you have struck a curious coincidence. To the minute, it is the anniversary of my wedding, so you will not expect me to be with you even in spirit.' He continued:

> If on the day when I was wed,
> And at the very hour,
> I were to show a solemn head
> At your Society (Limited)
> For decent burning of the dead,
> Then folk might say I'd turned sour
> Of wife and bairns and wedding bliss;
> While if I spoke stray marriage bells
> Might jangle with your funeral knells
> And shock the band of serious 'swells'
> You'd brought to bless your energies.
> So let me stay at home and read
> The marriage service with my mate
> And pray the other be delayed
> Unto a very distant date,
> Yet trust me, I'll do nought to hinder
> Your healthy efforts for our clay,
> To turn us all to honest cinder
> On the inevitable day.[3]

---

3. SBRCS AGM, 18/12/1908.

Nellfield Burial Scandal[4]

In 1898 litigation in Aberdeen generated publicity which cremationists were quick to exploit. The Baker Incorporation had a cemetery at Nellfield. William Coutts was its Superintendent.

The litigation arose from the discovery that a family grave had been deepened without consent, and the coffins and bodies within crushed to allow the coffins of strangers to be deposited in it. There were related trials, three civil and one criminal. In the first the children of the last family member buried in the grave sued the Incorporation. In the next two the Incorporation sued Coutts. Finally, Coutts was prosecuted for offences of violating sepulchres and perjury (NRS:AD 14/99/48 and JC 26/1899/1). The perjury consisted of tampering with the Incorporation's ledgers to conceal the number of bodies buried in graves and to falsify their identity.

The disclosures at the first trial prompted a host of applications from lairholders and others for graves to be opened and their contents checked. Visitors to the cemetery came armed with probes. There were four consecutive days of systematic excavation of the graves and walks of the cemetery ordered by the Sheriff. More graves opened at the request of lairholders were found to be in order than otherwise, but, nevertheless, far too many had been tampered with. The excavations revealed: bodies in the walks; lairs without bodies which should have been in them, and with bodies that shouldn't; lairs sold as 'clean' when they weren't; lairholders charged for deepening graves which had only been cleaned, if that; coffins and bodies smashed up; coffins placed one inside another with their contents in the topmost coffin; bodies doubled or fitted head to heel in the one coffin; and bodies and coffins buried in the toolhouse yard. The *Aberdeen Journal* published a daily table of results. When the Incorporation terminated excavations not ordered by the Sheriff the tally was: graves examined 248; satisfactory 178; unsatisfactory 70. By mid November the Incorporation had paid out £2,180 in settlement of about 200 claims.

The indictment against Coutts contained six counts of violating sepulchres and one of perjury – there could have been many more of each (NRS JC 71/33, HM Advocate v Coutts 1899; S. White 2016: 172–4). On the

---

4. This section is based on *Aberdeen Journal* 4/2/1899–6/2/1900, *Aberdeen Weekly Journal* 11/10–13/12/1899 and *Daily Free Press* 23/5/–13/12/1899.

fourth day of his trial Coutts pleaded guilty to just two counts of violating sepulchres. He was sentenced to six months' imprisonment.

Supporters of cremation immediately took advantage of the disclosures. Two letters in the *Aberdeen Journal* called for a crematorium. 'An old hand in the undertaking business' declared that 'if the public only knew what went on in the best regulated cemeteries when graves are being cleaned as the operation is called – and that operation is absolutely essential – they would soon become reconciled to the idea of cremation [...] I have long been convinced of the superiority of cremation over burial [...] and my convictions [...] were greatly strengthened by what came under my own observation of what went on in cemeteries that are above reproach'. On the day after Coutts's conviction Cameron and Farquharson and all the Directors of the SBRCS adverted to the disclosures at Aberdeen, 'which, there is reason to believe, will find parallels elsewhere if sufficient investigation be made', and called for support for the Society (*Glasgow Herald*, 12/11/1899). There were calls for the Town Council to establish its own cemetery. The Finance Committee of the Council was asked to report on this and, despite some opposition, on the establishment of a crematorium as well. A Police and Town Improvement Bill was being prepared and included in it was a clause, identical to section 92 of the Edinburgh Improvement and Tramways Act of 1896, prohibiting the establishment of a cemetery or crematorium within the City without the Council's consent. It also contained clauses about cemeteries, including one permitting the Corporation to regulate them by bye-laws. Later a clause was added empowering the Corporation to establish a crematorium. It appears it was practically identical to clauses in local Acts empowering local authorities to build crematoria, of which at that time there were five. No sooner had the clause been inserted in the Bill than it was deleted: the Bill should have defined the site on which the crematorium was to be built and the Council had not yet settled upon a site (Cremation Society of England 1900: 14).[5] The other clauses all survived after the bye-laws power was limited, in the face of opposition from cemetery owners, to the protection of public health and the maintenance of public decency (APIA 1900, ss 37–41).

5. Of the five local Acts the three most recent had specified a site, but the Leamington Corporation Act 1896 definitely had not, and the first, the Cardiff Corporation Act 1894, arguably had not.

The matter of the crematorium was raised during the contemporaneous Council elections, occasionally to comical effect. The stone masons were concerned at the effect cremation might have on the memorial industry and at a workplace meeting one candidate was asked whether he approved of the establishment of a crematorium and what effect it would have on the granite industry. He replied that he could not 'see any connection in the world' between a creamery and the industry. His error pointed out, it transpired that his attitude towards a crematorium was the same as his attitude to a creamery: neither should be built in Aberdeen. Other candidates were in favour of a crematorium. On the last day of November, Farquharson (1899, 1910), who had attended at least one of the exhumations, expounded the advantages of cremation and the disadvantages of burial, in the annual Aberdeen City Lecture; and a debate at the University Debating Society shortly after about whether 'cremation has become necessary' ended with twenty-four voting in favour of cremation and fourteen against.

Cremation Act 1902[6]

When his Disposal of the Dead Bill was lost in 1884 Cameron remarked that cremation would be able to proceed in a totally unregulated way. The legal implications of this slowly became apparent in England and Wales. Cremated remains could be deposited in churches and other places in which 'burial' was prohibited by the Burial Acts, because the 'burials' to which the Acts referred were those of uncremated bodies (In re Kerr 1894); and ashes could be buried without the production of a burial certificate. Rulings such as these posed no hindrance to the cremation movement except in so far as they might permit cremations in ways which would discredit it. In other contexts, however, they were an obstacle. Local authorities could lawfully do only what statute empowered them to. One empowered to 'bury' a body could not have it cremated (Poor Law Amendment Act (PLAA) 1844 s. 44; Public Health (Scotland) Act (PHSA) 1867 s. 43; Laski 1932) nor could Medical Officers of Health (MOHs), magistrates and Sheriffs, empowered

---

6. This section is based on CSA CRE/P/1/B/I; LMA PC/COR/1/53; NRS HH 61/108, HH 61/142; TNA HLG 29/69, HO 45/9474/244, HO 45/9476/927, HO 45/9531/40582, HO 45/9887/B17163, HO 45/10113/B11886, HO 45/1044/B18513/F3, HO 45/10144/B18513/F5, HO 45/10144/B18513/F6, HO 45/10144/B18513/F8, HO 45/B24279, HO 347/19/539, HO 45/9807/B633A, PRO 30/72/21, PRO 30/72/22; S. White 2003.

to order the burial of those who died of infectious disease, order their cremation PHA 1875 s. 42; IDPA 1890; PHSA 1867 s. 43). In Scotland this was changed in 1897 by a prescient but little noticed amendment to the Public Health Act – 'In this Act the word "burial" includes cremation' (PHSA 1897 ss 2 and 6)[7] – a change not replicated in England and Wales until 1936 (PHA 1936 ss 162, 163).

The Directors of the SBRCS had already turned their minds to cremating the unclaimed dead and in this amendment must have seen an opportunity. A committee of Robertson, Duncan and Mann was set up to find Poor Law authorities tempted by a fee of 8s for adults and 4s for children. The Governors of Govan Poorhouse and the Barony Parochial Board showed interest. But Glasgow Parish Council rejected the Society's approach (*Glasgow Herald* 2/3/1898 11f, 4/5/1898 12a). An amendment of the Glasgow Police Amendment Act 1890 might have been required: section 44, unusually, required the City's hospital, infirmaries and poorhouses to send unclaimed bodies for dissection after which they had to be buried (AA 1832 s. 13).[8]

As for building crematoria, local authorities were advised that legislation empowering them to establish cemeteries did not allow them to build or assist in the building of crematoria (Makepeace 1990: 8–9), although they could permit the deposit of cremated remains in their burial grounds. So authorities bent on providing crematoria had to promote individual Acts of Parliament to obtain the necessary powers. The first attempt to do so, by Tunbridge Wells in 1889, was blocked by the Home Office (HO) and Local Government Board (LGB) (Report on the Tunbridge Wells Improvement Bill 1889, cls 321, 322 [see under Tunbridge Wells Archives]).

At the Annual Meeting of the British Medical Association in 1891 Farquharson seconded a motion that its Parliamentary Bills Committee secure a change in the law to allow local authorities to build crematoria. A deputation from the Association of Municipal Corporations urged a similar course on the Home Secretary. At a meeting attended by Farquharson,

---

7. The amendment was moved unopposed among many others on the last day of the Committee Stage of the Bill (House of Commons 1897). *The Scotsman*, 4/6/1897 10a has a long report of this day's proceedings but does not mention this amendment. The *Glasgow Herald* did not report them.
8. The only similar provision is the Edinburgh Municipal and Police (Amendment) Act 1891 s. 77.

the Council of the Cremation Society (CS) had declined to patronise the SBRCS because it promoted the 'earth to earth' system of burial (ch. 2) as well as cremation. In 1892, however, the CS joined with the Church of England Burial, Funeral and Mourning Reform Association in a deputation to the Home Secretary to secure improvements in the system of death registration and Cameron was asked to introduce a Bill 'in furtherance of the objects of the Society'.[9] What Cameron, supported by Farquharson, secured was a Select Committee to enquire into 'the sufficiency of the existing Law as to the Disposal of the Dead, for securing an accurate record of the Cause of Death in all cases [...]'. It heard lengthy evidence from Thompson, Spencer Wells and Cameron himself and recommended the legal enforcement of the CS's procedures before cremation, namely two medical certificates, backed where necessary by a post-mortem and the retention of portions of the liver, kidney and stomach (House of Commons 1893). The HO relaxed its opposition to local authorities acquiring powers to build crematoria by local legislation and by 1901 fourteen had.[10]

The Bill that became the Cremation Act was the handiwork of the London County Council and was introduced, with a nod from the HO, in 1900 and passed two years later. It empowered burial authorities to establish crematoria and required their plans to have the approval of the LGB. It prohibited the erection of any crematorium, public or private, within fifty yards of a public highway, in the consecrated part of a burial authority's cemetery, and within 200 yards of a house whose owner, lessee or occupier had not consented to it. It required the Home Secretary to make regulations about cremation and imposed penalties for infringing them. The Bill was amended to exclude Scotland (and Ireland) expressly, the Secretary for Scotland's view being that there was no demand for it in Scotland. When a letter from the SBRCS failed to persuade the Bill's promoter to the contrary, Renshaw, supported by Bonar Law, sought to add a clause extending the Bill to Scotland by defining 'burial authority' in the Scottish context as any 'parish council or town council of any parish or burgh as defined in sections 2 and 3 of the Burial Grounds (Scotland) Act, 1855' and by replacing the Home Secretary

9. On the Association see Rugg 2013: 238–42. On its preference for burial see Lawrence 1889, 1891; and Parsons 2005: 212–15, 226. The Duke of Westminster combined being a staunch supporter of the Association with being a benefactor of the CS.
10. A list of the Acts is on the CS's website at www.cremation.org.uk

and LGB with the Scottish Secretary and the Local Government Board for Scotland (LGBS).[11] Farquharson was present to support the amendment and endorse the good accounts given of the crematorium in Glasgow, and the Lord Advocate offered no objection to it. The clause was passed by 199 votes to ninety. Twenty-nine Scottish members voted for it and eight against it. Some of the opposition to the clause came from those who saw in it a stepping stone to extending the Bill to Ireland, but equally some supported it for the same reason.

Because it was inconceivable that a parish council in England and Wales would be able to finance a crematorium, those ignorant of local government in Scotland were incredulous that a parish in Scotland would be able to do so. They sought to amend the new clause by taking parishes out of it. Renshaw pointed out, however, that some Scottish parishes were much larger than those in England and that in Scotland the parish council was the only authority having any connection with the burial laws. The amendment was defeated by 249 votes to 104, as was one to remove burial authorities having fewer than 10,000 inhabitants, T.W. Russell, the member for South Tyrone, chipping in that, 'The truth of the matter was that a Scotch debate might often be dull, but it was never ridiculous until Englishmen interfered.'

The bifurcation of responsibility in England and Wales between the Home Secretary and LGB reflected that over burial grounds. The Burial Act of 1900 had tidied matters up somewhat by allocating supervision of the sanitary and financial aspects of burial to the Board and matters of ecclesiastical law, such as consecration and 'surplice fees', and of crime and justice, such as exhumation, to the HO (Rugg 2013: 236–7, 261–2).

The problem in applying this template to Scotland was that the LGBS had never had anything to do with burial grounds. Such central supervision as there was was exclusively in the hands of the Secretary for Scotland apart from the approval of fees, which fell to Sheriffs (BGSA 1855 s. 14). Although Scottish Office (SO) officials realised that the Act would give the Board novel responsibilities, they raised no objection. Nor did they seek to have

11. The definition was subsequently amended to 'the parish council or town council of any parish or burgh as the case may be vested with the powers and duties conferred by section 2 and 3 of the Burial Grounds (Scotland) Act, 1855, or any Act amending the same', *P. Debs*, ser. 4, vol. 95, 1564–8 (HC, 26 June 1901). The wording about the Scottish Secretary and LGBS also had to be tidied up, *House of Lords Journal* (3 February 1902), 39.

sections which could have no application in Scotland expressly disapplied: these were sections 11, 12 and 13 and that part of section 5 which prohibited the erection of a crematorium on consecrated ground.

Cremation Regulations[12]

The regulations for England and Wales were drafted by a HO Departmental Committee.

Apart from the CS's crematorium at Woking there were four private crematoria and two municipal ones in 1902. The Rules of the former and the HO approved bye-laws of the latter varied little from the CS's (Troup 1903: Appendix III, Thompson 1901: Appendix B; Simon 1896; SBRCS 1904: 10). The regulations required by the Act were more extensive. They had to address: (1) the maintenance and inspection of crematoria; (2) the cases in which and the conditions under which 'the burning of human remains' might take place; (3) the disposition or interment of ashes; (4) the forms of the documents required for cremations; and (5) the registration of cremations (CA 1902 s. 7).

The regulations about items 1, 3 and 5 were few. The Committee married items 2 and 4 under the heading 'The Conditions under which Cremations May Take Place'. This was the largest section. It said nothing about the cases in which cremation might take place except by implication from those instances when it was not to be permitted, namely where the deceased was known to have left a written direction to that effect and where remains buried for less than a year had not been identified.

Observance of the conditions was to be secured by medical referees. These had to be appointed by cremation authorities and had to be doctors. Their task was to authorise or decline to authorise cremations on the basis of the forms and certificates required by the regulations. These required an 'Application for Cremation' and either (a) two medical certificates, one [Form B] from the deceased's doctor, the second [Form C] from a doctor of five years' standing appointed by the cremation authority (i.e. 'any burial authority or any person by whom a crematorium has been established' (CR

---

12. This section is based on **NRS:** GRO 1/648, 23/10/1914, HH 61/108, HH 61/126/239/64, HH 61/127/F4, HH 61/126/239/65, HH 61/126/239/67, HH 61/127/F3/239/68, HH 61/127/F2/239/92; **TNA:** HO 45/10249/B38635/F18, HO 45/10249/B38635/F28, HO 45/10197/B30770, HO 45/10249/B38626/F12, HO 45/10249/B38626/F13, HO 45/B32157.

1903)) or holding one of several public medical positions, or (b) a 'Coroner's Order'. Referees could require a post-mortem before authorising a cremation and could decline to authorise one without giving any reason.

Forms modified at referees' discretion could be used for the cremation of anyone who had died outside England or Wales. Referees could dispense with the forms, and the Home Secretary could suspend the regulations, in times of public health emergencies.

A much less rigorous procedure was prescribed for the cremation of still-born children.

The CS advanced seven objections to the prohibition of the cremation of those who had not wished to be cremated, among them that it was unauthorised because Parliament cannot have intended, without express words to that effect, to limit an executor's right to determine how a dead body was to be dealt with. Some at the LGBS shared the view that the prohibition was unlawful. One commented, 'It isn't clear how Regulation 4 and perhaps 5 can be defended as Regulations under sec. 7 of the Act.' (Regulation 5 prohibited the cremation of unidentified human remains).[13]

The SO was not as quick off the mark drafting regulations as the HO. Despite the Act's requirement that they be made, this did not happen until 1927. At first officials decided to await the result of the HO's deliberations. When they set about adapting the HO's draft for Scotland, the provisions relating to coroners and the role, if any, of procurators fiscal exercised them most. Troup, who had chaired the HO Committee, had told Dodds at the SO, 'I wish we had procurators fiscal in England. It would have made our work much easier,'[14] a sentiment reflected in the first draft of the Committee's Report. The first Scottish official to consider the draft took the hint and latched on to the possibility of making procurators fiscal medical referees. Fiscals, however, were never doctors (Shiels 2016). The Under Secretary at the SO thought the proposal impracticable and the Lord Advocate was totally opposed. So when the Home Secretary's regulations were published very little needed to be done to adapt them for Scotland and a draft was quickly prepared. The only substantial change required was to accommodate

13. Committee minute, 17/12/1903, NRS HH 61/127/F4. Letter from J. Swinburne-Hanham, Honorary Secretary, Cremation Society of England, to the Under Secretary of State, HO 7/3/1903, TNA HO 45/10249/B38635/F18.
14. Letter from C. Troup, Principal Clerk, HO to J.M. Dodds, Senior Clerk, Office of Secretary for Scotland, 21/1/1903, NRS HH 61/108.

procurators fiscal: fatal accident inquiries, whose remit resembled that of coroners to a very limited extent, were to have no place. By December 1903 draft regulations had been approved by the Lord Advocate. Almost as an afterthought the LGBS's observations were sought.

The Board appears not to have been consulted about the extension of the Act to Scotland (before 2 July 1902). Now it spotted that the legal implications of the Act and regulations were greater than in England and Wales because in the Scottish Public Health Act 'burial' was defined to 'include cremation'.

Section 79 of the Act empowered the Board in times of 'epidemic, endemic or infectious disease' to make regulations 'for the speedy interment of the dead'. Would this allow it to make regulations for their cremation? Dr J.B. Russell (see chs 2 and 3), the medical member of the Board (and a SBRCS Director), doubted it because the section used the word 'interment' rather than 'burial'. Because he thought cremation particularly suitable for dealing with deaths from infectious disease, the Board gave close attention to cremation Regulation 14. This allowed a medical referee to dispense with the usual certificates when a person had died from plague, cholera, or yellow fever on board a ship or in a public hospital, and the Home Secretary to suspend or modify the regulations in any district during an epidemic or 'for other sufficient reason' on the application of a local authority. The Board wanted itself and MOHs to be much more involved in the operation of Regulation 14. The SO rejected its proposal. It did agree, however, that the Board should be notified of the opening and closing of crematoria and of the appointment of medical referees.

A hiatus of three years followed. It is true that no local authorities in Scotland were clamouring to be allowed to build crematoria and the SBRCS does not appear to have been concerned that either it might be acting illegally[15] or to secure the protection of conformity to statutory requirements. The Act, after all, stated that the Secretary for Scotland 'shall' make regulations and made it an offence to carry out cremations otherwise than in accordance with them. When, in 1907, the Under Secretary for Scotland inquired about the regulations, the medical and legal members of the Board and the Solicitor General for Scotland agreed that there was no necessity for them.

15. This possibility did not arise in England and Wales because the Act and Regulations came into operation simultaneously.

The matter was revived in 1913, when the Edinburgh Cremation Society (ECS) was seeking land in Warriston Cemetery for a crematorium and asked the SO whether any regulations had been issued. The SO consulted the Board, which at first agreed that it would be as well to have regulations in place. Before a reply was sent, Leslie Mackenzie, the Board's current medical member, sent an underling to report upon operations at Glasgow. Adrian Smail reported that the crematorium was using documents almost identical to those in use in England and Wales which 'are rather elaborate but the Society have loyally adhered to them[16] so that no one can point a finger at them'. He also commented that the fee charged for the medical certificates (a guinea each) was probably a regrettable deterrent to cremation. Having ascertained that Mann would be willing to draft a set of regulations based on the Society's experience, Smail drafted a letter to him which was passed to the Board's medical and legal members. Mackenzie commented

> I see no objection to the suggested letter. The matter is not particularly urgent. The progress of cremation is slow. Personally, after a fairly careful study of Sir Henry Thompson's book some years ago, I could not feel satisfied that the precautions against foul play by poisoning (or even otherwise) were adequate and could, by any known administrative device, be made so. Hence I am not prepared to urge cremation forward. So long as it is on the present voluntary lines, the chances of foul play are not great, since, as a rule, only the more public minded persons will readily think of arranging for cremation. Regulations, therefore, may possibly be, with safety, made simpler than proposed here and so not impede the growth of the voluntary movement.[17]

Macpherson, the Board's legal member, concurred. The Board told the SO that it was having a completely new draft prepared based on Glasgow's experience, and a formal invitation was sent to Mann Jr with a strong steer that the Board would be willing to endorse regulations less elaborate than

---

16. Even to the extent of informing applicants for cremation that it was unlawful to cremate the body of someone who had left written directions to the contrary (SBRCS 1912: 17; NRS GRO1/648), something unlawful in England and Wales only because of Regulation 4. No such caution was included in earlier editions of the booklet (SBRCS 1904).
17. Minute by MacKenzie, 7/2/1914, NRS HH 61/127/F4.

Early Years, 1895–1918

in England and Wales. Eight and a half months later, the General Registry Office was told that 'the medical member is not disposed to hasten matters' and that 'the Board were disinclined to press matters'.

Despite the veiled invitation to draft simpler regulations, the Society's draft was more elaborate. It replicated the English and Welsh regulations so far as possible but transferred certain duties from medical referees to registrars. The reason was that at Glasgow certain clerical duties which in England and Wales fell to medical referees were being discharged by the Secretary or Registrar of the Society. The application for cremation was to include certain administrative matters not present in the English and Welsh form and the Register of Cremations would be more comprehensive. To the persons qualified to provide the second confirmatory medical certificate would be added 'an Examiner or Lecturer in Forensic Medicine or Medical Jurisprudence recognised by a Medical Licensing Authority'. At this time Scotland was far in advance of other parts of the United Kingdom in Forensic Medicine and Jurisprudence (Crowther and White 1988a; B. White 1983, 1988, 1994). In only one respect was the draft simpler than the English and Welsh regulations. It dispensed with the need for the application for cremation to be confirmed by a statutory declaration and this the Board readily accepted.

Smail noted the extra complications and proposed that a new draft be prepared. A year later Mackenzie apologised for not having attended to the matter. Smail once again advised the preparation of a draft. Nine months later, Smail's superior apologised for not having attended to the matter and it appears to have been put aside.

Maryhill from 1902 to the First World War

In the wake of the Nellfield scandal, the Board agreed to give every encouragement to 'gentlemen in Aberdeen' to build a crematorium and form a branch of the Society.[18] The same meeting discussed a report that the Glasgow Town Council was again considering purchasing land for a municipal cemetery. Neither succeeded at the time. The SBRCS booklet *Ashes to Ashes* (1904) lists cremation societies at Brechin, Edinburgh, Johnstone, Paisley and Perth.

18. In 1912, there was correspondence with 'Mr Watt of the *Aberdeen Free Press*' (Board minutes, 20/12/2012, p. 275), probably a member of the family which promoted Aberdeen Crematorium in the 1930s.

In 1902, director Buchanan referred to 'recent developments in England'. These will probably have included the passing of the Cremation Act 1902, the opening of Golders Green and the establishment of Hull (1901) and Leicester (1902) crematoria by their local authorities. Buchanan suggested to the Board that the Council might be invited to consider taking over the crematorium. Mann was asked to raise the matter with the City's Sanitary Committee but his report the following month resulted in the Society stepping back from this issue.

In 1904 Cameron succeeded Thompson as President of the CS, retiring from Parliament and moving to London. Cameron's period of office proved frustrating for him (Jupp 2006a: 94–7). Within three years of the 1902 Act local authorities had come to the fore in crematoria provision: City of London (1904) and, in 1905, Leeds, Bradford and Sheffield. Yet despite the example of these major conurbations, and increasing resort to cremation by the social elite, the general public remained committed to burial. Whilst a crematorium proposal for Eastwood Cemetery was dropped in 1906, Maryhill remained Scotland's only crematorium. On average there were twenty-eight cremations annually from 1903 to 1910. The disadvantages of maintaining a building used just once in a fortnight will have concerned both its Directors and its supporters.

Duncan continued as Chairman of the SBRCS until his death in 1922. Glaister Senior succeeded him. He had become the Society's Medical Referee and was first elected a Director in 1907. He and his son between them served the Society successively for half a century. Mann Senior died in 1910. The surgeon Sir Thomas Clouston joined the Board in 1913.[19] An indication of the liberal bent of the Society was its appointment of the first woman Director, Miss Margaret Ker, in 1914, followed by the second, Mrs J. D. Pearce, in 1920.

A number of financial decisions were taken in the summer of 1904: the ordinary cremation fee was raised to six guineas; the fee for the working classes was reduced by 30% inclusive of the burial of ashes. Chalmers and Duncan were to be remunerated for their professional work, respectively architecture and the examination of medical certificates, but each immediately promised their fees towards the overdraft. In 1906 the actual cost of a cremation to the Company was £2 4s 11d, leaving a surplus of £4 1s 1d from the ordinary six-guinea fee.

19. See Clouston 1912 for his pro-cremation arguments.

In 1907 an agreement was reached with the Cemetery Company based on the Society's principle that its debts would only be paid out of profits and not from revenue. The Society would pay up to 5s for the burial of an urn, and up to 1s 6d for the passage of carriages, hearses or vehicles through the cemetery to the crematorium.

In 1914 the Company finally paid off its overdraft and declared a profit; the Board introduced a fee of £2 for every member of a household whose head was an insured person as defined by the National Insurance Act. All cremationist propaganda pointed out that the more popular cremation became, the lower the fee could fall, but the years until 1918 continued to be lean. In December 1918 the Directors were at last able to report that the number of cremations for which a reduced fee had been paid had increased in each of the last three years.

The Society's persistent but low level of self-promotion matched its means. Public lectures were given, often by Chalmers. A new edition of the *Ashes to Ashes* booklet, planned in 1905, was not published until 1912. Undertakers were asked to use coffins more suitable for cremation, i.e. less expensive wood with no permanent metal fittings. Mann Jr and Chalmers agreed a 5% commission with undertakers to supply funerals.

Burial Reform, Premature Burial and Closed Churchyards

At successive AGMs, Duncan continued to speak of the inequality of pit burial. In 1908 the Board discussed the issue of premature burial, following a recent article one Director had read (Tozer 1907). At Manchester's Cremation Society, one-third of the membership had been composed of ladies 'whose chief reason for favouring cremation was the fear of being buried alive'[20] and this may have been the case in Glasgow. The Board then discussed providing a mortuary at Maryhill but this was considered impracticable and expensive. They also considered petitioning Parliament on the burial of ashes in Scottish kirk-yards which had been closed to further burials. This had recently been authorised in the closed cemetery at Johnston, west of Paisley. In 1913 the Board again asked Glasgow Corporation to permit the burial of ashes in closed churchyards.[21] Despite an encouraging

---

20. See Makepeace 1990; *UJ*, 15/2/1911, 28; Davies and Shaw 1995; and Bourke 2005 for the fear of being buried alive as an argument for cremation.
21. Consistory Courts in England had held that the Burial Acts did not prohibit the burial of ashes in burial grounds closed by Order in Council.

reply, the outbreak of war reorientated the Corporation's priorities: the Board recorded in 1915, 'No definite action having been taken by the Town Council, the subject was accordingly held over.'

Improvements at Maryhill

By 1905 Maryhill had been operating for ten years and had performed 156 cremations. The furnace, used just once or twice a week and in all weathers, needed attention; 'a cremation could [now] scarcely be carried out in safety'. Despite this warning, the issue was not addressed until April 1908 when Board member Houston proposed installing a new gas furnace. Chalmers obtained two quotations from furnace companies and proposed visiting crematoria in London to inspect their apparatus. He reported to the Board in January 1910 that a carbon oxide furnace was unsuitable as it required continuous firing (a problem encountered at Golders Green). Meanwhile the furnace – in its unheated building – had suffered considerable damage during the winter frosts. Tests were run to establish a natural draught to assist firing, and after formal discussions with the two furnace companies it was decided after all to adopt the carbon oxide model. Funeral directors themselves could cause problems for the furnace when using metal-lined coffins, a breach of Maryhill's own regulations.

The Company's satisfaction with the new hydraulic lift installed in 1907 may have encouraged them to consider further improvements: a marble slab for cooling ashes and plots for interred ashes. A Mr Pullen donated a memorial window to his late mother and this encouraged Littlejohn to approach 'some prominent Edinburgh people' to suggest the erection of additional windows. In 1912 a stained-glass window was installed in memory of a Mr Burnett. Two months later Mann Jr requested a three-light window in memory of his father. Other facilities for memorialisation were gaining in importance as cremation numbers slowly began to rise (thirty in 1909): a new style of urns in 1907 and new niches in 1909. What may have been the first 'family' set of niches was ordered by representatives of the late R.M. Patterson in 1911. In 1913, when there were forty-nine cremations, Mann and Chalmers planned an extension of the niches and the columbarium. The provision of heating in the chapel was not considered until 1911, when Glaister suggested installing an anthracite stove. The question was not raised again until the 1915 AGM.

In 1906, after over 200 cremation services, the Directors again addressed the question of music. By now they may have been considered that an organ would be a real attraction; Mann himself donated a harmonium. Not until 1917 was any further suggestion recorded that congregations might appreciate organ music. This time Mrs Allan donated an organ. It is possible that Chalmers did not discuss with Mrs Allan whether the organ was suitable for use just once a week in an isolated building: the organ was kept in store, incurring costs, until it was finally decided that it could not be installed.

The First 'Wrong Body' Cremated[22]

In 1911, Maryhill unknowingly cremated the wrong body, the first known occasion of this happening. On Tuesday, 9 May, the famous illusionist Sigmund Neuberger ('The Great Lafayette') was to perform at the Empire Palace Theatre on Nicolson Street (now the Edinburgh Festival Theatre). The previous Saturday, his adored dog 'Beauty', a gift from magician Harry Houdini, had died. Glasgow's Piershill Cemetery agreed to bury it (on Wednesday, 10 May), but only on condition that Lafayette on his death would himself be buried alongside the dog. Lafayette, however, had long before made arrangements to be cremated.

The performance was 'The Sultan and the Lion's Bride' in which an actress was to be thrown into a cage with a lion. The illusion consisted in Lafayette changing places with a double and entering the cage disguised as a lion while the animal was taken out through a trapdoor. However, an electric wire above the stage fused and the scenery caught fire. The iron safety curtain was lowered but crushed the cage. When firemen reached the stage area later that evening, they found eight bodies, but two, including Lafayette's, were unaccounted for. A disfigured body dressed in the Sultan's costume and with Lafayette's sword was found on the floor. The sword made identification practically certain; and this was confirmed by Lafayette's manager. The body was sent by train to Glasgow for cremation at Maryhill. It was announced that Lafayette's ashes would be buried in the vault at Piershill the following Sunday.

On the Wednesday, Nisbet, Lafayette's London manager, arrived in Edinburgh. He became worried when he learned that valuable rings usually worn by Lafayette had not been found on the fingers of the corpse sent for cremation. At 5.30 pm rings found on another body showed that this was Lafayette.

22. See *Variety* 11/5/1911; Boyle 2009; Fraser 1996; and Mann 1954. I am grateful to Dr Brian Parsons for supplying these references.

By now Charles Richards, Lafayette's double at the performance, had been cremated and the ashes returned to a mortuary in Edinburgh. Beauty had been buried at Piershill. Lafayette's body was driven to Maryhill where it arrived just after midnight, 'Out of hours for any cremation but special dispensation had been sought and granted' (Fraser 1996: 62). The coffin was opened and when officials were satisfied that it really did contain the body of Lafayette, the required forms were completed and the cremation took place at 2.00 am.[23]

Thousands lined the route when Lafayette's ashes were taken to Piershill on Sunday, 14 May. Neuberger was Jewish and the local rabbi refused to conduct the funeral service as the grave was in unconsecrated ground; instead a Church of Scotland minister read the burial service. Had there been no mistake the burial of the ashes would have provided most welcome publicity for Maryhill. The way things turned out can only have confirmed the Glasgow public's suspicions about cremation and hardened its opposition to it.

Before the First World War there was little enthusiasm in Glasgow for either cremation or burial reform. Maryhill's cremations averaged twenty-nine per year between 1907 and 1910; thereafter, they rose steadily to fifty-seven in 1914 and eighty-seven in 1920. The War years depressed the spirits of the Glasgow Society: no shareholders attended the December AGMs in either 1916 or 1917. There were seventy-four cremations in 1918, representing 0.09% of Scotland's 78,372 deaths that year.

The Edinburgh Cremation Society, 1909–1918

The initiative that led to an Edinburgh Cremation Society (ECS) came on 3 December 1908[24] when Dr W.G. Aitchison Robertson, addressed the city's Sanitary Society on 'Cremation' (W.G.A. Robertson 1909). He was MOH for Edinburgh and a lecturer on Medical Jurisprudence and Public Health at Edinburgh's School of Medicine. The ECS would work vigorously for

---

23. Lafayette's death was announced with an obituary in *Variety*, 11/5/1911. The cable was dated 10 May and had been sent before the misidentification had been discovered.
24. *The Scotsman*, 4/12/1908. An earlier attempt to form a CSE had been made c.1895 (see ch. 3).

nineteen years before forming the Edinburgh Cremation Company in 1928 and opening its crematorium at Warriston a year later.[25]

Robertson was not alone in his purpose. There were already links between Edinburgh and the Society at Glasgow, particularly through Littlejohn. Probably more important was the minor but growing advocacy of cremation expressed by individuals within the Scottish public health movement whose supportive articles appeared in the fortnightly *The County and Municipal Record* (e.g. Frew 1906).[26]

A second meeting, on 8 December, was advertised as 'Several parties interested in the erection of a crematorium in the Edinburgh district will be glad to meet others [...].' A Councillor Cameron took the chair. The main speakers were Drs Aitchison Robertson and William Robertson (MOH for Leith).[27] Over sixty people were present 'including about a dozen ladies', a radical sign, given the traditional gender separation at English and Scottish funerals. Reviewing the progress of cremation, Cameron suggested that crematoria should be commercial,[28] perhaps reflecting his Council's fiscal conservativeness. Aitchison Robertson then illustrated public health aspects of current burial practice with slides of 'dead bodies undergoing putrefaction'. A Dr Alexander Walker spoke of 'the strong feeling that existed in the medical profession in favour of cremation.'[29]

Solicitor Dan Easson formally initiated the Edinburgh cremation movement when he chaired a meeting on 24 February 1909.[30] Aitchison Robertson and Harvey Littlejohn (son of Sir Henry) were also present. To illustrate the defects of the existing burial system, Littlejohn could draw upon his father's earlier research. Cremation was far more economical than burial, particularly given the scarcity of urban space. He estimated that

25. It is a matter of great regret that the Society's archive has not been found. Letters from Mr Neil Munro, Company Secretary of Edinburgh Crematorium Ltd, to the author, March 2009 and July 2011.
26. For Frew, presumably a practising Christian (see Bibliography), cremation would no more be an obstacle to the doctrine of the Resurrection than burial.
27. *The Scotsman*, 7/12/1908.
28. *The Scotsman*, 9/12/1909.
29. Ibid. References in *The Transactions of the Cremation Society of England* suggest that lantern slides (as yet undiscovered) were a feature of the ECS' publicity.
30. *The Scotsman*, 24/2/1909; UJ, 15/3/1909. Easson was an Edinburgh solicitor whose wife shared his support for the cremation movement.

nearly 1.25 acres were allocated for new graves annually in Edinburgh. As for expense, the average cost of burial for 'the poorer classes' lay between £6 and £8, which excluded the cost of a private grave. For wealthier families, funeral costs could range up to £150. 'With a crematorium in Edinburgh in constant use the cost would be within the reach of the poorest.' Littlejohn avoided religious and forensic issues and did not mention that crematoria could be provided by local authorities.

It is unclear why or whether a Cremation Society had not already been established in Edinburgh.[31] After all, 35% of Glasgow cremations were estimated to come from Edinburgh.[32] Littlejohn Sr had been a member of the SBRCS for some years. As MOH he had been painstaking in arguing for the reform of burial conditions in Edinburgh: perhaps he did not want a private crematorium to compete with the public burial facilities for which he had long argued. And perhaps few Edinburgh citizens were willing to follow the lead of a Glasgow-based society which, even after fifteen years' work, was doing fewer than one cremation per week.[33]

The Society held its inaugural meeting in the City Chambers, Edinburgh, on 3 February 1910.[34] It sought Town Council support at the earliest stage. Lord Provost Brown accepted the Chair, although he carefully remarked that this did not absolutely commit him to the cremation cause. Brown was followed by Farquharson, recently retired from Parliament,[35] who asserted that 'Cremation could now be carried on without opposition either from the law or from Mrs Grundy.'

The adoption of the Society's Constitution was proposed by the Rev. William Main who commented that 'a thrill of horror always went through him when he witnessed the committal of a dead body to the earth'. The Rev. George Christie, who was elected with Main to the Executive Council, would become a leading figure in the Edinburgh cremation movement. It is not yet clear how representative these two were of other Midlothian clergy.

31. See ch. 3, n. 12.
32. *UJ*, 15/2/1911.
33. Mr Duncan MacCallum, then Secretary of the FBCA, personal communication, August 2009.
34. *The Scotsman*, 4/2/1910.
35. See Farquharson (1899) for his pro-cremation arguments. Inexplicably, his two volumes of autobiography (1911, 1912) carry no references to his cremation activities.

Early Years, 1895–1918

The meeting then elected office-bearers: Littlejohn became President;[36] the two Robertsons were appointed to the eleven-strong Executive Council, as was Mrs Easson; Easson was elected Secretary and Treasurer. The aim of the Society was 'to promote the practice of cremation by means of meetings, lectures, publications or otherwise' and its ultimate object, reported the *Undertakers' Journal*, was 'to have a crematorium erected in the City [...] Should the society fail to induce the Town Council to do this, the question of floating a company on the lines of the SBRCS Glasgow will, it is said, probably be considered.'[37]

An Edinburgh Crematorium: Seeking a Site

By the AGM of April 1910, 300 people had given their names as favouring cremation (even though subscriptions amounted to only £4 11s 6d). The Society's publicity may also have influenced a citizen of Dumbarton, Mr Archibald Denny, who wrote to Dumbarton Town Council during 1910 as 'a loyal Son of the Rock' (i.e. a Dumbarton resident) to offer the Council £100 for the establishment of a public crematorium in or near the town. The Council accepted the gift, but it remained unspent a year later.[38]

Within a month came the first attempt to persuade one of Edinburgh's cemetery companies to build a crematorium. The city 'was rapidly extending westwards, and surrounding [the privately owned] Dean Cemetery' wrote a *Scotsman* correspondent.[39] Instead of enlarging its burial ground, it should build a crematorium. A fortnight later, a candidate for a vacant ward asked for his policy on crematoria and noting the 'great deal of discussion about the Dean Cemetery', favoured a crematorium to obviate cemetery extension but as a private not public enterprise.[40] The Society's First Annual Report noted that one of the Edinburgh cemetery companies [unnamed] had power under its Articles of Association to erect a crematorium but the

---

36. The Vice-Presidents were Sir Alexander R. Simpson, Lady Constance Lytton, Lady Steel, Professor Thomas Hudson Beare, Clouston and Littlejohn Jr. Like the SBRCS, the ECS sought the sponsorship of leading social and professional figures.
37. *UJ*, 15/3/1910.
38. *UJ*, 15/1/1911. See, further, ch. 7.
39. *The Scotsman*, 28/3/1910.
40. *The Scotsman*, 13/4/1910.

Society also considered that 'public opinion should be further educated' before any cemetery company was formally approached to build one.[41]

A new figure emerged at the second AGM on 17 May 1911: Edward, Lord Salvesen, a distinguished judge who had been Attorney General for Scotland in 1905.[42] Salvesen, supported by Easson, would henceforth lead the Edinburgh Society for thirty years. His successful leadership of the campaign to provide Edinburgh with a zoo had some similarity with his campaign for a city crematorium. The single sentence about the crematorium and the many pages about his founding the zoo in his memoirs are not an accurate reflection of his importance to the cremation movement in Scotland (Salvesen 1949: 213).

At that AGM two observations were made by Duncan, visiting from the SBRCS. He reported that the Vatican was understood to be reconsidering its position on cremation. This was confirmed by the publication of the latest edition of *The Catholic Encyclopaedia*, where William Devlin's article on cremation (Devlin 1908: 483) was more measured than the Church's stances in 1886 and 1888 (see ch. 2). Duncan's second point picked up on earlier remarks by Salvesen about Westminster Abbey's decision[43] to accept only cremated remains in Poets' Corner. Duncan suggested cremated remains might be buried in churches and that St Giles' Cathedral, at the heart of the nation's capital, should set aside a place for the burial of the ashes of Scotland's great men.[44]

The ECS Council reported steady progress in 1911.[45] It had approached the directors of one of Edinburgh's private cemeteries and they had responded 'sympathetically'.[46] Meanwhile the ECS had applied to the Corporation for its consent to a crematorium being established in a city cemetery. Section 92 of the Edinburgh Improvement and Tramways Act 1896 required any person or company wanting to build a crematorium within the city to obtain the consent of the city if the land on which it was to be built had been purchased after Whitsunday 1896. The minimum cost, with one chapel and

41. *UJ*, 15/6/1911.
42. For Salvesen's life, see Salvesen 1949.
43. Matthews 2004: 222–5.
44. *The Scotsman*, 18/5/1910.
45. *The Scotsman*, 27/5/1912. See also *UJ*, 15/6/1912, 174.
46. This was probably Warriston Cemetery (Dr Susan Buckham, personal communication, May 2012).

Early Years, 1895–1918

two incinerating chambers, was estimated at £3,000, and pledges totalling £400 had already been received. At the 1912 AGM, Littlejohn reported that the Town Council had responded that 'provided a suitable site could be obtained, there would be no objections to the building'.[47]

Consent to the building of a crematorium in Warriston Cemetery, in the north of the city, was considered by Edinburgh's Public Health Committee on 26 November 1912. The Committee recommended that the Council grant the request, provided the plans to be submitted accorded with regulations. This initiative cannot have proceeded much further as the Society made a further approach in July 1913. The Society asked the Heriot Trust to feu 0.4 of an acre in Warriston Cemetery.[48] This offer was presumably rejected. Hindsight suggests that the 1913 discussions with Warriston's Directors may have been the time when the ECS began to think about forming its own crematorium company. This may also have been prompted by the Society's discussions with their preferred architect.

The choice of architectural firm is of singular interest. In 1913 the ECS appears to have turned first to the Edinburgh practice of Sydney Mitchell and Wilson. Mitchell had been appointed architect to the Commercial Bank of Scotland and the Board of Lunacy in Scotland, from which stemmed a number of his most important works during the 1880s. However, given its date, the crematorium design is likely to have been by E.O.A. Jamieson, who took over the business after Mitchell's retirement in 1911 and Wilson's death the following year. Whether or not the firm was recommended by the Dean Cemetery Company or the Society, some considerable acumen was shown, even at this early stage, in recognising the power of architectural 'reputation'. Here was an established, well-respected firm that had built across the city for decades and which would surely legitimise the cremation movement in the public mind.

The unpublished sketch plan shows a design based on a church model, with a square tower and plain rectangular windows. Planned to seat 100, the 'chapel' had a simple barrel-vaulted roof. The catafalque was placed centrally and the coffin was to be removed horizontally. The columbaria running along the sidewalls were perhaps influenced by the arrangement at Manchester Crematorium.

47. *The Scotsman*, 27/5/1912.
48. *The Scotsman*, 10/7/2013.

The First World War brought an almost complete stop to the promotion of cremation in Edinburgh, as in Glasgow and south of the border. The Edinburgh Society was not to revive its campaign for cremation until 1921.

Towards a Radical Influence on Scottish Funerals

In 1912 further support for cremation came from migrant Scots Presbyterians in London. St Columba's Church of Scotland in Pont Street decided to consecrate a crypt chapel for the repose of cremated remains.[49] This initiative was probably that of their minister for twenty-five years, the Rev. Dr Donald MacLeod. He had publicised his request for his own body to be cremated and his ashes placed in what would become the crypt. Perhaps some Presbyterian traditionalists thought that burial aisles were being reintroduced: a hint of some dissension may be sensed in the *Undertakers' Journal* reporter's words, 'It is hardly necessary to defend the step which has been taken'; after all, 'the desire to lay to rest the dust of Christian people in or near the earthly temple in which, when alive, they worshipped, is as old as the Christian Church itself.' This had, of course, been the practice encouraged by the Church since the fourth century[50] but forbidden by John Knox.[51]

This prompts the observation that the Scottish cremation movement added two more radical features to Scottish funerals. J.A. Chalmers had designed his crematorium for Maryhill with a chapel as an essential and central feature. In this he had followed those at Woking and at Manchester. But traditionally Scottish burials began in the home and proceeded by road to the burial ground. Chalmers stated that he designed his building with Masonic features so as to welcome Masons (Chalmers c.1927), but it is as if he felt intuitively that Scottish cremation funerals should include a specifically religious location, in addition to the two traditional places of home and burial ground. His design at Maryhill was to set four precedents for all future crematoria in Scotland: he ensured the committal service would be

---

49. *UJ*, 15/10/1912 reproduces the words of the Consecration Prayer. St Columba's Church and crypt were destroyed by enemy action during the Second World War (James Mathers, personal communication, November 2011).
50. Rowell 1974; P. Brown 1981.
51. Given the Scottish Reformation's decision not to consecrate future kirk-yards (see ch. 1), it is of interest that St Columba's Church wished to consecrate their crypt.

indoors; in a religious setting; and where music would be available. Finally, the chapel was thus substituted for the graveside as the location for the final stage of the funeral journey.[52] Chalmers' design deliberately encouraged a sense of the sacred (in a Presbyterian context), foreshadowing the Kirk's 1897 decision to permit ministers' participation in religious rituals at the committal of the body.

The Persistence of the Burial Tradition

Some awareness of how 'sentiment' checked the adoption of cremation is suggested by commentators in the *Undertakers' Journal* between 1911 and 1917. One editorial doubted whether public feeling about cremation was really one of hostility to the act of cremation itself. 'More probably it has its root in disinclination to depart from ancient custom.' The conservative grip on burials was 'one more instance of the adherence of the Scot, rightly or wrongly, to old prejudices. The tenacity of "Sandy" to custom is proverbial [...] Strong sentiments still rivet Scotsmen to the graveyard.'[53]

Another *Undertakers' Journal* columnist pinpointed one of the lynchpins of conservatism in family funerals and their location. The vast majority of deaths took place at home. (At that time the proportion of mothers dying in childbirth and of children dying before their fifth birthday was high. Thirty years would pass before the introduction of the National Health Service [1947] and the accelerated trend towards dying in hospitals. The home was the normal, natural and cheapest place for dying.) There should therefore be no surprise that 'one thing differentiates the Scottish from the English funeral. It is that the religious service must be held in the "hoose".'

In England, an Anglican liturgy for funerals had emerged from the Catholic Church liturgy, albeit truncated and reformed, at the Reformation (Rowell 1977). In England, therefore, there was no need for the house to be the setting for the funeral: the burial was always preceded by an authorised Anglican liturgy, at the lychgate and then at the graveside. In Scotland, under John Knox's edict, not only was the house the only place in which prayer could be offered by the minister, it was the most appropriate place as the bereaved family were the object of the prayers. Prayers for the dead were forbidden.

52. See ch. 1.
53. *UJ*, 15/2/1911.

The *Undertakers' Journal* suggested that the Scottish tradition needed amendment when it wrote that certain people 'would like to abolish this traditional service in the home of the deceased and have it at the church' by which, as one reforming voice put it, 'we should be spared the ghastly spectacle of a funeral being regarded by all the unkempt wives and children of the neighbourhood as an occasion for gathering and "glowering"'. This was a tradition enforced by the massed and cramped housing conditions of nineteenth- and early twentieth-century Scottish cities. Within three decades of the *UJ*'s comment, both the corpse and death itself were being sequestered from the public to the private sphere.[54] Instead of traditional death-bed scenes in a family and domestic context, policed by the culture of the local neighbourhood, people increasingly died in the institutional setting of hospital or nursing home.

---

54. Mellor and Shilling 1993.

Colour plate 1. Daldowie Crematorium, Glasgow (1955), William Robertson Watt, County Architect of Lanark. (Photograph, Hilary J. Grainger)

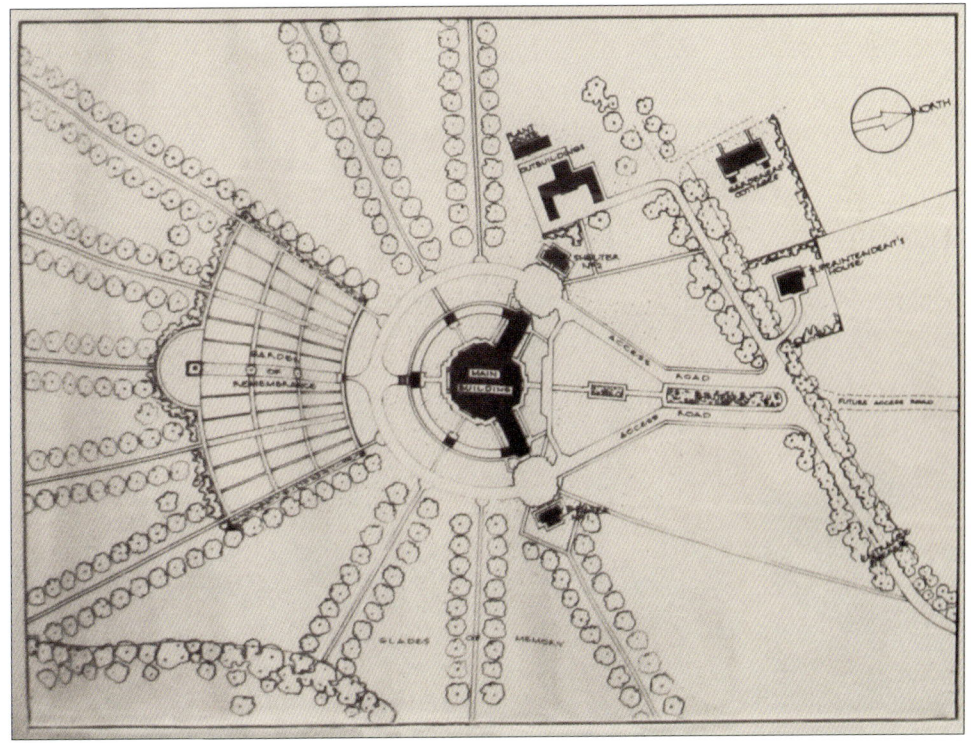

Colour plate 2. Site plan of Daldowie Crematorium, Glasgow (1955). (Plan in the possession of the Cremation Society of Great Britain)

Colour plate 3. Daldowie Crematorium, Glasgow (1955), William Robertson Watt. The Pergola. (Photograph, Hilary J. Grainger)

Colour plate 4. Daldowie Crematorium, Glasgow (1955), William Robertson Watt. Entrance to the East Chapel (Photograph, Hilary J. Grainger)

Colour plate 5. Daldowie Crematorium, Glasgow (1955), William Robertson Watt. Interior of the East Chapel. (Photograph, Hilary J. Grainger)

Colour plate 6. (*right*) Daldowie Crematorium, Glasgow (1955), William Robertson Watt. Interior of the Chapel of Remembrance. (Photograph, Hilary J. Grainger)

Colour plate 7. (*below*) Craigton Crematorium, Glasgow (1957), James Maitland Steel. (Photograph, Hilary J. Grainger)

Colour plate 8. Greenock Crematorium, Inverclyde (1959), Stuart Clink, Inverclyde Council Architect (of Cullen, Lockhead & Brown, Hamilton). (Photograph, Hilary J. Grainger)

Colour plate 9. Greenock Crematorium, Inverclyde (1959), Stuart Clink, Inverclyde Council Architect (of Cullen, Lockhead & Brown, Hamilton). Entrance hall with view into the chapel. (Photograph, Hilary J. Grainger)

Colour plate 10. Greenock Crematorium, Inverclyde (1959), Stuart Clink, Inverclyde Council Architect (of Cullen, Lockhead & Brown, Hamilton). Chapel interior. (Photograph, Hilary J. Grainger)

Colour plate 11. (*left*) Greenock Crematorium, Inverclyde (1959), Stuart Clink, Inverclyde Council Architect (of Cullen, Lockhead & Brown, Hamilton). View of side window of chapel. (Photograph, Hilary J. Grainger)

Colour plate 12. (*below*) Cardross Crematorium, Argyll and Bute (1960), John Watson of Watson, Salmon & Gray. (Photograph, Hilary J. Grainger)

Colour plate 13. Cardross Crematorium, Argyll and Bute (1960), John Watson of Watson, Salmon & Gray. Chapel interior. (Photograph, Hilary J. Grainger)

Colour plate 14. View across the Clyde and surrounding Argyll hills from Cardross Crematorium. (Photograph, Hilary J. Grainger)

Colour plate 15. *All Embracing Truth*, sculpture by Hew Lorimer RSA, FRBS, standing at the end of the loggia of Cardross Crematorium, Argyll and Bute. (Photograph, Hilary J. Grainger)

Colour plate 16. The Linn Crematorium, Glasgow (1962), Thomas Smith Cordiner. (Photograph, *Pharos*, February 1963, p.9)

Colour plate 17. Blackley Crematorium, Manchester (1957), Leonard Howitt, Manchester City Architect. (Photograph, Hilary J. Grainger)

Colour plate 18. The Linn Crematorium, Glasgow (1962), Thomas Smith Cordiner. (Photograph, Hilary J. Grainger)

Colour plate 19. The Linn Crematorium, Glasgow (1962), Thomas Smith Cordiner. (Photograph, Hilary J. Grainger)

Colour plate 20. The Linn Crematorium, Glasgow (1962), Thomas Smith Cordiner. Interior of St Mungo (main) chapel. (Photograph, Hilary J. Grainger)

Colour plate 21. The Linn Crematorium, Glasgow (1962), Thomas Smith Cordiner. Interior of the Room of Remembrance. (Photograph, Hilary J. Grainger)

Colour plate 22. Masonhill Crematorium, South Ayrshire (1966), Clark Fyfe, County Architect's Department. (Photograph, Hilary J. Grainger)

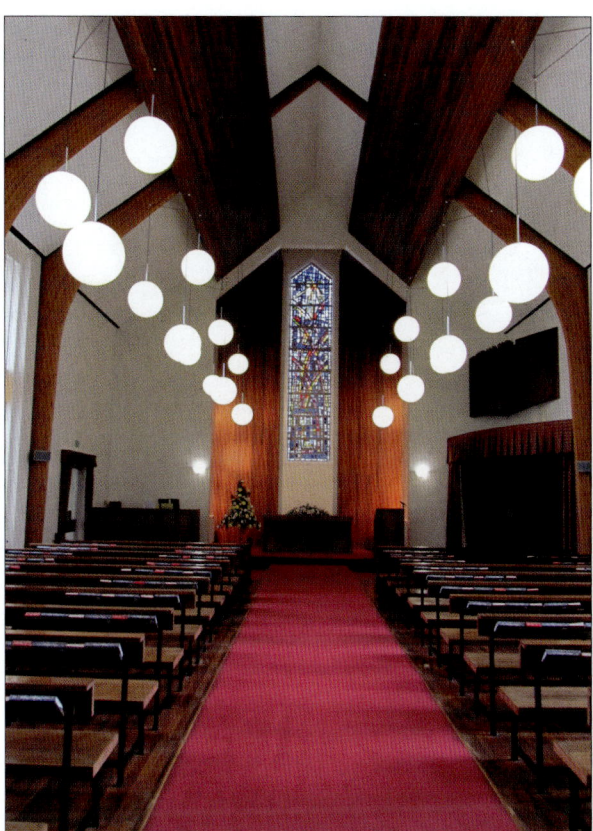

Colour plate 23. (*right*) Masonhill Crematorium, South Ayrshire (1966), Clark Fyfe, County Architect's Department. (Photograph, Hilary J. Grainger)

Colour plate 24. (*below*) Masonhill Crematorium, South Ayrshire (1966), Clark Fyfe, County Architect's Department. Chapel windows. (Photograph, Hilary J. Grainger)

Colour plate 25. Dalnottar Crematorium, Clydebank, West Dunbartonshire (1967), Sir Frank Mears & Partners, Edinburgh. (Photograph, Hilary J. Grainger)

Colour plate 26. Dalnottar Crematorium, Clydebank, West Dunbartonshire (1967), Sir Frank Mears & Partners, Edinburgh. (Photograph, Hilary J. Grainger)

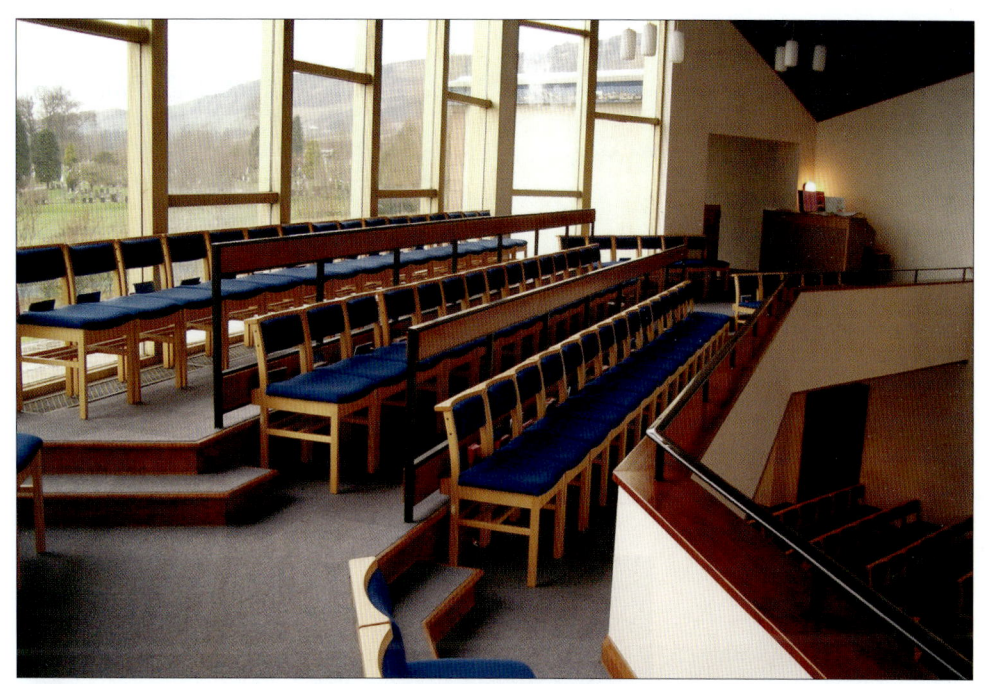

Colour plate 27. Dalnottar Crematorium, Clydebank, West Dunbartonshire (1967), Sir Frank Mears & Partners, Edinburgh. Interior of chapel showing the view over the Clyde and Renfrewshire Hills. (Photograph, Hilary J. Grainger)

Colour plate 28. Kirkcaldy Crematorium, Fife (1959), Sanger & Rothwell, Oldham. (Photograph, *Pharos*, May 1959)

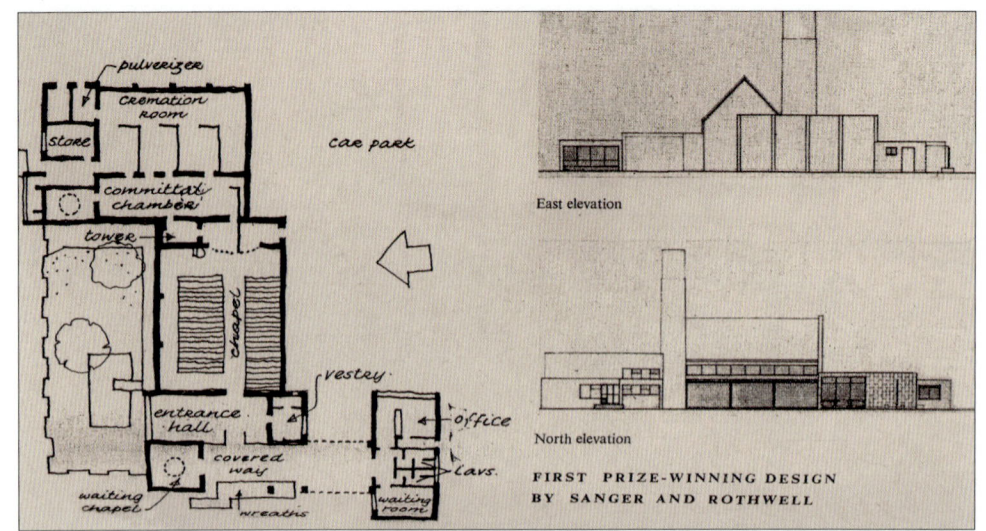

Colour plate 29. (*above*) Prize winning entry by Sanger & Rothwell, Oldham, for the Kirkcaldy Crematorium Competition held by Fife Council in 1953–54. (Drawing published in *Architects' Journal*, 10 June 1954)

Colour plate 30. (*right*) Oldham Crematorium, Greater Manchester (1953), Sanger & Rothwell, Oldham. Interior of chapel showing side window. (Photograph, Hilary J. Grainger)

Colour plate 31. Kirkcaldy Crematorium, Fife (1959), Sanger & Rothwell, Oldham. Chapel interior showing view onto the landscape. (Photograph, Hilary J. Grainger)

Colour plate 32. Kirkcaldy Crematorium, Fife (1959), Sanger & Rothwell, Oldham. Chapel interior. (Photograph, Hilary J. Grainger)

Colour plate 33. Falkirk Crematorium, Falkirk (1962), Alexander James Macaskill Currell, Burgh Architect and Planning Officer. (Photograph, Hilary J. Grainger)

Colour plate 34. Falkirk Crematorium, Falkirk (1962), Alexander James Macaskill Currell, Burgh Architect and Planning Officer. (Photograph, Hilary J. Grainger)

Colour plate 35. Falkirk Crematorium, Falkirk (1962), Alexander James Macaskill Currell, Burgh Architect and Planning Officer. Interior showing side windows. (Photograph, Hilary J. Grainger)

Colour plate 36. Falkirk Crematorium, Falkirk (1962), Alexander James Macaskill Currell, Burgh Architect and Planning Officer. Chapel windows showing view onto the Gardens of Remembrance. (Photograph, Hilary J. Grainger)

Colour plate 37 (*above*) Perth Crematorium, Perth & Kinross (1962), George Kerr Stuart, Perth Deputy Burgh Surveyor. (Photograph, Hilary J. Grainger)

Colour plate 38 (*right*) Perth Crematorium, Perth & Kinross (1962), George Kerr Stuart, Perth Deputy Burgh Surveyor. Interior of Chapel. (Photograph, Hilary J. Grainger)

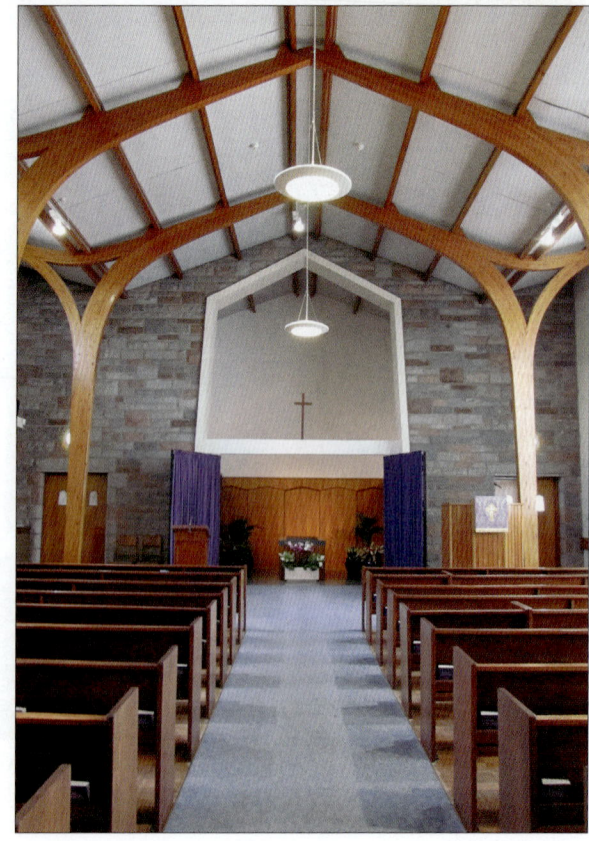

Colour plate 39. (*left*) Perth Crematorium, Perth & Kinross (1962), George Kerr Stuart, Perth Deputy Burgh Surveyor. Hall of Remembrance showing stained glass window by Alexander L Russell. (Photograph, Hilary J. Grainger)

Colour plate 40. (*below*) Mortonhall Crematorium, Edinburgh (1967), Sir Basil Spence, Glover & Fergusson. Entrance to the main chapel. (Photograph, Hilary J. Grainger)

Colour plate 41. Mortonhall Crematorium, Edinburgh (1967), Sir Basil Spence, Glover & Fergusson, showing the Chapel of Remembrance in the foreground. (Photograph, Hilary J. Grainger)

Colour plate 42. Mortonhall Crematorium, Edinburgh (1967), Sir Basil Spence, Glover & Fergusson, showing stained glass in the main chapel by Sir Basil Spence. (Photograph, Hilary J. Grainger)

Colour plate 43. Mortonhall Crematorium, Edinburgh (1967), Sir Basil Spence, Glover & Fergusson. View from the Calvary Cross toward the crematorium. (Photograph, Hilary J. Grainger)

Colour plate 44. Dunfermline Crematorium, Fife (1973), Fife County Council. (Photograph, Hilary J. Grainger)

Colour plate 45. Dunfermline Crematorium, Fife (1973), Fife County Council. Interior of chapel showing windows with views into the landscape. (Photograph, Hilary J. Grainger)

Colour plate 46. Dunfermline Crematorium, Fife (1973), Fife County Council. View showing chapel windows. (Photograph, Hilary J. Grainger)

CHAPTER FIVE

Cremation in the Depression: Failure and Success, 1918–1939

Introduction

Two traumatic events dominated the years 1918–1939: the aftermath of the First World War and the economic Depression. Scotland lost 60,000 men at the Front (Royle 2007). War memorials became a vital part of Scottish bereavement strategies. Prayers for the dead, long a Presbyterian abhorrence, were now encouraged by some Church of Scotland leaders (S.J. Brown 2016). It is likely that belief in the resurrection of the body diminished, as in England, and certain that Scots were attracted by popular Spiritualism with its emphasis on the immortality of the soul (Church of Scotland 1922).

Industry flourished during the War, stimulating global competition to Scotland's traditional exports, but economic decline set in swiftly after 1918. The War affected rural employment; by 1920 one-fifth of Scottish estates were on the market. The urban migration of labour increased pressure on the housing supply; there were rent strikes and mass labour meetings which helped stimulate Labour Party popularity. The world crash of 1929 precipitated Scotland into an economic depression where social policy priorities were health, housing and jobs. As a social priority, funeral reform took a much lower place.

Calls for Funeral Reform in Aberdeen

In 1917 a correspondent to an Aberdeen newspaper deplored the artificial flowers and *immortelles* which 'disfigured' Allenvale Cemetery. This seems to have prompted a public meeting about funeral reform in the Council

Chamber, and attendees included funeral directors, cemetery managers and clergy.[1] On 30 October, a Church of Scotland minister, T.D. Watt, argued for a more rational use of people's time at funerals: mourners endured long delays, both outside the home before the coffin was 'lifted' and at the graveside. Dr Matthew Hay, Aberdeen's Medical Officer of Health (MOH), supported Watt: black clothes were unnecessary[2] and 'gloomy emblems' only survived 'in remote Highland glens'. 'Recent years had seen a liberalisation of the public's ideas as regarded funerals.'[3]

Watt's rationalisation of time and money dedicated to funerals as 'waste' can be set in the context of burial arrangements at the Front and of the wartime economy, when work was dangerous and time at a premium, women were pressed into paid work, and materials for funeral clothing and hospitality were scarce. Watt's recommendations for simpler funerals were adopted unanimously and the Lord Provost (as Chairman) circulated them to local clergy, undertakers and cemetery managers.[4] In the *Aberdeen Press and Journal* (*APJ*) nine months later new correspondents echoed October's rational approach. 'Common Sense' deplored the use of 50,000 acres of 'beautiful countryside' as plots for burying 'our beloved dead'. 'R.I.P.' argued that an Aberdeen crematorium would end time-consuming journeys to Glasgow.[5]

In 1921 journalist Edward Watt called for an Aberdeen crematorium. Watt's war experience had strengthened his support for cremation: 'Millions of demobilised soldiers [...] have experienced for themselves the loathsome repulsiveness of decaying humanity which is the same in the grave as in No-man's-land [...] amongst those millions must be thousands who would prefer to dispose of their dead by the speedy and purifying action of fire.' Bourke has commented that soldiers' experiences during the War shifted 'the emphasis of [cremationist] rhetoric [...] [afterwards] it was no longer seemly to remind men of bodies lying on the battlefields [...] as they underwent the indignity of slow decomposition.'[6] Watt called on Aberdeen

---

1. *UJ*, 15/6/1917.
2. See Taylor 1982.
3. *UJ*, 15/11/1917.
4. Ibid.
5. Ibid., 10/5/1918.
6. See Bourke 1999: 223; Chapman 1985: 252; McKim 1944.

Failure and Success, 1918–1939 111

Council to apply for the necessary powers within their next Parliamentary Bill. His call was ignored until 1928, when he had become a City Councillor.[7]

Maryhill Crematorium 1918–1930

Meanwhile, Maryhill remained the sole crematorium in Scotland. While cremations rose steadily (from seventy-four in 1918, to ninety in 1924 and 174 in 1929), this still represented fewer than four funerals each week. Neither the funeral industry nor the Scottish churches nor the general public seemed yet inclined to change from burial.

The immediate post-War years brought new leadership to the Scottish Burial Reform and Cremation Society (SBRCS). (A similar process occurred with the CS when Cameron retired as President in 1920: the energetic Scotsman Peter Chalmers Mitchell, Director of the London Zoo, became its Chairman (Mitchell 1937)). In 1922 Ebenezer Duncan died, after leading the Society for thirty-four years. Glaister Senior succeeded him as Chairman and with new Directors, including John Biggar (accountant, Socialist and future Provost), brought fresh energy to the leadership along with (now Sir) John Mann. Now based in London, Mann again attempted to resign as Honorary Secretary in 1921, but was persuaded to continue in the post. Easson of the ECS joined the SBRCS Board in 1926.

Wider UK developments gradually facilitated Scottish cremation (Jupp 2002, 2006a). By 1930 there were nineteen crematoria in England and Wales (forty-eight by 1939). The Co-operative Movement funeral-directing section opened in the 1920s (Parsons 2009). Funeral directors exploited cremation's economic advantages as horse-drawn carriages were succeeded by motor hearses; encouraging clients to choose cremation was to fit more funerals into one day (Howarth 1996, 1997; Parsons 2013). In 1922 the CS held the first of a series of annual conferences and in 1924, with Sir John Mann's help, established the Federation of Cremation Authorities (FCA)[8] for owners of crematoria, both public and private (Jupp 2006a: 103–4).

With the SBRCS's balance exceeding £2,000 in 1924, quotations were sought for a new organ (£1,240). Chalmers superintended improvements

---

7. Watt noted at Kaimhill's opening in 1938 that it 'marked the culmination of a forty years' movement in Aberdeen'.
8. The FCA was renamed the Federation of British Cremation Authorities (FBCA) in 1937, becoming independent of the Cremation Society.

which were formally opened in 1926, with heating, lavatories, better lighting and more memorial niches (Chalmers c.1927). The more confident mood is discernible in the Board minutes of 4 July 1927, which included discussion of a design for a new columbarium described by Chalmers. Memorials brought regular income. Inspired by Yeates' 1924 FCA conference paper (Yeates 1924), Chalmers adapted the twin themes of religion and aesthetics, with two full-sized marble angels, each dropping flowers into the urns at their feet. New stained-glass windows expounded the theme of ashes 'reposing among the angels' (see above, p. 80). Angels were a contemporary theme, encompassing a non-sectarian view of the supernatural realm and a more positive doctrinal vision of the after-life than that imposed in the Knox vision (Cumming 2005, 2016).

The Crematorium That Never Was: Kilbowie, Glasgow, 1927–1931

In October 1927 a Councillor Pilkington on Glasgow City Council proposed a 'Municipal Cemetery with or without a crematorium'.[9] This initiative seems to have come out of the blue. It is not known how aware Pilkington was of the history of Glasgow's burial provision or the progress of Maryhill, contemporary discussions in Edinburgh or the financial crises imminent in Glasgow and in the western world.

At least three attempts to persuade Glasgow City Council to build a municipal cemetery had failed in the forty years before 1900. Now, with franchise extension and the rise of organised Labour, Glasgow's politics experienced a sea-change. Ten Labour MPs were elected in 1922. By 1926, Labour had fifty City Councillors. Pilkington's initiative represented a new expression of the 'municipal Socialism' which had earlier characterised Glasgow's government.

A Special Committee met on 23 April 1929 to hear the Town Clerk's cautiously optimistic feasibility report.[10] It recommended the Corporation to provide a municipal cemetery; concerning a crematorium, the Committee proposed inspecting 'the new crematorium in Edinburgh'. Almost immediately there was opposition: in June, a Councillor Roberton moved the proposal for a new crematorium be rejected. Twenty-eight members voted for the motion, and twenty-five for the amendment. Was it the crematorium, the cemetery or municipal ownership issue that had drawn opposition?

9. GLA. Glasgow Town Council minutes (GTC), C1/3/77, p. 2385.
10. GLA. Corporation of Glasgow: Report (D-TC/6/606/2 No. 14).

Nevertheless, the pro-crematorium motion was carried by three votes. By November the Town Clerk had identified, among possible sites, the 63.9-acre Auchertoshen Estate at Kilbowie, in the south-east of the city.[11]

In November Councillors Pilkington and Macwhannel met with Maryhill's Biggar, Easson and Glaister 'to discuss the advisability of erecting a municipal crematorium in connection with a municipal cemetery'.[12] The SBRCS had decided against a rival crematorium in the city, for their own client base was insufficiently established. The Board minuted, 'It was felt by both parties that it would probably be a mistake to erect another Crematorium in the city and it was suggested [again] that the Corporation might consider taking over the existing crematorium or coming to some arrangement with the Directors whereby cremations would be undertaken by the Society for the Corporation. Nothing definite had been decided by the Corporation.'[13]

On 23 April the Special Committee agreed to recommend to the Corporation a purchase, at £110 per acre. On 12 June, Pilkington's project resisted another objection, the recommendation being approved by thirty-three votes to eighteen.

On 4 September the Public Assistance Committee (PAC) took responsibility for managing the cemetery and also considering 'the unexhausted portion' of the remit concerning a crematorium. Then, suddenly, the minutes fall silent, recording no formal Council activity on the cemetery/crematorium project until the next February. A week is a long time in politics. How much can happen in four months?

On 29 January 1931 Councillor Pilkington tendered his resignation from the Council. In June, the Corporation rescinded its decision for a municipal cemetery.

The choice of a site was but one of a series of obstacles. The accelerated decline in the national economic situation was probably the major issue that checked the city's support. A second obstacle was the political opposition from a minority of Councillors; whatever their reasons, the anti-cremation stance of Glasgow's 15% Roman Catholic minority will have had an influence.[14] A third was the consequence of local government reorganisation in

11. GLA. Corporation of Glasgow: Report: D-TC/6/600/4 No. 17.
12. SBRCS Board minutes, 11/12/1929; SBRCS Board minutes, 8/5/1929.
13. SBRCS Board minutes, 11/12/1929.
14. Dominic Maguire, personal communication, March 2010.

1929: the PAC was handed the responsibility for the Kilbowie project at a time when the calls upon its budget were about to spiral upwards. When Pilkington resigned, the project lost its leadership.

The Edinburgh Cremation Society, 1918–1928

In 1921, the ECS revived its crematorium project. In 1920 an Act of Parliament had united the independent cities of Edinburgh and Leith. The enlarged City of Edinburgh also gained part of Midlothian. The boundary change included a number of burial grounds which the Corporation was now obliged to maintain. It also widened the Society's search area. In February 1924, Edinburgh's Public Health Committee considered Councillor Millar's proposal for a municipal crematorium and agreed to a deputation from the Society's Executive Committee of the ECS on 18 March, which Lord Salvesen would lead.

Meanwhile, the Lord Provost's Committee was negotiating for 29 acres within the former Leith boundary, the Easter Warriston estate. Its owner, Colonel Agnew, was willing to sell but wished to occupy the house until his death.[15] The Burgh Assessor reckoned the estate would be ideal for housing and a recreation ground. Given the rapid post-war suburbanisation, the City Council had to juggle many priorities. It had also to manage its newly-acquired cemeteries which, with the passing of the Church of Scotland Act 1925, would now include another eleven parish churchyards.

In January 1926, Easson asked the Council for 'a site to be reserved in the Easter Warriston Estate for the erection of a crematorium'. After ten weeks the Council decided to take no action.[16]

On 26 January 1927, Lord Salvesen led a deputation to the Lord Provost's Committee to support Councillor Raithby's motion 'to consider whether the time has not arrived when the Corporation should proceed with the erection of a Municipal Crematorium'.[17] The Corporation now replied that while they 'should not themselves undertake the provision and running of a crematorium', if the ECS were to provide one, 'the Corporation would be

---

15. Edinburgh City/Town Council minutes, Central Library, Edinburgh. CR TCE, 30/7/1925, following the *Lord Provost's Committee Report* of 1/7/1925, pp. 580–582.
16. Ibid. CR TCE, Council meeting, 1/4/1926, with reports from sub-committee 'B' on 17/3/1926 and the Lord Provost's committee of 17/3/1926.
17. Ibid. CR TCE, Council meeting, 6/1/1927, p. 155.

prepared to cooperate with them [...] to find a suitable place'.[18] The onus was thus firmly placed upon the ECS to raise funds for a crematorium site and persuade the public of its benefits.

In May 1927 Lord Salvesen had written that 'under existing law no crematorium might be built within 50 yards of a public highway. By contrast, an ordinary cemetery might adjoin a public road, so why should a modern crematorium be regarded as an eyesore or as a source of nuisance?'[19] The 1902 Cremation Act also prevented the siting of a crematorium within 200 yards of a residence. This 'radius clause' made it 'almost impossible to find a new site for a crematorium' in Edinburgh. Now, however, Salvesen had his eyes on Easter Warriston House. Salvesen had been born and brought up in Leith and, walking to school, university and later his chambers, knew the area intimately.[20] Easter Warriston House lay outside the two radii.

On 16 May 1927 Colonel Agnew died at his home.[21] The way was now open for the Council to make decisions about the Warriston estate.

With etiquette discouraging precipitate action, the CSE planned carefully. In January 1928 it acted. It advertised a public lecture by Easson on 16 January with Salvesen in the Chair and Dr William Robertson, now Edinburgh's MOH, among the speakers. Chairing a crowded meeting, Lord Salvesen asserted Edinburgh was behind the times.

There was not a capital city in the world, with a population such as Edinburgh had, that was without its crematorium, and it was the bounden duty of the municipality, if they did not erect a crematorium themselves, to give facilities for other people to do so.

The Society had been on the lookout for a site for many years. Urban land, argued Salvesen, was not only increasingly scarce but subject to competing priorities like playing fields. It was more important to provide for the living than the dead. The context of his argument was the importance of public health and welfare, which had climbed the political agenda with the accession to local and national power of the Labour Party. ('Save the land for the living' was the motto of the CS.)

---

18. Ibid. *Report by the Public Health and Lord Provost's Committees.* CR TCE, 7/4/1927, p. 374.
19. Salvesen 1927.
20. See Albert nd (NLS MS 9130)
21. *Scotsman* 17/5/1927. Agnew had served under General Havelock at the first relief of Lucknow.

Easson drew on novelist Thomas Hardy's example, referring to his cremation that very day. He noted that while the poet's heart was to be buried (in Dorset), the remainder of his body was to be cremated at Woking and his ashes interred in Westminster Abbey.[22] Councillor Raithby's motion 'that this meeting, recognising the necessity and importance of providing in Edinburgh facilities for cremation, urges the Town Council to grant a suitable site now',[23] was carried unanimously.

Salvesen had kept his trump card until the end. The reason for the meeting, he revealed, was that the Council now had a site at its disposal, eminently suitable for a crematorium. This was one of the Council's own properties, and near Warriston.

Two days later the Joint Sub-Committee of Housing, Public Parks and Transport discussed the allocation of Easter Warriston Estate. They recommended a four-fold allocation: to Parks, Housing and Streets and Building Committees and, finally, to the Treasurer's Committee, Easter Warriston House with grounds totalling 2.8 acres.

The City Treasurer's Committee suggested a figure of £3,000 for the house and grounds. In April 1928 the Property Sub-Committee examined the Society's acceptance, with its request for a one-year option while it established a private company. The Committee agreed to this, but with the following condition: 'the return to be paid in respect of money raised for and in connection with the crematorium will not in any year exceed 6 per cent' (to avoid any stigma of profiteering from the dead). At full Council on 5 July the agreements were offered and accepted.

The purchase agreed, the Society moved quickly with its architectural plans. It chose Robert Lorimer, architect of the Scottish War Memorial on Castle Hill, Edinburgh. Salvesen's commission of Lorimer was a major coup.[24] Lorimer's designs were available by August 1928, as soon as Edinburgh Crematorium Limited (ECL) was launched. The writ to sell Easter Warriston House and its land was signed on 9 November 1928.[25] A series of factors, political, economic and social, had prolonged the search for a site for nineteen years.

22. See Jalland 2010: 110–18 and Matthews 2004: 222–5.
23. *Scotsman* 7/1/1928.
24. The Lorimer and the Salvesen families were old friends (Andorsen 1949).
25. Edinburgh City/Town Council minutes, Central Library, Edinburgh. CR TCE, Council meeting, 9/11/1928, p. 17.

Edinburgh: An Architectural Statement

The prominence of architecture in the public mind in Edinburgh was of significance to the cremation movement. Scotland's capital since the fifteenth century, Edinburgh was remodelled on a grand scale in the early 1800s with the intention of creating a city of unrivalled visual harmony and discipline based on Greek antiquity. Edinburgh's New Town, first laid out in the 1780s, was further developed to house the city's professional and business classes and by 1830 its elegant houses, squares and streets housed some 40,000 residents, near a quarter of Edinburgh's population (Devine 2012: 329). Hailed in 1820 as 'The Athens of the North' by the poet Hugh William Williams, Edinburgh was set in a spectacular natural landscape. Architecture was part of the psyche of the city and its role in the promotion of cremation was never likely to be underestimated by the ECS, given the social standing and educational background of its membership. This became all too apparent when the plans for a crematorium began to crystallise in 1928. The choice of architect was now squarely in the hands of the newly formed ECL which was clearly mindful of the associative, symbolic and indeed emotional value of architectural style. Expectations would have been high.

Warriston Crematorium

There was to be no compromise and no diffidence, the architectural ambitions of Edinburgh's cremationists had grown substantially since 1913 and it was with supreme confidence that they turned to Scotland's leading architect, Sir Robert Stodart Lorimer (1864–1929) and his partner John Fraser Matthew (1875–1955). Lorimer boasted not only a national profile, but was also known personally to Lord Salvesen (who, with solicitor Dan Easson, had led the ECS since 1911).[26] Lorimer's father, James, Regius Professor of Public Law at Edinburgh University, had been a friend of Salvesen's family since the 1880s, which perhaps accounts for Lorimer designing Salvesen's Norwegian holiday home Risøbank Manor in 1901. In 1913 he also designed a new bandstand for the Edinburgh Zoological Park, another of Salvesen's projects. The Edinburgh social network, let alone that of Salvesen, was undeniably effective in securing Lorimer's commission for Warriston.

26. Dan Easson played an enormous role in the Scottish cremation movement, serving on the Boards of the SBRCS and the companies in Edinburgh and Aberdeen. He was greatly assisted by his wife (shown in plate 9 at the opening of Warriston Crematorium in 1929).

The decision to appoint Lorimer invites comparison with the London Cremation Company's thinking in 1902 when the Company approached the eminent late Victorian architect Sir Ernest George (1839–1922) to design Golders Green Crematorium, the 'flagship' building of the CS and its London Cremation Company. This represented a key moment in the architectural expression of cremation in Britain for a whole variety of reasons, one being that it witnessed the involvement in crematorium design of an architect of national standing who, the London Cremation Company believed, would 'command the confidence of the public'.[27]

Warriston was Edinburgh's Golders Green, being the first crematorium in the capital, the only difference being that unlike George, Lorimer was not allowed carte blanche in terms of architectural expression – his design, in great part, would be determined by an existing building. But while the architecture differed, the symbolic message was the same: here was an architect of national standing, coincidentally like George a leading domestic architect, who would ensure the confidence of Edinburgh's discerning residents.

The commissioning of Lorimer was a masterstroke in the battle for hearts and minds. After working in London he began practising in Edinburgh in 1893, where his work was to remain largely domestic, partly as a result of the social and professional circles in which he moved, but also because large commercial commissions demanded considerable staff reserves which were never a feature of his practice. His houses were characterised by a Scottish romanticism and a respect for Scottish craftsmanship. Elected an associate of the Royal Scottish Academy in 1903, Lorimer's public profile was enhanced in 1909 by his appointment as the architect for the Thistle Chapel in St Giles' Cathedral. By 1928 he was a figure of commanding stature, having been Scotland's leading architect since 1911.

But if such impeccable credentials were not enough, Lorimer had a distinguished and singular association with the architecture of commemoration and remembrance. In 1918 he was appointed an architect for the War Graves Commission and recalled the 1920s as a decade dominated by the 'endless flood of memorials of all shapes, sizes and costs' (Savage 2005: 133) – indeed, he exhibited little else at the Royal Scottish Academy from 1920 to 1926.

Of perhaps even greater significance was Lorimer's selection in 1919 from six architects invited to produce designs for the Scottish National War

27. London Cremation Company minutes, 23/1/1901, p. 23. For the key role of Golders Green Crematorium, see Grainger (2000, 2005, 2011).

Memorial proposed in Edinburgh. This commission proved to be a vexatious and long drawn out affair, which took its toll on his health. It was finally completed in Edinburgh in 1928, the year in which he was approached by the ECL to convert Easter Warriston House.

To date five conversions of cemetery chapels had taken place in England and Wales – at Lawnswood, Leeds (1904); West Norwood, London (1915); Hendon, London (1922); followed by Pontypridd, Rhondda (1924); and Arnos Vale, Bristol (1928). While conversions would become increasingly popular in England, especially post-war, on account of ease of planning permission and cost, there were *no* cemetery chapels in Scotland – accounting perhaps for only three conversions having been undertaken, one of a house at Warriston, the other two of churches at Moray (1999) and most recently at Houndwood (2015).

Matters moved swiftly. Lorimer was appointed in August 1928 and instructed to produce plans for the alterations and the erection of a Superintendent's lodge. By October, plans to alter the property, now in a poor state of repair, had been submitted to the Town Council together with those for the gate lodge. The architects issued schedules of work and there was discussion as to whether or not to install a coke or gas furnace. By 25 October plans had been passed by the Dean of Guild Court and submitted to the Scottish Board of Health (SBH), which returned them without any observations. The costs amounted to £5,507 for the main building and a further £964 for the gate lodge. The Secretary also submitted copies of a report on furnaces compiled as a result of visits to Sheffield, Bradford and Golders Green crematoria. Possession of the property took place on 5 November, by which time there was a suggestion of building a mortuary on additional ground acquired by the Company to the north of the house.

Easter Warriston House was a substantial, two-storey villa built in 1818 for the banker Andrew Bonar. The property, by its very nature, blended into the architectural fabric of Edinburgh, thereby mitigating one of the most obvious forms of objection. Lorimer removed the internal walls to create a white-painted vaulted chapel lit by tall arched windows on the south side. He extended the building at the east end to form an apse with a tall, tripartite stained glass window into which the catafalque was placed as the focus of the chapel. Lorimer provided alternative designs for the facades.[28] The more chaste versions were approved on 11 October 1928.

---

28. In the possession of ECL.

Interestingly, Lorimer eschewed George's innovation at Golders Green, of a porte-cochère (covered entrance) for the comfort of mourners, perhaps on account of the desire to maintain the existing appearance of the house, but more likely because there were steps up to the main entrance, determined by the basement arrangement necessary for a descending catafalque. It was agreed that the furnace room, originally intended to be in an extension to the north at basement level, would be accommodated instead within the existing building.

Lorimer brought a lifetime of experience to the design of the interior. Two church designs might have contributed to his thinking. St Peter's Roman Catholic Church in Morningside (1906) and St Andrew's, Aldershot (1926) share a number of features, including the placing of the altar in a recess. St Andrew's has a tall east window as befits a Presbyterian church; the reticence of the interior, with its simple arched openings finds a strong echo at Warriston where, even in death, the citizens of Edinburgh were afforded something of the urbanity of the surroundings they had enjoyed in life.

A two-storeyed columbarium to the north was entered by paired, arched openings to the east and west of the two-storey organ. The niches, which eventually enclosed the ashes of the most prominent members of the ECS, were installed the following year. At the opening on 3 October 1929, attended by about 250 people with clergy of four denominations, 'the Directors expressed their satisfaction with the completion of the building, the installation of the stained glass window, and also the pipe organ.'[29]

A number of alterations have been made over the years; the addition of cloisters, a second Cloister Chapel, 1958 and other minor changes, including the remodelling of the main chapel in 1967 and the addition of an entrance porch. Notwithstanding the restrictions of the adaptation of an existing building, time has shown that Lorimer was to exert an indelible influence on the design of Scottish crematoria; two of his lasting legacies being the tall east window and the centrally placed, descending catafalque.

Cremation Regulations[30]

Work on the regulations had stopped in 1914. It was resumed in 1923 as

29. ECL minute books, vol. 1928–1958, p. 34.
30. This section is based on **NRS:** GRO 1/648, GRO 5/1924, HH 61/127/F3, HH 61/127/F5, HH 61/127/F6, HH 61/142, HH 61/144, HH 61/994; **TNA:** RG 48/445, RG 48/446, RG 48/458.

the result of an enquiry from a registrar of deaths. The SBRCS did not cremate anyone whose death had not been registered and, as proof of this, required the Schedule I (ch. 1), which it retained. Consequently there was no Schedule to present to the keeper of the cemetery in which ashes were to be buried.

In 1923 a perplexed undertaker told the General Registry Office (GRO) that the SBRCS had informed him that for a cremation he would need an 'Order for Burial' also called 'Form D' obtainable from the local Registrar, but the Registrar knew nothing of Form D and could give him only a Schedule I 'which is for burial and no use for cremation'. The Secretary at the GRO minuted that the Order for Burial was the Society's term for a Schedule I and that 'as cremation is a form of burial, Schedule I properly falls to be delivered to the Officials of the Crematorium [...] it being illegal to cremate without it'. But the enquiry led Gray to ask about the draft regulations and to draw attention to the difficulties he faced without them. Smail was now a Head of Section at the Scottish Board of Health.[31] He knew of moves to build a crematorium in Edinburgh, was aware that cremations were increasing slowly, but saw no more need for regulations than previously. The Secretary to the Board, however, thought otherwise. 'The making of regulations is mandatory, and it is surprising that no regulations have been issued for Scotland – especially as there is a crematorium. It will look rather odd to issue the regulations 22 years after the Act was passed but at the same time I feel some action should be taken in view of the increasing number of cremations and the possibility of other crematoria being established.' Because the Cremation Act was concerned with 'matters affecting or incidental to the health of the people' and the Board had already been vested with the Secretary for Scotland's powers in respect of burial grounds, the Board asked for the Secretary's powers under the Act to be transferred to it. The Scottish Office (SO) rejected the request: the regulations were as much about the prevention and detection of crime as about the protection of public health. It agreed, however, that regulations should now be made.

The English and Welsh regulations had been amended in 1914, consolidated in 1920, and further amended in 1925 and 1927. The 1927 amendment followed from the introduction of the registration of stillbirths, which were

---

31. The Local Government Board for Scotland had been dissolved and its functions and members transferred to the SBH by the Scottish Board of Health Act 1919. This also transferred the GRO from the SO to the SBH (Kyd 1956).

of increasing concern to doctors and medical statisticians (Rose 1976; Davis 2009). In Scotland stillbirths were not registered[32] nor were there any statutory requirements about their burial. So there was temptation to treat a child who had lived only a few minutes as stillborn and avoid the need to register it and pay for a proper burial. Infanticide was often concealed thus. Children stillborn in hospitals and maternity institutions were often incinerated.

The Scottish regulations were lying before Parliament when the SO learned that the SBH had been alerted to several cases of the disposal of children 'who have lived only a few moments'. Three in Glasgow and Edinburgh were being investigated by procurators fiscal. In two the children had ended up in a hospital furnace. The cases raised questions about the adequacy of registration procedures and whether incineration, particularly of the stillborn, would constitute an offence against the Cremation Act.

Regulation 15 would lay down the conditions for the cremation of stillborn children. Section 7 of the Act authorised the making of regulations about the burning only of 'human remains' (ch. 1). Both the Legal Secretary to the Lord Advocate's Department and J.M. Vallance, the Solicitor to the SBH, doubted whether a stillborn child was 'human remains'. 'It seems to me,' wrote Vallance, 'that the expression "human remains" means remains of a human being and in the absence of authority on the subject—and I can find none—I am of the opinion that a child that has never breathed [...] cannot be said to be a human being.' That being so, Regulation 15 was invalid. Furthermore, the incineration of the stillborn in hospital furnaces and kitchen stoves would not contravene Regulation 3, which required cremations of 'human remains' to take place in crematoria. The SO decided it was too late to withdraw the regulations but, once they were in force, enquired whether the Home Office (HO) had encountered any difficulties with its regulation.

The HO's reply was as reassuring as was possible in the absence of any judicial determination of the meaning of 'human remains' (Ministry of Health 1927). When Vallance learned of it he commented that he could 'quite understand that it is thought proper to adopt the line that the Cremation Act applies to the remains of a still-born child and personally if

32. Comparing the Scottish Registration legislation with that of the English and Welsh, one may question whether the Scottish did not require the registration of stillbirths. The latter required the registration of every 'child born alive', the latter only of 'any child born'.

I were an administrator I should take that line although I would realise that if the point were taken in court the Act might be held not to warrant the regulations dealing with still-born children'.

Once the regulations had come into force, the question of whether still-births were 'human remains' had to be directly faced. Smail doubted whether the regulations would be workable if the English interpretation of 'human remains' were adopted. 'In his view it is a question whether some intermediate way cannot be found for keeping a finger on the pulse of what goes on – both as regards the handing over of the bodies of children, live-born or still-born, for medical purposes, and the storing of bodies by undertakers.' A way round the problem would be to accept that a hospital incinerator could be a crematorium. This solution was never seriously contemplated. In 1930 the Registrar General, having taken the advice of the Crown Agent, told the Secretary of a maternity hospital, 'I have made enquiries as to the Maternity Hospital practice of cremating still-born foetuses being strictly in order, and am advised that it is so. I, however, again urge on you the great importance of strictly drawing the line at still-born foetuses [...] In terms of the Cremation Act, Hospital Authorities are not at liberty to cremate the remains of live-born children.'[33] It is difficult to see how this advice could be given if a stillborn child was 'human remains'.[34]

Eight years later the registration of stillbirths was introduced in Scotland (RSBSA 1938). As the legislation was being passed the Lord Advocate was told of doubts about whether 'human remains' encompassed the stillborn and asked for the point to be investigated. Once the Act had been passed the Registrar General wondered whether he should include in the certificate of stillbirth the footnote appended to the English certificate. This ran 'It is an offence against the Cremation Act, 1902, to dispose of the remains of a still-born child by burning except in a crematorium [...].' He learned from the Crown Agent that Crown Counsel 'entertain some doubt on the legal point

33. At this time there was no statutory definition in Scotland of a stillbirth, just as there had not been in England and Wales before 1926. For the differing criteria for a stillbirth in both jurisdictions see Crowther and White 1988b: 859 and, generally, Morgan 2002: 261.
34. For examples of uncertainty about the relationship between the registration of stillbirths, their disposal by burial or cremation, and the procurement and disposal of human tissue under the Anatomy Acts see in particular **NRS:** HH 61/142, GRO 5/1924).

but are not disposed to differ from the view acted upon by the Department here and in England unless the Courts otherwise determine'. To cover his back and to the dismay of the Registrar, the Agent suggested the notice appended to the form should read 'Attention is directed to the provisions of the Cremation Act 1902 and relative regulations regarding the disposal of human remains by burning', thus avoiding the categorical statement on the English and Welsh form. This parrying of the question had its foreseeable consequence. 'Does this mean', asked a doctor four months later, 'that one can no longer dispose of the bodies of still-born children by burning them (with the consent of the parents) in the hospital furnace and that they must be given decent burial as though they had lived?' After consulting the Department of Health for Scotland (DHS) the Registrar replied that he could not give an authoritative answer but that the official view until the courts determined otherwise was that 'human remains' did include the stillborn and that 'such remains cannot therefore lawfully be disposed of by burning in a hospital furnace or incinerator'. Crown Counsel's doubt was fresh in the minds of those considering whether to amend the regulations to require cremation authorities to notify the local Registrar of the cremations of stillborn children: this 'would seem possible [...] if it were clear that [...] "human remains" [...] could be properly applied to the remains of a still-born child'.

The three other matters that particularly exercised officials as they considered the draft regulations between 1924 and 1928 were: the relaxation of the regulations in public health emergencies; the relationship between the regulations which (a) required deaths to be registered before cremation, (b) specified the certificates required before a medical referee could authorise a cremation and (c) allowed their modification for the cremation of persons who had died outside Scotland; and (d) the role of procurators fiscal.

Warriston: The First Decade

On 6 July 1928 Salvesen founded the Edinburgh Crematorium Company Ltd (ECL), with Easson as Company Secretary.[35] The Company was incorporated on 11 July.[36] Three days later, the prospect invited offers for £10,000-worth of shares. The response was remarkable. On 31 July the Directors reported that the capital had been oversubscribed by £1,909.[37]

35. ECL Board minutes, 6/7/1928.
36. Ibid., 3/8/1928.
37. Ibid., 3/8/1928.

Failure and Success, 1918–1939

The Company's policy was to allocate all applications for smaller groups of shares in full. This maximised the spread of ownership. While thirteen of Salvesen's relatives backed his venture, nearly 300 other individuals bought parcels of shares.

The Directors decided they would increase the capital of the Company to £13,000 and called an EGM for 11 August to raise it.[38] Following the favourable vote, they could proceed with an outright purchase of Easter Warriston House and grounds and rebuilding. By late October Lorimer's adaptations for the crematorium and the garden lodge had been passed by Edinburgh's Dean of Guild.[39] With the money now raised Dr William Robertson resigned as a Director as he felt it inappropriate to occupy this position while he still served as the City's MOH.[40]

On Thursday, 3 October 1929, the Crematorium was officially declared open by the Lord Provost.[41] Four clergy took part in the dedication. Representing all the major Protestant denominations, they signalled the legitimacy of cremation as acceptable for the disposal of the dead.

Ten years' progress

Earlier this century an elderly lady came forward who had been a relative of the Agnews. She described Easter Warriston House on the eve of its conversion:[42] the upstairs columbarium took over the nursery, and the cremator the basement wash-house. During 1928–9, the chapel was carved out of the first two floors of the main house. Coffins reached the cremator via a descending catafalque from the chapel. The furnace was gas-fired and made by Askams (Chamberlain 2002). The chapel could seat 150 people (at memorial services it held 350).

The Warriston project was an immediate success. There were twenty funerals in the first three months. The Company encouraged visitors on Sunday afternoons; 10,000 in the first twelve months. Warriston immediately drew funerals from Glasgow's catchment area. In 1930 Warriston reached 125 funerals, to Maryhill's 121. Thereafter Edinburgh steadily pulled ahead annually, reaching 730 in 1936. Its success then exercised a positive

---

38. Ibid., 3/8/1928.
39. Ibid., 25/10/1928.
40. Ibid., 31/8/1928.
41. The official programme, ECL archives. See Plate 9.
42. Jim Nickerson, ECL, personal communication.

effect upon Maryhill. In 1939 Glasgow reached 498 and Edinburgh 1,218. Edinburgh had now the second busiest crematorium in the UK.

The net income from these funerals was augmented by the considerable demand for memorials. The Directors wisely chose not to sell niches outright but on twenty-five-year renewable leases. By 1934 the niche space in the gallery was almost filled up, and other areas of the building were used for panels and plaques. The commercial success of the Crematorium meant that the 6% dividend (see p. 116 above) for 1928–9 was first paid in 1932. In 1933, the entire year's dividends were paid from that one year's profits. The next ten years saw a steady development of Warriston's buildings, equipment, gardens and facilities.

Funerals at Warriston

What was the character of a funeral at Warriston? There are a few clues to picture the content of a service: first, mourners were not rushed, for instance in 1932 there were only 266 funerals (fewer than one per day). This required minimum staffing: from 1929 to 1937, Easson as Secretary also acted as Superintendent. From 1934 the organist deputised for him and in 1937 a Superintendent was appointed and provided with his own lodge.

Second, there was originally no service book. At the 1942 AGM a Dr Dryerne suggested that 'something might be done at the services, to help mourners who did not know the procedure and especially the chief mourners'.[43] Service cards should be printed. That year, the Church of England had started to debate an authorised order of service for cremations (Jupp 2006a: 135–42). Anglicans, however, had the advantage of funeral liturgies from their 1662 and 1928 Prayer Books, which clergy had recently but unofficially adapted for cremation. Dryerne's point was thus more substantial than it appeared: in asking for a formal service order, he was asking for Scottish funeral congregations to have a liturgical role and not only their clergy.

Third, what did ministers do? They would probably have read Scripture, given an address, offered prayers and chosen hymns.[44] Even this content became restricted with the steady increase in funeral numbers: in 1937 services were restricted to twenty minutes whenever another funeral was to follow immediately.

43. ECL AGM, 14/4/1942.
44. See Davies 2002 who, drawing on Bloch 1992, has explored the concepts of 'words against death' as a crucial component in death ritual.

Fourth, Warriston had installed an organ almost from the outset. In 1939 the Board, learning that some mourners wanted music but were unable to afford it, made the organist's post permanent, at £125 per annum (plus car allowance). Next year, the organ was played at 822 of the cremation services (55% of the annual total).

On this limited evidence, one may conclude that just under half of funerals consisted entirely of the spoken word, uttered mainly by the minister. When the Crematorium's promotional material speaks of 'deeply reverent services', one has to conclude that the thoughts, prayers, beliefs and emotions of the mourners themselves must have contributed much to the reverent atmosphere.

The cost of funerals

These first Scottish cremationists kept their word about funeral economies. Warriston charged eight guineas from 1929; for those insured under the NHI Scheme (and their families), it was £4. In April 1933 the normal charge was cut from eight guineas to six. On 9 March 1934 the Secretary was authorised to 'use his discretion' in reducing fees where relatives were unable to pay the full charges, or in children's funerals. In 1937 the normal fee was reduced to five guineas with £3 for Old Age Pensioners and those insured. That same year the Board agreed that a reduced charge of £1 7s 6d be made for the cremation of a poor person for which the Council was paying.

The ECL benefited from several advantages denied to the first cremationists in Glasgow forty years before. By 1939, cremation had shown itself to be the leading alternative to burial; Edinburgh's Town Council was from the outset more open to cremation. The city had a smaller population than Glasgow; its stronger middle and professional class element threw into relief the strong working-class component of Glasgow. The capital's Catholic (and therefore pro-burial) minority was far smaller, while its stronger Episcopalian minority was less opposed to cremation.[45] Maryhill chose to become a non-profit-making company and repaid its debts after nineteen years. Warriston had agreed a 6% dividend with the Council and paid this after just three years.

---

45. The Episcopalian Church followed the Church of England who, following the Cremation Act 1902, gave cremation its tacit support.

The 1930s: Four More Private Crematoria

The Company had good reason to broadcast their progress. In 1935 the 541 cremations represented 10% of the city's deaths; 60% of cremations had come from the insured classes. In 1936 Warriston had cremated a higher proportion of its local population than any other crematorium in the United Kingdom.[46] Within Edinburgh itself, the 899 cremations in 1937 represented 12.5% of the City's deaths.[47] The success of the ECL quickly inspired further cremation growth in 1930s Scotland. By 1936, two more private crematoria had opened, at Dundee and Paisley, and a crematorium company had been incorporated at Aberdeen. By 1939 a further private crematorium had opened at Seafield Cemetery, Leith. Each displayed different design features.

Dundee Crematorium

By employing a purposeful Romanesque style executed in red brick, with powerful detailing and sturdy buttressing, local architect T. Lindsay Gray designed Dundee Crematorium in 1938 to look wholly ecclesiastical. In arrangement the chapel is very like an Episcopal church, although here the east chancel contains not only an altar but also a central, descending catafalque. The nave culminates in a substantial eastern tower, which besides being ornamental carried the flues from the cremators. The chapel with its barrel roof, round-headed nave arcades and ashlar-panelled dados in the aisles, accommodated 200 mourners. The quality of the detailing throughout is high.

The commissioning of Gray (1905–1979) at the age of thirty-one returns to the pattern of engaging a young, relatively inexperienced architect of promise. He had only one church in Monifieth, designed in 'economical Gothic' and a few church alterations to his name before designing the Crematorium, but those who knew Gray recalled that his 'assured military style, great structural competence and imperturbability commanded the confidence of corporate clients and churchmen alike'.[48]

Aberdeen: Kaimhill

As at Dundee, hopes for a municipal crematorium proved unsuccessful in

46. ECL AGM, 16/4/1937.
47. ECL AGM, 29/4/1938.
48. Dictionary of Scottish Architects http://scottisharchitects.org.uk/architect_full.php?id=201253 accessed 2 May 2012.

Aberdeen and so the Aberdeen Crematorium Ltd was formed in 1934. Its architects were R. Leslie Rollo and Hall whose design marked a departure in style. Little is known of this partnership, but Aberdeen remains a fine, little altered example of a 1930s Modernist building, cruciform in shape. The horizontal emphasis and blocky massing in square and coursed, pink and grey granite, rather than the more commonly seen whitewashed render, is skilfully elevated by Rollo's utilisation of soaring verticals in the chapel windows. Despite its Modernist vocabulary, the catafalque remains central and descended.

Paisley Crematorium

The Paisley Cemetery Company had been formed in 1842 when the thirty-acre Woodside Cemetery, one of the most visionary of early Scottish cemeteries, was laid out at the west end of the town. By the early 1930s the Directors of the Company had come to acknowledge the rising popularity of cremation. Opened in 1938 by Lord Salvesen, the Crematorium was designed by prominent local architect James Steel Maitland (1887–1982). Maitland was an interesting figure – a painter, wood carver, theatrical scene painter and costume designer as well as an architect. As his Crematorium design shows, Maitland was not only an admirer of the strength and elegance of Scotland's native architecture, but also sensitive to both the nature of a commission and its site. His design combines a local idiom with something of the gravitas of funerary buildings, perhaps enhanced by the surrounding memorials, which had to be accommodated in the positioning of the building. The interior was almost Art Deco Moderne, with echoes of the simplicity of Lorimer's Warriston interior with its central, descending catafalque in front of a tall window. With its local references and modern interior, Paisley Crematorium bridged the gap between tradition and modernity. In 1957 Maitland went on to design Craigton, Glasgow's third crematorium.

Seafield Crematorium

The move towards the more overtly modern style, promoted at the Glasgow Exhibition in 1938, was writ large at Edinburgh's second crematorium, in Leith, built the following year at the eastern end of Seafield Cemetery, which had been laid out originally in 1887. The Leith Cemetery and Crematorium Company had opted for a successful local commercial architect, W.N. Thomson and Co. and Seafield's Art Deco styling represented a conspicuous departure from church architecture. Constructed in reconstituted granite, it assumed originally a somewhat harsh presence, now considerably softened by Virginia creeper. Commentators point to its 'decorous jazz-modern' (Gifford, McWilliam, Walker, Wilson 1984: 477) subdued cinema style. But elements of gravity remain, notably the monumental pseudo-Classical portico, which dominates the façade. Thompson consulted examples south of the border and it is not insignificant that the Company had in its possession plans of Arnos Grove Crematorium, Bristol (1928), originally a Classical style cemetery chapel, which may well have inspired the lofty columns of the portico at Seafield. The chapel, lit by specially designed individual brackets, and the apse and catafalque both lit by concealed flood-lighting, added a sense of theatre.

Seafield differs markedly from Warriston, both in terms of architectural style and choice of architect. The dead of Leith 'went out' in style, perhaps in tune with the times or perhaps in deliberate contrast to their more conservative counterparts at Warriston.

Burial of Ashes in Edinburgh[49]

After the regulations had come into force the difficulty that had revived work on them in 1923 cropped up again. Now, however, there was slightly less room for manoeuvre because a medical referee could not authorise a cremation unless a Schedule I was produced to him, and cremation authorities had to keep all certificates relating to cremation for at least fifteen years. Cemetery keepers were insisting on the production of a Schedule I before the burial of ashes. In Glasgow the Crematorium would issue an extract from the Cremation Register for 5s, in Edinburgh for 2s 1d. Although the GRO did not believe that section 44 of the 1854 Act applied to the burial of ashes, it advised that a cemetery keeper, uneasy at allowing one without the production of a Schedule I, could always protect himself by reporting it to the Registrar on a Schedule H.

Several ways of facilitating the burial of ashes were considered but were discounted because they would have required amendment of the 1854 Act. Eventually Easson devised a certificate which recorded that a Schedule I had been produced to the cremation authority and kept by it, and gave the date and place and date of the registration of death and of the cremation. At its head was written 'This certificate is to be delivered by the undertaker or person having charge of the funeral to the person having charge of the

---

49. This section is based on **NRS:** GRO 1/648, HH 61/138, HH 61/141.

place of interment, previous to the interment taking place.' Although non-obligatory it was thought that cemetery keepers would accept it, especially as the SO, DHS and Registrar General approved it. There was no charge for a Schedule I but there had to be one (of 1s 1d) for this: the Inland Revenue advised that being an extract from a register it was subject to stamp duty. Smail wondered whether the new certificate should be brought to the attention of the SBRCS but a SO official minuted, 'I think we can let the Glasgow Society alone until they worry SO.'

Revision of the Regulations[50]

The revision and consolidation of the regulations in the south in 1930 caused the SO to review its regulations and replace them in 1935. Considerable effort was put into determining how the 1927 regulations should be amended in the light of the changes made in England and Wales, but in the event the alterations made were slight. They would have been greater had the DHS and Easson had their way, but SO officials elected to keep change to a minimum and, except for good reason, stick closely to the English and Welsh regulations.

Since doctors qualified as required to sign the second confirmatory medical certificate were proving hard to come by, the Scots very willingly followed England and Wales in requiring them henceforth to be only of five years' standing. Both jurisdictions also introduced a ban on the second certificate being given by relatives of the deceased and partners of the doctor giving the first.

The Scots did not, however, follow the English and Welsh in transferring the power of appointing medical referees from cremation authorities to a Secretary of State. But examination of this matter did reveal an irregularity. Regulation 10 required cremation authorities to appoint 'a' medical referee and 'a' deputy medical referee. Glasgow had appointed more than one deputy, and Edinburgh had appointed two medical referees and one deputy when its crematorium opened, and another deputy in 1933.[51] The SO and

---

50. This section is based on **NRS:** GRO 1/648, HH 61/128/F1, HH 61/128/F5, HH 61/128/F160, HH 61/128/2, HH 61/906/1, HH 61/906/3, HH 61/906/4, HH 61/994.
51. See too the appointment of a replacement deputy medical referee in 1935 before the new regulations came into force. The difficulty the SO had in establishing whether it had been informed of these appointments suggests that it did not regard it as particularly important that it should be informed.

DHS agreed that this was irregular but equally that it should be possible for more than one deputy to be appointed. The revised Scottish regulations made clear, as the English and Welsh ones did not, that while a cremation authority might have more than one deputy, it could have only one referee.[52]

The Scots saw no need to follow England and Wales in replacing the power of the Secretary of State for Scotland to make any inquiry he thought fit into the carrying out of the regulations with an obligation on referees to make such reports to the Secretary as might be required. Nor did Scotland follow England and Wales in permitting a cremation authority to scatter ashes left in its charge unclaimed. The only option remained 'decent burial'. Edinburgh's practice of burying ashes without an urn or marker prompted one official to doubt that this was 'decent'.

Most effort was devoted to the documentation required for the cremation in Scotland of persons who had died elsewhere – the particular problem here being to decide what could be substituted for a certificate of the registration of death – and the reformulation of Regulation 12 which set out the functions of medical referees. As regards the former, the new regulations made particular provision for deaths in England, Wales and Northern Ireland and left deaths elsewhere to be accommodated by the Secretary of State for Scotland's power of dispensing with the regulations. As regards the latter, Regulation 12 was reformulated but with little alteration to its substance.

The Origins of Daldowie Crematorium, 1933–1939

The future burial needs of the Glasgow conurbation were to be addressed not by the old guard of which Maryhill's John Mann was representative, but by another John Mann (no relation), a railway guard and a Labour County Councillor. When Daldowie was finally opened in 1955, Mann recalled that he had first raised the matter of a crematorium in the Public Assistance Committee (PAC) in 1933 and was challenged with 'cowardice and all sorts of things'.[53] On 13 November 1936 Mann began his second campaign for a county crematorium. He sought public funding from within the elected political system to provide Scotland's first municipally owned crematorium.[54]

52. What the Edinburgh Society did, if anything, to regularise the position of its two medical referees is not known.
53. *Glasgow Herald*, 18/2/1955.
54. Lanarkshire County Council Archive, Mitchell Library, Glasgow. CO1/3/1/65 vol. 36, PAC sub-committee, 13/11/1936.

A note of opposition was raised at the PAC sub-committee in November 1937. A Councillor Clifford moved that no further action be taken over the crematorium. Mann won 'by a large majority'. It is not clear on what principles or prejudices Clifford's opposition was based. The ICF had been launched earlier that summer with a specific remit to persuade the Catholic Church to remove its fifty-year ban on cremation, so opposition may reflect Roman Catholic interests.[55] Nevertheless, the County Council had now accepted the principle of a county-controlled crematorium.

Attention now turned to suitable locations.[56] The County Architect suggested the Daldowie Estate, previously acquired by the Drainage Committee for sewage works. The sub-committee inspected Daldowie. Mann's progress was again obstructed: in 1939 the Council divided 50:50 on the proposal that John Mann and the Town Clerk might attend the Joint Conference of Burial and Cremation Authorities at Portsmouth. Even so, sometime during 1939 Lanarkshire County Council awarded the crematorium project a small grant of £10,000, the first local authority in Scotland to do so.[57] Within months Britain was at war. Daldowie was one of many civil projects immediately put on hold.

The Maturing of Maryhill, 1930–1939

Maryhill entered a new phase following Warriston's rapid success. Bound by its constitution, Maryhill diverted its growing profits into extending and beautifying its buildings and reducing its fees.

A drop in funerals in 1930 proved only temporary. Glaister told the Society's 1930 AGM that the two main causes were the opening of Warriston and the unusually low death rate in Glasgow that year.[58] A year later, Bailie Biggar told how an emerging characteristic of the rising cremation figures was 'due to a certain class of death, viz. malignant disease'.[59] Thus, two evolving characteristics of twentieth-century mortality were becoming apparent

---

55. See Davies, Kent and Keizer 2005: xxvi–xxvii.
56. Lanarkshire County Council Archive. CO1/3/1/71 PAC crematorium sub-committee minutes 14/3/1939: sub-committee p. 1782 and appendix, pp. 1783–8.
57. When Lanarkshire County Council finally decided in 1939 to proceed with the construction of a crematorium, the Finance Committee laid aside £10,000 for a modified scheme (*Glasgow Herald*, 18 Feb. 1955 p. 10a)
58. SBRCS AGM, 12/2/1930.
59. SBRCS Board minutes, 23/12/1931.

in the local Scottish statistics: the decline in the death rate and, in part consequence, the salience of certain causes of death, especially cancer and long-term chronic conditions.

The death of Glaister Senior in 1932 and the retirements of John Ker (1930) and Sir John Mann (1933) brought fresh leadership. The new Chairman was Bailie J.M. Biggar. His political role in Glasgow enhanced the profile of the SBRCS. While he had been opposed to the Kilbowie project, he became increasingly positive about encouraging cremation in other Scottish cities, and expressed his hope in 1938 that, 'a time would come when each town in the Kingdom would have its own municipal crematorium'.[60]

Board member D.W. Hardie gave twenty-six public lectures on cremation during 1934 and his role in the Co-operative movement underlines the growing importance of this new player in funeral directing.[61] The industry was also being galvanised by the National Association of Funeral Directors' search for increased professional status through better training (Parsons 2009) and the work of Lord Horder's reformist Council for the Disposal of the Dead (Jupp 2008).

In March 1933, at Biggar's first Board meeting, the agenda included new plans for the building. Repainting, electric light and a repositioned catafalque were all discussed, with a twenty-five-year limit for memorials instead of perpetuity 'as after that time, very few people were interested in the urn in question'. Over the next six years Maryhill introduced a Garden of Rest, a new organ, a telephone, a ladies' lavatory, heating, increased seating, a clergy vestry, a Superintendent's office and a tower for the columbarium (costing by 1938, £6,475). These extensions were finished in the autumn of 1939 but the planned opening date was delayed by the outbreak of war.

Towards an Aberdeen Crematorium

In September 1928, Edward Watt, now a Councillor, gave the City Council notice of a motion 'to consider and report on the practicability of establishing a municipal crematorium in or near the City'. Aberdeen's inter-war housing development had started slowly and estates were still available near the city. For MOH Harry Rae, supporting the idea, the issue was whether

60. SBRCS AGM, 30/12/1938.
61. The Co-operative movement developed its funeral directing section in the 1920s. See Parsons 2009, who reports an undertaking service being provided by the Co-op branch at Alloa, Clackmannanshire.

Failure and Success, 1918–1939 135

the crematorium should be public or private. The Council soon chose the latter and promised support, but the next year the global economic crisis descended and the crematorium issue lay dormant for four years.

In 17 September 1934, Councillor Ceiron Jones, a Unitarian minister and a Socialist, revived the proposal but as a public project and the Council sounded interested.[62] What had encouraged Jones? After all, Glasgow had dropped their Kilbowie project and Lanarkshire rebuked Councillor Mann. The deteriorating economic situation did not presage public initiatives like cremation, especially with a national rate of 1.33%. Yet Maryhill and Warriston were increasingly busy, Dundee's crematorium was nearing completion, and in England municipal crematoria projects were accelerating. By 1939, forty-seven (twenty-one in 1933) would be opened as English urban councils successively realised the advantages of cremation, both to impoverished families and to themselves. Local authorities in England, however, were given greater support by central Government than those in Scotland, a general grievance that would be felt for decades to come.[63] The issue came before Aberdeen's Finance Committee in December 1934. Jones was now a Bailie and Watt City Treasurer. By May 1935 a sub-committee had been set up and the full Council given its concurrence.

When the Finance Committee met in September, it received a letter 'on behalf of a group proposing to build a private crematorium' and asking the city whether 'in view of this development, the Council are to proceed further with the proposal to establish a municipal crematorium in Aberdeen'.[64] A signatory to the letter was City Treasurer Watt. This move galvanised the Council's choice: public or private? At October's Finance Committee Bailie Jones' motion won by three votes to two, with Watt abstaining.[65] Six days later, at a full Council meeting, Jones' motion was defeated by seventeen votes to fourteen.[66] Whether or not Watt knew that he would

62. Aberdeen Council minutes (Aberdeen Central Library reference LO 941.25) 1933–4, p. 548; Council meeting of 17/9/1934, p. 548; Council meeting 1/19/1934, p. 572.
63. See Harvie 1981.
64. Aberdeen Council. Minutes of the Finance Committee, 11/9/1935. (1934–1935, p. 686).
65. Aberdeen Council. Minutes of the Finance Committee, 1/10/1935. (1934–1935, p. 705).
66. Aberdeen Council. Minutes of Council 7/10/1935 (1934–1935, pp. 707–8).

be elected Lord Provost within days, his decision to abstain was entirely appropriate.

The way was now clear for the private company. On 18 November the Council received the plans of a crematorium which Aberdeen Crematorium Ltd proposed to erect on a site at Kaimhill, in south-west Aberdeen.[67] On 12 December, at the Town Planning Committee, Jones moved that the plan be not sanctioned and won by four votes to three.[68] However, at the next full Council meeting on 6 January 1936, Jones was defeated by nineteen votes to seven.[69] The Kaimhill project could now move ahead.

Lord Provost Watt, as Chairman of the Aberdeen Crematorium Ltd, gathered a team of prominent citizens as his co-Directors. When the Company was incorporated on 1 February 1936, they included Dan Easson, Archibald C. Morrison (Watt's successor as City Treasurer) and Mary Fenella Paton of the Paton cotton family.[70] Each member had taken fifty shares. There were altogether seventy-eight shareholders. The great, the good and the respectable had been effectively canvassed for their support.

The dedication service: signs of doctrinal realignment

With the building work proceeding, the Episcopalian Bishop Frederick Deane, Bishop of Aberdeen and Orkney, preached at the dedication service.[71] Deane characterised popular Christian belief in the resurrection of the body as now superstitious and outmoded, a change from traditional belief speeded by the violent destruction of soldiers' bodies by high explosives in the Great War, as opposed to civilians 'buried [whole] in the ground'.[72] Deane said 'he spoke as the mouthpiece of a great body of enlightened opinion among Christian people'.

---

67. Aberdeen Council. Minutes of Council 18/11/1935 (1935–1936, p. 12).
68. Aberdeen Council. Minutes of the Public Health Committee 12/12/1935. (1935–1936, p. 115).
69. Aberdeen Council Minutes of Council 6/1/1936 (1935–1936, p. 117).
70. Memorandum and Articles of Association of Aberdeen Crematorium Ltd (1936). James Dewar was Company Secretary.
71. See Deane 1938 and *Aberdeen Press and Journal* (*APJ*), 15/4/1937.
72. There are parallels between Bishop Deane's judgements and those of Principal Major and Bishop Gore; see Gore 1924, Major 1922, Jupp 2006b and for the wider context Bourke 1996.

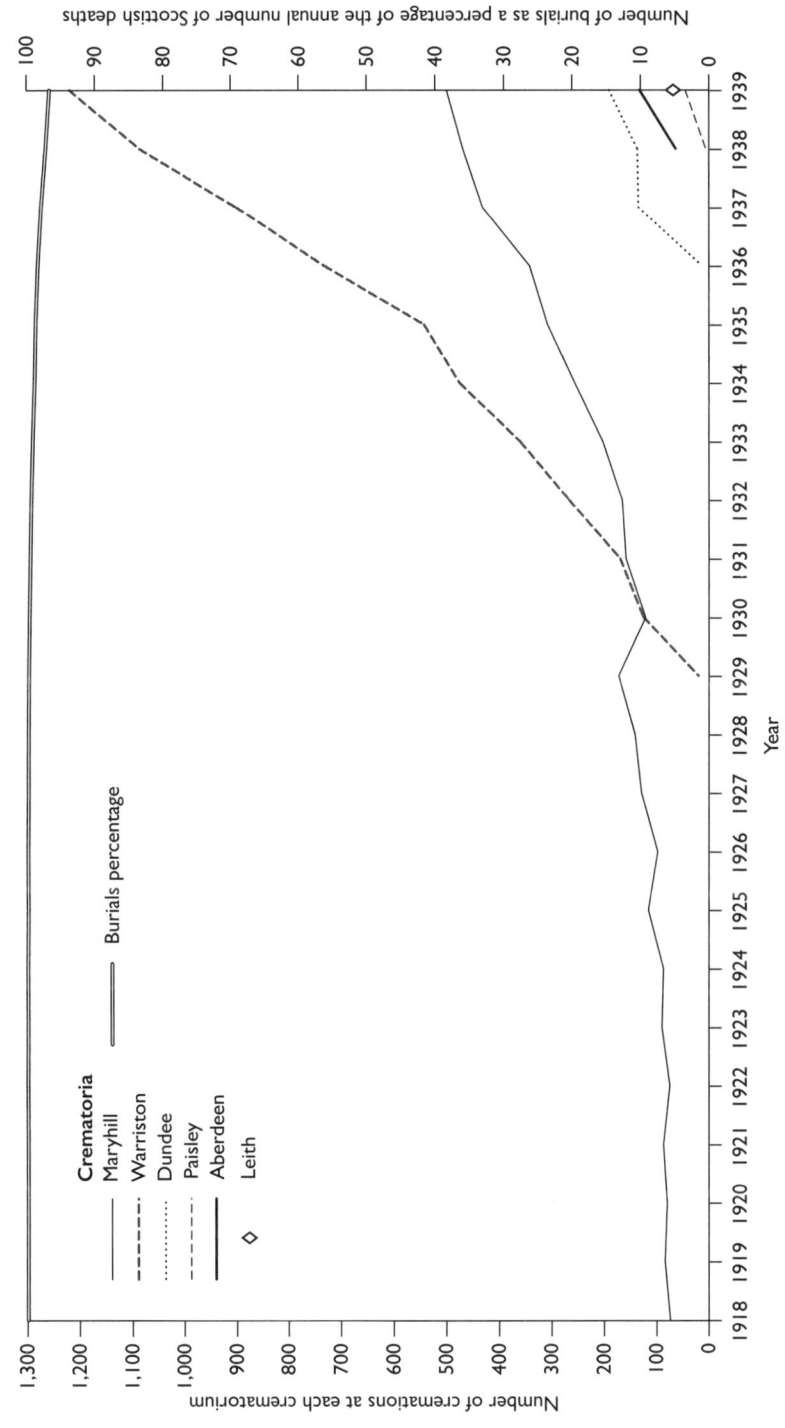

Graph 1. The graph shows the annual numbers of cremations at each of the first six crematoria in Scotland in the inter-war period, 1918–39. It shows the continuing slow growth at Maryhill (Glasgow, opened 1895) and the effect of Warriston (Edinburgh)'s immediate success both upon Maryhill and in stimulating four more crematoria. All were privately owned. The graph shows that burial was still the overwhelming preference of Scottish families, over 96% in 1939.

The previous year, the CS had polled Britain's bishops for their views on cremation. Bishop David of Liverpool had responded:

> It is already agreed among the best educated Christians that the quickest, cleanest and most seemly disposal of the dead is provided by cremation [...] in spite of prejudice against it which arises from a mistaken belief that in the resurrection the identical particles of the earthly body are reassembled and become 'the body that shall be'.[73]

Deane's themes of enlightenment and education, of the practical and economic advantages of cremation, and of modern attitudes to the mode of human existence in the next life were one with Bishop David's.

The Crematorium was opened on 14 March 1938. By year's end 1939 it had carried out 195 funerals. Meanwhile Paisley had been opened in 1938 and Seafield, Leith in 1939.

Now with all six crematoria privately owned, it may have seemed that Scotland was merely extending its century-old reliance upon private enterprise for the disposal of its dead. The outbreak of war temporarily halted the promotion of cremation, but with three exceptions. In 1939–40, the Government had to decide between burial and cremation as the more efficient mode of disposal for people killed in mass air raids. The second was Mann's revival of his Daldowie plans in 1943. Thirdly, the Kaimhill scandal in 1944 would raise critical questions about future cremation practice but prove to be the watershed between the pre- and post-war eras for Scottish cremation, and between private and public crematoria.

---

73. *Pharos* 2(1) (Oct. 1935), 18ff.

CHAPTER SIX

The Second World War and the Aberdeen Scandal, 1939–1952

Law of Cremation in War Time[1]

In September 1938 the Munich crisis alerted the Government to the inadequacy of the country's civil defence preparations (O'Brien 1955: 153ff; Rugg 2004; Jupp 2006a: 127–35). Local authorities were advised on how to deal with domestic civilian war fatalities. The Ministry of Health (MH) issued Circular 1779 and Memorandum 222 to authorities in England and Wales, the Department of Health for Scotland (DHS) Circular DP 2 and a memorandum to authorities in Scotland. The only important difference between them was that in England and Wales the law would be changed to permit authorities to bury persons who had died from war operations before their deaths had been registered. Scotland had never required registration before burial. In each jurisdiction, however, a death did have to be registered before cremation.

'So far as the interests of the Cremation Societies are concerned,' minuted a Staff Officer at the Scottish Home Department (SHD), 'I doubt if they would consider it good propaganda if the use of their crematoria by local authorities came to be associated [...] with a cheap and easy method

---

1. This section is based on CSA CRE/P/5; NRS HH 61/140; **PA**: HL/PO/JO/10/10/1213/1132, HL/PO/JO/10/10/1213/1148; **TNA**: CAB 75/5/9, HO 45/10249/B38626/F42, F44, F46, F48, HO 45/11050/152635/F37, HO 45/18142/F47, HO 45/20597/F1, F3, F5, F15, F18, F23, F24, HO 45/21880/802517/F97, HO 144/21621/F51, HO 186/1225.

of disposing of masses of unclaimed dead [...] [I]f pit or trench burial is allowed to remain as the only method open to local authorities it will possibly serve to create a prejudice in the public mind against earth burial and thus stimulate an interest in cremation.' Cremation interests did not see it thus. They lobbied hard for authorities to be permitted to cremate war casualties and for the legal restrictions on cremations to be relaxed. In England and Wales they drafted a scheme which amounted to a virtual nationalisation of existing cremation facilities, augmented by mobile crematoria and even pyres, and large-scale compulsory cremation (Piggott 1939). They were told that the Government had no intention of relaxing the law. Equally they were told that the Government had none of making it more difficult to arrange cremations.

Legislation implementing Circulars 1779 and DP 2, however, did make it more difficult. Regulation 30 of the Defence Regulations authorised local authority clerks and commanding officers to certify deaths as due to war operations; and required local authorities to 'inter' anyone whose death had been thus certified if not satisfied that adequate arrangements had been made for their 'interment'. Since cremating a body was not 'interring' it, an authority knowing mourners were planning a cremation could not be so satisfied. Strictly speaking, the authority would have to threaten to commandeer the body unless the mourners agreed to arrange its burial. Presumably this was why the Cremation Society's (CS) propaganda had it, not entirely accurately, that 'the cremation of civilian war dead arising from air raids will not be permitted'.

Cremation was restricted in other ways too, by the circumstances of domestic war fatalities and limitations on coroners' powers, leaving applicants for cremation to find and pay for a pathologist to do a post-mortem in order to obtain the necessary certificate, or to bury the body, wait a year, and exhume it.

Eventually, in July 1940, an amendment to Regulation 30 changed the word 'interment' to 'disposal' and permitted medical referees to authorise cremations on the basis of a certificate from the Registrar of Deaths that a death was due to war operations. For this a medical certificate of the cause of death was not required: it could be based on a certificate from a local authority clerk or commanding officer.

Scotland could have dealt with the legalities differently. Under its Public Health Act, bodies could be buried or cremated. Moreover the powers of Secretaries of State to suspend or modify the cremation regulations 'during an epidemic or for other sufficient reason' were differently drawn. In 1914 the Home Office (HO) had taken the view that, because the Home Secretary could act only on the application of a local authority, Regulation 14 did not permit suspension or modification of the regulations simultaneously countrywide. In Scotland the Secretary of State's power was not dependent on an application from anyone. Furthermore, in Scotland there was less statutory regulation of the investigation of violent deaths than in England and Wales.

Salvesen implored successive Secretaries of State for Scotland for a different dispensation in Scotland, but the DHS was determined that wartime conditions should not be made the occasion for requiring local authorities to cremate dead bodies or for increasing their powers to do so. It looked as though Scotland was going to fall in almost exactly with the line being proposed in England and Wales when its Law Officers insisted that a certificate from a Registrar that a death was due to war operations would suffice for cremation only if based on a medical certificate that the death 'was due to a specified cause which is consistent with death directly due to war operations'. Edinburgh Crematorium Company's offer of free cremations of the bodies of unidentified war dead did not advance its cause: amended Defence Regulation 30, which permitted cremation, still did not allow unidentified bodies to be cremated.

Thus, in wartime resort to cremation became harder in Scotland than in England and Wales for two reasons. The first was that in Scotland a certificate from a doctor showing a medical cause of death had to be produced to the Registrar of Deaths. The second reason was that in Scotland the cause had to be certified as 'directly' due to war operations (raising nice issues of causation).

Dewar Trial[2]

A trial in October 1944 threatened to have profound consequences for the development of cremation. James Dewar, the manager of Kaimhill Crematorium in Aberdeen, was convicted of stealing 1,044 coffin lids and

---

2. This section is based on **CSA:** CRE/P/2/G, CRE/P/1/B/VI; **NRS:** JC 71/77, JC 36/150, HH 61/127, HH 61/127/F5, HH 61/128/2, HH 61/135, HH 61/136, HH 61/140, HH 61/704, HH 61/906/3; **TNA:** ASSI 45/105/1, HLG 45/1471, HO 45/17512/47, HO 45/17512/52, HO 45/17513/655502/F52A, HO 45/25619/F1, HO 45/25619/F5, HO 45/25619/F6, HO 45/25619/F7, HO 45/25619/F8, HO 45/25619/F9.

two coffins from the 1,488 cremations carried out between 1938 and 1944, and Alick Forbes, an Aberdeen undertaker, was convicted of resetting (receiving) 100 coffin lids. Dewar was imprisoned for three years, Forbes for six months.

Dewar was a town councillor, a bailie, a police judge, a JP and an officer of the National Fire Service. He was a Vice-President of the Scottish Branch of the National Association of Cemetery and Crematorium Superintendents (NACCS). He was the first Secretary of the Aberdeen Crematorium Company and its Managing Director, and he was Superintendent and Registrar of the Crematorium. Almost from the start he gave away wood from coffins. He let the fire service have some as well as friends and family. In wartime such material was in short supply.

The trial was moved from Aberdeen because of adverse publicity following news of Dewar's arrest. His counsel told the High Court in Edinburgh of stories of gold teeth removed from bodies sent for cremation and of the temperature in the cremator being lowered to allow bodies to burn slowly so that fat could be collected and sold to fish and chip shops. Flowers from wreaths were being resold to local florists.[3]

The Council of the CS was extremely concerned. Dewar had told the police that the removal of lids and their use as firewood 'is a general practice through the whole crematorium movement, and the same lids can be found at Woking and other crematoriums', a claim he repeated at his trial. The conviction the previous July of an Aberdeen doctor of making false declarations in cremation certificates was little remarked[4] although his doing so was brought to light by the police investigation of Dewar (Westland 1958; Glaister 1945: 148), but the Dewar trial lasted four days in a court festooned with exhibits – coffins, shrouds, coffin lids, a rabbit hutch, a writing bureau, a tea tray, a birds' egg collection box, radio cabinets, desks and seed boxes – was presided over by a judge with smelling salts to hand, and received nationwide publicity.

3. For examples of these rumours circulating as poems and children's rhymes see Mackenzie 2006.
4. Dr Harry Mackay had signed nine second confirmatory cremation certificates in which he had falsely stated that he had spoken to the doctors providing the first certificates. He escaped being struck off the Medical Register, 'General Medical Council Special Session: False Statement in Cremation Certificates', *Supplement to the British Medical Journal*, 28/7/45, p. 16b.

The Council retained the Dean of the Faculty of Advocates, J.G. MacIntyre, to keep a watching brief over the proceedings and paid the expenses of crematoria Superintendents called by the prosecution to refute Dewar's claim. George Noble, a Council member and former Secretary of the CS, advised the Superintendents of the line of questioning faced by those who had preceded them.

In the absence through illness of Edward Watt, the Chairman of the Board, evidence about the discharge of the Board's responsibility for the management of the crematorium was given by a fellow Board member who had far less contact with Dewar than Watt. Noble accurately reported that he 'was very weak [...] and it was evident that Dewar had jumped from Secretary and Registrar to Superintendent and Managing Director and had virtually complete control'. The Board did not carry out inspections of the Crematorium's operations nor had it ever been officially inspected.

The Society's solicitor had hoped that the judge would allow MacIntyre to make a statement on the Society's behalf. This was a naive hope. But Sir David King Murray, the Solicitor-General, did tell the jury

> these proceedings were in no sense directed against the system of cremation [...] The evidence [...] from all over the country [...] showed very clearly that these conditions [i.e. due propriety and respect] could be and were realised in connection with cremation where there was proper supervision of the crematorium.

In fact Murray was far from sure that what had happened at Aberdeen was not being repeated elsewhere. After the trial counsel advised the Society against issuing a statement to the press because 'the Society was plainly in no position to give an assurance that malpractices did not take place at other crematoria'. Herbert Jones, the Society's Secretary, wrote to a Council member, 'I personally have been given confidential information of practices at crematoria which are of a most undesirable character, and the Solicitor-General had similar information, which he did not divulge.'[5] Three months later the furnaceman at Darlington Crematorium and a local undertaker were sentenced to eighteen months' imprisonment for stealing coffin lids from the crematorium between 1939 and 1944.

5. See, too, letter from H.J. Squires to the Minster of Health, 23/10/44, with hearsay evidence of the removal of coffin lids and fittings ('this coffin ramp'), TNA HO 45/25619/F4a.

Although Noble reported that he had heard that Lord Cooper was in favour of cremation, the Lord Justice Clerk began his charge to the jury

> Reverence for the dead and respect for the sanctities which surround the last rites are amongst the most deep seated sentiments of the human race […] During the last four days you have heard much which […] must have come as a shocking revelation of the extent to which that reverence can be violated and those sanctities desecrated. You may even think […] it is high time that the process of cremation, as conducted hitherto at Aberdeen, was subjected […] to the most stringent inspection and control, in order that a story such as this may never be told in a Scottish Court again.

The Cremation Regulations provided for official, but not obligatory, inspection of crematoria in several ways.[6] This omission was deliberate (Troup 1903: 14). Professor John Glaister, the Chairman of the Scottish Burial Reform and Cremation Society (SBRCS), quickly let it be known that regular official inspections would be welcomed by those responsible for crematoria in Scotland and that at Maryhill unannounced inspections of the Crematorium were made by an officer of the Society. But he, as well as the officials in Edinburgh responding to Lord Cooper's call for inspection, were not quite right in thinking that there had been no governmental inspections. Although possibly not in the exercise of an authority conferred by the regulations, Smail had inspected Maryhill in 1913 and 1926, and Warriston before its opening in 1929. In England and Wales the MH had occasionally inspected crematoria but had no programme of inspections.

The immediate consequence of Lord Cooper's words was the DHS's taking over the SHD's responsibility for the oversight of the Cremation Act and Regulations, thus uniting responsibility for burial, cremation, anatomy, mortuaries and death registration, an arrangement first proposed in 1924 (ch. 5) and then in 1940 during discussions about the amendment of Defence Regulation 30. Drs Hood, the Deputy Chief Medical Officer, and Sutherland, a Departmental Medical Officer, were appointed inspectors within the week.

---

6. In 1935 the HO produced a report based on responses to a questionnaire to medical referees.

The Superintendent at Woking gave evidence at the trial. Stanley Walker specifically denied that lids could be found lying there and that removing lids would assist combustion. A medical textbook, edited by one of the medical referees at Warriston, quoted the Superintendent of Woking as having written, 'The average time required for the complete cremation of an adult body, if enclosed in a coffin, is an hour and a half, but without coffin one hour, provided the temperature of incinerating chamber is up to 1,800F' (Smith and Cook 1934: 565). Walker denied being the source of this information. He had been Superintendent since 1925 and said that the advice came from sixty years previously.[7] An instruction in force at Golders Green Crematorium that coffin lids must be left secure was denied, not very convincingly, to indicate that lids were being removed.

After the trial Easson's widow told two officials at the DHS that 'her husband had visited Woking Crematorium sometime between 1931 and 1937 and had told her that a number of lids were lying about which he said were afterwards used for firewood'. On appeal Dewar's counsel sought to adduce this evidence to buttress Dewar's claim that he believed he was entitled to keep lids because he believed this was done at other crematoria. The difficulty was that neither to the police nor at his trial had Dewar mentioned Mrs Easson. He had mentioned meeting a lady at a cremation conference who had told him that 'she disliked Woking Crematorium because they do not bother to take the lids away from public gaze' but that lady was not Mrs Easson. Moreover, being hearsay, her testimony would have been valueless to refute the Superintendent's direct evidence at the trial. The court refused to hear it. Dewar's and Forbes' appeals were dismissed (Dewar v H.M. Advocate 1945).

The cross-examination of prosecution witnesses suggests that Dewar believed that the police had been tipped off about the retention of coffin lids at the Crematorium by the recently established Scottish Area Federation of the National Association of Funeral Directors (NAFD), which objected to the Crematorium's involvement in undertaking. 'This is a conspiracy,'

---

7. The source was W. Sargeant who had been appointed to Woking in 1902, having previously been Superintendent of the crematorium in Liverpool. The advice first appeared in F. Smith (1905: 632), was not removed from the edition published four years after the trial (Smith, Cook and Stewart 1948: 565), was introduced into the second edition of Sydney Smith's own textbook (1928: 222) and repeated up to and including the last edition (Smith and Smith 1955: 238).

Dewar testified, 'I know who is behind it', but he did not tell. The investigating detective had been expecting a tip-off from the Association: he had heard that a 'secret' meeting of the Association had discussed contacting the police. In the event an attendant at the City Hospital mortuary alerted the police about the reuse of coffins bringing bodies to the mortuary: his suspicions aroused, he had marked them. When the Town Council was considering whether to buy the Crematorium the NAFD petitioned the Secretary of State not to allow the Council to conduct funerals 'beyond those necessary for the cremation of human remains'. This was unnecessary. It had no power to act as an undertaker.

Aberdeen: The First Council-owned Crematorium in Scotland

In December 1944 Kaimhill's shareholders accepted Aberdeen City Council's (ACC) offer of £20,294 8s for Kaimhill, which thus became the first publicly owned crematorium in Scotland. In January, the loan application was approved by ACC and then by the Secretary of State within a fortnight. The Parks Superintendent and City Chamberlain were asked to propose a scale of charges and to draft regulations. In March, some Councillors successfully argued for the removal of the differential charges, not only for people living within and without the city boundaries but also for certain classes of widows. Sunday funerals had long been a tradition in England, especially popular with the poorer classes. The Aberdeen 'reformers' now won another vote for cremations on Sundays (after 11.00), reducing the double fee proposed. The Council, as a new Cremation Authority, applied to join the Federation of British Cremation Authorities (FBCA). On 16 June the DHS approved the site and plans of the (now renamed) Aberdeen Crematorium.[8] The cremation numbers that had dipped following the trial recovered within three years.

The origins of NACCS's Scottish Branch

The first professional association of UK Cemetery Superintendents was established in 1913 and renamed the National Association of Cemetery Superintendents in 1918. In 1932 it became the National Association of Cemetery and Crematorium Superintendents.[9] Yet, even by 1939, only 3.3%

---

8. Aberdeen City Council minutes 3/9/1945, p. 750.
9. In 1947, the NACCS was renamed the Institute of Burial and Cremation Administration (IBCA).

of Scottish funerals included cremation (3.8% UK) and it appeared that burial would long continue as people's choice.

The NACCS Scottish branch was founded on 9 January 1943, its Secretary being R.C. Macmillan, Director of Parks and Cemeteries, Kirkcaldy (Macmillan 1951). It quickly attracted sixty members, providing a sustainable professional network. Soon represented at national level, it hosted the 1949 NACCS national conference, in Glasgow. Its first Chairman, T.L. Reid, managed Paisley's private cemetery and crematorium, but most members possessed only cemetery experience.

Reid was an emphatic advocate of crematoria (Reid 1943). He foresaw crematoria planned regionally: one for Kilmarnock and South Ayrshire, another for Ayr and so on. John McKim, also from Paisley, was strongly pro-cremation too, recalling his First World War experiences: 'I look on a dead body as a menace to the community, and hold that its prompt removal and quick dissolution are common-sense essentials in a well-ordered community' (McKim 1944: 8). The Branch minutes are particularly detailed and informative from 1943 to 1951 but give the impression, however, that the priority of most members was to improve cemetery service, with better training and recruitment, rather than to promote cremation. Immediate problems included arrangements for the burial of war-time casualties, both civilian (Dalgleish 1944) and military (Chettle 1941; Pettigrew 1948): the Imperial War Graves Commission was often represented at the Scottish branch meetings.

The NACCS Memorandum

In early 1944, the NACCS published a *Memorandum on Planning for Post-War Reform in the Disposition of the Dead* (NACCS 1944). For its time, this was a radical document. It was influenced by the pre-war reform movement; the stimulus of the Beveridge Report; increasing competition from privately-owned crematoria; an antipathy to funeral directors; and recollections of the pauper funeral.

Most civilian deaths still occurred at home. So bereaved relatives were subject to advice, both neighbourly and professional: undertakers, memorial masons, florists and cemetery proprietors. The war had shown the need 'for a central public authority in each locality to accept full responsibility for such disposal'. The *Memorandum* proposed that responsibility for the disposal of the dead should be a monopoly of local government whose role in disposal, post-war, should be deliberately expanded.

The *Memorandum*'s root conviction was that 'the disposal of the dead, from the moment of death until the completion of the final disposal, is one function; new legislation should deal with it as such'; 'the consolidation of complex and piecemeal burial legislation into one single Act of Parliament' was a priority. Local authorities had been handicapped by a lack of finance and the need for central government borrowing permission. Local government should have a monopoly in crematoria and the role of private enterprise should be 'terminated as soon as possible [...] Competition in providing burial and cremation facilities, and any form of financial inducement which encourages specific interests in the disposal of the dead, should be abolished'. Funding remained delicate: should the cemetery department 'be financed entirely by the revenue it produces or subsidised out of public funds so as to provide an inexpensive service?' The NACCS favoured full state responsibility. Town planning being a major preoccupation in wartime Britain, especially featuring in reconstruction plans, the *Memorandum* recommended that all schemes should provide for both cemeteries and crematoria.

The Scottish branch regularly discussed post-war planning of cemeteries and crematoria and approved the draft *Memorandum* in September 1943. A major obstacle was the very complexity of burial law (Fellows 1940). Few participants, however, could have believed that all burial legislation could practically be consolidated into one Act; for this rationale flew in the face of individual sentiment, traditional customs, bereaved families' budgets and the vested interests of funeral directors, the first port-of-call for bereaved families.

A strong Socialist ethos lies behind the call for the nationalisation of the funeral directing industry, a call which was focused in MP Garry Allighan's address to the NACCS 1947 Conference (Allighan 1947). This had been much favoured by Prime Minister Clement Attlee, although never Cabinet policy (Wilson 1977: 278). Nationalisation was also encouraged by Joan S. Clarke on Beveridge's team; her 'Funeral Reform' in the *Fabian Review* of January 1943 was reprinted in the NACCS Journal (Clarke 1944).

The Post-war NACCS Scottish Branch

Unlike in England and Wales, the drive behind Scottish crematorium provision came eventually from central Government, the Department of Health for Scotland (DHS), who had been given responsibility for cremation after the Dewar trial. Meanwhile, the Scottish branch minutes reveal that no cremation issues dominated their meetings; the lawn cemetery model particularly appealed (Rugg 2006). At the 1949 Glasgow NACCS conference, Macmillan and Dalgleish promoted the garden cemetery model as less costly to maintain and as more convenient for mourners (Macmillan 1949; Dalgleish 1949).

In November 1950, the new Secretary, Graham Blair, organised a day seminar in Paisley. He had invited William Pearson of Leeds, NACCS' National President to take part (Pearson 1951). Pearson praised his Scottish audience for pioneering the lawn cemetery model and then expounded on how he saw cremation developing. This address to his Scottish peers may be interpreted as a green light for adopting cremation. In England a cremation rate which had reached 13.86% in 1949 (11.07% in Scotland) hinted at an irreversible process of change.

Pearson's paper anticipated a distinguishing characteristic of future Scottish crematoria in being sited separately from cemeteries: 'I believe it is in the interests of the [cremation] movement—that as these new crematoria will be erected up and down the country they should be commenced on a fresh basis, and outwith the surrounding cemetery.'[10] He also recommended the committal of the coffin at the *end* of the service and the restriction of memorialisation to the Book of Remembrance.

Re-organising for Post-war Funeral Reform

Post-war change in British funeral customs came from several directions. The 1942 Beveridge Report included financial support for the British population from 'the cradle to the grave'. Attlee introduced new benefits for bereaved people as early as 1946. The Death Grant (£20 in 1948) was designed to reduce funeral costs and ward off the predations of the Industrial Assurance industry.

In 1944, the Church of England formally signalled its support for cremation. In May 1944 the Upper House of the Convocation of Canterbury agreed that 'Cremation of a dead body is lawful as a preparation for Christian burial or disposal in consecrated ground' (*Chronicle of the Upper House of Convocation*, 25 May 1944: 187). No clearer sign of Anglican support could have been given that by the cremation of the left-leaning Archbishop Temple, on 31 October 1944.

In 1947 the CS and the FBCA (Jones was Secretary of both) launched the Cremation Council of Great Britain (CCGB), seeking to work more closely with Government departments. Few Scottish local authorities had the advantage of Lanarkshire's pre-war permission for a crematorium; other Scottish local authorities found themselves lower down the queue for DHS support.

10. Pearson 1951: 23.

Aneurin Bevan played a unique role in the promotion of cremation as Secretary of State for Health whose remit included housing and local government (Bevan 1946). But with the NHS and housing as Bevan's first priorities, his MH rejected every application for permission to build a crematorium from 200 UK local authorities. The CCGB repeatedly pressed the MH with fifteen of the most urgent requests: when these were reduced to five, Bevan gave way. In December 1948 the MH gave permission for the building of six crematoria and one chapel conversion, but all were in England.

In 1946, the CS decided it would no longer participate in joint conferences of burial and cremation interests as it judged that such co-operation was detrimental to its cause. This exacerbated tensions between the CS and the FBCA (E. Turner 1988; Jupp 2006a: 145). In 1950 the Federation recommenced the annual joint conference with the IBCA, a conference dominated by local government staffs and representatives.

The Second World War experience changed British funerals. As Howarth has summarised, 'The exigencies of a society at war forced the survivors to abbreviate their normal mourning rituals; life had to go on [...] a relatively low-key approach to funeral ritual was established' (Howarth 1997: 120–34). The Scottish cremation rate rose from 3.33% (1939) to 7.48% (1945). Scottish funeral directors had discovered cremation's advantages. Scotland's first funeral home was opened in Perth (1939). This innovation encouraged families to allow funeral directors to take care of the corpse, enabling them to achieve economies of scale in coffin-making and greater control over the funeral process. The War had ended the import of Belgian black horses and funeral directors' reliance on motor hearses grew, enabling more funerals in the working day. In 1942 the Scottish Area Federation of the NAFD was established and quickly gained 200 member firms. After 1945 bereaved families increasingly used funeral directors' Chapels of Rest, a change further stimulated by the new NHS from 1948. The location of death thereafter shifted steadily from home to hospital. All these factors contributed to bereaved families ceding more control over funerals to funeral directors.

Interdepartmental Committee on the Cremation Regulations[11]

The Dewar trial provoked other suggestions apart from inspection. Cremation authorities should not be allowed to be undertakers. Undertakers

---

11. This section is based on **CSA**: CRE/P/6/C/Box 2, CRE/P/6/A; **NRS**: HH 61/113, HH 61/129, HH 61/130, HH 61/131, HH 61/132; HH 61/134, HH 61/136;

should be state registered. Crematoria should be publicly controlled. A Departmental Committee should be set up to investigate methods of cremation. Relatives should be permitted to witness cremations. Members of the newly formed Proprietary Crematoria Association (PCA) were concerned about the public's reaction if it learned they were selling precious metals and jewellery left in the ashes after a cremation and giving the proceeds to charity.

Officials in both Edinburgh and London now had little doubt that what had happened at Aberdeen was an isolated aberration. Herbert Morrison, the Home Secretary, told Parliament that he had no evidence that the Cremation Regulations were not being 'scrupulously observed' but he was investigating whether they needed amendment.

To make good on Morrison's answer, the HO convened a meeting with representatives of the MH and the DHS. It became apparent that widely differing attitudes to inspection were held on either side of the border. All Scottish crematoria but Aberdeen's had been inspected by Christmas. It seems the intention was that each crematorium should be inspected at least annually. It is probable that this was achieved in 1953, 1954, 1955 and 1956. The MH checked only that the site and buildings of public crematoria accorded with approved plans and had no interest in how cremations were carried out. All agreed, however, that they did not know enough about the process of cremation and decided to await the submission of the Scottish inspectors' reports.

One of the matters discussed was when or whether to involve outside bodies in the discussions. Meantime the HO had been approached by the CS. When the Aberdeen coffins case hit the headlines the Society had been contemplating the promotion of a Private Member's Bill to relax some of the statutory restrictions on cremation. At the end of 1944 its Council had resolved 'that a Code of Practice should be drawn up for the conduct and operation of crematoria, embracing all aspects of the matter'. Despite Jones's frustration at the indifference of the FBCA to the Dewar trial, the

TNA: DPP 1/17, HLG 45/1620, HO 45/10249/B38626/F18, HO 45/10249/B38626/F37, HO 45/25619/F6, HO 45/25619/F15, HO 45/25619/F24, HO 45/25619/F30, HO 45/25619/F31, HO 45/25619/F32, HO 45/25619/F33, HO 45/25619/F35, HO 45/25619/F37, HO 45/25620/F43, HO 45/25620/F54, HO 45/25620/F58, HO 45/25620/F88, HO 144/1757/425994, HO 144/20185, HO 282/2, HO 282/25, HO 299/10, RG 48/2188; Troup 1903; Strutt 1950.

Federation was to be informed of the resolution and offered the Society's help in drawing up the code.

Early in 1945 Sir George Elliston, then MP for Blackburn and a member of the Society's Council, attended the HO to discuss the revision of the Cremation Act and Regulations and the prospect of Government support for a Private Member's Bill. He was given some hope of HO backing, but this would have to await perusal of the Scottish inspectors' reports.

About the proposed code the HO said that it would be willing to be consulted but would have no authority to approve it (a perplexing remark given the Home Secretary's power to make regulations about cremation).

There appears to have been an independent initiative for a code in Scotland. In reviewing the reports of the Scottish inspectors before Christmas, Robert Howat, an Assistant Secretary at the DHS, commented

> Later, however, we might consider whether we should not prepare a code of procedure [...] which could be issued to the cremation authorities for voluntary adoption [...] If we kept up our inspections, the 'code' would have a special use [...] of course, it would be a joint affair with the Home Office. One rule should no doubt be that the lid must not be removed from a coffin once the coffin has reached the crematorium.

The Federation appointed a subcommittee including Jones and Noble to draft the code. It and an accompanying 'Instructions to Funeral Directors' were approved at the Federation's AGM in September 1945. Among its clauses were that 'No official of a Cremation Authority shall conduct the business of a funeral director', 'No portion of the coffin or its contents shall be removed following the Committal Service', 'The utmost care shall be taken to ensure that the ashes resulting from each cremation shall be kept separate' and 'Care should be taken to separate [...] metals from the ashes, and [...] they should be retained for subsequent disposal in accordance with the directions of the Cremation Authority, or higher Authority.'

Whether the HO had been consulted before the code was issued is not known: the DHS certainly had not. When Hood saw it he commented that relations should be told that valuables should not be enclosed in the coffin at all. Sutherland favoured the procedure at Paisley where metal fittings – which had to be detached from coffins – were put in the cremator at the side of the coffin, removed from the ashes and buried separately in the crematorium grounds. 'But,' he wrote, 'I suppose the code is better to err on the side of the angels, and anyway it was drawn up by delegates of the operators themselves.'

Hood remarked that it might not be possible to keep the ashes from each cremation separate: this was not happening at Warriston. The cremator had to cool before ashes could be removed, and when they were to be removed from the crematorium or otherwise preserved, this was done. In most cases, however, the ashes were dispersed in the crematorium grounds, and with the number of cremations carried out daily it was not possible to allow the cremator to cool to keep the ashes separate. In this case, the cremations were carried out one after the other, but the ashes were collected in bulk the next morning.

Although Morrison had discounted the necessity for a committee to investigate changes to the regulations, the HO soon decided that one should be convened. Occasionally a trial draws attention to the possibility of cremation being used to conceal evidence of crime. It happened with the trial of the Seddons in 1912 and with that of Dr Armstrong in 1922. And it happened again in 1947 just as the Interdepartmental Committee began its deliberations. Two months before its first meeting the wife of a Dr Clements died at Southport. An anonymous tip-off led the coroner to halt the funeral, after which both Dr Clements and the pathologist who had performed a post-mortem on Mrs Clements committed suicide. An inquest jury returned a verdict that Mrs Clements had been murdered by her husband. Cremationists were disconcerted by her being his fourth wife. The first two had been buried after Dr Clements had signed their death certificates. The third had been cremated at Liverpool too quickly for the police to intervene. A month after the closing of the inquest, Austin Strutt, an Assistant Secretary at the HO and the Committee's chairman, opened its first meeting with the words, 'Whilst their thoughts had been turning towards an easing of the Regulations, the recent Southport case had brought a sharp realisation of the dangers even under existing safeguards' and the Committee decided that the first person to be invited to speak to it would be Professor Webster, the Director of the West Midlands Forensic Laboratory, who had conducted an enquiry into the Clements case.[12]

The Committee included a representative from the DHS, namely Howat. Its remit was limited to reviewing the Cremation Regulations, which in

12. The committee also heard from Cyril Banks, the Medical Referee of Nottingham Crematorium, who, presented with an application for cremation, had alerted the police to the possibility of murder in the Nurse Waddingham case in 1936.

Scotland were the responsibility of the Scottish Office, not the HO. The SHD, despite its interest in the prevention and detection of crime, was not invited onto the Committee. No Scottish organisations or witnesses submitted memoranda directly, or gave evidence in person, to the Committee, as English ones did. The Secretary of the SHD, when he saw the Committee's report, remarked, 'I do not think we would have acquiesced in the appointment by the Home Secretary of a Committee covering Scotland.'

About inspection the Committee was surprisingly sanguine. It did recommend that inspection should be possible at any time, not just 'at any reasonable time', but saw no need for regular inspections of crematoria: the Scottish inspectors had given the Scottish crematoria clean bills of health; Kaimhill was regarded as an isolated aberration; and most new crematoria were likely to be local authority controlled and supervised. The Committee's confidence in the superior rectitude of public authorities may have been influenced by the CCGB telling it of three crematoria which had been opened and closed shortly before the recent war. The Committee reported that these 'had been established by private bodies which were inadequately equipped and unsatisfactory in their conduct, but [had] closed down on the outbreak of [...] war before their operation had time to cause scandal'. Howat had queried whether the Committee should not obtain independent verification of this and the PCA denied it roundly, claiming that Jones, the Council's Secretary, had told it that the Committee had 'misconstrued' the Council's evidence. It had not.

The Committee heeded the plea of the CCGB and others for the same controls to apply to public and private crematoria and recommended that the 'siting and establishment and [...] plans of all new crematoria shall be subject to official approval before the crematorium opens'. Since this would require amendment of the Cremation Act, it was, strictly speaking, outwith the Committee's remit. The Committee had decided at its first meeting, however, that it would report upon proposals to amend the Act.

Of these there were two others which the Committee supported. The first was the removal of the requirement for an application for cremation to be attested by a statutory declaration. The other was the introduction of ministerial control of fees charged for medical certificates. The Act required charges or fees for 'the burning of human remains' in public crematoria to be ministerially approved. A fee for a medical certificate is not a fee for 'the burning of human remains'. With the National Health Service came a review to reduce and simplify the certificates provided by doctors and to determine which were covered by doctors' terms of service and so came free of charge. It was hoped that cremation certificates would be so regarded or that the Board of Trade and Central Price Regulation Committee would be able to regulate fees for them. With these hopes dashed,[13] the Committee recommended that the fees should be uniform across the country and subject to an upper limit set by the Home Secretary. The HO had initially accepted that, if the MH agreed, charges by private crematoria should be subject to approval by the Ministry, but this proposal found no way into the Committee's report.

Fees were one of the two matters most canvassed before the Committee. The other was whether to retain the three certification Forms B, C and F and in particular Form C. Opinion about it was evenly divided among the witnesses to the Committee, with even medical referees split. In the end the Committee proposed a solution along lines first suggested by the Deputy Chief Medical Officer of the DHS: medical referees would be abolished and Forms C and F combined and given in England and Wales by Medical Officers of Health (MOH) assisted by panels of doctors chosen by local authorities, and in Scotland by the hospital service.

The CS had always protested against the prohibition on cremating anyone who had left a written direction to the contrary. The Committee approved not only the ban's retention but its extension, following the precedent to be set in the National Assistance Bill. Under this a local authority obligated to deal with a dead body was to be empowered to have it cremated; but as a result of the Lord Advocate's intervention, the Bill was amended so the authority would be prohibited from doing so if it had reason to believe that cremation would be contrary to the deceased's wishes (NAA 1948 s.50(1), (6)). The Committee recommended that it should be unlawful to cremate someone 'known to have held views or beliefs inconsistent with cremation'.[14]

---

13. The Safford (1949: 30, 60) Committee on medical certificates ruled that Forms B and C were not medical certificates because they were reports of investigations.
14. The Anatomy Act 1832 s. 7 prohibited the dissection of persons who had expressed objections to their corpses being so used in writing at any time or verbally in the presence of two witnesses during their terminal illnesses. The Corneal Grafting Act of 1952 s. 1(2) would prohibit the removal of eyes from a corpse if the deceased, having once expressed an objection to this, had not withdrawn it.

The other major matter considered by the Committee was the Code of Cremation Practice. The Committee welcomed it and recommended that some of its provisions should be incorporated in the Cremation Regulations. Three, as formulated by the Committee, were identical in substance to the Code's. These were: that no-one should be permitted to enter the committal room except with the express permission of the Superintendent of the crematorium; that the ashes from each cremation should be kept separate and when sent by rail or post should be so in suitable containers; and that each coffin should be cremated separately – the Committee made no comment on the practice expressly permitted by the Code of cremating a mother and her stillborn child in the same coffin. The matters about which the Committee would have regulations more precise than the Code related to interference with a body or a coffin at the crematorium and the disposal of metals. The Committee made no comment on the Code's prohibition of officials of a cremation authority acting as funeral directors.

Of the twenty-seven recommendations made by the Committee the two that evoked most disagreement among the consultees of the Committee were those relating to the treatment of metals at crematoria and the second medical certificate. HO officials proposed to cut the Gordian knot over the first by suggesting that metals could be removed with the consent of relatives. The second certificate posed much more of a problem.

The HO consulted the MH. Dr James Fenton, an Acting Principal Medical Officer at the Ministry who had been an MOH himself, persuaded Strutt that the issuing of the certificate could be left to MOHs without involving doctors. Both apprehended that this would antagonise the British Medical Association (BMA) which was opposed to a combined certificate and to the involvement of MOHs. Hoping that it would temper the Association's opposition to the combined certificate, they decided to accept the Association's suggestion of a fee of two guineas plus a mileage allowance for issuing Certificate B (and Certificate C) but, before doing so, to ask the MH officially whether this would be in line with other medical fees that it had to approve.

Since the Ministry had no responsibility for setting or approving fees for cremation certificates, the only knowledge it had of them was from complaints. There was confusion. Some thought that more was charged for Certificate B than for Certificate C and some less. Some thought that more was justifiable and some less. Eventually, fortified by the Ministry of National Insurance's rather surprising agreement that a fee of two guineas would not be unreasonable – the Ministry had to fund the death grant – the HO arranged a meeting with representatives of the BMA and Society of Medical Officers of Health at which the Association reiterated its opposition to any statutory regulation of the fees – although it was prepared to countenance local committees of the Association recommending 'suitable' fees – and both the Association and the Society, which had not previously expressed any views on the Committee's recommendation, opposed any involvement of MOHs in the proposed procedure. Although not reflected in these exact terms in the approved note of the meeting, Howat was told, 'Strutt summed up by saying that the difficulties in introducing the Committee's scheme appeared to be insuperable [...] He gave it as his impression that the scheme appeared to be dead.'

Meanwhile there had been consultations in Scotland. Glaister, Kerr and the Glasgow Procurator Fiscal were strongly opposed to the abolition of medical referees. The Lord Advocate, on balance, favoured retaining the present system while strengthening Certificate C. At a meeting at the DHS, Glaister and Kerr reiterated their views and the BMA's representatives echoed the view of their London colleagues. Howat was becoming increasingly frustrated. He wrote to his superior,

> that the Home Office appear to be wavering a bit on the proposal for a combined certificate. It would, I feel, be decidedly unfortunate if the issue were decided merely in the light of medical opinion, which [...] is by no means unprejudiced. After all, the cremation certificates mean a good deal of money to the profession; and, again, the Medical Referees do not want to think that their jobs could be done by others [...] The arguments advanced by the Medical Referees [...] were rather over-stated [...] I had a word with Dr Walker (a BMA representative at the meeting) [...] after our Scottish meeting, from which I gathered that his view was that Scottish doctors might [...] be willing at least to consider the abolition of Form C in Scotland even if a similar step was not considered in England.

Shortly after he wrote to Strutt,

> Frankly, I am deeply perturbed at the way things are developing. It looks as if we dare not do anything [...] if the doctors see fit to object [...] It does seem rather a poor show if the net result of all our consideration of the medical aspects of cremation is going

to be that doctors get an official blessing to certain somewhat generous fees – fees which even then are not binding on them. For my part, I would much prefer the fee issue left alone until we had cleared our minds about certification.

Cremation Act and Regulations 1952[15]

Because there was little chance of parliamentary time being found for Government legislation to enact the committee's recommendations which required it (including the statutory regulation of fees) and because the HO did not regard them as having high priority, all that could be done was to draft amendments to the cremation forms and obtain the BMA's commitment to regulate fees. A draft letter to the Association was prepared in which the word 'maximum' was inserted between 'suitable' and 'fee'. At this point, however, Joseph Reeves, the MP for Greenwich and a member of the CS's Council, aided by the HO, secured a First Reading for a Ten Minute Rule Cremation Bill, long contemplated by the Society (Reeves 1952). It contained a clause empowering a Minister to prescribe maximum fees for cremation certificates. It would also facilitate local authorities combining to provide crematoria[16] and allow them to provide crematoria even if they did not have a cemetery; make the site and plans of private crematoria subject to the same requirement of ministerial approval as public ones; remove the necessity for statutory declarations to attest applications for cremation; and reduce the limit in the radius clause from 200 to 100 yards.[17] The letter to the BMA was put on hold.

While the CS and FBCA were harmonious partners in the CCGB, the Federation had supported the amendment of the radius clause. Now it

---

15. This section is based on **CSA**: CRE/P/6/A; **NRS**: AD 64/4, AD 64/408/5, HH 61/109/, 18, 20, 24, HH 61/129; **TNA**: HO 282/25, HO 282/40, RG 48/2188.
16. Lawyers differed about whether local authorities which were not burial authorities could do this, and there was concern that a ratepayer, opposed to cremation, might challenge an authority which sought to do so.
17. The first drafts of the Bill would have allowed cremation authorities to select the ministers of religion to perform services at their crematoria. The Society was persuaded to drop this as being too controversial and likely to scupper the Bill. It had also wanted to remove the prohibition on erecting crematoria on consecrated ground but was persuaded not to pursue this as being too uncertain in effect because of the complicated legal effects of consecration.

joined with the Association of Municipal Corporation, whose members owned 70% of crematoria, to oppose not only this but the development of any more private crematoria except as replacements for those already existing. 'This is it,' wrote Reeves about the observations the Federation had submitted to the HO; 'Unless we can smother this document and all that is behind it we are lost.' Gilbert Mitchison, the Labour MP for Kettering, did the Association's and Federation's work in committee on the Bill. Possibly because all but one of the crematoria in Scotland were private Mitchison sought – unsuccessfully – to exclude Scotland from the Bill. In fact the DHS and the Lord Advocate's Department were at first unsure whether they wanted the Bill extended to Scotland because a Bill was being finalised to consolidate Scottish burial and cremation law (ch. 8). Apart from the Scottish Bill's provision about the radius clause (which was more radical than the provision in Reeves' Bill) the two Bills were compatible and the Department eventually decided that no difficulties would arise from the Bill's applying to Scotland.

In committee Mitchison defeated the amendment to the radius clause but failed to secure local authorities a monopoly of the development of crematoria. There was no controversy about the Bill's doing away with the necessity for statutory declarations to support applications for cremation. There was some over the statutory regulation of fees for cremation certificates.

Power was to be conferred on a Secretary of State to prescribe maximum fees not as an amendment to section 7 of the 1902 Act but as a stand-alone section, thus avoiding the unprecedented step of charging excessive fees a crime. But the clause did not require fees to be prescribed. Mitchison objected to this and, although unable to change it, did secure an undertaking from the HO Minister that should the HO not come to a satisfactory voluntary arrangement with the BMA about maximum fees the Home Secretary 'will certainly wish to use' the power.

Mitchison also secured an amendment to require an application for cremation to be independently verified. Regulations would be required to say by whom. To ensure these came into operation at the same time as the Act, the activation of the Act was delayed for three months and regulations under the 1902 Act were made subject to the ordinary negative resolution procedure. Even so, time was short and the HO decided that it would not extend the new regulations to implement the other changes recommended by the Interdepartmental Committee (and in particular to the wording of the cremation forms – even Form A) but would confine them to itemising the class of persons competent to verify an application for cremation. There was a 'surprising amount of controversy' about who should be included, most particularly with the DHS about whether a doctor who had given either of the medical certificates should be able to verify an application for cremation. Both sets of regulations came into force in September 1952. Doctors were to be able to verify applications for cremation in any circumstances either side of the border.

CHAPTER SEVEN

Glasgow and the West, 1945–1967: The National Context of Post-war Planning

The experience of war seems to have been a key factor in the rising public preference for cremation by Lowland families. The first year of war saw an increase of 25% in Scottish cremations (1939: 2,343 (3.33%; with total UK cremations 3.51%) the last, 4,689 cremations (7.48%; with total UK cremations 7.8%). From 1940 to 1944, the cremation rate in Scotland exceeded that of England. Thus, it seems that legal restrictions on cremation had had little practical effect in Scotland.

In 1945 Scotland's cemetery managers did not assume that within a generation cremation would overtake burial as the nation's preference.[1] The two largest conurbations, Clydeside and Midlothian, continued to rely upon private cemetery provision. In the straitened economic circumstances, all capital projects faced restrictions and crematoria, additionally, needed authority and borrowing consent from the Department of Health for Scotland (DHS). From 1888 Scotland's cremation movement had been initiated by voluntary societies and private initiatives; after 1945 local authorities worked hand in hand with the DHS to take over the leadership.

The Role of the Department of Health for Scotland

A document in the National Records of Scotland, probably composed in early 1954, is a key indicator of the role of national government in local

---

1. See ch. 6.

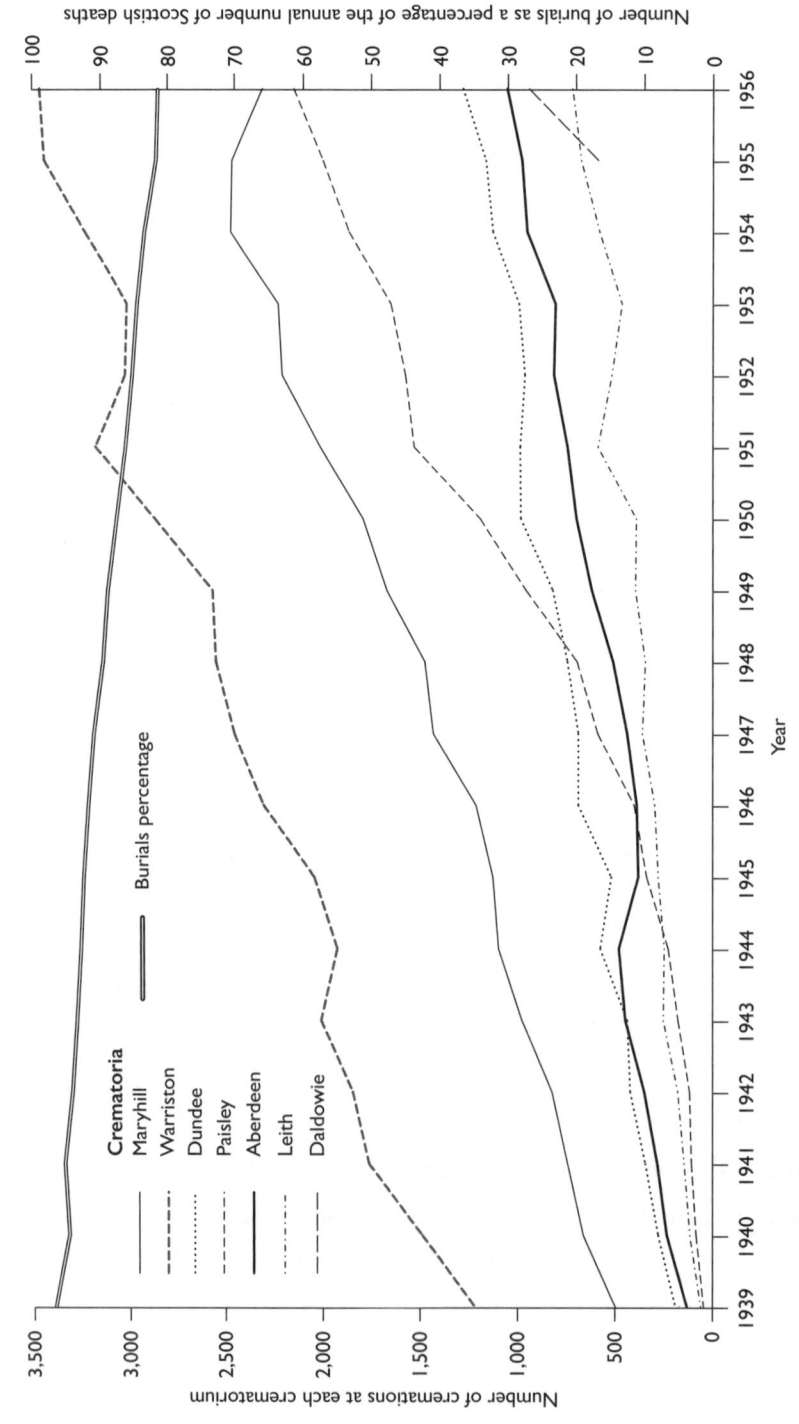

Graph 2. The graph shows the annual numbers of cremations at each of Scotland's first six crematoria, 1939–56, and the first year of Daldowie. Daldowie was the first of the great phase of crematoria building by Local Authorities. The first six crematoria played a vital role in making cremation an acceptable alternative to burial; just under one fifth of Scottish funerals involved cremation in 1956.

decision-making.[2] It focuses on the Clyde basin, listing established crematoria as Maryhill and Paisley with Daldowie nearing completion, and then describing tentative proposals for new crematoria. The author lists the catchment areas and where they overlap. He considers the criteria for establishing a crematorium in the Clyde basin that would pay its way: it should be accessible to between 50,000 people and preferably 100,000, most living within five miles' car drive from the proposed site (the DHS had consulted funeral directors on this issue). The strong but minority Catholic presence in the area has been overlooked. Furthermore, the author makes no mention either of how cremation numbers have risen in Scotland since 1939 or, comparatively, with England and Wales.

At the Cremation Society's (CS) conference in Ayr in 1955 the Under-Secretary of State for Scotland surprised delegates by revealing the front-runners for approval as Kirkcaldy, Kilmarnock (later, Ayr) and Greenock, with Falkirk, Dumbarton (later, Cardross), Clydebank and Castlemilk (later, The Linn) behind them.[3] His address signalled the formal, public support of the Scottish Office for cremation (Stewart 1955).

All these projects save one endured a long gestation: Daldowie (1955) took twenty-two years, Greenock (1959) took ten years, Cardross (1960) thirteen, Ayr (1966) twenty-nine, and Clydebank (1967) took only three years. In the east, the time-line was even longer: Dunfermline (1973) thirty-eight years, Kirkcaldy (1959) twenty-one, Mortonhall (1967) nineteen, Perth (1962) and Falkirk (1962) each seventeen. No crematorium was to be built in the west after 1967 for thirty years; in the east after 1975 for eighteen. This chapter now addresses three major post-war projects in the west: Daldowie, the Necropolis and the Linn.

Daldowie: The Project Resumes[4]

In 1943 Councillor John Mann was appointed Chairman of Lanarkshire's Social Welfare Committee, whose responsibilities included burial grounds. Mann immediately revived the Crematorium Sub-Committee, and in

2. NRS HH 61/690 'Selection of Crematoria Sites in the Clyde Basin, with Special Reference to the South Bank', no author and undated but c.1954, documents 235 and 236.
3. *Pharos* 21(3), 2.
4. For minutes of relevant meetings, see Lanarkshire County Council minutes at the Mitchell Library Glasgow, in the series commencing CO/1/3/1/83.

February 1944 inspected two sites, the 'Ice-house Field' at Daldowie, which had been considered suitable in 1939, and the Murray Memorial Chapel in Lanark Cemetery, which might be adapted as a crematorium.[5] Further discussion was halted with the Normandy invasion.

At the election in July 1945 Lanarkshire returned its first majority Labour administration. Mann was elected County Convenor. The tasks facing Lanarkshire were many; Mann had to postpone his plans for the crematorium. Yet in September 1946 he recalled his Crematorium Sub-Committee after thirty months. He was now ready to proceed with his personal crusade.

County Architect W.R. Watt produced alternative proposals for Daldowie, the major decision being between two chapels or one. The designs offered an imposing building on a large area of land, the Ice-house Field or Chuckie Hill, each flanked by the Clyde. The committee preferred the two-chapel design, at an estimated cost of £70,000. Formal approval was given by the full County Council at its November meeting, and a letter seeking approval sent to the Secretary of State via the DHS. In September 1947 the Town Clerk reported that the DHS had intimated it would in principle approve the Daldowie site.

During the winter, Committee Chairman Lindsay died and Councillor R.L. Brodie succeeded him. The Secretary of State had not yet authorised the beginning of building work so in October 1948 Brodie's committee itemised necessary preliminary works. Intent on its Lanarkshire project, it may have resented offers of collaboration from neighbouring councils as an intrusion. In October 1949, at the instigation of Motherwell Town Council, some neighbouring Councils discussed providing crematoria on a joint basis. Brodie defended his Daldowie scheme stoutly and moved swiftly to request the DHS for a starting date on its construction.

The DHS responded within five weeks. While it was prepared to secure as early a starting date as possible, it suggested that the Daldowie proposals be pursued on a more modest scale. The Town Clerk met with DHS technical officers and offered concessions. Revisions were discussed in February 1950. The work was to be completed in three phases over a period of five years. The first phase would be the building of a large chapel, the crematory chamber and furnaces, the Chapel of Remembrance and the administrative offices, over two years. The second would include the second chapel and the mortuary and the third the ancillary work with the columbarium and

5. LCC, CO/1/3/1/83 1944, p. 612.

Garden of Rest. The DHS had decided in January 1950 that, subject to local planning permissions, it would approve the proposals but in July 1950 ruled out the columbarium.

In April 1951 a special meeting considered Watt's revised cost estimates for the whole project. The total sum, based on the lowest tenders received, was £211,256. The scale of post-war inflation may be gauged by the fact that the costs of the crematorium buildings had risen from £46,000 (1946) to £114,630 (1951). In July word came that the Secretary of State had approved the plans (subject to minor modifications) for Phase One. The Ministry of Works (MOW) awarded a starting date of 1 August 1951.

The laying of the foundation stone

The date of 26 September 1952 represented a personal triumph for Mann. His speech is revealing.[6] He praises the public health reformers of the 1840s and 1850s but omits Glasgow's almost entire neglect of its responsibilities to provide public cemeteries. His account of the origins and development of the Crematorium emphasises the economic advantages to the Council but lays no great stress on the money and trouble bereaved families will be saved. His history of the cremation movement makes no mention either of the Cremation Society of Great Britain or of the Scottish Burial Reform and Cremation Society's pioneering work at Maryhill. While commenting with hindsight, however, it is improper to detract from Mann's achievement. He had, over nineteen years, initiated, argued and fought to establish Scotland's first publicly commissioned crematorium.

Three years in the building

Brodie and Watt were kept busy. Much was achieved at the meeting of March 1953. The DHS had given Watt permission to continue from Phase One without a break in the masons' programme, including works from Phases Two and Three to ensure the building was wind- and water-tight. The MOW also agreed that 1 August 1951 should now be regarded as the starting date for the whole project, thus removing a number of timing and financial restrictions for the County Council.

The Councillors were intent on providing a public service that would replace the urban culture of burial, which they believed had disadvantaged

---

6. Mann's speech was printed as an Appendix (pp. 2169–71) to the Welfare Services meeting of 13/10/1952, p. 2168, CO1/3/1/100. See *Glasgow Herald*, 27/9/1952.

generations of bereaved Clydeside families. The March 1954 meeting debated the delicate issue of charges. The first years would certainly see an excess of expenditure over income but the aim would be to achieve a balance after six years. The Committee boldly anticipated 500 cremations in the first full year, building up thereafter to 2,500 cremations in the sixth year. This calculation produced a cremation fee of eight guineas for the cremation fee, comparing favourably with other crematoria in Scotland. Lanarkshire's Councillors operated on the principle that the cremation fee should be as all-inclusive as practicable and 'incidental charges for odds and ends' be kept to a minimum. After comparing other crematoria fee levels, they decided to make music and floral decorations part of the inclusive price and, as the Chief Medical Officer was to act as Medical Referee, no separate certificate fee need be charged (though he could have requested it; see ch. 8, n. 51).

Over the next months a range of decisions was made. Thomas L. Reid, the Superintendent and Registrar of Paisley, was selected for the Superintendent's post at a salary of £820 p.a., and then offered the combined post of Superintendent and Registrar but at the salary already agreed. There would be a panel of four organists and when the number of cremations in a week reached fifteen a full-time organist would be appointed. Hymnbooks were to be bought for both Church of Scotland and Church of England services. Mann would officiate on the opening date, now fixed for 1 October 1954. There were hitches: overtime payments were conceded; the electric furnaces were delayed; and the opening date twice rearranged. The Crematorium was officially opened on 17 February 1955.

Daldowie first exceeded 2,500 cremations in 1966 (2,616 for the whole year) but by that time the Linn, open for only four years, had reached 1,519. If Daldowie had been intended to encourage the Glasgow area to adopt cremation, it had certainly succeeded.

The Glasgow Necropolis[7]

In 1939 Glasgow's Maryhill had conducted 498 cremations; by 1945, 1,127. The SBRCS had gained greater influence when its Chairman, Baillie John Biggar, was elected Provost of the City of Glasgow in 1941. He suggested that the Society approach the City Council with a view to providing a new

7. For Necropolis Committee and other Merchant House minutes, see the Mitchell Library, Glasgow.

site for a publicly-owned crematorium, either at Aitkenhead Park or at Castlemilk.

Biggar died unexpectedly on 8 August 1943. His successor was Professor John Glaister, as ardent a cremationist as his father, but without Biggar's political authority. Thus the opportunity that Biggar might have had as Provost to persuade the City Council to build its own crematorium was lost. The initiative for a second Glasgow crematorium moved first to the Merchants House and later to the City Council.

In September 1945 a member of the Merchants House revived the proposal for a crematorium at the Necropolis (which had been twice rejected in the 1930s). The Necropolis Committee was asked to consider the issue. It called for an Ordnance Survey map covering the Necropolis. This was to examine the restrictions of the 200-yard radius clause required by the Cremation Act 1902. In May 1947 a surveyor reported that all the ground in the Necropolis was within 200 yards of some dwelling-house. The Committee opted to promote a Provisional Order to circumnavigate these restrictions. This would take time. The Merchants House, as a private organisation, obviously could not apply for Government financial support.

In October 1947 the Merchants House discontinued its Necropolis Committee, its members' failure to show any enthusiasm to take decisions for its future impelled the Directors of the Merchants House to take decisive action. Henceforward, the Finance Committee would supervise the both the cemetery and crematorium project. In February 1948 it authorised a deputation to call upon the Secretary of State as a preliminary for promoting a Provisional Order (PO). The Secretary declined an interview. Applications for POs had to be in by 27 March 1948 or be delayed until November. The Directors gave their consent to pursuing the Order on 14 June 1949 and their PO was confirmed on 28 July 1950.

Meanwhile, the Finance Committee passed a recommendation from the sub-committee on Necropolis finances for raising grave fees, as the burial ground was a continuing drain upon the Merchant House's resources. A successful crematorium might revive the cemetery. A Crematorium Sub-Committee was set up, enlisting leading Merchants House Directors. In April 1952 it reviewed the architect's drawings. A statement of costs was ready by May and a Memorandum prepared for the quarterly meeting of Directors in June.

The June meeting proved decisive for the Necropolis project. The Crematorium Committee argued that in time the crematorium would not only pay for itself but also cover the loss on the Necropolis. Ideally, two chapels would accommodate twenty-four funerals in a day. The profitable level was 6,000 cremations a year; this would take time to establish (Warriston had only achieved 3,000 for the first time in 1951). However, the crematorium would cost £100,000, its running costs would be £16,700 annually and the loss on the Necropolis would continue. The Merchants House had limited capital reserves of which the crematorium project would take one half. The assembled Directors will have asked themselves whether this was a risk worth taking, reflecting that in a Catholic city, some 15% of the population was prohibited from choosing an alternative to burial. It was agreed that the Crematorium Committee would reconsider their proposal.

Having met with their architect and reviewed his reduced estimate four days later, the Committee asked the Collector to report to the Finance Committee. The Collector's report raised insuperable problems. First, though the architect had produced a simplified crematorium at £55,000, its single chapel could accommodate only twelve funerals a day. This would just cover the costs. Secondly, to invest in a crematorium would skew the Merchants House's image by making funerals its major and public priority. Some Directors may have felt that the House, with its charitable purposes, would prefer not to be seen to profit from cremation.[8] Other Directors acknowledged that the dignity of the House would be put at risk. Yet if the House set fees below those of the private crematoria, the Necropolis' financial position would be made worse. No mention was made of Daldowie's imminent foundation stone ceremony.

On 10 March 1953 the Merchants House Directors voted to accept the recommendation of their Sub-Committee that the proposal to build a crematorium at the Necropolis should be indefinitely postponed.

There is an issue of happenstance. How different might it have been if Lord Provost John Biggar had not died unexpectedly in 1942? Here was a leading Socialist, anticipating a Beveridge-planned Welfare State, a cremationist by conviction and Chairman of the SBRCS, with its existing crematorium. If Biggar had survived, he might have been in exactly the right position to position a Glasgow Council crematorium project second in the queue for Government funding behind neighbouring Lanarkshire.

8. The 1966 litigation (see p. 174 below) would be an illustration of the principle that making a profit on a service does not necessarily prevent an organisation being a charity.

Then the Merchants House would never have needed to reconsider its own Necropolis project but could have concentrated on reviving its burial ground, plans which did not materialise until the 1980s (Crawshaw 1990).

Glasgow City Council[9]

The cost of delay

When Glasgow Corporation's Parks Committee received its agenda papers for their meeting in September 1945, the issue of the once handsome Western Southern Necropolis, now in liquidation, confronted them. Their bold response was 'to consider the whole question of the burial grounds in the city and report' and to entrust this task to a sub-committee. The City Council's minutes over the next five years suggest nothing was done. This only delayed an inevitable decision: the Council took over responsibility for the whole Southern Necropolis in 1952 (Hutt 1996).[10]

In March 1951 the Parks Department (Parks) was made formally responsible for 'additional cemetery accommodation and for crematoria to meet future requirements'. Two years later, a Special Sub-Committee on Burial Grounds and Crematoria (SSC) was appointed and recommended to Parks the reservation of an eighty-acre site south of the Carmunnock Road and east of the Linn Park estate, to contain both a cemetery and a crematorium. Parks backed this recommendation. In the period immediately after 1918, many private estates had been sold, thus making available sites well outside the 200-yard radius clause. The Linn, like Daldowie, was one: its 180 acres had been bought by Glasgow Corporation in 1919.

Planning for a crematorium

In August 1954 Parks asked the Secretary of State to agree in principle to the Carmunnock proposal; and began to prepare plans and estimates. The Town Clerk wrote to the DHS and waited patiently. By November an amended proposal relocated a cemetery at Castlemilk extending to 40 acres and an alternative site for the crematorium on adjacent land within Linn Park extending to 15.5 acres. Attention now focuses on the crematorium.

9. For minutes of relevant meetings, see Glasgow Council minute books at the Mitchell Library, Glasgow, in the series commencing CO/1/3/112.
10. In the late 1960s the City Council adopted the policy of taking over the old private cemeteries in Glasgow (The Corporation of Glasgow – Parks Department 1967; W.H. Smith 1969).

Two principle issues confronted Parks' plans. The first was delicate: a commercial proposal to build a crematorium in Craigton Cemetery had already received planning approval in principle by the Corporation. If the Craigton project went ahead, would the growing public interest in cremation be strong enough to accommodate a third crematorium? Indeed, could the DHS use Craigton to negate the Linn scheme? The Depute Town Clerk sought the Department's views.[11]

A second obstacle was more quickly solved. The City's Architects' Department had been asked to prepare plans nearly a year earlier. Now in November 1955 the City Architect replied that, owing to present commitments, it was not possible to produce the design at an early date. At this point the Town Clerk produced his master-stroke. He persuaded the Committee that met on 14 November to appoint Thomas S. Cordiner to undertake the work in association with the City Architect and the Director of Parks. Cordiner's appointment swiftly accelerated the Linn project.[12]

Meanwhile the Department considered Craigton. The DHS felt it was no longer practical to keep individual services such as crematoria within a total figure for Scotland. In his departmental note of 2 December (see Note 9) 'WJM' confirmed there was now no question of Craigton and the Linn being in direct competition for a limited capital allocation for crematoria. However, the Department's priority remained to keep local authority spending within the limits of the annual budget for capital expenditure. The Craigton scheme, for which Glasgow had by now felt obliged to give planning approval, would 'in the eyes of [...] the Department somewhat diminish the urgency of the Castlemilk scheme'. However, the Department would question 'fairly strongly' the scale of the Linn project: £250,000 seemed excessively large. 'We feel very doubtful about the idea of a "giant" crematorium – perhaps larger than Daldowie – which seems to be in view.'[13]

Bargaining with the DHS

A meeting between the DHS and Glasgow Corporation was arranged for March 1956.[14] For the Department, Howat was doubtful about the projected

11. NRS HH 61/690, untitled note by W.J. MacLehose to document 9, 2/12/1955.
12. See below.
13. NRS HH 61/690 McCulloch to Gavin, note on document 15, 17/2/1956.
14. Ibid., 'Crematorium at Linn Park, Castlemilk, Glasgow. Note of meeting

cost. Garside, Director of Parks, said that the substitution of the Castlemilk site for Carmunnock had reduced from eighty to fifty the acreage required for the joint project, still serving 'a population of up to 600,000 people'. It included six cremators serving two chapels. The latter would seat 120 people each but the aisles would allow twice that number. Baillie Cockburn pointed out that the Corporation already had heavy expenditure maintaining the city's old cemeteries. To limit the further growth of this burden, he was very anxious to provide for crematorium facilities on an adequate scale.

Howat responded that the Department thought it unlikely that a crematorium at the Linn would serve a population of more than 200,000 persons. Current mortality rates were 2,400 deaths a year. A single-chapel crematorium with just two cremators could handle 2,000 cremations a year. Then he gave the Glasgow representatives an encouraging steer. They should put forward a detailed case showing the urgency of building further cemetery provision and of the eastern section of the new road. Meanwhile, he concluded, discussions could be started at once with a view to a revised scheme for a single-chapel crematorium.[15]

A site meeting was held on 21 March 1956.[16] Garside rejected the estimate of 200,000 as the Linn's potential catchment population; 300,000–400,000 from all parts of Glasgow was more likely. Existing crematoria were already running at capacity at peak periods. Could the Department approve a small family chapel to supplement the main one? Gordon of the DHS suggested that, even allowing for a catchment of 300,000 people, one crematorium with three cremators should be able to meet any foreseeable demand. This moment seems to have been a breakthrough. An agreement was recorded that the main chapel should seat 150 people but be capable of taking 100 more. Furthermore there should be no columbarium. (This echoed the theme adopted at Daldowie that, as the whole building was a memorial to the dead, a columbarium was not specifically required.)

---

with Glasgow Corporation on 16/3/56' signed by McCulloch. Original ref: WS/55/GLW/2, pp. 216–19.
15. Ibid.
16. NRS HH 61/690, pp. 211–14. 'Crematorium – Linn Park, Glasgow. Meeting in the City Chambers, Glasgow, on Wednesday, 21 March 1956, at 10.30 a.m.' (signed by McCulloch).

Thereafter, and for seventeen more months, there are no more DHS notes on the progress of the Linn, during which time Craigton Crematorium was opened (1957). Glasgow Town Council was allowed to progress its Linn project without much supervision and the DHS minutes offer no explanation for its non-interruption. The Parks Committee met in June 1957 'to recommend [...] that a crematorium be provided at an estimated cost of £240,000'. The Town Clerk then applied to the DHS for borrowing consent.

The undiminished scale of the project clearly took the Department by surprise. It found Glasgow's proposals excessive. Technical Officers for the DHS and for Glasgow met on 17 December 1957,[17] with no Councillors present. They took out their scissors. It was then agreed that the initial work could be cut back to £190,000 by a series of measures: shortened covered ways to chapels; parking areas halved; carriageways narrowed; building of eastern road access to be delayed. The DHS wrote to the Corporation. The letter's penultimate paragraph marks the first Scottish reference to environmental protection. The Clean Air Act 1956 had been the UK Government's first serious legislation about air pollution. It was agreed that the Linn should fit smoke density indicators.

In October 1958 Connell and Gordon of the DHS organised a site visit to the Linn cemetery to check on its progress. The Glasgow Town Council contingent turned up in force including Bailie Flanagan (Chair, Parks), Hood (Depute Town Clerk), Garside, Cordiner and his deputy Watson. They insisted on adding the Crematorium to the meeting's agenda. The DHS minutes hint that its delegates had felt ambushed. However, the stratagem, if such it was, worked: it was agreed that Hood would make a formal approach to the Department for borrowing consents for the Crematorium,[18] including £27,000 to extend the car park, and £20,000 for an access road so the direct labour force working on the cemetery could start on the Crematorium.[19] The Department proved sympathetic, MacLehose writing, 'I think the pressure of one cortège upon another at Warriston Crematorium is a warning that it is reasonable to provide a really adequate space for cars to park and for the

---

17. NRS HH 61/690, note of meeting of 17/12/1957, by Pollock and Gordon, documents 162 and 163.
18. NRS HH 61/690, note of meeting of 21/10/1958, by Connell and Gordon, document 63 (copy of minutes by Gordon to Russell, 27/10/1958), pp. 125, 126.
19. Ibid.

incoming and outgoing traffic to move.'[20] In January 1959 the Department gave permission.

The Crematorium was finally opened on 22 October 1962 at a cost of £224,000. In the remaining three months of that year it carried out 137 cremations and in the next full year, 1,005. In 1970, it conducted 2,136 cremations, with Craigton 1,245, Maryhill 2,440 and Daldowie 3,240. Cremation in Glasgow was now an established alternative to burial.

The Roman Catholic Church: An Unexpected Decision

On 2 May 1964, a surprise announcement precipitated further changes in Scottish attitudes to cremation. The Roman Catholic Church had lifted its ban on cremation for Catholics.[21] The decision had been taken the previous year but secrecy had been imposed by the Holy Office. The delay probably owed something to the death and funeral of Pope John XXIII in June 1963. The decision itself owed much to the International Cremation Federation, founded in 1937 with a specific intention to persuade the Catholic Church to lift the ban (Jupp 2006a; see above, chs 3, 4).

The Vatican's statement recognised that 'the burning of the body […] has no effect on the soul, nor does it inhibit Almighty God from re-establishing the body again'.[22] It acknowledged that the 1886 ban had been imposed largely because of secular and political opposition to Catholics' dominance over cemeteries and burial rites. However, the Vatican emphasised its preference for burial, insisting that the Catholic funeral liturgy was never to be held at a crematorium nor were Catholic clergy to conduct the funeral liturgy. This insistence was removed in 1966 through the intervention of Fr John McDonald, a professor of moral theology.[23] This permission was soon adopted in Scottish Catholic dioceses, with a specific form of service for Scottish dioceses approved in 1973.

These decisions will have encouraged local authorities with Catholic ratepayers. Nevertheless, Catholic families were slow to change. Some Scottish

---

20. MacLehose to A.G. NRS HH 61/690, Departmental notes in document 64, 17/12/1958, p. 30.
21. *The Tablet*, 13/6/1964. See Vaughan 1890; Jupp 2006a: 163–8; McGinnell 2006, 2015.
22. Quotations from *Acta Apostolicae Sedis Official Commentary*, 24/10/1964, section III, 5: 13, 822–3, quoted in *Pharos* (February 1965), 15.
23. *Pharos* (November 1966), 91, 93; McDonald, personal communication, 1991.

funeral directing firms catered exclusively for Catholics or Protestants.[24] The underlying Catholic preference for burial persists (McGinnell 2006: 15; 2015). Yet, in a wider context, the Vatican decision reduced the influence of religion in British funeral choice. For the majority of Christians in Britain, cremation was from now on a matter of personal choice (Jupp 2006a: 168).

Charitable Status of the Scottish Burial Reform and Cremation Society

Since 1954 the SBRCS had been allowed charitable relief on the payment of income tax. One cannot but suspect that the opening of the Linn explains why, three weeks before the Crematorium came on stream, the Corporation turned down the Society's application for the 50% charitable rate relief to which it had just become entitled on its Maryhill crematorium (LGFPSA 1962 s. 4(1)(a)). More than three years later the Scottish Courts dismissed its claim but the House of Lords, which included the Scottish Lord Reid, unanimously upheld it.[25] The Society's surplus of £70,000 caused at least one of the Scottish judges to raise an eyebrow at its assertion that its charges were minimal. Another commented sardonically on the 'dialectical difficulty' of the Corporation's contending, on the one hand, that cremation was not a benefit to the public while, on the other, running a crematorium itself. Most surprising of all, perhaps, was that two of the Scottish judges required evidence (which was not advanced) that cremation was a public benefit, and only one, apart from Lord Reid, expressly accepted that the Burial Acts of the nineteenth century and the Cremation Acts warranted him in taking judicial notice (i.e. no evidence required) that it was. Following its success the Society dropped 'Burial Reform' from its name.

The Architectural Climate

The post-war period in Scotland was one in which modernist architecture became inextricably linked with ambitious utopian visions representing a new social order based on equality and improvement, whether for the living or the dead. The country witnessed an unprecedented programme of

---

24. Interviews with Glasgow funeral directors, 2011.
25. Scottish Burial Reform and Cremation Society v Glasgow Corporation 1966, 1968, NRS CS 258/1966/4002, 4003.

national reconstruction. This was an age of architectural opportunity. In the words of architects Alan Reiach and Robert Hurd, 'Here is a new Scotland to be built.'[26]

Two Scottish architectural traditions had emerged at the beginning of the twentieth century. To the west, in Glasgow, a rational, progressive style rooted in Beaux-Arts classicism, and to the east in Edinburgh a traditional ideal embodying Scottish national values.[27] Both continued through the 1920s and 1930s. The 1938 Glasgow Empire Exhibition showed Beaux-Arts modernity having added influences drawn from European and American Art Deco. In the early 1950s, while traditional ideas persisted in Edinburgh, there was now a growing consensus that the forward-thinking modernist style practised in Glasgow was better suited to a Socialist state's ambitions and the building of 'a new Scotland'.

The thirteen crematoria built between 1955 and 1975 represent, in microcosm, the architectural expression of the progressive social policies of local authorities which were working for the greatest good for the greatest number. Crematoria took their place among public and civic buildings, schools, fire-stations, old peoples' homes, shops, banks, technical colleges, training centres – all little engines of modern post-war urban life. Architects considered the designing of a crematorium as an opportunity to serve the public, although most of them would be afforded only one such chance.

Daldowie: Architecture as Remembrance

Daldowie, the UK's seventy-fifth and Scotland's seventh crematorium opened in 1955. County Architect William Robertson Watt (d. 1963), together with his Deputy D.C. Bannerman, prepared two sketch plans in 1946 – one involving a single chapel, the other two chapels and a mortuary chapel. The latter was approved, subject to minor alteration, by the DHS and the cost capped at £68,800. Watt is thought to have visited some '30 or 40 crematoria with members of his committee'[28] in seven years. John Arnott, who worked with Watt on the project, argued that since crematorium design

---

26. Reiach and Hurd 1941, quoted in Glendinning 1997: 3; Grainger 2012.
27. For a full account of post-war developments in Scotland see Glendinning 1997: 1–45.
28. Arnott 1957: 46–53, 46. In 1946 the Council visited Woking, Golders Green, Streatham Park and Islington. CO 1/3/1/88 Lanarkshire CC minutes 1946, vol. 2. They also visited Maryhill, Warriston and Dundee.

was 'a subject relatively untouched in the realms of technical literature' and given the fact that about '60 out of the 90 crematoria built in this country in the last 50 years had been conversions',[29] then the only way architects could gain experience was by visiting existing crematoria. Watt recalled the design being drawn on a piece of paper in a hotel while he and representatives of the County Council were undertaking a tour of established crematoria in London.[30] But building restrictions halted progress until 1949 when site preparation finally began. The crematorium was built in three phases: 1951–3; 1953–5; 1955–6.

Daldowie was the first Scottish crematorium to be built for sixteen years and more importantly, the first built entirely by a local authority and at an eventual cost close to £250,000 – widely in excess of its predecessors. Described as 'the largest and most ambitious crematorium scheme to have been carried out in this country for many years',[31] it heralded the 'heroic age' of local authority crematorium building between 1955 and 1975.

Although traditional in style, it marked a shift from the architectural pluralism of its predecessors to a clear architectural concept – that of the physical embodiment of remembrance, Arnott arguing that, 'The whole conception of this scheme is that the building should in itself be a memorial to those who are cremated at Daldowie.'[32]

Contemporary style was avoided, the architect believing that mourners

> are attending under emotional stress, paying their last respects to one who meant a great deal to them, and at a time like that they probably require a feeling of solidity, stability and tradition and the comfort of permanence and some sense of the continuity of life, expressed in the design of the building; it is no time for disquiet caused by unusual structural techniques. No one wants this.[33]

Perhaps prompted by the classical house formerly on the site, Watt's design fostered a sense of continuity while acknowledging 'the standard set by the War Graves Commission in their memorials' since this

---

29. Arnott 1957: 46.
30. *The Glasgow Herald*, 18/2/1955.
31. Arnott 1957: 46.
32. Ibid., 50
33. Ibid., 48.

was 'timeless architecture'[34] represented by classicism. The Technical Secretary of the Federation of British Cremation Authorities (FBCA) believed the Council 'had created a place of simple dignity and beauty [...] a great example to the world and given 'a lead in Great Britain'.[35] In so doing, Glasgow had recaptured some of the architectural ground from Edinburgh.

Daldowie was executed in cream stone from Northumberland, the architect quipping that 'Unfortunately all the Scottish quarries were engaged in the hydro-electric scheme and consequently we had to go to England for stone.'[36] This remark speaks volumes about the preference that Scots showed for local materials. The crematorium is hexagonal. The projecting chapels, lying on axial lines radiating from the core of the scheme are drawn together as a circle by a pergola. The entrances to the chapels are the points at which the circle is broken, perhaps symbolising death. The cremating chamber lies at the core, above which rises a copper dome containing the flues from the cremators. Significantly, there is no visible chimney. Watt must surely have been aware of G. Berkeley Wells' design for Reading (1932) and J.P. Chaplin's for Northampton (1939) both featuring domes with flues brought over into the centre of the cupolas in order to camouflage the chimneys. The chapels are rectangular, simple in style, light and airy and with clear views of the grounds and polished Peterhead granite catafalques positioned in apses. There is also a dignified austerity about the small but richly decorated Chapel of Remembrance, where the internal columns supporting the dome are of Portland stone.

Daldowie initiated new rituals. Watt and Arnott believed a crematorium ought ideally to occupy a new site and the larger the better. An architect designing for an existing cemetery site 'has automatically got a certain atmosphere before he starts: he is not starting on a virgin site and he is not creating his own atmosphere. You are bound to see headstones on the way to the crematorium and that, I think, is not the atmosphere which should be associated with a crematorium'.[37] Daldowie occupied a generous site on a former estate. Mourners cross a 'threshold' from the busy roads to undertake the long, hearse-driven processional route through the estate

34. Ibid., 48.
35. *Glasgow Herald*, 18/2/1955, 10.
36. Arnott 1957: 50.
37. Ibid., 51.

grounds, thereby initiating a new ritual, involving time and distance where the journey in itself might offer spiritual significance in its engagement with the natural surroundings. There are no porte-cochères. Entry is direct and mourners leave by a choice of door from the entrance vestibule, either to the pergola walk or directly to the car park.

The second change of ritual involves the method of removal of the coffin. The dominance of burial in Scotland had cast a long shadow and accordingly coffins descended in all Scottish pre-war crematoria. Here, for the first time, they are removed horizontally, although this had not been the original intention.

This was also the first time that Scottish architects had talked about the psychological impact of a crematorium. There should be no association with a cemetery, they argued, 'no suggestion of the many thousands who have gone before; the attempt should be made to create the feeling that each, as it were, is the first to be there, and that the crematorium is there for that particular service only. It is largely a question of atmosphere and psychology.'[38] This view anticipated the phenomenological analysis of buildings in the 1970s, which reflected on the importance of 'experiencing' architecture.

The last crematorium in Scotland to adopt a traditional style, Daldowie occupies a pivotal point between past and present, being innovative in its integration of disposal, ritual and remembrance and the idea that natural surroundings might play a role in assuaging grief, an idea adopted enthusiastically thereafter in Scotland.

Craigton Crematorium

Craigton, Glasgow's third crematorium, opened in 1957. It was a joint project between the Co-operative Group and the funeral directors Wylie & Lockhead. The only privately owned of the period, while interesting, is much less imposing. Its architect James Steel Maitland, responsible for Paisley Crematorium in 1938, described himself as an 'Unrepentant Traditionalist' (Maitland 1952: 319), at a time when the boundaries between 'national' traditionalism and 'international' modernity were beginning to break down after the war. Constructed from brick faced in cream roughcast, the crematorium forms a single-storey group with flat roofs interrupted only by the pitched slate roof of the chapel, the chimney being attached at the rear of the crematory.

38. Ibid., 51.

Greenock and Scandinavian Modernism

Greenock Town Council, estimating only thirty years of burial space left, initiated its crematorium project in 1949 but had to await DHS (1953) and Secretary of State (1956) approval. The Council had to obtain a Provisional Order to obviate the 'radius' clause. Greenock Crematorium followed Craigton in 1959 and was designed by Inverclyde Council's architect Stuart Clink (1912–1981) of Cullen, Lockhead & Brown, a long-established practice based in Hamilton. The Crematorium is located within the cemetery, where a new road wound uphill to the grounds of the former Caddlehill House where, so far as possible, trees were preserved to create a verdant backdrop to the new building. Clink looked to the well-mannered and humane Swedish Modernist style rooted in social welfare, popular in England as a result of the Festival of Britain in 1951. The Council was well attuned to the needs of a contemporary society, hard hit by the war, especially on Clydeside. The design acknowledged both the modernity of cremation and advances in secular thinking.

Greenock, constructed from handmade mellow red brick with synthetic stone dressings, had a Westmorland green slate roof providing a striking contrast to its light walls. One of the defining features of the design is the five-bay flat-roofed loggia, with pylon-like openings running along the entrance front. No attempt was made to disguise the tall, broad chimney with its copper cap. The attention to detail is notable, for example the block panel with the coat of arms of the Burgh of Greenock in relief. Once again materials were of a very high quality. The floor of the entrance hall is formed with travertine tile with inserts of Emperor Napoleon tile and a border of rosso levanto marble, and the walls are lined with a simple panelling of limba, a light-coloured timber used throughout for all the furnishings and fittings.

The entrance hall, at right angles to the main axis of the chapel, has a doorway on the opposite side of the building, offering an alternative exit leading to the formal garden beyond. On the main axis of the building, an extension of the entrance hall forms a Hall of Memory housing the Book of Remembrance. A plate-glass screen divides these two spaces from the main chapel. Clink clearly followed the lead of Sanger and Rothwell at Kirkcaldy (1954) in opening up the chapel and bringing the formal garden 'within' the building. A second chapel designed to accommodate small funerals is entered from the loggia. Wherever possible, flower boxes are integrated into the building, in keeping with contemporary style. The original decoration was very much of the period, with hourglass lamp fittings and the wall housing the 'sanctuary' for the catafalque painted in a very rich purple with gold fleur-de-lys motifs contrasting with the light pastel shades of the walls. Greenock illustrates two distinctive approaches adopted by local authorities in Scotland; that of often venturing beyond their own Architect's Departments in commissioning architects of local standing and of invariably seeking to employ the best quality materials that budgets would allow.

Cardross: Simplicity and Landscape

Argyll and Bute Council had reserved a ten-acre site for a cemetery and a crematorium in 1947.[39] While the cemetery opened in 1950, the Council had to wait another seven years before DHS authorised the building. John Watson (1903–1977) of Watson, Salmond & Gray, designed Cardross Crematorium in 1960. An arresting geometric and studiously plain building, with cream harled walls and green copper roofs, it commands a magnificent view across the Clyde and surrounding Argyll hills. This was the first of Scotland's crematoria to occupy such an exposed site and as such prompts some consideration of the important role that landscape and its relationship with the Scottish psyche would assume in the future. At the Glasgow Empire Exhibition the emphasis had been on Beaux-Arts modernity, but 'Amongst the "technically efficient" ranks of exhibition pavilions [...] were islands of romanticism, such as the re-run of the "clachan" exhibit from 1911, with its thatched house and painted castle. Scotland's "national identity" was now firmly identified as a landscape issue' (MacInnes, Glendinning and MacKechnie 1999: 101).

At Daldowie the vehicular approach had been made more meaningful by the exploitation of the estate grounds. At Cardross the wider drama of the natural Scottish landscape and the sense of place, of *genius loci*, was harnessed, encouraging a sense of belonging and continuity in supporting mourners in their acceptance of the profundity of death.

This is a clean-lined, thoughtful composition, dominated by the chapel with its shallow pitched roof and long clerestory windows. The arched opening of the porte-cochère, surmounted by a pyramidal roof with finial, marks the entrance. Designed on two axes at right angles, the chapel is arranged

---

39. In 1910, a Mr Archibald Denny had offered Dunbarton Council £100 towards a crematorium, *UJ*, 15/1/11. (see ch. 3)

along the main east–west spine, while the cross north–south axis accommodates the waiting room, porte-cochère and entrance hall. The interior is light and airy and the polververa and light green Swedish marble catafalque occupies a central position in the apsidal end of the chapel. A vertical strip of Porto Santo marble rises behind the catafalque, both accentuating the height and concealing the light source, thereby adding an element of drama. Four segmental arches open to the south aisle, and lead to a small marble-lined Chapel of Remembrance. The whole has a modern, yet classical feel with the axial link from the west of the vestibule to the gardens.

At the end of the loggia is a dramatic figure, sculpted by Hew Lorimer (1907–1993) RSA, FRBS, son of architect Robert Lorimer, representing 'All Embracing Truth' inspired by John Masefield's poem *Truth*. There are also decorative semi-circular plaster panels representing the seasons in the entrance hall together with the County coat of arms by Douglas Bisset.

The Linn: A Modernist Statement

In the early 1960s there was a feeling of optimism among some Scottish architects that the welfare-state standards defined in the 1940s were finally being provided for everyone through the medium of modern architecture. Nowhere was this more effectively demonstrated than in Glasgow. The city's fourth crematorium would arguably be the finest. Completed in 1962, the same year as Basil Spence's Coventry Cathedral, the Linn Crematorium captured something of the spirit of a country in which 'the driving force behind Modernism was a huge desire to sweep away the fusty old world of density and decay, and to replace it with something bright and new' (MacInnes, Glendinning and MacKechnie 1999: 105). Glasgow was at the forefront of progressive housing at this time. The Corporation had experimented with multi-storey flats in the late 1940s and early 1950s, but it was not until comprehensive redevelopment and Government subsidy began in the late 1950s that the experiments really took root. Over 100 high-rise blocks were envisaged and built. Most original was Sir Basil Spence's great wall of slabs in Hutchesontown–Gorbals, built in 1960–6, with sweeping concrete pylons and hanging garden decks. This was a new, optimistic dawn heralding improved conditions for the living and also, it would transpire, for the dead.

Glasgow City Council's Architect's Department was too busy to undertake the commission so the city turned instead to Thomas Smith Cordiner (1902–1965), a leading Glasgow architect, well-known for his schools and churches. He had been responsible for some nineteen Roman Catholic churches across the city, designed between 1947 and his death in 1965. The Linn was opened just two years before the Vatican lifted its ban on cremation. In his professional role Cordiner was capable of working with all denominations, as demonstrated at St Paul Provanmill in 1948–51, a rare Church of Scotland commission. Cordiner was a progressive. He made extensive use of concrete portal frames – the most common means of cheap construction throughout the 1950s – in his churches, notably the barn-like St Margaret Mary, Castlemilk (1956–7) and most dramatic of all, the A-framed Immaculate Conception, Maryhill (1955–6).

The Linn, on its elevated site, is one of the most dramatic designs of the 1960s, and made a bold statement about the modernity of cremation in defiance of the traditional views held in Scotland. Its overall symmetry is underlined by the stepping of the dramatic cantilevered canopies of the long covered walks leading down to the south of the site, which return to enclose the rear courtyards. Cordiner chose to look beyond Scotland for an architectural expression of cremation in a powerful industrial city. His quest clearly led him to Blackley Crematorium in Manchester by progressive City Architect Leonard Howitt, opened in 1959, with which The Linn shares a number of features (Grainger 2013). Cordiner's design also owed a debt to the progressive Beaux-Arts tradition, so strong in Glasgow, and betrays his training with Burnet, Son and Dick, successors to J.J. Burnet and Thomas S. Tait, the leaders of the style. In common with Daldowie, The Linn shares, if not the architectural vocabulary, then some of the monumental presence, of the work of the War Graves Commission.

The sweeping south façade, constructed of pre-cast concrete frames of a regular pattern pierced with translucent coloured glass blocks, serves as the dramatic centrepiece of the design. Here no attempt was made to reference local materials or traditions; the structure was instead created with reinforced concrete surfaces finished with mineralite aggregate. External walls were faced with light brown rustic bricks. Interestingly, the first set of drawings submitted to the City Council had included a pool in front of the south front, an idea later abandoned on the grounds of economy. This would have been the first employment of water in the landscaping of a Scottish crematorium.

The two self-contained chapels, St Mungo and St Giles, seated 310 and thirty-two respectively. Common to both is the Room of Remembrance housed on the lower ground floor overlooking the gardens, the back wall of which is richly panelled in beech and is the background for seven carved panels depicting the Beatitudes. The chapels are also distinguished by the use of high quality marble. The pierced openings of the façade give a shadowless light to the interior of the St Mungo Chapel, where natural lighting is by clerestory windows offering a glimpse of trees on the hillside behind. Additional seating is provided in the transepts, which can be isolated by curtains. The Crematorium cost some £200,000.

The Buildings of Scotland describes the Linn as '[l]ong and low but with a strongly mannered silhouette' (Williamson, Riches and Higgs 1990: 539). Its overall debt to Blackley is obvious, notably the curved south façade with its dramatic canopies and tapering piloti stretching out on either side. Blackley and the Linn represent two of the most theatrical and ambitious post-war crematoria. And in so far as it is possible to identify the projection of a civic identity in a building, these crematoria both promote and reflect the progressive social thinking on the part of two important industrial cities.

Ayr Crematorium

Of all the western counties, Ayshire experienced the longest delay. A crematorium at Ayr was first proposed in 1937, with a first DHS application in 1939. In 1945 Kilmarnock Town Council proposed its own crematorium and negotiations between the two towns and the County Council lasted until 1960. In contrast to the ascending approach to Greenock Crematorium, with its commanding view of the Clyde, Masonhill Crematorium is set in 7 acres of countryside to the south-eastern edge of the seaside town of Ayr. It is approached by a long downward road, which finds the crematorium in a wide, open situation. Dating from 1960–6, it was designed by the County Council Architect's Department under the direction of Clark Fyfe (1914–2005), the County Architect and Planning Officer, at a contract price of £122,000. The architect in charge was Douglas R.C. Hay (b. c.1935). Standing in 6.25 acres, a little over two miles from the town centre, the harled and slated building comprises four distinct areas: the entrance hall, departure area, cremation area and chapel. The building complex is made up of interconnecting geometrical shapes, dominated by the lofty, broadly traditional but nevertheless rather 'modishly styled' chapel (Close and Riches 2012: 175), with its pitched roof and white concrete vertical louvred windows, some with coloured glass. The shapes of the openings to the entrance portico and chimney are reminiscent of Greenock, suggesting that architects were looking to one another for prompts.

The chapel seating 120 is entered through glazed aluminium double doors. The interior is simple, accentuating the bold Baltic redwood portal frames set in plastered butts between white concrete louvres. There are long stained glass windows at either end by Pierre Fourmaintraux, dating from 1965. Significantly, Ayr offers the first Scottish example of a catafalque positioned to one side of the apse, allowing mourners an alternative focus. The back and side walls of this area are lined with forest green marble and the catafalque table is clad front and sides in a contrasting dark green serpentino marble matching the apse table. The furniture is simple in design and constructed from the protected species of afromosia hardwood on black metal frames. The Chapel of Remembrance is adjacent to the upper departure foyer, although there is also access direct from the formal Garden of Remembrance so that it can be entered in privacy. Ayr was the first crematorium in Scotland to include a sculpted fountain pool surrounded by paving and screened walls. A large window in the Chapel of Remembrance overlooks a separate enclosed garden for private meditation, showing just how sensitively this aspect of the design had been thought through. Mourners leave under an open portico similar in style to that of the entrance, with columns forming bays for floral tributes.

Clydebank Crematorium

Dalnottar Crematorium, Clydebank (1964–7) was unashamedly modern. Located in Dalnottar Cemetery, it stands in a wooded area at the foot of the Kilpatrick Hills and is positioned to offer a magnificent view from the chapel window to the lower reaches of the Clyde and the Renfrewshire Hills. West Dunbartonshire Council commissioned the architectural practice of Sir Frank Mears and Partners based in Edinburgh, and the architect is thought to have been Horace Arthur Rendel Govan (1908–1989). Described as 'a clutter of lower roofs gathering around the pitched planes of the chapel roof falling from a chimney tower in the east' (Gifford and Walker 2002: 342), the Crematorium was constructed with steel reinforced concrete and brickwork of fyfestone, with red granite in chips or dust from Corrennie in Aberdeenshire to give some warmth to the external masonry. The sloping chapel roof is in slate and the chimney stands directly behind the catafalque. The chapel, almost triangular in plan, seats 200 and originally had parquet flooring and benches. The catafalque recess, placed centrally, stands below a stained glass window by Scottish artist Carrick Whalen. Once again, great attention is paid to materials, in this case high quality woods from Africa,

Graph 3. The graph shows the growth in cremation numbers for the nine sites in south-west Scotland, 1955–77, the 'golden age' of Scottish crematorium building. The newer crematoria, especially Daldowie and The Linn, have provided wider funeral choice for bereaved families south of the Clyde and contributed to a steady decline in the Scottish national burial rate. By 1977 there were more cremations than burials. This major change in funeral customs took place in just two generations.

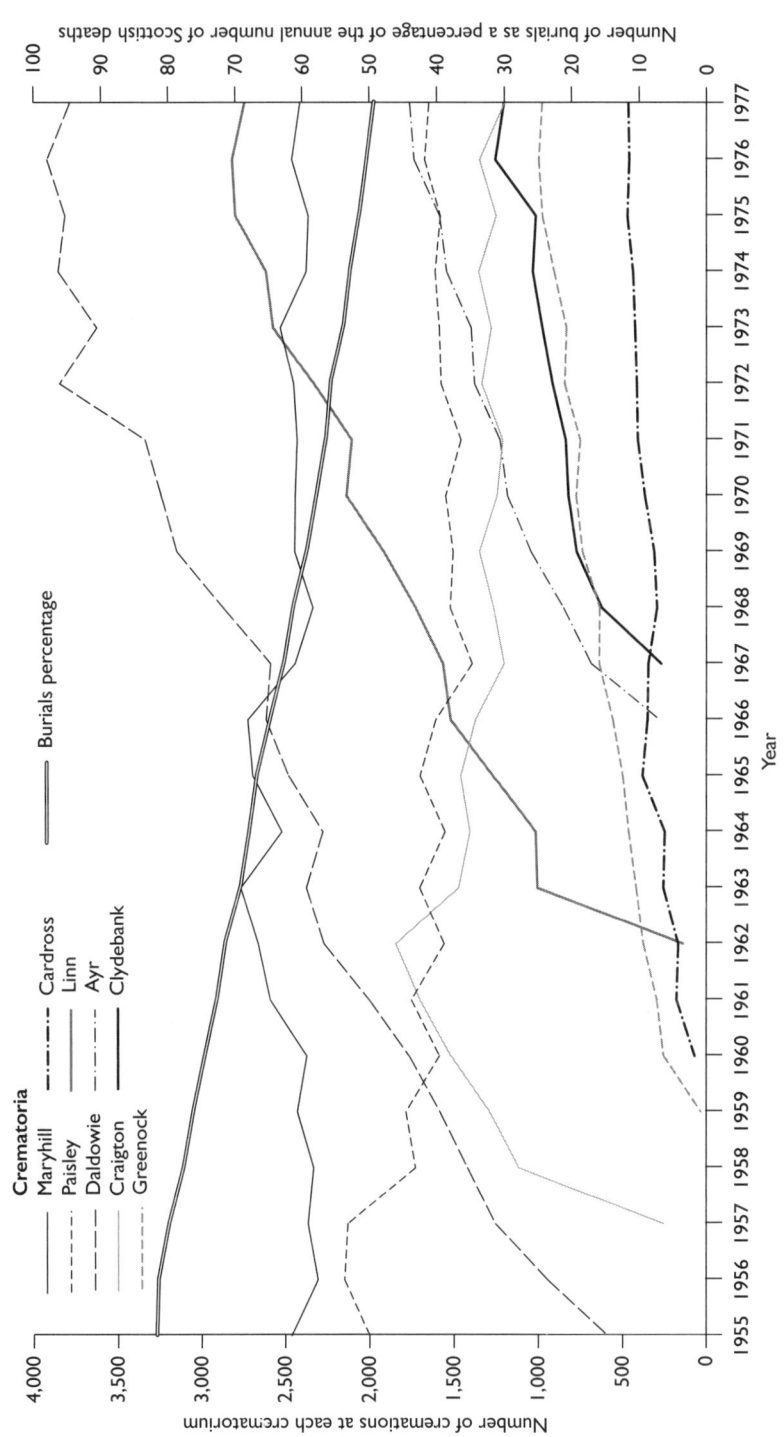

Burma and South America, including afromosia. The outward facing windows are gold anodised aluminium. Mirror image waiting rooms allow mourners to enter the chapel from both east and west. A separate Chapel of Remembrance also commands magnificent views. The contract price was £156,323.

The DHS had adopted as one of its avowed principles the provision of crematoria to cover the most populous areas between the Clyde and the Forth, keeping within the national Welfare Services budget for Scotland. Glasgow and the west had set the bar high in terms of progressive crematorium design during the 1960s. Glasgow's record was remarkable – the first crematorium in 1895 and all three post-war crematoria completed by 1962. Edinburgh would be hard pressed to match this achievement. Although Mortonhall would open some five years later in 1967, it would remain the capital's only post-war crematorium and the only one to be publicly owned.

CHAPTER EIGHT

Edinburgh and the East, 1945–1967

Paradoxically, the nation's health had improved during the War. With more equitable food and healthcare distribution, infant and maternal mortality rates continued to fall. The new Labour Government's Welfare State promised more social equality and better life chances. These, including the National Health Service, better schooling, housing and welfare payments all helped to extend longevity, making death increasingly an event for old age. Meanwhile, cremation commended itself to local authorities and increasingly proved attractive to a society more geographically and socially mobile, and whose familiarity with deaths at home was steadily declining.

Between 1945 and 1967, four publicly-owned crematoria were built in eastern Scotland: Kirkcaldy, Perth, Falkirk and Mortonhall in Edinburgh.

Framing Grief: Kirkcaldy Crematorium

The architectural move towards Modernism in the East was sealed in 1953 by Fife Council's decision to hold a competition for the design of Kirkcaldy Crematorium. The promoters hoped 'that the crematorium will constitute a positive step forward in the design of this type of building' suggesting 'that the scheme should not necessarily follow typical ecclesiastical precedents but rather that competitors should attempt to provide a dignified contemporary design fulfilling both the functional and the architectural requirements of the programme'.[1] The site for a crematorium in Kirkcaldy had first been reserved in 1939.[2] By 1949 Fife County Council, Dunfermline and Kirkcaldy

---

1. *The Architect and Building News*, 17/6/1954, p. 724.
2. *Dunfermline Press and West of Fife Advertiser*, 14/1/1939.

Town Councils had made rival proposals and, in the winter of 1951–2 asked the Department of Health for Scotland (DHS) to decide between them. Kirkcaldy was chosen.

The competition was agreed in March 1953, a proposed budget of £79,500 settled in November and by January 1954 competition entries were pouring in. Building began in 1956, but delays ensued and Kirkcaldy finally opened in 1959.

The competition assessor recommended to the Council by the Royal Institute of British Architects, was Dr Ronald Bradbury (1908–1971), a former Director of Housing in Glasgow (1943–8) and thereafter City Architect of Liverpool. The 237 entries included those from Lorimer & Matthew, Peter & Alison Smithson and Basil Spence, all later to become high profile architects in the UK and abroad. Somewhat surprisingly, the winners were the little known provincial firm of Sanger & Rothwell from Oldham in Lancashire. Their design bore a striking resemblance to their innovative conversion of a Nonconformist chapel in Hollinwood Cemetery, Oldham of the same year, where they had removed the entire sidewall of the chapel and installed a floor-to-ceiling window to offer a view of a garden. *The Architects' Journal*, which in common with the rest of the architectural press had paid scant attention to crematorium design hitherto, devoted a four-page illustrated article to the conversion in April 1954.[3] While the text mentioned the window, it had no particular comments about it. But this innovation was to have far-reaching implications, not only for crematorium design in Britain, but also for the development of a new physical and psychological context for the process of mourning in Scotland. Not only are the configurations of the three main groupings of buildings at Oldham and Kirkcaldy the same, so too is much of the design and detailing of the chapel.

Bradbury acknowledged 'a simplicity and directness' in Sanger & Rothwell's plan which was immediately apparent: 'The general layout and positioning of the scheme on the site is moreover straightforward and well considered' and after minor alterations the design 'will be a building achieving a very high degree of working efficiency and of an attractive architectural character.'[4] He also noted, 'The chapel is attractively proportioned, and the opening of the lower side aisle-wall with a continuous range of windows to the garden will give the correct relationship between the garden and the interior of the

3. *Architects' Journal*, 29/4/1954, pp. 520–3.
4. *The Fife Press*, 29/5/1957.

chapel',[5] but he too failed fully to appreciate the significance of this innovation in which the distinction between a crematorium chapel and a church had been drawn at a stroke.

Architecture undoubtedly has a role to play in encouraging the expression of feeling, and consideration of the psychological impact of architectural space was nothing new to architects. But these assume a heightened significance in the planning of spaces designed to accommodate grief and mourning. The chapel had always been at the core of crematorium designs, carrying with it both the promise and the burden of assuaging grief. But it was merely one component in a much more complicated nexus of unfamiliar experiences encountered by mourners. It is they who invest the building with meaning as best they can in trying circumstances. The Kirkcaldy chapel challenged the accepted ecclesiastical norm of an enclosed, private space as best suited to fulfil the emotional needs of mourners preparing for the committal of a loved one. What was so innovative about this design was the rethinking of the relationship between the physical and the psychological.

It challenged the longstanding architectural conception of the chapel, by fracturing the enclosed space and by so doing, changing the dynamics of what took place in that newly configured space. The design also introduced a natural dimension to a hitherto material construction. There is no record of what prompted Sanger & Rothwell to open up the chapel, but in privileging the feelings of mourners the design was in many ways in tune with contemporary thinking.

In 1957, two years before Kirkcaldy opened, the French philosopher Gaston Bachelard published *The Poetics of Space*, in which he argued that it is space, not time, which invokes memories (Bachelard 1957). By opening up the chapel to other horizons both in the physical and psychological sense, Sanger & Rothwell offered new opportunities for experiencing feelings of grief and for drawing on memories. The psychological framework was reconstructed by bringing nature into the chapel. The non-religious mourner could draw solace from the symbolism of the cycle of life in nature, or merely succumb to the soothing sights of vegetation and water. The opening up of the chapel therefore readdressed the relationship between spatial arrangement and inner condition and by so doing exceeded the functional aspects of crematorium architecture.

5. Ibid.

Sanger & Rothwell's design offered an alternative focus for those who found it too distressing to look at the coffin. There was no intention, however, to diminish the psychological importance of the catafalque, which at both Oldham and Kirkcaldy formed part of a wider contemporary scheme of design intended to suggest that death and mourning were now to be 'experienced' as part of contemporary life and no longer linked inextricably with religious belief which was losing some of its hold. The chapel might now be seen to represent a form of what could be characterized as 'secularized sacredness'.

At Oldham and Kirkcaldy, Sanger & Rothwell also anticipated emerging theory about death and mourning. Architect Jane Drew claimed in 1965 that 'No longer is mourning socially recognised as important, as it has been through history, and expression of feeling is not encouraged' (Drew 1965). That same year sociologist Geoffrey Gorer (Gorer 1965) argued that death no longer had a place in modern life, and thereby the process of mourning was undermined. Kirkcaldy, however, provided a contemporary context in which mourning might take place.

While the 'open chapel' model was adopted almost universally south of the border, becoming one of the defining features of post-war designs in England, it received a mixed reception in Scotland. Arnott argued in 1956,

> There is one aspect of contemporary design which I would like to warn you against, and one which has been used in at least one crematorium, and that is the idea of bringing the garden into the chapel. Now that is usually expressed by having the Garden of Rest and Remembrance immediately outside the chapel. Remember this, that if you can see the Garden of Rest from inside the chapel you can see inside the chapel from the Garden of Rest, and to me the essential feature in any chapel should be its sense of privacy [...] [furthermore the garden would be out of bounds while services were taking place, as] you cannot have men using a motor mower while a service is going on (Arnott 1956: 48–9).

For the most part, the 'closed' chapel held sway in Scotland, perhaps because of more deeply-rooted religious feeling attaching to traditional chapel design. The majority perpetuated the lofty, enclosed space that had prevailed pre-war. Cardross, Perth and Ayr, for example, although they have windows, offer no views. Greenock and Falkirk, however, both followed Kirkcaldy with their generous side windows looking onto gardens.

The wider lesson drawn from Kirkcaldy, albeit played out in the relationship of the building to its immediate surroundings, would not be lost in Scotland. It would lend weight to the heightened significance of the landscape. Although the seven crematoria opened during the 1960s were conspicuously different in design, they often shared magnificent sites commanding stunning views of the local landscape; Cardross, Falkirk, The Linn and Clydebank in particular; and the exception being Mortonhall, which was in a more contained urban but wooded setting. Landscape was by now acknowledged as playing a significant role in comforting mourners and no nation was more wedded to an attachment to a sense of 'place' than Scotland, where familiarity and locality is held dear. While the commodified space of the chapel continued for the most part to respect tradition, in so far as this was a space where rituals took place, the notion of 'place' was afforded a new significance. The locations of crematoria in cemeteries, or more often in old estates or on entirely new sites, now allowed a drive, often long, through familiar countryside to the place of committal. This engagement with local landscape, albeit through the windows of a mourning car, recreated for a contemporary society the procession from house to burial place, which had traditionally taken place on foot.

Falkirk and Perth, 1962

Falkirk and Perth, opened in the same year, represent the two contrasting forms of chapel design. In May 1945, Falkirk Town Council (FTC) approved a crematorium but other priorities, especially housing, intervened. By 1952, the shortage of burial space had become acute.[6] Scotland's Under-Secretary of State J.H. Stewart MP was supportive.[7] Despite proposals from Alloa and Stirling, the DHS confirmed Falkirk as its choice but delayed approval until December 1960.

Falkirk Crematorium was by Alexander James Macaskill Currell (1915–1962) who had been appointed Burgh Architect and Planning Officer for the town in 1948, where he was largely responsible for its development plan and wholly responsible for the Council's post-war housing estates. His background may well explain the character of the crematorium, which is very much in keeping with post-war thinking and aesthetics in England.

6. *Edinburgh Evening Dispatch*, 11/11/1953.
7. Stewart 1955.

Falkirk exemplifies high quality and contemporary design, sharing characteristics with many UK crematoria of a similar date. It is situated on a seven-acre site at the north end of a cemetery which had been laid out in the 1870s. Plans were considered between May 1959 and February 1960[8] and Falkirk Crematorium opened in 1962 at a cost of £80,000. The composition is dominated by the lofty chapel opened up to the west by large double glazed windows giving a vista across the gardens laid out by the Parks Department, under the supervision of Roy Irvine, Superintendent of Parks and Cemeteries. The furnishings and detailing are designed to be simple and the original colour scheme in the chapel involved white walls above a seven-foot six-inch high walnut-panelled dado, with exposed structural columns painted a deep blue.

The north wall is particularly striking, with its walnut panelling interrupted by a central marble centre section housing an oak cross, lit by concealed lighting. Mourners leave by a side door into a covered loggia where flowers are placed. At the point of committal the coffin is lowered, the movement concealed behind a rich blue velvet pall. A wing to the right of the entrance hall contains the vestry, offices, waiting room and toilets. Adjacent to the entrance hall is the Chapel of Remembrance, with striking stained glass windows. The design again takes into account the surrounding landscape, capitalising on the magnificent views across the Carron Vale to the Denny Hills. The lawns and flowerbeds form an integral part of the scheme and wed the building to the landscape. The traditional brick in a sandy colour is in keeping with surrounding buildings allowing the building to take its place in the community.

In February 1945, Perth Town Council (PTC) approved a crematorium in principle but six years passed before the County Council agreed to support the plan. In September 1957 PTC, defying its own Finance Committee, acquired the Hunting Tower Estate.

While the Burgh Surveyor John Penman (1899–1974) prepared plans in 1957, the Perth Deputy Burgh Surveyor, George Kerr Stewart (1921–1982) was responsible for the final design in 1959–62. Best described as 'modern-traditional' it is distinguished by its materials. It is constructed partly in Aberdeen granites of varied colour from selected quarries and partly faced with brick with fyfestone pre-cast exposed granite aggregate concrete slabs.

8. Falkirk Archives A997/1/1960/2414.

Only the pitched roof of the chapel, with its undisguised 'campanile-like' chimney, interrupts the predominantly flat roofs of the composition.

The main feature is undoubtedly the chapel, where laminated timber trusses with cantilevers over the side aisles were introduced. The line of these enclose the smaller area designed to foster intimacy during the service. The catafalque at the east end of the chapel is teak panelled and forms a contrast with the cherry wood panelling of the enclosing walls. Wrought iron gates, backed with curtains, separate the apse from the chapel.[9] The latter is an enclosed space lit by ten clerestory windows with stained glass by Alexander L. Russell, depicting a series of Christian symbols.

The Hall of Remembrance is immediately to the left of the entrance and opposite the chapel doors. It forms a distinguishing feature, overtly Christian in its symbolism. Plastered and painted white, it allows reflected colours from the stained glass, again by Russell in the west window, to be appreciated. This depicts the risen and ascended Christ, clothed in the garments of his regal majesty. His right hand is raised in blessing, and his left hand holds a cruciform pastoral staff, the symbol of redemption. In the centre of the base of the window is the Pascal Lamb, with the banner of St Andrew, the symbol of the atonement, and St John the Baptist, the patron saint of the City and Royal Burgh of Perth. Stained glass characterises many churches in Perth, and despite the modernity of the design the character of the lofty chapel and the abundance of stained glass offer a sense of tradition and continuity for mourners.

Edinburgh: The Search for a Site

In April 1946, A.T. Harrison, Recorder of Edinburgh City Burial Grounds (Recorder) advised the City Council that within two years there would be no burial space in Colinton parish nor, after five, in Liberton.[10] These two large parishes, small villages until the mid-nineteenth century, with mansions and estates, were incorporated within the City of Edinburgh in

---

9. *Pharos* 28(2), 9 noted that 'the Scottish tradition of the nearest relatives taking a symbolic part in the last rites at the committal service [by holding the cords] has been retained by the arrangement whereby two relatives or friends of the deceased may go forward and close the wrought-iron gates as an act towards the end of a service'.
10. Edinburgh City Council (ECC) General Purposes Committee, Parks Sub-Committee (PS-C), 8/10/1946.

1920. Both parishes witnessed private house-building in the inter-war period and post-war Council housing which, in Liberton, helped increase its population by 80% between 1951 and 1961 (Keir 1966; Ferenbach 1975: 44).

Both parish kirk-yards had been extended in 1926. Twenty years later, burial space was running short. Available land was not only scarce but coveted by a number of rival institutions. Over the next ten years the search for suitable cemetery sites ran into opposition from interests seeking to satisfy the needs of agriculture, education, housing and defence. All cemetery decisions had to be authorised by the DHS and the Secretary of State.

In October 1946, the General Purposes Committee (Parks Sub-Committee) instructed the Director of Parks, the City Engineer and the Town Planning Officer (TPO), 'to report on a site for the possible establishment of a combined cemetery and crematorium'.[11] This was the first official reference to the public crematorium project. Whether the original prompt was the lack of burial space, the popularity of Warriston and Seafield, or the Beveridge Report, is not clear but, as a member of the Scottish NACCS Branch, the Recorder would have been alert to all these factors.

Throughout 1947 the TPO kept in mind the burial needs of the two parishes.[12] In the City's new planning proposals, he allocated 30 acres south of Hunter's Tryst. However, the soil was too rocky and the site too far from Liberton. It was to be some years before the Council realised that one site could serve both parishes. Meanwhile, the Civic Amenities Committee (CAC) worked for Colinton and Parks, Markets and Gardens Sub-Committee (PMS-C) was responsible for Liberton.

Colinton's preferred site centred on Fernieflat Farm.[13] While there was some opposition to a crematorium, site-tests revealed its suitability for burial. In January 1949 the CAC reviewed progress.[14] The owner grew feeding-stuffs for a dairy herd and was unwilling to sell. The Town Clerk was instructed to negotiate 10 acres nearby. The soil proved suitable and the owner willing, but the land needed extensive drainage, so the Parks Superintendent (PS) recommended an alternative site, already Council-owned, on the Redhall estate. Although part was under consideration for a school, the TPO promised to support the use of the remainder for a cemetery. It was now February 1950.

11. ECC PS-C, 8/10/1946, p. 328.
12. ECC PS-C, 9/12/1947, p. 17.
13. ECC PS-C, 13/1/1948, p. 71.
14. ECC CAC, 25/1/1949, pp. 275–6.

The PS did not overlook Liberton. He and the TPO recommended 10 acres at Muirhouse Farm, south of Burdiehouse Burn. For reasons unknown, the Liberton issue was placed on the agenda of the Lord Provost's Committee (LPC) a political move often used to marginalise an issue. At any rate, the Town Clerk suggested that the city might buy Liberton Manse and the Kirk Session's ground nearby for a crematorium.[15] The Manse had strong associations with Robert Louis Stevenson but the main obstacle was the housing lying within 100 yards' radius.[16]

In April 1951, the LPC decided to lease for grazing that part of Redhall Farm eyed by Colinton for burial. The PMS-C protested that Colinton had exhausted its burial space and appealed to the LPC to reconsider.[17] In hindsight, this seems to have been the moment at which ECC realised the importance of its committees' concerns, so that the searches for more burial ground at Colinton and Liberton now ran parallel with each other, until 1955 brought an eventual solution.

The LPC attended to Colinton's request and allocated 6 acres on the Council's Redhall farm estate. On 17 March 1951 an Act of Council gave formal powers to proceed. Then the Craiglockhart Residents' Association (CRA) protested to the Secretary of State. By November 1952 the Secretary's decision was still awaited and the CAC now realised that the City Education Committee also had its eye on Redhall Farm.[18]

Perhaps the CAC and the Education Committee realised there was hope in collaboration. They had a joint meeting and a site visit.[19] They may also have contacted the Secretary of State about his delayed response to the CRA. The DHS then offered an alternative site, but this turned out to be owned by Merchiston Castle School, which had already opposed a cemetery bid; that site too was affected by the 'radius clause'. Mindful of the CRA's objections, the DHS offered three more alternative sites. Checking revealed that two of them had already been rejected for cemetery use and the third belonged to the Territorial Army. The CAC and the Education Committee conferred again, rejecting all the DHS sites. Each wanted Redhall Farm and

15. ECC CAC, 19/9/1950, p. 100.
16. ECC CAC, 28/11/1950, p. 163.
17. ECC PMS-C, 10/4/1951, p. 299.
18. ECC CAC, 25/11/1952, p. 183.
19. ECC Special Joint Sub-Committee of Education and CA Committees, 23/12/1952, pp. 197–8.

they agreed to share it. When the DHS admitted in January 1953 that the Department of Agriculture had objected to two of the sites it had proposed only two months before, the minds of the Councillors hardened: Redhall must be the cemetery site. The Town Clerk and Council supported them.[20]

Liberton had its own struggles with the DHS. In November 1951 the PMS-C approved the Muirhouse Farm site for a cemetery[21] and then sought DHS approval. In June 1952 the DHS rejected Muirhouse Farm as it had 'an established dairy herd of 59 cows', and was overlooked by housing. Instead, the DHS offered Liberton three other sites; 34 acres at Burdiehouse Burn, 8 acres at Gracemount Farm and 12.8 acres at Mortonhall Estate.[22]

The PMS-C agreed Mortonhall was the only possible site.[23] It had a secluded and woodland setting, and adjoined an old burial ground. The Sub-Committee requested 15.2 acres to accommodate both a cemetery and a crematorium. Mortonhall's owner, unwilling to sell, offered five alternative sites. The PMS-C visited all five before its February 1953 meeting and confirmed its original choice.[24] The CAC agreed to seek a CPO if the soil proved suitable.[25]

The City Council's resolve over Mortonhall was stiffened; this may have assured both the CAC and the CRA that a Mortonhall site would remove the need for a separate burial site for Colinton. In July 1953 the DHS recommended Colinton sites other than Redhall Farm. The PMS-C proposed a deputation to the Secretary of State. The Chairman, Convenor and Town Clerk met him on 11 December, with a Ministry of Agriculture representative present. The DHS then recommended a site at Fernieflat Farm (16 December) but the CAC insisted on Redhall and asked the Minister to reconsider.[26] Twice more the DHS insisted on Fernieflat (18 February and 4 March 1954) and the CAC reluctantly visited the site in September 1954. Before writing to the DHS the Town Clerk had taken the precaution of approaching Fernieflat's owner, who strongly objected to any change from agricultural use.[27] Undeterred,

20. ECC CAC, 27/1/1953, p. 233.
21. ECC PMS-C, 30/11/1951, p. 144.
22. ECC PMS-C, 10/6/1952, pp. 22–3.
23. ECC PMS-C, 14/10/1952, p. 143.
24. ECC PMS-C, 3/2/1953, pp. 237–8.
25. ECC CAC, 24/3/1953, p. 281.
26. ECC CAC, 26/1/1954, pp. 157–8.
27. ECC CAC, 26/10/1954, p. 104.

the Council then applied for planning approval for both the Fernieflat and Mortonhall sites. On 12 April 1955 the PMS-C was informed that while the SOS was still considering Fernieflat Farm, the Secretary had approved Mortonhall.[28] Each site would need a CPO.

On 28 April a special meeting of the ECC agreed that, using its powers under the Burial Grounds (Scotland) Act 1855, it would acquire the Mortonhall site by compulsory purchase.[29] It was a coincidence that the city's procedure to provide burial ground came from an Act of Parliament passed exactly 100 years before (see chs 1 and 2).

This decision seems to have removed the pressure on the Council to search for a burial site at Colinton. Perhaps Councillors, prompted by their cemetery managers, had become aware that one Scottish funeral in six was now a cremation. Warriston and Leith had conducted 3,806 cremations between them in 1954. Extended ownership of cars and telephones, with better refrigeration techniques, all contributed to developing funeral directing practice and, with petrol no longer rationed, access to out-of-town crematoria was facilitated.

Yet, once the CPO decision was made, matters slowed down. A draft plan for the cemetery and crematorium site of 25.27 acres was prepared by October 1955.[30] In September 1956 the Sheriff of Lothian and Peebles gave his approval and the owner agreed to sell. In July 1958 the City bought Mortonhall estate for £6,000.[31] Three months later, the Council asked the City Architect, Alexander Steele, to prepare plans.[32] These were approved in September 1959.[33] Despite some hesitation over dedicating the cemetery – not the Presbyterian tradition – the cemetery was dedicated on 16 April 1960.[34] This event followed the CAC meeting on 12 April where two surprise decisions were taken.[35] First, Mortonhall would be a lawn cemetery (Rugg 2006) and, secondly, the City Architect recommended that an outside firm of architects be appointed to design the crematorium.

28. ECC PMS-C, 12/4/1955, pp. 255–6.
29. ECC City Corporation special meeting, 28/4/1955, pp. 668–71.
30. ECC PMS-C, 11/10/1955, p. 84.
31. ECC PMS-C, 8/7/1958, p. 27.
32. ECC PMS-C, 14/10/1958, p. 54.
33. ECC PMS-C, 1/9/1959, p. 38.
34. ECC CAC, 12/4/1960, p. 136.
35. ECC CAC, 12/4/1960, p. 136.

Mortonhall was Edinburgh's first municipal cemetery of the modern era, opened 100 years after Henry Littlejohn had first called for this step 'as a sanitary measure of no small significance' (see ch. 2).

Pride and Prejudice: Edinburgh Mortonhall

The story of Mortonhall Crematorium illustrates very eloquently the compromises over cost that architects had often to make to produce civic buildings of quality, as opposed to municipal buildings of mediocrity – an all too familiar story. The principal players were the architect, Sir Basil Spence (1907–1976); his partner J. Hardie Glover (1913–1994); Alexander Steele (1906–1980), the City Architect of Edinburgh; and his Deputy, Leslie Roland Penman (c.1904–1998). In October 1958 the PMS-C instructed Steele to draw up plans for the proposed crematorium, but the Edinburgh Architect's Department, in common with its counterpart in Glasgow, was dealing with large housing programmes and so it was eighteen months later that Steele recommended to the CAC that an outside firm of architects be employed.

In appointing Spence in 1960 Edinburgh Corporation secured an architect of considerable international standing. In 1951 he had won the competition to design the new Coventry Cathedral, destroyed in 1940 during an air raid. The Mortonhall contract was on a fixed price basis for labour and materials. In accepting, Spence specified that his partners in Edinburgh would supervise work and attend meetings 'but I can undertake to design the building and supervise all the details. This, I think, is the vital part'.[36]

Penman provided site plans and an outline brief. 'The siting and boundaries of the area were to accord with the proposals in the 1957 Development Plan for the City and Royal Burgh of Edinburgh and would cover an area of 28.928 acres in total.'[37] The cemetery would occupy 13 acres to the west of the site, with the crematorium lying immediately to the east, just within undulating woodland. The main entrance to the cemetery and crematorium was to be from Howden Hall Road on the east, by way of the original east carriage drive to Mortonhall. The brief included 'a chapel to seat 300; another to seat 50; a Chapel of Remembrance; vestry; rest rooms and toilets; large waiting room; 3 gas cremators, with space for a fourth; a freezing chamber to receive

36. Royal Commission on the Ancient and Historical Monuments of Scotland (RCAHMS), MS2329/SCT/43/1/11–12.
37. RCAHMS, MS 2329/SCT/1/89–91.

four coffins; office and a workers (staff) retiring room. The buildings were to be non-denominational in character and after committal the drawing of a curtain to conceal the bier is favoured. Circulation routes should ensure that groups of mourners and their respective cars are kept apart'.[38] In January 1961 the contract was extended to include staff cottages, one a four and the other a five apartment dwelling.

The city considered progress to be slow and requested plans by March. Spence responded, 'The Parks Sub-Committee must realise that this represents a great opportunity for a fine piece of architecture and I must make a request for ample time to think the scheme out before I commit myself to sketch plans.'[39]

There was a suggestion that Committee members might visit 'crematoria in the Manchester area' which would have doubtless included Blackley (1959). By April Penman was 'anxious to know how things were progressing', and Glover reported that 'final sketch plans were unlikely for yet some considerable time, although a great deal of thought had already been given to the scheme.'[40] In April 1961 Spence wrote to Steele with frustration on hearing that the budget was £80,000: 'I am extremely concerned about the crippling restrictions it will impose on me. This operation will turn into one of economical planning rather than an attempt to get the best crematorium in Britain [...] As far as I can see, this will have to be a utilitarian brick and harl job to get the accommodation you require and satisfy the budget.'[41] Steele responded, 'I have however been doing some arithmetic and, having regard to the size of the project, think that you will find it more easy than you anticipated to provide a nice building.'[42] Steele then opined that descending catafalques had fallen out of favour and objected to Spence's proposal to build in stone. Plans were finally submitted on 24 October, but Steele's report to the Committee suggested that things had gone awry, many of the shortcomings of the present scheme resulting from a lack of discussion between Spence and the city. Steele wrote, 'There can be little doubt that the design submitted is stimulating but I would hope that in the final event there might be a re-assessment of the scale of the building where one cannot hope

38. Ibid.
39. RCAHMS, MS 2329/SCT/43/1/75.
40. RCAHMS, MS 2329/SCT/43/1/109.
41. RCAHMS, MS 2329/SCT/43/1/105.
42. RCAHMS, MS 2329/SCT/43/1/104.

to attain the uplift and sense of exhilaration which can be created in religious structures of greater scale and similar shape.'[43]

Steele's report quibbled about the costs, now based on a design developed to the completed sketch plan stage. The area had increased from 7,000 to 9,000 square feet and the pool proposed by Steele had been replaced by 'a much more elaborate and expensive type.'[44] A litany of concerns about the circulation and planning were raised, Glover telling Spence, 'I think he [Steele] must be rapidly put in his place on this whole project. Unfortunately both he and Penman have, in the past, separately designed Crematoria, and consider themselves complete experts in this matter [...] I feel personally that he is not in any way the person to carry this out on our behalf, since he is obviously biased regarding the whole scheme.'[45]

Spence was furious: 'It appears that his main idea is to put his great fist into the scheme and destroy it. I would rather resign than let this happen.'[46] In January 1962 Spence justified his choice of a descending catafalque, 'partly because the ground affords this possibility and partly because of the architectural treatment. The finish of this Chapel is simple and austere, the introduction of curtains would completely ruin the conception and go against what is the primary thought. I feel this very strongly. The interiors should be simple and austere. This is not a cosy suburban chapel but a dignified and austere crematorium chapel for the city of Edinburgh.'[47]

In February 1962 the Committee agreed, but in March Penman wrote with further queries. This letter was clearly the final straw and Spence wrote to Sir John Greig Dunbar, the Lord Provost, a week later,

> The nub of the matter is that Steele is behaving like a bloody fool, is unbearably autocratic, bossy, rude, tactless and is determined to foul up my design for your Crematorium [...] Glover has been on to me this morning to say that the cost will have to be cut drastically. As I made clear at the last meeting, I am not interested in doing an inferior article, which will certainly be the case if Steele has his way.

43. RCAHMS, MS 2329/SCT/43/1/99–100.
44. Ibid.
45. RCAHMS, MS 2329/SCT/43/1/97–8.
46. RCAHMS, MS 2329/SCT/43/1/96.
47. RCAHMS, MS 2329/SCT/43/1/63.

I must say that I have refused many millions of work recently (including two entire new Universities) and with taxation as it is I am only interested in doing good work. With Steele behaving like a pompous ass this will be impossible and I may have to resign [...] this job is giving me more trouble than Coventry cathedral.[48]

After looking into the matter, Dunbar suggested that Steele was under some pressure from the CAC and the City Treasurer 'who are being most difficult'.[49]

A meeting was arranged between Spence and the Lord Provost and relevant city representatives on 17 April 1962 and some six months later final requirements were agreed. These involved the positioning of a small office for the Superintendent, the waiting room and the Chapel of Remembrance, which was to be greatly reduced in size. Glover concluded, 'In order to avoid having too many small elements dotted around, I thought it might be feasible to link the Waiting Space structure with the Remembrance Chapel and, at the same time, move the pond from the East to the West which, in turn, links it with the Garden of Rest in this area.'[50] Spence agreed, saying, 'I think it may even be an improvement so I would crash ahead.'[51]

Construction began in September 1964, but cost continued to be a problem, Spence designing the stained glass himself as the Council could not afford an artist. In August 1966 agreement was reached over the shape of the concrete cross, inspired by that at Gunnar Asplund's Woodland Cemetery, Stockholm (1935–40). In October Glover and Spence were exchanging notes about the candlesticks, the cross in the chapel and the design of the city coat of arms for the entrance gates, which Spence thought

> looked like a postage stamp on this great wall which is handsome in its appearance [...] So far as the cross is concerned, I think that this looks puny and apologetic. I would much prefer something let into the ground behind the catafalque, free standing and much bigger [...] Do have a look at the interior of Ronchamps and you will see exactly what I mean. I am certain the cross on the wall will destroy the monumental character that we have now [...] Forgive

48. RCAHMS, MS 2329/SCT/43/1/54.
49. RCAHMS, MS 2329/SCT/43/1/40.
50. RCAHMS, MS 2329/SCT/43/1/10.
51. RCAHMS, MS 2329/SCT/43/1/34.

me for being so outspoken but I feel that the Crematorium should be one of the best buildings we have done recently.[52]

Mortonhall finally opened on 7 February 1967 at a cost of £230,000.

> The crematorium is tucked into the side of a hill and the main approach skirts a tiny memorial chapel containing a book of remembrance, to reveal a small and a larger chapel in the woodland clearing, their southern walls rising in sharp profile like jagged masonry shards [...] The combination of angled walls and narrow window apertures and the use of indirect lighting was something explored by Spence in a wide range of buildings in the 1960s, including the Chapel of Unity at Coventry.[53]

The pyramid roof of the large chapel acts as a vestigial spire and admits light into the interior over the catafalque, a Baroque conceit to create drama and one reminiscent of Blackley, Manchester; a concrete cylinder performs the same role in the smaller chapel.

The building's international credentials were impeccable: Gunnar Asplund's Woodland Cemetery and Le Corbusier's pilgrimage church at Ronchamps, eastern France of 1954. Spence argued, 'If I can get quality [...] if I can get something in the building that helps to enrich people's lives – oh that sounds pompous [...] But one can give comfort to people, comfort against fears and frustration. I think that there is a great social need for good architecture.'[54]

In 1970 Mortonhall for the first time conducted 1,000 cremations in the year.

Doctors' Fees for Cremation Certificates[55]

By 1953 the DHS had reluctantly fallen in with the Home Office's (HO) decision to settle the issue of maximum fees before finalising amendments to the medical certificates. With the Cremation Bill passed, consultations about the draft letter to the British Medical Association (BMA) resumed. The DHS's view was that two guineas was generous for the

---

52. RCAHMS, MS 2329/SCT/43/1/134–5.
53. Fenton and Walker 2012: 113, 116.
54. RCAHMS, MS 2329/X/19/16/118.
55. This section is based on **NRS:** HH 61/113, HH 61/129; **TNA:** HO 282/2, HO 282/125.

present certificates and that the maximum for their replacements should be less. The draft was amended. The Association would be told that 'the Secretary of State regards the Association's proposed maximum fee as reasonable and appropriate both for the present certificates and for the modified certificates which he intends to prescribe under the amending Regulations' and be asked to recommend this to its members.

Unsurprisingly the BMA wished to know what modifications the HO had in mind. The DHS had begun to revise Form C and a copy was sent to the Association. The Association denied that it had ever accepted two guineas as a maximum fee. It told its members that the changes envisaged to Form C were not substantial, that its Council had approved a draft of the new form, and that while it was willing to recommend two guineas as a suitable fee for both certificates, it was unwilling to recommend that two should not be exceeded.

Meanwhile the HO had learned that many doctors were giving Form B gratis or for a small fee and was concerned that a recommendation from the Association that two guineas was suitable for both certificates might lead doctors to increase their fees for Form B. It wrote to the Association that, 'if the recommendation is to be in terms of a suitable fee rather than a maximum fee it would be inappropriate for any recommendation to be made in regard to Certificate B'. The Association's response was to draw its members' attention to the decision of its Annual Representative Meeting in 1951 that two guineas was suitable for both certificates and to point out that NHS hospital doctors, while obliged to give Form B gratis, unlike GPs and private doctors, were entitled to charge for Form C, a licence which some were suspected of exploiting to make up for the income forgone for Form B. Evidence of such overcharging, provided by the Co-operative Union, was in the hands of the HO's contemporaneous Working Party on Funeral Charges, on which Howat represented the DHS. Ever reluctant to exercise the power given it by the 1952 Act to set a limit to the fees charged by doctors, the HO regarded the impasse with the Association as far less unsatisfactory than the Department. The Department had always wanted the HO, in its dealings with the BMA and in answers to parliamentary questions about fees, to be much more threatening. 'We can't stop the HO being pleased,' minuted Haddow, 'but we aren't'; 'Personally, I cannot help feeling that the Association has been guilty of something approaching sharp practice,' wrote Howat. The Department asked to be disassociated from any compromising reply to the Association. Despite reports in subsequent years of doctors charging unreasonable or excessive fees, the power to prescribe fees for cremation certificates has never been exercised, and in Scotland, together with the certificates themselves, was abolished in 2016 (below, ch. 9).

Burial and Cremation Law Consolidation[56]

The Bill which had caused doubt in the DHS and the Lord Advocate's Department (LAD) about whether Reeves' Bill should be extended to Scotland (ch. 6) was the work of a Local Government Law Consolidation Committee. Its origins lay in the work of an earlier committee appointed in 1937 to consolidate the law relating to local government and public health in Scotland (Jeffrey 1943: 5). The outbreak of war terminated that Committee's efforts. But in 1942 Vallance, a member and prime mover of the Committee, drafted a series of clauses anent burial and cremation. In 1948 another Committee was appointed with Vallance as a member and a remit similar that in 1937 (Fisher 1953a: 5). Vallance's draft was retrieved and in 1953 the Committee's second report was accompanied by a draft Burial and Cremation (Scotland) Bill (Fisher 1953b, 1953c).

Both Committees had been charged with reporting on 'what amendments of the existing law are desirable for facilitating consolidation and securing simplicity, uniformity and conciseness' and the first had been advised by the Secretary of State to ignore amendments which 'are likely to raise controversial issues'. This would be to ensure that advantage could be taken of the simplified procedure for passing consolidation Bills.

The most, and very, controversial proposal of the second Committee concerned the radius clause. Section 5 of the 1902 Act prohibited the 'construction' of a crematorium within fifty yards of a public highway and 200 yards of a house whose owner, lessee or occupier had not consented to it. Compliance with these restrictions was secured by the necessity of ministerial approval for its site and plans. Section 5 had made it very difficult for the Edinburgh Society to find a site for a crematorium, was to make it

---

56. This section is based on **NRS:** AD 63/408/1, AD 63/408/2, AD 63/408/3, AD 63/408/4, DD 5/1837, DD 5/1840, DD 5/1847, HH 60/823, HH 61/111, HH 61/112, HH 61/135, HH 61/687, HH 61/908/1–3, HH 80/865, HH 80/899; **TNA:** BD 11/2943, CAB 134/1976, CAB 134/1977, CAB 134/1993, CAB 134/1997, CAB 134/2001, HLG 45/1468, HLG 45/1569, HLG 45/1571.

difficult for local authorities wishing to expand into crematoria building after the war, and would be tested by private developers at the start of the next century. It gave rise to two particular problems. The first was its uncertainty. 'Crematorium' was defined by the Act as a 'building fitted with appliances for the burning of human remains and everything incidental and ancillary thereto'. The definition's last six words[57] admitted doubt about the point from which the distance was to be measured: was it from the cremation chamber, the perimeter of a cremation authority's land, or some other spot within the site?[58] Since the Act did not define 'construct' it was unclear how, if at all, section 5 applied to an extension, or the adaptation of a structure, to a crematorium. The second problem was that a cremation authority which had acquired land for a crematorium could be prevented from building on it if, before construction was begun and perhaps even before it was complete, a hostile owner put up a house within 200 yards or an owner, lessee or occupier, formerly consenting, changed their mind.

Until about 1949 the conventional understanding appears to have been that the distance was to be measured from the cremator chamber. Then, or possibly after the Ministry of Health's responsibility for approving the site and plans of crematoria was transferred to the newly created Ministry of Local Government and Planning in 1951, a different in-house lawyer decided that the distance should be measured from some point nearer, or perhaps on, the perimeter of the cremation authority's land. After protests from local authorities and the Cremation Society (CS) the Ministry relented. 'Ancillary thereto' was to be interpreted as ancillary to the burning, not ancillary to the building: the ground on which ashes were scattered had to be outwith the prescribed limits but ornamental gardens, roadways and lodges need not be (S. White 2013; Ministry of Housing and Local Government (MHLG) 1956: 26; MHLG 1957–78). The only way of circumventing section 5 was to obtain a private or local Act of Parliament disapplying it, as five local authorities in England and one in Wales had done by 1950 and as the Merchants House

---

57. These had been added to allay the Local Government Board's apprehension that without them a burial authority would be unable to spend money on such appendages as chapels and waiting rooms.
58. At the other end the distance was probably to be measured from the walls of the house rather than from its curtilage (or policies) (Wright v Wallasey Local Board 1887).

of Glasgow and Greenock did in 1950 and 1952 (MHGCOCA 1950 s. 3(4), GCOCA 1952 Sch. 13(2)) and Edinburgh City Council sought unsuccessfully to do in 1953.

Vallance's draft narrowed the classes of person entitled to veto the construction of a crematorium (and the provision of a public burial ground), and defined 'crematorium' as 'any building fitted with appliances for the purpose of burning human remains' including 'any chapel, memorial hall, or other premises or thing incidental or ancillary thereto', and 'construct' to include 'adapt for use as a crematorium any premises which were not immediately previously used for that purpose or extend any existing crematorium'.

Despite opposition from the DHS the Committee struck out the radius clause and the requirement for the site and plans of crematoria to have ministerial approval, considering that the public interest this protected could be left to planning laws. The Department felt it advantageous to have definite standards set down in statute, enforced by the Secretary of State, which planning authorities might otherwise disregard. The Committee's view was that 'it was against modern trends to allow a single person arbitrarily to refuse to concede the use of land to a local authority for burial grounds purposes'. For a householder's veto it substituted a right of objection to a sheriff whose determination would be final. It toyed with the idea of limiting the right of objection to house owners only but extending it to any owner in the 'locality' of the proposed development.

In the wake of Parliament's decision in 1952 (see ch. 6) to extend the requirement of ministerial approval for the site and plans of crematoria and to leave the radius clause unamended, the Committee reluctantly backtracked. But it still insisted that the neighbours' veto be replaced by a right of objection to a sheriff and that the class of person entitled to object be more limited than those presently entitled to a veto. It also modified Vallance's definition of 'crematorium' to 'any building constructed and equipped for the purpose of burning human remains and includes any chapel, memorial hall, or other premises ancillary thereto', and his definition of 'construct' to 'includes erect, and a reference to the construction of a building of a particular kind includes a reference to the adaptation of a building as a building of that kind'. In the process the reference to 'extending' a crematorium was lost and, despite the Committee's decision to restore it, it was never restored. Nor was the Committee's decision to outlaw the burning of human remains elsewhere than in a crematorium reflected in the drafting.

The Bill's amendments to the law exceeded those necessary to facilitate consolidation. Parliamentary time could not be found for the Bill. Work on it was put aside but at the start of 1955 was revived as was hope of passing it as a consolidating measure. The DHS was still concerned at the Bill's severe curtailment of neighbours' rights and felt that its drafting had been too much influenced by local authority interests. Earlier Howat had suggested that a fair balance could be achieved by placing the onus on the local authority to appeal to the sheriff against an alleged unreasonable withholding of consent by a householder or lessee and this suggestion was endorsed by the Secretary of State for Scotland and adopted by the Committee. Work was again interrupted by the General Election of 1955 and not resumed until the start of 1956 and then, apparently, only briefly. When the Bill was resurrected in 1958 it was modified to give effect to the Committee's decision and was approved by the three local authority associations. The Secretary of State for Scotland sought Cabinet approval for the parliamentary draftsman to revise the Bill to have it ready for introduction when opportunity arose, telling the Home Affairs Committee (HAC) that 'it seems unlikely that the suggested procedure would be regarded as unreasonable and be seriously opposed'.

Immediately this approval had been obtained the Department decided that the Bill would go forward as an ordinary Bill (and not as a consolidation or quasi-consolidation measure) and pressed the draftsman to proceed urgently. The draftsman, however, declined to draft until approval had been obtained to introduce the Bill and this prevented a redraft being produced until 1966.

A restraint on the progress of the Bill came from a similar consolidation exercise being undertaken in London. Bills had been drafted in 1954, 1956 and 1958 but nothing had come of them. In 1962 Lord Colville introduced a Bill drafted by the National Association of Parish Councils. English and Welsh burial legislation was much more complicated than Scottish. England and Wales had two statutory codes relating to the provision of public burial grounds, one based on the Burial Acts, the other on the Public Health (Interments) Act 1879 (Rugg 2013). Parish Councils were concerned only with the former and Colville's Bill tidied up the law for their benefit. The MHLG wanted a unified code based on the latter. Colville was persuaded to drop his Bill by a promise that the Government would soon produce a Bill and invite him to introduce it (S. White forthcoming).

The Scottish authorities had never contemplated handing their Bill to a private member. The decision to do this with the English and Welsh Bill prompted the Scottish Home and Health Department not only to envisage this, but to attempt to spur on the drafting so as to have a Bill ready for introduction at any moment. The Secretary of State approved this so long as the parliamentary draftsman could find the time to produce a Bill. He did not.

Meanwhile Colville was harrying the Government for the Bill promised him. To placate him the Cabinet approved the employment of the parliamentary draftsman to work on the English and Welsh Bill, but suggested that, if this failed, an invitation to promote the Scottish Bill might, in the words of the Scottish Office, 'keep him happy': Colville was a Scot and had been Secretary of State for Scotland. The Scottish Bill received Cabinet approval a little while later, the material about the radius clause being presented as 'a compromise proposal [...] unlikely to be controversial'. Within four months a Bill had been drafted in accordance with instructions finalised in 1960. The Cremation Acts of 1902 and 1952 were to be repealed. The plans and site of any crematorium or extension to a crematorium were to require ministerial approval. Owners, occupiers and lessees (holding leases having a period of not less than two years to run) of a house within 200 yards of land proposed to be used for a crematorium (or within 100 yards of land proposed to be used for a burial ground) were to have fourteen days of being notified of the proposal to lodge an objection with the proposer, who could then either drop the proposal or apply to the sheriff for permission to proceed with it. 'Crematorium' was to be defined as 'any building constructed and equipped for the purpose of burning human remains and includes any chapel, memorial hall, garden or other premises ancillary thereto'. 'Construct' was not defined. The draftsman commented, "We are now at a crossroads with regard to this Bill and [...] somebody somewhere must decide whether we intend to produce the Fisher Committee's Bill, subject to minor adjustments necessitated chiefly by the lapse of time, or whether our objective is a new Bill framed according to new thinking.'

While the provisions of the English and Welsh Bills about local authorities' powers and responsibilities for the provision and maintenance of burial grounds and crematoria eventually found a statutory home in the Local Government Act 1972, work on the Scottish Bill petered out in 1966 with nothing in the statute book to show for twenty years of effort.

Working Party on the Cremation Regulations, Human Tissue Act 1961, Cremation Regulations 1965 and Cremation Regulations (Scotland) 1967[59]

With the Cremation Act 1952 passed and the minimal consequential amendments to the Cremation Regulations made, the HO put aside further action on the recommendations of the Interdepartmental Committee. The DHS, however, set about drafting amendments to implement them. While this was intermittently progressing the HO received a deputation from the CS asking for action about excessive fees being charged for cremation certificates and about differences of opinion among medical referees of their function. This, the Society claimed, was shown by the report of the proceedings at the Society's Annual Conference in Ayr (CS 1955: 7–15), puzzlingly because differences of opinion are not apparent in the report of the Conference proceedings. No doubt, though, there was concern about variations in referees' discharge of their function[60] because it was at this meeting that steps were taken to form the Association of Crematorium Medical Referees (S. White 2002b). Both Glaister and Kerr addressed the Conference. Kerr's view was that, apart from very minor points, the Regulations did not need changing: what needed changing was the approach of doctors and funeral directors towards them. With this both Department and HO agreed. The HO did nothing except agree to send representatives to the next Conference. The Department got on with redrafting the Scottish Regulations, had produced a draft by July 1956 and sought the HO's reactions to it.

A year later the HO replied with the news that the Federation of British Cremation Authorities had been invited to submit recommendations for amendments to the Regulations. Since 1955 the Federation had been harrying the HO over its tardiness in acting upon those unimplemented of the Interdepartmental Committee (ch. 6). The HO had not thought it right to consider this while the police investigation of, and legal proceedings against,

---

59. This section is based on **NRS:** HH 61/133, HH 61/134, HH 61/143, HH 61/144, HH 61/1055; **TNA:** CAB 134/1995, CAB 134/1993, CAB 134/2054, CAB 134/2056, DPP 2/2572, HO 282/25, HO 282/26, HO 282/27, RG 48/3239.
60. The Brodrick Committee reported sixteen years later that there was variation in: (1) referees' understanding of the requirement that they be satisfied that the cause of death had been 'definitely ascertained'; and (2) the extent to which they requested a post-mortem or referred cases to coroners before authorising cremations (Brodrick 1971: paras 27.19–27.23).

Dr Bodkin Adams were ongoing: Adams was eventually acquitted of murdering his patients but, subsequently, in July 1957, convicted of falsifying their cremation certificates. Nine months later the Federation submitted its proposals. Perhaps the most interesting of these were that the requirement of ministerial approval of charges for cremation should be extended from municipal to proprietary crematoria, and that approval should not be given to 'the establishment of competitive cremation facilities in some districts whilst others have no such facilities'. 'We are committed to a meeting and it's becoming increasingly clear that we are committed to preparing regulations,' an official minuted resignedly. At the meeting the Federation was made the offer of a working party to draft Regulations, which it reluctantly accepted.

Reporting back on the first meeting of the Working Party in January 1959, the DHS's representative minuted

> I had imagined that the substance of the existing Regulations would, in general, stand, strengthened by the incorporation of the Committee's recommendations which, apart from the major ones (12 to 15) relating to the arrangements for medical certification, were said, in 1950, to be generally acceptable. But the Chairman of the Working Party (Mr Stotesbury) made it clear in his opening statement that the Home Office had in mind a drastic revision of the Regulations and certainly did not contemplate incorporating all the recommendations of the Interdepartmental Committee. The ensuing discussion on Regulations 1 to 5 and 16 [...] showed how far the Home Office are thinking of going in eliminating 'dead wood'; it looks as though nothing much is going to be left of Regulations 1 to 5 [...]
>
> After the meeting I spoke to Mr Stotesbury and expressed my surprise. He replied that the Chairman of the Interdepartmental Committee [...] is a lover of controls and that he (Mr Stotesbury) and those to whom he works are not. The current Home Office view is that cremation authorities must be assumed to be responsible bodies who will have the good sense to see to it that the cremation cause does not suffer because of ill-conducted crematoria. They are, therefore, aiming at excluding from the Regulations any provision that amounts to no more than a pious hope (see, for example, recommendation 2 of the Interdepartmental Committee

[viz. as to the 'integrity, demeanour and technical competence of cremation staff']) and any provision which cannot really be enforced.

The Home Office view is, of course, in line with modern trends and if they and the cremationists are satisfied that their Regulations – at least those relating to the conduct of crematoria – may be weakened, we, with our much less experience of cremation, can hardly question their proposals. We are, however, concerned, because the change in the Home Office outlook will have its effect on the Scottish Regulations: it is obviously desirable that the English and Scottish Regulations should be similar – except, of course, where they must differ because of the different legal systems.

As a prediction of the results of the Working Party, this assessment turned out to be very wide of the mark. The most radical of the possible reforms would have been the abolition of Form C or some amalgamation of Forms C and F and, perhaps, the employment of full-time salaried Medical Referees operating on a regional basis. But proposals such as these, as before, ran into the unyielding opposition of the BMA. The Association now had a fresh arrow in its quiver. Its Assistant Secretary was about to publish a study purporting to show that numerous murders must be going undetected (Havard 1960) and this informed the Association's position that a doctor giving Form B should continue to have to state the cause of death 'definitely'; that the requirement for a doctor giving Form C to 'see and question' the doctor giving Form B should not be relaxed to allow the latter to consult the former by telephone; and that only doctors of at least ten years' standing with wide experience in the practice of medicine should be eligible for appointment as Medical Referees, thus excluding most Medical Officers of Health (MOH) from the position (BMA 1959). This last demand was a compromise, though hardly much of one, between two committees of the Association, the Private Practice Committee on which general practitioners were represented, and the Public Health Committee which looked after the interests of MOHs.[61]

61. There was a further issue concerning MOHs. Most local authorities were seeking to appoint their MOHs as Medical Referees of their crematoria. The Public Health Committee of the BMA obtained counsel's opinion that MOHs could not be required under their usual terms of service to perform this function (or, in other words, if they consented to take it on they could require payment for

The Working Party did produce the draft of a completely revised set of Cremation Regulations for England and Wales. Its HO members came to realise, however, that a compromise would never be agreed about Form C between the cremation and medical interests. In 1963 the HAC decided that it should be retained.

The HO had resisted repeated calls for the Home Secretary to prescribe maximum fees for cremation certificates but thought it would be impolitic to lay new Regulations before Parliament without simultaneously prescribing fees. When the draft Regulations were circulated for comment consultees were told the Home Secretary would be fixing maximum fees after consulting about their level. The BMA now suggested three guineas for each form without an increase in the mileage allowance, which the HO thought 'not unreasonable'. The HO, however, rejected the Association's request that fees be prescribed for Form D (given by a pathologist for carrying out a post-mortem) – the labour being too varied to be suitable for a standard fee – and Form F (the medical referee's authorisation to cremate) – not a 'medical certificate' within section 3(1) of the 1952 Act. The MHLG told the Working Party that it would be willing to exercise its power under section 9 of the 1902 Act to prescribe such a fee on the application of a cremation authority, but this could only be for public crematoria.

Once it had been decided to retain Form C, further work needed to be done to settle its terms. While this was being undertaken, the HO, in response partly to pressure from the BMA (BMA 1964), set up a Departmental Committee to report on death certification and coroners, and the problem of Form C (and consequently the contents of all cremation forms) was handed over to this Committee. It took seven years to report. It decried the alarmist nature of Havard's (and the BMA's) conclusions about the extent of undetected homicide, made recommendations for changes to the procedures for the registration of death whether via coroners or not, and proposed the abolition of all cremation forms and the post of Medical Referee (Brodrick 1971). Only now (2016) are separate cremation forms and medical referees about to be abolished in Scotland as well as in England and Wales (ch. 9).

   it). 'Medical Officers of Health: Counsel's Opinion', *Supplement to the British Medical Journal*, 3/1/1959, 3; and 'MOH and Crematorium Appointment: Dispute with Borough Council', *Supplement to the British Medical Journal*, 12/12/1959, p. 19.

With the revision of the forms handed over to the Brodrick Committee, there were few matters for the new Regulations to address. They were introduced in 1965 in England and Wales (CR 1965) and 1967 in Scotland (CSAR 1967). Householders known to the applicant replaced the limited classes of persons qualified to countersign an application for cremation. It became possible for unidentified human remains to be cremated and, more importantly, for those who objected to cremation to be cremated. Early on the Working Party had decided that the present Regulation caused difficulties and that the Interdepartmental Committee's proposal would be virtually unworkable. The HO, despite anticipating possible objections from the Roman Catholic Church, decided that Regulation 4 would be revoked. An applicant for cremation, however, still had to say whether any near relative of the deceased objected to the cremation. The Regulations also prescribed the contents of the certificate required for the cremation of bodies donated and dissected under the Anatomy Acts, a disposition made possible by the Human Tissue Act 1961. The Scottish Regulations in addition empowered Scottish cremation authorities to scatter ashes as well as to bury them.

CHAPTER NINE

Cremation: Social and Cultural Change, 1967–2016

Introduction

This chapter first addresses changes in funeral behaviour in the two decades between the building of Hazelhead (1975) and Friockheim (1993) when no new crematoria were built in Scotland (see ch. 1). Yet the era saw considerable change in particular influences on Scots' funeral behaviour. Four issues are selected: population trends, the environment, the funeral directing industry, and family ritual and religion.

Demography

Scotland's population remained static for most of the twentieth century (Anderson 1996). It was characterised by lower birth rates, increasing life expectancy and outward migration with little inward replacement. Infectious diseases declined as the primary cause of deaths, to be replaced by long-term chronic conditions, plus cancers and strokes. Longevity was slowly extended. Nevertheless, a gender gap in life-expectancy persisted and death rates continued high in poorer urban areas. Between 1971 and 1991, the number of deaths persisted at around 61,000 annually.

Several factors reduced people's exposure to and familiarity with death (McFarland 2010). First, death became increasingly an event of old age. Second, the location of deaths was changing: after 1947 the NHS came to provide an institutional environment for births and deaths. In 1963 46% of deaths occurred at home (1993: 26%) and 51% in hospitals (1993: 63%) (Scotland's Population 2007). Third, with better refrigeration techniques

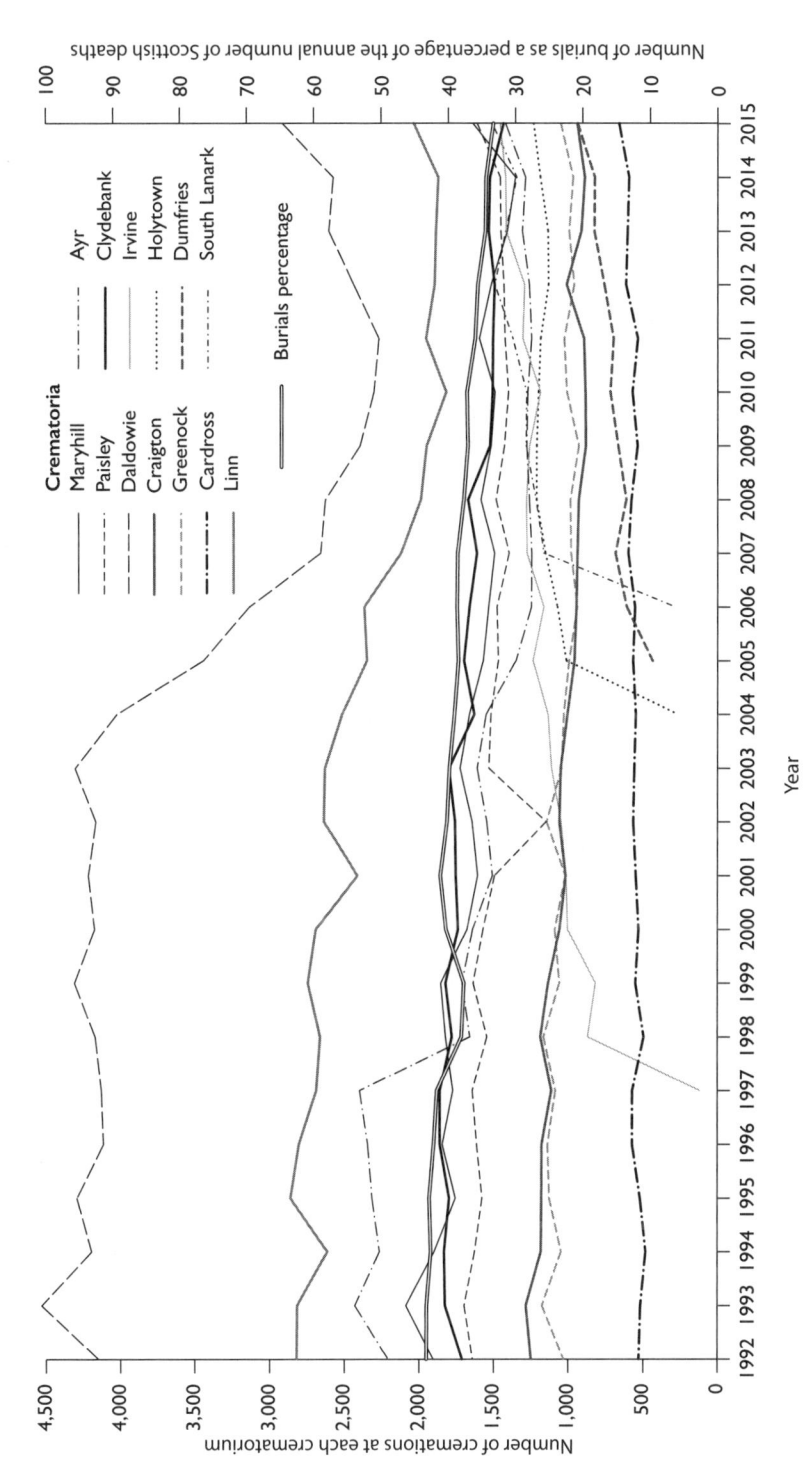

Graph 4. The graph shows the growth of cremation in south-west Scotland. The newer sites – Irvine, Holytown, Dumfries and South Lanark (the sole publicly built crematorium in the south-west) – draw business from older, especially Daldowie and The Linn, and increase accessibility for more local communities. From 1975 to 1995, Local Authorities had built no crematoria, slowing the increase in cremations. The re-entry of the private sector into crematorium building from 1993 helped raise the national cremation rate to 66.7% by 2015. The persistence of burial remains to be explained.

available, funeral directors could offer custody of the corpse on their own premises in the interval before the funeral.

A fourth factor was the character of post-war housing development. New building styles (especially tower blocks) proved uncongenial for traditional customs of watching the corpse; 'modern council housing design and the dispersal of established communities to new towns and peripheral estates were already imposing their own constraints on the funeral day' (McFarland 2010: 260–1).

Funeral choice was affected by post-war population movement. With the relocation of both housing and changing employment opportunities, core urban populations fell (Glasgow by 22% between 1971 and 1981) and a process of counter-urbanisation saw people moving to country and coastal areas. This severed families' access to their traditional burial sites, while increasing their access to crematoria during the building phase of 1957–67.

Environmental Concern

From before the Clean Air Act 1956, the hazards of industrial emissions and nuclear power were evoking a public consciousness about man-made threats to the earth and its atmosphere. Protest groups like Greenpeace (1971) arose. Membership of the European Union (1972) introduced external pressures to UK environmental concern. The Thatcher Government passed its Environmental Protection Act 1990 (EPA).

The Act directly affected British crematoria (Chamberlain 2005). From 1 January 1991, crematoria could only operate with prior authorisation from local Environmental Health Officers. All emissions were now to be monitored. The policy was given the acronym BATNEEC (Best Available Techniques not Entailing Excessive Costs).[1] Local authorities, owning most crematoria (and all post-war crematoria save Craigton in Scotland as at 1991), had to comply. This required revising budgets, retraining staff and fitting new filtration equipment by April 1997. Costs were estimated at £70 million for the UK's (then) 225 crematoria. Local authorities felt uneasy about passing this sum on to bereaved families, for only in 1989 they had been required to ensure that their cemetery services annually covered their costs and had to raise burial fees.

Mercury (from dental amalgam) remained the most hazardous emission and, as its industrial emissions declined, crematoria became exposed as

1. The cynically-minded coined the acronym CATNIP (Cheapest Available Technology Not Involving Prosecution).

the major mercury polluter. The UK was a signatory of the OSPAR (Oslo–Paris) Convention for the Protection of the Marine Environment of the North-East Atlantic. Its recommendation 2003–4 called for application of BATNEEC to prevent the dispersal into the atmosphere of mercury from human remains. The UK was to set the lead in reducing mercury emissions. The Cremation Society (CS) and the Federation of British Cremation Authorities (FBCA) established the Crematoria Abatement of Mercury Emissions Organisation (CAMEO) in 2005 to enable a national system of burden-sharing aiming to reduce mercury emissions by one half by 2020.[2]

The EPA, as amended in particular by the Pollution Prevention and Control Act 1999, had three major effects on cremation and burial in the UK: the involvement of consumer groups targeting levels of funeral costs; the revival of 'green' burial; and the return of the private sector in crematoria provision. Some local authority crematoria responded to the environmental challenge by selling their crematoria (or outsourcing the management alone) to private firms; other local authorities, without existing crematoria, now began to rely on private provision for many of the new-builds.

Funeral Directing

The EPA affected funeral directors' work. Coffins had been made of chipboard, their bonding including synthetic resins and cellulose lacquer. The formaldehyde content of upgraded chipboard was to be reduced by two-thirds. Bitumen, pitch, metal and melamine were banned. PVC, polyester and acrylics were now unacceptable for coffin linings or shrouds.

Cremation offered funeral directing firms economies of scale (Parsons 2014; and forthcoming). From 1900, the funeral directing service steadily became more professionalised (Parsons 2014; and forthcoming; McFarland 2010: 267–8). Until the 1960s most funeral companies had been family-owned. The only exception was the Co-operative Societies' funeral directing departments, which grew in number from the 1920s (Parsons 2014; and forthcoming). With the 1970s came a series of acquisitions; in the 1980s the Co-ops and three other conglomerates dominated the UK funeral-directing market. In 1986, Scotland's Co-operative firms conducted nearly 33% of funerals, with 52% in Glasgow (Monopolies and Mergers Commission 1987: 4).

Many 1980s developments in funeral directing and cemetery and crematorium ownership were inter-related and affected other areas of the

2. CAMEO Information Update, February 2005.

human experience of bereavement. They prompted increasing Government surveillance of the industry, with enquiries into the Co-op's acquisition of House of Fraser funerals (1987) and SCI's acquisition of PHKI and Kenyons (1995); and a Private Finance Initiative (1995) encouraging local authorities (unsuccessfully) to sell crematoria to the private sector. Investigations into pre-paid funeral plans followed. Consumer groups took up funeral reform, highlighting such issues as informed choice, costs and 'green' issues. Media attention ensured that the subject of death began to shed its twentieth-century cloak of invisibility. The Scottish disasters of Piper Alpha (1989), Lockerbie (1989) and Dunblane (1996), followed by the death of Princess Diana (1997), evoked awareness that personal loss was no longer a prerequisite of mourning (McFarland 2010: 275). Mourning patterns were changing.

Family Rituals and Religion

In 1965 Gorer found Scottish rituals of mourning to be among the most traditional in the UK. These included attendance at the death bed; the paying of respects; burial rather than cremation; black armbands; abstaining from leisure activities; grave visiting (Gorer 1965). More recently, McFarland's field-work with funeral directors and nurses in rural and urban Scotland enabled her to identify the 1970s as a watershed in closing the gap between urban and rural funeral practice (McFarland 2005, 2008).

In 1965, more Scots died in hospital than at home and 33% were cremated. In 1972, Geddes characterised the 'Scottish way of death' as one of rising funeral costs and depressed funeral benefits; of the decline of funeral pomp and black mourning wear; of large funeral receptions as the exception rather than the rule. In short, Scottish funerals were not so much traditionally restrained as deliberately underplayed. 'Despite a conservative adherence to tradition, the Scottish way of death is changing,' wrote Geddes (1972); the key feature of this change was cremation, with an 80% rate in Edinburgh.

A decline in religious observance was also apparent from 'the long 1960s' (S.J. Brown 2009: 188; McLeod 2007). In 1956 Church of Scotland membership had peaked. Key indicators of religious affiliation now declined: church weddings, communicants and Sunday Schools. The withdrawal of women from their traditional role in transmitting religious belief and adherence became marked. Only a fifth of children baptised became communicant members by 1972. More recently, despite the heavy load borne by some Kirk ministers at funerals (Reid 2002: 46), C.G. Brown has produced evidence to show how death has figured quite prominently in some Scots' narrative of abandoning religion; and the increase of funerals conducted by secular celebrants has been marked (C.G. Brown 2016).

Studying older Aberdonians in the 1980s, Williams discerned 'a Protestant legacy' in their attitudes to bereavement. The Reformation had divided Christians' attitudes to the dead body. 'While Catholicism could easily accommodate this vile flesh because it was always what the purified soul had to escape, Protestantism had to get rid of it, because it could no longer serve to image the immediate passage of the soul to its felicity' (Williams 1990: 152). While this connects with the original Presbyterian attitude to burial (ch. 1), it suggests why those inheriting a Reformed culture might have welcomed cremation. As the third millennium began, McFarland (2010) and C.G. Brown (2016) have both highlighted the increasing secularity of funerals.

While statistics of funerals are rare, a 1995 survey into grave reuse revealed growing heterodoxy in beliefs (Davies and Shaw 1995: 93–4). Of those claiming Church of Scotland affiliation, 22% believed death to be the end of life, 6% believed in the resurrection of the body and 6% believed in forms of reincarnation. Of the Catholics sampled (in Glasgow and English cities), 14% believed death to be the end of life, 18% believed in resurrection and 11% believed in reincarnation. Traditional Christian beliefs about death had clearly been ill-communicated and had become widely dismissed.

Hazelhead and Inverness Crematoria

The eighteen years (1975–93) between the opening of Hazelhead and Friockheim have earlier been characterised as 'the great gap'. Scotland's era of big public building projects was at an end. The regional and investment differences are particularly significant: in the west, no publicly funded crematoria were opened between Clydebank (1967) and South Lanarkshire (2007). In the east, no publicly-funded crematorium was built after 1967 (Mortonhall). The new-build crematoria after 1995 were all privately-built with the exception of South Lanarkshire; ever since 1975 (Hazelhead) Scotland has opened only two publicly-funded crematoria. This chapter now focuses on the new crematoria at Hazelhead, Aberdeen (1975) and Inverness (1995).

From Kaimhill to Hazelhead

Kaimhill's cremations increased steadily after 1944 (480) reaching 1,515 (1960) when a quarter of Scots funerals were cremations. Meanwhile the 1952 survey of Aberdeen, *Granite City*, omitted the crematorium, implying that town planners were relying upon private burial provision (Chapman et al. 1952: 126). Kaimhill's 400-yard diameter was now filled with housing. Recurrent problems eventually forced the Council to seek a replacement. The ongoing issue was Kaimhill's location in the growing city's south-west.

A new organ required a building extension whose eventual cost was £19,000. In the early 1960s local tenants were complaining to Councillors of 'obnoxious fumes'; all three furnaces needed attention. Meanwhile, mourners' cars jammed local roadsides. In January 1962 Aberdeen City Council (ACC) first spoke of a new crematorium on a new site, leaving Kaimhill as a memorial chapel.[3] In May, the ACC shelved the issue.[4]

By 1968 pressure had further increased on Kaimhill. The Scottish cremation rate was now 38% but the weakening economy squeezed available funding for public projects. In April 1968 ACC discussed the future use of the Freedom Lands at Hazelhead[5] including a replacement crematorium. City and County Council Clerks conferred and in October 1970 the County offered 25% of the now £430,000 estimate. Despite continuing Government struggles with inflation, the city's Finance Committee agreed in April 1971 that the crematorium was its number one priority. Confidence induced by the discovery of North Sea oil possibly influenced the decision.

In January 1972 the County increased their offer, providing their own preferred site at Jessiefields was chosen, and ACC accepted. The estimate had increased to £661,699 when tenders were allocated in May 1973. The Middle East crisis then precipitated a dramatic rise in fuel costs, itself fuelling Aberdeen's new prosperity. When Hazelhead was opened on 27 October 1975, cremations at Kaimhill (2,000 per year) ceased. The buildings were sold to a funeral director. Its coffins scandal continues in local memory.[6]

A Crematorium for Inverness

At intervals over thirty years, crematoria proposals within Inverness-shire Councils had proved fruitless.[7] When, in June 1988, local funeral director W.T. Fraser offered to Inverness District Council (IDC) to build a crematorium,

3. ACC, 2/10/1961, 8/1/1962.
4. ACC, 4/5/1962; Parks and Recreation Committee (P&R), 19/2/1968; ACC, 11/3/1968.
5. Anon 1929; Morgan 2009.
6. See the website for *Leopard*, the magazine for north-east Scotland, collected by Norman McKenzie.
7. E.g. 1969 and 1972, *Inverness Courier* (IC), 24/11/1972. See Jupp 2010.

Inverness' Environmental Health Committee (EHC) welcomed the idea immediately. It had earlier agreed that land could be reserved for a crematorium at the Council's new (1982) Kilvean cemetery, built to ease demand on the 1864 Tomnahurich cemetery. The IDC gave its support on 25 July. Then came two more bids: from local funeral director John Fraser & Son, and the Crematorium Company, part of the Great Southern Group (GSG). The Highland Regional Council preferred public ownership.

These bids encouraged the EHC, given Inverness' rising population of incomers from the south, the expansion of its suburbs and increasing cemetery subsidies. In November the Crematorium Company applied formally to build a crematorium within Kilvean cemetery. The HRC approved GSG's plans in January 1989. These included two chapels, car parking, but without overnight mortuary facilities. The project would be seen through by Councillors Cattell and Hone, Chair and Vice-Chair respectively of the EHC.

GSG was granted planning permission in June 1989. Unexpectedly, in September, GSG's Crematorium Company withdrew from the project, pleading inability to raise the £400,000 required. Two reasons might be offered: first, GSG had now amalgamated with the conglomerate PHKI, entailing a reconsideration of commitments. Secondly, the EPA was imminent, requiring expensive emissions filtration. The latter affected Inverness Council: if a crematorium was to be built by public funds, would rate-payers agree? The Council now voted to encourage new private bids.

There was a third complication, both political and religious. The new Major Government inherited a policy to reorganise Scottish local government. If, therefore, the town-dominated Inverness District were to be combined with neighbouring (rural) Highland authorities, there might be public opposition sufficient to block it. One source was the Free Presbyterian Church of Scotland (FPCS), representative of the strict Calvinist position about attitudes to death and funerals. Its Inverness minister, the Reverend Dr Donald Boyd, told the *Glasgow Herald* many ministers and their congregations strongly opposed any change in the traditional style of Highland funerals.[8]

The FPCS had seceded from the Free Church in 1893, counting the latter's 1892 Declaratory Act a serious break with the Westminster Confession of Faith.[9] Whilst the FPCS numbered just 4,000 (1997), it had helped sustain

8. *Glasgow Herald*, 14/4/1990.
9. Anon 1896; Drummond and Bulloch 1975; McPherson n.d. [1970]; J.L. MacLeod 2000; Caswell 2009.

the cultural distinctiveness of a major part of Scotland and its grip on popular culture had only begun to weaken in the 1970s (C.G. Brown 1997: 72). The FPCS believes that only God knows whom He has predestined for eternal life in heaven (McPherson n.d. [1970]: 375). Consequently, there is nothing that the living can do for the dead (Caswell 2009, 2016). FPCS funerals are performed in line with these beliefs. The coffin is not brought into the church; there is neither eulogy nor music; the dead are neither named nor prayed for; and the body is buried, not cremated. The FPCS is opposed to Spiritualism, prayers at the graveside and national war memorial services (McPherson n.d. [1970]: 382). The FPCS position on cremation now needed to be publicly articulated.

Inverness EHC's response to the FPCS was that while it respected its opinions, a crematorium was an appropriate development for the area. Increasingly, as religious opposition intensified, the EHC debated the crematorium project in private session. Local historian James Miller has commented on the frequency of this tactic when Councillors faced sensitive planning and development issues (Miller 2004: 308). Councillors' minds were concentrated when the last private bid was withdrawn in July 1991. A fortnight later, the IDC agreed to provide for a crematorium within its future capital programme.

Encouragement for crematorium proponents came from the opening of Friockheim Crematorium (Angus) in 1993. After visiting Friockheim, the EHC accelerated its efforts and on 3 December 1993 the Council's Parks and Recreation Committee unanimously approved of a £7.5 million leisure and conference centre, the figure including a £1.2 million crematorium. With the full Council vote arranged for 13 December, commentators sensed rising tension, the *Glasgow Daily Record* noting 'the Council are facing a race against time to get started before local council reorganisation [...] Hard-line churchmen have spent years opposing a plan for a crematorium'. On 13 December the full Council approved the plan.

The FPCS continued to press their case: the project was financially unviable, cremation was a gruesome process and it would 'change the character of the Highland funeral'.[10] Dr Boyd arranged a public meeting.[11] The

---

10. *Scotsman*, 22/4/1994.
11. *IC*, 26/4/1994.

Inverness Courier (*IC*) criticised the Church's position.[12] Boyd collected 1,700 signatures supporting his call for a public debate.[13].

On 24 May 1994 the Highland Regional Planning Committee approved the plans unanimously. The IDC, having prepared its tender documents in advance, posted them immediately.[14] A project team was convened to build the Crematorium. Despite continuing press criticism of FPCS positions,[15] with the HRPC decision made, the controversy was losing its heat. Scotland's Kirk and Catholic Church both accepted cremation. The FPCS was the main religious and local organisation openly campaigning against the project. The national assembly of the FPCS in June confirmed its position[16] but it was too late to affect the Inverness decision. The Church's opposition to cremation drew largely on Scriptural precedent. First, cremation did not show sufficient respect for the dead; second, the Bible associated the burning of the body with God's Judgement; third, the burial of Jesus Christ in the New Testament provides the model for the Christian funeral; and fourth, Christians bury their dead in expectation of their resurrection.

Inverness Crematorium was opened on 26 July 1995. Today the controversy is one about which the Inverness interviewees consulted had largely but politely refused to comment, as if the matter was a family embarrassment best forgotten.

In a process accelerated by the removal of the Catholic ban, cremation had increasingly become, for the majority of Christians in Britain and for the non-churchgoing public, a matter of personal choice and convenience (Jupp 2006a: 168). In retrospect, the exhausting struggles experienced by Inverness Town Council may have encouraged other local authorities to return to Scottish Victorian policies of relying upon private provision for the disposal of the dead (Hussein 1997).

12. *IC*, 26.4.1994.
13. *Aberdeen Press and Journal* (*APJ*), 10/5/1994. On 20 May his local FPCS Lochaber Presbytery rejected the crematorium as 'unnecessary, impractical and morally wrong' (CSA).
14. *IC*, 27/5/1994.
15. *IC*, 3/6/1994.
16. Resolution on Cremation. *Free Presbyterian Church of Scotland: Proceedings of Synod together with Report and Accounts 18 May 1994*. I am grateful to the Revd George Hutton (Inverness) for discussing with me the FPCS position on cremation.

The Architecture of Dunfermline, Hazelhead, Friockheim, Inverness, Irvine, Moray and Holytown

By 1967 Scotland had produced two of the finest crematoria in the UK: The Linn, Glasgow (1962) and Mortonhall, Edinburgh (1967). Both were local authority owned and both challenged the strong tradition of burial in Scotland by confidently – indeed, defiantly – adopting a wholly Modernist idiom generally eschewed in England, but significantly later adopted in Wales. In so doing they exposed the mediocrity of much crematorium design in England. During the 'heroic phase' of crematorium building between 1955 and 1975, local authorities had sought to provide crematoria that were at once functional and humane and accorded with the architectural climate of being 'openly responsive to the mass society of the 20th century' (Glendinning and MacKechnie 2004: 195). In Scotland, as in England and Wales, by 1970 the heyday of local authority provision was over and it fell to the private sector to consider the financial viability of crematoria in less densely populated areas, where mourners had hitherto been forced to travel long distances to their nearest crematorium. This pattern reflected the situation across the UK, where the surge of building had taken place between 1950 and 1970 with 149 crematoria opening in the 1960s, dropping to sixteen in the 1970s and a mere seven during the 1980s.

There was a slowing down in building generally in Scotland during the 1970s. Large-scale reconstruction programmes ceased largely as a result of economic crisis and heavy industry being under threat. This was mirrored by a corresponding halt in the building of crematoria, there now being enough to satisfy Scotland's urban needs. The main centres of population along the Glasgow–Edinburgh corridor were now well served, with provision as far north as Aberdeen. Dunfermline (1973) and Hazelhead, Aberdeen (1975), the only two crematoria built in the 1970s, just before the eighteen-year interregnum, would be the swansongs of major local authority statement buildings.

Dunfermline and Aberdeen: The Modernist Finale

Dunfermline Town Council, voting for a crematorium in 1945, had lost out to Kirkcaldy in the DHS' 1952 decision. In the 1960s Dunfermline revived its proposal. Its scheme was approved by the Secretary of State in 1970, and the crematorium was opened by Fife County Council on 22 January 1973. Dunfermline Crematorium was Modernist in idiom. Designed by Council architect George Alexander Stenhouse, it nestles in the hollow of an undeniably beautiful site. Constructed in a light-coloured brick, with metal fascias and cedar window frames, its low-lying intersecting planes are reminiscent of Frank Lloyd Wright's designs, as are the ways in which the undisguised chimney anchors the building to the site and the internal and external spaces interact. The glazed wall on either side of the catafalque offers a view of a bank of trees. The opening up of the chapel pioneered by architects Sanger & Rothwell at Oldham (1953) and Kirkcaldy (1959) was taken up by Fife Council once more at Dunfermline, in the belief that nature could exercise a compulsive hold on human emotions and invite a depth of human attachment deeply consoling for mourners.

Aberdeen, Scotland's most north-easterly city, is one with character and a sense of purpose. BBC journalist, broadcaster and Aberdonian James Naughtie argues,

> A city must have a sense of itself, or it hardly counts as a city. Aberdeen has never found it difficult to manage that. Glasgow and Edinburgh have seemed to be great lumbering beasts baying at each other across a landscape between the Firth and the Clyde, which sometimes appears to have been laid waste in a battle for supremacy. The one so big and dark, the other so conscious of its outward elegance – surely Aberdeen has benefited from wanting to have no part of it. They can fight for their territory and wage their various social struggles, but somehow the North-East can stay happily remote.[17]

Remoteness, landscape and climate are three natural characteristics that have come to define a city famed for its unforgiving weather. Constructed from the granite hewn from its environs – a hard, resistant, sparkling rock – Aberdeen's very architectural fabric articulates powerfully everything that the city stands for, the granite contributing to the mysterious alchemy that has fashioned the city's identity.

Aberdeen's second crematorium, Hazelhead, stands not only as the last of phase II of Scottish crematoria, but also as one of the final statements of modernist crematorium building. It is a singular building, broad and expansive, signifying a particular moment in Aberdeen's development. By 1970, the city was bucking the downward economic trend as a result of the discovery of oil in 1969. In the final decades of the last millennium Aberdeen reconfigured

17. Naughtie 2000: 1.

itself from an economy based originally on textiles, fishing and granite, to an international hub for the oil industry. Its expansion included not only specialist industrial buildings, but also housing for the increasing numbers of international oil workers. Indeed, throughout the 1960s and 1970s Aberdeen City Architect's Department, under the leadership of George M. Keith, was concentrating its efforts on designing progressive housing right across the city, most of which involved high density, multi-storey schemes. Included amongst the earliest was housing at Hazelhead, an area four miles out of the city. This represented the peak of municipal house buildings in the 1960s in Scotland, with its high-rise flats, low blocks and terraces.

The change in demographics doubtless helped prompt the building of a second crematorium and the site chosen was Hazelhead, close to Jessiefield Farm where the crematorium is surrounded by 30 acres of attractively landscaped grounds, 20 acres of which constitute the Garden of Remembrance. The site is adjacent to 600 acres of woodland. The City Architect's Department appointed Cosimo Pacitti as 'project architect', with main responsibility. Born in 1931, Pacitti had trained in Aberdeen and by 1964 was living in Rutherglen, suggesting that he was in practice in Lanarkshire. He joined the Aberdeen Architect's Department led by Ian Alexander Fergusson in the late 1960s and this appears to have been his first job.

The crematorium is a concrete-clad building, with two large chapels, simple in style and almost asymmetrical in arrangement. It represents a different kind of Modernism from the unified monumental forms of Spence at Mortonhall. Here the internal spaces are more fluid and unified in both mass and space, in keeping with the progressive churches of the time by Gillespie, Kidd & Coia. A striking modern cross arrangement surmounting the chimney adds a further contemporary note to the design. The approach, contrasting its lightness of finish with the dark green of the surrounding trees, is both dramatic and majestic.

The deep expansive canopies and the 'battered' walls constructed from inclined 'off-white' pre-cast panels with an exposed aggregate finish of coarse Skye marble chippings give the building a singular presence. The choice of materials is significant in a city that sets such store by granite. The aggregate finish, which catches the light, is mimetic of Aberdeen granite, which commentators mention in the same breath as the weather, maintaining that it sparkles across the city after rain. A pre-cast splayed concrete kerb runs along the bottom of the walls, forming a base above the granite paving, creating the impression of a building emerging organically from the ground upon which it stands. The crematorium is low-lying, as if hunkering down in defiance of Aberdeen's unrelenting weather. But there is a comforting stillness about the solidity of the white shapes over which the clouds roll. The building conveys a sense of purpose, a sense of self-worth. It is a clean, light and healing building.

The canopies act as both receivers and dispersers of entry, enveloping mourners and offering them immediate physical and psychological shelter. The bereaved are somehow cradled as they enter the unusually spacious single volume of the main chapel designed to hold 270 mourners. Pacitti trod a fine line between economy and emptiness. Despite being one of the largest chapels of its kind in the UK, and certainly in Scotland, Hazelhead escapes anonymity by virtue of two features. First, the brightness of the interior; here concealed lighting along the sidewalls creates an ethereal effect. Second, the chapel has no window to the landscape beyond. This is a rather late example of a traditional chapel space, but its very closed character is a sensitive solution in a city where remoteness binds people together and promotes a collective form of self-reliance. The chapel speaks of a desire for a space in which they might feel part of some larger totality and relate to the community to which they belong. Mourners are further emotionally bound by their shared focus on the dominant, freestanding catafalque. The same approach is adopted in the smaller chapel, which nevertheless accommodates some ninety-six mourners.

Strikingly modern stained glass windows were commissioned for the entrance hall from the American designer Harvey Salvin, and symbolise the changing seasons and the elements of earth and water. These too are bright and uplifting in colour. In the 1990s the crematorium was extended to include mercury filtration equipment in accordance with the EPA legislation. The interior of the utilitarian area of the crematorium is wholly Modernist in idiom, resembling the efficiency of a hospital interior, with its broad corridors, modern plant and clinical reception areas for both funeral directors and coffins. The original intention of architects has not been diminished in any way by the extension (2010), which fits perfectly with the Modernist functionality of the building.

Hazelhead was not only the final example of Modernism in Scottish crematorium building, but it also stands as a perfect embodiment of the remoteness, singularity and character of a city out to challenge the supremacy of the 'great lumbering beasts' of Edinburgh and Glasgow. By the time of its opening in 1975 the days of Modernism in Scotland were at an end and the third phase of crematorium building beginning in 1993 would mirror its wider abandonment in Scotland as a whole.

Private Perspectives: The Move towards Vernacular

By the time Scotland emerged from its eighteen-year interregnum in crematorium building, architectural taste and approaches to funeral requirements had changed. In the third phase of Scottish crematorium building seven out of nine crematoria were privately owned, matching the pattern in England and Wales, where only two out of the thirty-two crematoria opened from 1990 were local authority owned. It therefore fell to the private sector to determine the aesthetics of these new spaces required to address an increasingly wide range of social, economic and psychological needs. The private sector had neither allegiance to Modernism nor the desire to sponsor a Modernist collectivist aesthetic, and in the expansionist postmodernist era it inclined, somewhat inevitably, towards a more conservative approach.

A visual analysis of Scotland's final nine crematoria suggests two things. Firstly, a rejection of local authority Modernism in favour of a broadly vernacular idiom and secondly, a resultant homogeneity of style, a form of 'internationalism' with a small 'i' resulting from a greater engagement with architectural trends popular in the UK. Taking first the vernacular: although Modernists saw the return to vernacular forms as encouraging a sentimentalising of the past, characteristics such as a sense of place, hierarchy, scale, harmony, enclosure, materials, decoration and community unquestionably tapped into a rich vein of traditional values popular with large sections of the public both north and south of the border. During the 1980s many people found these essentially 'human values' embodied in vernacular architecture both attractive and reassuring, particularly in the context of crematorium design, where mourners were looking for more familiar, domestic spaces. With one exception, Scotland's third phase crematoria all subscribe to the vernacular principles above. The exception is Moray Crematorium, the conversion of the Grade II Gothic Enzie South Parish Church of 1886, undertaken in 1999. Moray is one of only three conversions in Scotland, the others being Warriston (1929) and Houndwood (2015).

Inglis & Carr of Kirriemuir heralded the change with their design for Parkgrove, Friockheim, Angus, in 1993 for Ken Parkes, a private individual, who had joined forces with funeral director Ernest Taylor from Forfar, to build the crematorium. The architects described the design as drawing 'its inspiration from abstracted classicism, with the use of strong intersecting axes, reinforcing the ritualistic and processional functions traditionally associated with burial.'[18] It invokes the traditional nave and transept of a church, with intersecting roofs culminating in the masonry flue, which is expressed simply and honestly. The architects suggested that, 'The ceiling finishes to the porte-cochères and the continuity of the surface finishes between internal and external areas help to reinforce the dialogue between the inside and outside. These devices have produced an architecture extroverted and outward looking rather than introverted and gloomy.'[19] They also preferred the use of natural materials, adding

> The use of 'high-tech' materials has been avoided throughout the building with traditional masonry, timber and slate forming the main aesthetic. This conservation-minded approach has been extended into the landscape. It is hoped that this building, in its handling of materials and spaces and its overall response at both a conscious and subconscious level [...] that the lives of the bereaved relatives will be enriched by the sense of place and purpose created here.[20]

Inverness Crematorium followed, designed in 1995 by Graham Rennie of the Highland Council for Inverness District Council. Built on a tranquil and rural location on the western outskirts of the city, it is traditional in design and construction and respectful of Highland traditions in its quest to assume a role in the local community. The chapel, with its long pitched roof, dominates the design, interrupted only by the chimneystack, which in turn is pitched with skew gables to acknowledge local building traditions. There are two chapels, to allow for both large and small family funerals. Here, glazed areas overlook garden courts from which members of the public are excluded, thereby ensuring privacy and quiet. Both catafalques are housed in central recesses and the Book of Remembrance is housed in the separate Tower Chapel, approached though the wreath court. Once again, reference is made to the crowstep gables of the locality.

The Emergence of Homogeneity

Holmfirth Bridge, Irvine, was designed in 1997 by Martin Critchell, of

18. *Resurgam* 36(1) (Spring 1993), 4.
19. Ibid., 5.
20. Ibid., 6.

Critchell, Harrington & Partners, to whom the Great Southern Group (GSG) had turned for the design of its crematorium at Bodmin, Cornwall in 1989, and where Critchell's preference for domestic scale is immediately apparent. This domestic 'feel' was continued at Aberystwyth in Wales, designed in 1994 for the Crematoria Investment Company Ltd (having taken over GSG) and three local District Councils, and Heart of England Crematorium at Nuneaton in Warwickshire, built in 1995 again for the Crematoria Investment Company Ltd. Doubtless because of his work in Wales and England, Critchell was approached by the Caledonian Cremation Company to design Holmfirth Bridge.

Critchell produced another simple domestic solution, with harled walls, a grey tiled roof and discrete chimney. The chapel, marked externally by a tall gable, has a boarded ceiling and by now characteristic floor-to-ceiling window behind the altar, giving panoramic views across the Ayrshire countryside, including the River Irvine and the span of the Holmfirth Bridge. On approach from the car park to the porte-cochère, there is a large pool crossed by a wooden bridge. The beautiful location, on the banks of the River Irvine, provided the opportunity to combine the Garden of Remembrance with riverside walkways. Critchell's domestic vocabulary was intended to comfort and console by dint of familiarity. There is a balance between private and public in all his work, which translates well in his crematorium design. Mourners are provided with an architectural and landscaped environment, which allows for both public ritual and private contemplation. The manager of Holmfirth Bridge reports that mourners always make very positive comments about the landscape, where through the chapel window kestrels have been seen to rise during services. The style of the building has attracted some interesting responses from the public; it has been mistaken for a golf club, hotel and restaurant, on the grounds of its excellent parking facilities and welcoming ambience.

Holytown (2004) was a Dignity project, its architect Philip Baldry of Art-Tech Ltd, Concept Studio, Great Yarmouth. This is couched in a modern vernacular style, leading one visitor to mistake it for a carvery, once again raising the question of the confusing associative values of architectural style. The building, comprising three principal elements, stands on a hillside in North Lanarkshire and is characterised by its white harled walls and deep-pitched roofs which anchor the complex to the site.

Roucan Loch, built outside Dumfries in 2005, was by Robert Potter & Partners. Established in 1964 with offices in Ayr, Dumfries, Glasgow and

Stranraer, the practice is broad-based and was responsible for the postmodern J.M. Barrie House (1984–6) in George Street, Dumfries. Roucan Loch, the only facility serving Dumfries and Galloway, is set in 10 acres of natural countryside, bordered to the north by mature Scots Pine woodland, and to the south by the loch itself. The building has a glulam timber structure and uses western red cedar externally and yellow pine internally. The timber works sensitively with the peaceful natural landscape to create a tranquil space. The windows on both sides of the service room frame views to the woodland and the loch. Both the employment of timber and the setting anticipate the private Catholic Fuente Nueva chapel, built the following year on the banks of Rupanco Lake in Chile. Both are positioned close to water and both convey a feeling of quiet spirituality. Roucan Loch was designed specifically to host small services for a maximum of forty people, held in addition to a main service in the Church or Chapel of Rest.[21] The Crematorium was commended by the Glasgow Institute of Architects in 2005.

In 2006 the same firm designed South Lanarkshire, Blantyre, the only local authority crematorium of this period. Dignity was involved initially, but pulled out of the project because of some uncertainty on the part of the local authority. This was to be the first project in Scotland to incorporate mercury filtration from the outset. The construction was fraught with difficulties. Some argue that the building is poorly sited in a lower 'saucer' and drainage is only adequate until there is heavy rain. But the salient drawback is that mourners look up towards the dual carriageway. From a stylistic point of view, Blantyre begins to represent a somewhat homogenous style common to its contemporaries south of the Border. The clock tower bears an undeniable likeness to a Tesco supermarket. Interestingly, the firm went on to project manage the much acclaimed Crownhill Crematorium for Milton Keynes Council, where the chapel has an uplifting interior. Crownhill's chapel has fine acoustics and is used by the local orchestra for practice and performance. It is also used for weddings, providing powerful evidence of a new crematorium assuming an extended role within a local community.

Livingstone was the first of two crematoria designed for the Westerleigh Group in partnership with West Lothian Council by Stride Treglown,

---

21. Case Study 14, SUST Sustainability in Architecture, Architecture + Design Scotland.

a leading English practice based in the south-west. Opened in 2010, it conforms to the modern vernacular canon, which the owners contend 'has a light, natural look, in sympathy with its rural surroundings'.[22] A sculpture depicting three deer – a reference to the resident herd of fallow deer on the site – was commissioned from Mor Design following a long consultation process with the local community as part of the planning agreement with the Council and led by the authority's Arts Officer.

Scotland's first crematorium to serve the Borders was opened in 2011. Again by Stride Treglown for the Westerleigh Group, the project met with fierce opposition from Melrose and District Community Councillors and 1,350 members of the public, including the Save Scott's Countryside Group, concerned about its proximity to Abbotsford. *The Borders Telegraph* reported one objector as saying it 'was the biggest disaster since the Romans arrived in Melrose'.[23] It is situated adjacent to the Wairds cemetery, which is within the Eildon and Leaderfoot National Scenic Area on the slope of Eildon Hill North which enjoys protected status. Objectors were taken to look at the recently opened Livingstone Crematorium, which they concluded was 'relatively unobstrusive', 'simply designed', 'tastefully decorated' with 'an attractive use of wood and natural stone'. The style, by now recognisable, was not the problem, the objectors conceding that it could be 'the right building in the wrong place'.[24] Interestingly, Martin Critchell, Robert Potter & Partners and Stride Treglown all had experience in the healthcare sector, suggesting a parallel with places of healing and comfort.

The modern vernacular, however, was not without its critics. In 2003, Hugh Thomas, the architect of three English crematoria, the much-admired Bury St Edmunds (1989), Banbury (1999) and Sittingbourne (2003), talked about what he perceived to be the problem of aesthetics in provincial architecture, where there was great opposition to modern design:

> So, am I stuck with having to produce crematoria in a 'traditional' style?
>
> [...] What is meant, clearly, by those who insist upon a traditional style, is something recognizable within their own vocabulary of

22. http://www.westerleighgroup.co.uk/news.html#westlothianopening, 11/4/2013.
23. *Border Telegraph*, 11/11/2009.
24. *Border Telegraph*, 30/11/2010.

church, barn, farm buildings, and now presumably, Tesco – and all in heavily appropriate materials. But slate is not local to the east of England; nor Velux rooflights, nor is the whole concept of a crematorium.[25]

In March 2013 *The Times* reported that Tesco's plans to build a supermarket in Sherborne in Dorset had been met with fervent resistance from the local community. Tesco's architects' visions were covered in messages on Post-it Notes, none positive: 'You/Tesco are not to be trusted and are not wanted'; 'Tesco has no style or grace, loud and brash [...] a hateful organisation'.[26] Indeed the kindest thing written about the design for the new store was that 'it looked like a crematorium'.[27] And so, within a period of ten years, Tesco supermarkets were being compared with crematoria, rather than the other way round. The designs of Scotland's recent crematoria have largely countered this comparison.

Modern crematoria are often criticised for being impersonal and meaningless non-places. Bristol architect John Nash argued in 1989 that poor standards of design tended to 'trivialise and depersonalise peoples' lives, diminish society and family values and make the proper wholesome remembrance of those who have died difficult to achieve'.[28]

An Ecclesiastical Footnote

Given the lack of cemetery chapels for conversion, two examples point to the possibilities offered by church conversions. Enzie South Parish Church, Broadley, near Buckie in Banffshire, rebuilt in a Gothic style by Bruce & Sutherland in 1885–7, closed as a result of the amalgamation of local congregations. It was bought by local funeral directors, Christies, and converted into a crematorium in 1998–9 at a cost of £400,000 inclusive of land. One of its distinguishing features, the canopy which descends over the coffin, has prompted much discussion, being described variously as looking like 'the keel of a ship', 'an old-fashioned haystack' and 'the canopy of a pram'.

Until the opening of the Borders Crematorium in Melrose in 2011, there had been no provision in the Scottish Borders and until 2015, residents

25. Correspondence with the author, May 2005.
26. *The Times*, 19/3/2013.
27. Ibid.
28. Nash 1989: 84.

of Berwickshire had to travel long distances of up to fifty-seven miles to Mortonhall, Edinburgh and Melrose Crematoria. The Grantshouse and Houndwood church (1836) is a handsome Italianate building with round arched windows and doorways, whinstone walls and red sandstone dressings. The tower is its defining feature, with a pyramidal roof with wide eaves and round-headed windows to each face and a blank circular feature below each opening. The church was B-listed in 1971 by Historic Scotland, but closed in 2003, and was bought by the Edinburgh-based Carlton Group with a view to reopening the church and converting part of it into a crematorium. At Grantshouse and Houndwood, the architectural story of cremation building comes full circle. The modest Grantshouse and Houndwood Parish Church is one of only a handful of known buildings by James Chalmers, the architect of Maryhill Crematorium, and was built in 1887–8 with Andrew Robson. James Chalmers was in partnership with Andrew Robson from 1885 as Chalmers & Robson; this partnership was dissolved by 1889.

In the light of the recommendations of the Burials and Cremation (Scotland) Act, church conversion might well present the way forward for Scotland.

A National Perspective

There are several notable differences between Scotland's attitude towards crematorium design and that of England and Wales. The first is that Scotland was not faced with the dilemma of adopting the economic solution of the cemetery chapel conversion. Forty-nine of England's 276 crematoria are conversions, compared with Scotland's one house conversion and two church conversions. By definition, Scotland therefore spent more on its provision *pro rata* than England. The second trend is the alacrity with which Scotland abandoned any reference to ecclesiastical architectural styles, preferring to adopt contemporary idioms as a more appropriate choice for its crematoria. Third, Scotland looked to appoint high calibre architects. Local authorities not only encouraged good, modern design, but were also quite prepared to look beyond their own departments to engage local, national, or in the case of Edinburgh, international architects of sound reputation. Fourth, it followed that there was an insistence both on high quality, local materials and local craftsmen wherever possible, to engender a sense of place and ownership. Historically, Scotland has acknowledged the role that architecture can play in fostering and reflecting a sense of continuity at both a local and a national level. But perhaps the most telling difference is in the recognition and exploitation of the power of landscape, whether in existing cemeteries, old estates or new sites. The Scots hold dear the national landscape and therefore its role in the acceptance of death and the processes of mourning and collective remembrance has, quite understandably, become something of a national signature.

Radius Clause[29]

In 1980 that part of section 1 of the 1952 Cremation Act which required the site and plans of a proposed crematorium to have ministerial approval was repealed (LGPLA 1980 ss 188, 194, 195 and Sch. 34, part XVI). The reason given in briefing documents was 'site approval duplicates controls available to local authorities under planning legislation and, as far as crematoria chimney heights are concerned, under the Clean Air Act 1968'.

It was because of the necessity of ministerial approval that the examination of the meaning of sections 2 and 5 of the 1902 Cremation Act described earlier took place (ch. 8). Either Ministry officials spotted potential infringements of section 5 in plans submitted to them, or neighbouring landowners or occupiers drew them to the Ministry's attention. In one case Wandsworth Borough Council complained that one point of a crematorium building erected by Lambeth Borough Council was only forty-eight yards from a footpath in Wandsworth's area; and Durham had to revise its plans because of the proximity of its proposed crematorium to a footpath. The need to comply with section 5 led some authorities to resort to fairly drastic expedients. Weymouth Borough Council secured the consent of a council tenant by threatening to evict him. Perhaps the last exercise of the power to turn down plans was in 1979 over the crematorium Barry Town Council proposed to build in its cemetery. Astoundingly, the technical adviser to the Council was reported as saying that 'there was no way we could have known' that the consent of the occupiers of dwellings within 200 yards of the crematorium was required!

The Ministry regarded the granting of its approval of site and plans as quite independent of any planning considerations and they strictly enforced section 5 (according to their understanding of it). The fact that a proposal had received planning permission did not restrict the Minister's discretion; and, conversely, planning authorities appear to have had no regard to section 5 of the 1902 Act. Their attitude has been 'We administer the Town and

---

29. This section is based on **TNA:** HLG 45/1303, HLG 45/1452, HLG 45/1493, HLG 45/1554, HLG 120/2868.

Country Planning Acts: the Cremation Act is not our business.' An identical stance is taken by the Scottish Environment Protection Agency in granting operating permits under the Pollution Prevention and Control Act 1999 to crematoria. A recent example of this approach in Scotland is the conversion of Houndwood parish church to a crematorium. The room housing the cremator is within fifty yards of a public highway and 200 yards of the home of a householder who did not originally consent to the conversion. When the FBCA protested to Scottish Borders Council (SBC) at its grant of planning permission for the conversion, the Council replied 'It is a basic principle of planning law and practice that the planning system should not intervene in matters that are properly controlled through other legislation. Therefore, it would not be appropriate for a planning application to be refused because the development may contravene some other legislation, such as the Cremation Act 1902' (see Walker 1997: para. 73). This approach was endorsed by the Scottish Government, although about this both the Government and SBC have spoken with forked tongues. Only a year earlier in consulting on the recommendations of the Burial and Cremation Review Group (Brodie 2007) the Government had broadcast its view that 'current legislation requires that in order to achieve planning permission' any new crematorium must comply with section 5 of the 1902 Act (Scottish Government 2010: para. 98, question 45). Analysis of the public's response to the consultation showed 'a very high level of agreement that the requirements specifying minimum distances between new crematorium buildings and houses or roads should be maintained when granting planning permission' (Social Research 2010b: 1, 5). In particular, SBC responded, 'We firmly believe that the current legislation specifying minimum distance be maintained with regard to planning permission submissions and the granting of the necessary authority' (SBC 2010: 10).

The consequence of the 1980 repeal is that enforcement of section 5 became discretionary, it being left to aggrieved neighbours to resort to whatever private law remedies were available should they wish and could afford to do so and to procurators fiscal to prosecute for an offence against section 7 of the Cremation Act. This makes it illegal, not to build a crematorium within the prohibited limits, but to carry out cremations in a crematorium so built. Each cremation will constitute a separate offence and not only will the cremation authority commit it: depending on their knowledge, employees of the authority, funeral directors, applicants for cremations, perhaps even mourners would be guilty.

Colour plate 47. Hazelhead Crematorium, Aberdeen (1974), Aberdeen City Architect's Department led by Ian Alexander Fergusson. Project architect, Cosmo Pacitti. (Photograph, Hilary J. Grainger)

Colour plate 48. Hazelhead Crematorium, Aberdeen. Extension dating from 2010, Aberdeen City Architect's Department. (Photograph, Hilary J. Grainger)

Colour plate 49. Hazelhead Crematorium, Aberdeen (1974), Aberdeen City Architect's Department led by Ian Alexander Fergusson. Project architect, Cosmo Pacitti. (Photograph, Hilary J. Grainger)

Colour plate 50. Hazelhead Crematorium, Aberdeen (1974), Aberdeen City Architect's Department led by Ian Alexander Fergusson. Project architect, Cosmo Pacitti. Entrance canopy. (Photograph, Hilary J. Grainger)

Colour plate 51. Hazelhead Crematorium, Aberdeen. Extension 2010, Aberdeen City Architect's Department. (Photograph, Hilary J. Grainger)

Colour plate 52. Parkgrove Crematorium, Friockheim, Angus (1993), Ingliss & Carr, Kirrimuir. (Photograph, Hilary J. Grainger)

Colour plate 53. Parkgrove Crematorium, Friockheim, Angus (1993), Ingliss & Carr, Kirrimuir. View from the porte-cochère. (Photograph, Hilary J. Grainger)

Colour plate 54. Parkgrove Crematorium, Friockheim, Angus (1993), Ingliss & Carr, Kirrimuir. Chapel Interior. (Photograph, Hilary J. Grainger)

Colour plate 55. Parkgrove Crematorium, Friockheim, Angus (1993), Ingliss & Carr, Kirrimuir. Porte-cochère. (Photograph, Hilary J. Grainger)

Colour plate 56. Inverness Crematorium (1995), Graham Rennie, Highland Council. (Photograph, Hilary J. Grainger)

Colour plate 57. Inverness Crematorium (1995), Graham Rennie, Highland Council. Tower Chapel housing the Book of Remembrance. (Photograph, Hilary J. Grainger)

Colour plate 58. Holmsford Bridge Crematorium, Irvine, North Ayrshire (1997), Martin Critchell, Critchell, Harrington & Partners. (Photograph, Hilary J. Grainger)

Colour plate 59. Holmsford Bridge Crematorium, Irvine, North Ayrshire (1997), Martin Critchell, Critchell, Harrington & Partners. (Photograph, Hilary J. Grainger)

Colour plate 60. (*above*) Holmsford Bridge Crematorium, Irvine, North Ayrshire (1997), Martin Critchell, Critchell, Harrington & Partners. (Photograph, Hilary J. Grainger)

Colour plate 61. (*right*) Holmsford Bridge Crematorium, Irvine, North Ayrshire (1997), Martin Critchell, Critchell, Harrington & Partners. Chapel interior. (Photograph, Hilary J. Grainger)

Colour plate 62. Holytown Crematorium, North Lanarkshire (2004), Philip Baldry of Art-Tech Ltd, Concept Studio, Great Yarmouth. (Photograph, Hilary J. Grainger)

Colour plate 63. Holytown Crematorium, North Lanarkshire (2004), Philip Baldry of Art-Tech Ltd, Concept Studio, Great Yarmouth. (Photograph, Hilary J. Grainger)

Colour plate 64. Holytown Crematorium, North Lanarkshire (2004), Philip Baldry of Art-Tech Lt., Concept Studio, Great Yarmouth. (Photograph, Hilary J. Grainger)

Colour plate 65. Roucan Loch Crematorium, Dumfries (2005), Robert Potter & Partners. (Photograph, Ruth Jardine)

Colour plate 66. Roucan Loch Crematorium, Dumfries (2005), Robert Potter & Partners. (Photograph, Ruth Jardine)

Colour plate 67. South Lanarkshire Crematorium, Blantyre (2006), Robert Potter & Partners. (Photograph, Hilary J. Grainger)

Colour plate 68. South Lanarkshire Crematorium, Blantyre (2006), Robert Potter & Partners. (Photograph, Hilary J. Grainger)

Colour plate 69. West Lothian Crematorium, Livingston (2010), Stride Treglown for West Lothian Council. (Photograph, Brian Parsons' Collection)

Colour plate 70. West Lothian Crematorium, Livingston (2010), Stride Treglown for West Lothian Council. (Photograph, Brian Parsons' Collection)

Colour plate 71. West Lothian Crematorium, Livingston (2010), Stride Treglown for West Lothian Council. (Photograph, Brian Parsons' Collection)

Colour plate 72. (*right*) West Lothian Crematorium, Livingston (2010), Stride Treglown for West Lothian Council. Sculpture by Mor Design. (Photograph, Brian Parsons' Collection)

Colour plate 73. (*below*) Borders Crematorium, Melrose (2011), Stride Treglown for the Westerleigh Group. (Photograph, Hilary J. Grainger)

Colour plate 74. (*left*) Borders Crematorium, Melrose (2011), Stride Treglown for the Westerleigh Group. Entrance. (Photograph, Hilary J. Grainger)

Colour plate 75. (*below*) Borders Crematorium, Melrose (2011), Stride Treglown for the Westerleigh Group. Porte-cochère. (Photograph, Hilary J. Grainger)

Colour plate 76. Borders Crematorium, Melrose (2011), Stride Treglown for the Westerleigh Group. Crematorium with Wairds Cemetery in the foreground. (Photograph, Hilary J. Grainger)

Colour plate 77. Houndwood Crematorium, Scottish Borders, (2015). Conversion of Grantshouse and Houndwood Church by the Carlton Group. (Photograph, Brian Parsons' Collection)

Cremation of Body Parts[30]

In the decades either side of 2000 two cultural shifts were to affect the operations of crematoria. The first was a reaction against the paternalism of the medical profession, the other an increased sensitivity to the products of pregnancy loss.

Disclosures in the 1990s that organs removed during post-mortems of children had been kept by English hospitals were followed by similar disclosures about Scottish hospitals. Some of these retentions were unauthorised. Others were authorised according to the terms of the Human Tissue Act 1961 but parents who had consented to the removal of 'tissue' did not realise that tissue could include whole organs. Parents, having as they thought buried or cremated their child, were faced with arranging second (and even third) funerals for belatedly recovered body parts. Some were told that because the Cremation Regulations made no express provision for the cremation of body parts they could not lawfully be cremated. Some were even told that body parts had to be disposed of as clinical waste. Crematoria that were prepared to cremate body parts might require a fee for doing so. As a result, the Cremation Regulations both sides of the border were amended to regulate this (CAR 2000; CAR 2006; CSAR 2003; S. White 2000a, 2000b) and even more far-reaching changes were made to the Human Tissue and Anatomy Acts (HTA 2004; HTSA 2006).

Reform of Death Registration and Abolition of Cremation Certification

Between 1974 and 1998 Dr Harold Shipman killed at least 215 of his elderly patients, many of whom were cremated. In 2000 he was convicted of murdering fifteen. Six had been cremated after he had signed Form Bs, some falsely or misleadingly (J. Smith 2002: Appendix E). An inquest found twenty-four more to have been unlawfully killed. There was concern about the failure of the death registration and cremation certification process to detect his murders. (Dr Havard was still on hand to claim vindication for his views about the extent of undetected homicide that had been dismissed by the Home Office Working Party on the Cremation Regulations and the Brodrick Committee [Havard 2000].) In response, the Minister for Health

---

30. Kennedy et al. 2000; Redfern et al. 2001; O'Hara 2002; Department of Health et al. 2001; Department of Health 2003; Maclean 2001, 2002.

set up an enquiry under section 2 of the National Health Service Act 1977. It was to be chaired by Lord Laming. It would sit in private, but report publicly. In association with this enquiry and to feed into it, the Home Secretary put together an Interdepartmental Working Party to review the procedures involved in the certification of deaths and the authorisation of burials and cremations (Home Office 2000a; Clifford 2000). In March, the Working Party issued a questionnaire to interested parties; in July it produced an analysis of those responses; and in October it circulated a document setting out three options for reform (Home Office 2000b, c, d).

At the same time the Minster for Health asked the Chief Medical Officer to commission a clinical audit of Shipman's practice. A year later it was published. One of the purposes of the second cremation certificate (Form C, as it then was) is to detect and prevent homicide by a doctor providing the first certificate (Form B). As Shipman completed Form Cs for the patients of doctors who had provided Form Cs for his patients the audit was able to compare his approach to completing Form C with that of these other doctors. It is the richest of ironies that, after the many years' criticism of the irresponsibility with which doctors completed Form Cs, a medical mass murder (Shipman) was so much more conscientious and meticulous than any of the other doctors as to be held up in an official report as an exemplar of how it should be done (Baker 2001: 47, 113).

Meanwhile a group of relatives of Shipman's known or suspected victims and several media organisations had applied for judicial review of the Minister's decision that the Laming enquiry should sit in private. They were successful and in January 2001 Dame Janet Smith, a High Court judge, was appointed under the Tribunals of Inquiry (Evidence) Act 1921 to conduct a public enquiry, with power to compel witnesses to give evidence. She was to criticise six doctors for lack of vigilance in completing Form Cs (J. Smith 2003: 353–87) but all were subsequently cleared of serious professional misconduct by the General Medical Council (C. Dyer 2004; O. Dyer 2005a, 2005b). Her third report dealt with death and cremation certification and the roles of police and coroners in the reporting and investigation of deaths. It was complemented by a review which had been established by the Home Office into very much the same subject. There were other enquiries at this time into the handling of dead bodies and the retention of organs (Clarke 2001; O'Hara 2002; Palmer 2003; S. White 2001). The result of these endeavours, eventually (Department of Health 2007, 2008), was legislation which provides for the establishment of a medical examiner system (CJA

2009 ss 18–21). This, when brought into operation, will deliver what the CS had advocated since its early days and what the Brodrick Committee had recommended – the standardisation and tightening of the procedures before burial and cremation can take place with no extra certificates required for cremation. As an interim measure in England and Wales a revised set of Cremation Regulations was issued, the most innovatory feature of which was a right given to applicants for cremation to inspect the Form B and C (now renamed 4 and 5) certificates before cremations (CEWR 2008 reg. 22).

Scotland responded to these events with the establishment in 2005 of a group mainly to review legislation relating to cremation and burial, but keeping an eye on the English and Welsh developments relating to death certification. Following a consultation about the recommendations of the group (Scottish Government (Reid Howie Associates) 2010a) provision was made, as in England and Wales, for the scrutiny of death certificates and the doing away with medical certificates for cremation and medical referees (CDSA 2011; CDSACPO 2015). In England and Wales all deaths will be scrutinised by medical 'examiners', but in Scotland medical 'reviewers' will scrutinise a proportion only.

Disposal of Human Remains after Cremations – Non-viable Foetuses, the Stillborn and Babies

Legislation about the remaining recommendations of the Group might not have been so fast arriving had it not been for the coming to light in December 2012 of how ashes from the cremation of stillborn and neo-natal children had been dealt with at the Council-owned Mortonhall Crematorium in Edinburgh. Their parents had been told that no ashes were recoverable from such cremations; but ashes had been recovered and buried in the grounds of the Crematorium, either in its Garden of Remembrance or in a rutted area adjacent to refuse skips whose appearance, in Dame Angiolini's words, 'was wholly inappropriate to the solemnity and decency of interment'. The section of the cremation register recording what had happened to them had been inaccurately or misleadingly completed and the actual cremations, carried out overnight with the secondary combustion chamber turned off, were in breach of the Crematorium's operating permit. After a short internal inquiry (Rosendale 2014) the Council appointed Dame Elish Angiolini, a former Lord Advocate, to establish what had happened following the cremations of foetuses, stillbirths and infants and to report on the conformity of procedures at Mortonhall with professional standards (Angiolini

2014). Because the police and procurator fiscal were investigating whether crimes had been committed the Investigation could not start in earnest until the following April when the procurator fiscal decided that no prosecutions would be brought. Meanwhile the revelations about Mortonhall had caused parents to ask questions of other crematoria in Scotland and research by the BBC suggested that what had happened at Mortonhall was not confined to Mortonhall. Consequently the Government set up a commission, under the chairmanship of Lord Bonomy, to review policies, guidance, practice and legislation relating to the recovering and disposal of remains from the cremations of babies and infants (Bonomy 2014).

Unless parents made other arrangements, hospitals and pathology departments in Edinburgh sent the stillborn and neo-natal dead and, in later years, foetal remains, for cremation at Mortonhall, for which parents did not pay but from which they were told by medical staff there would be no recoverable ashes. Rarely were parents told that ashes would be recovered from cremations at the two privately owned crematoria in the city and, when they were, they were led to believe, mistakenly, that they would have to pay for this. Advice given by the FBCA and the Institute of Cemetery and Crematorium Management (ICCM) in slightly different terms and except in the very early years, was not that ashes were never recovered but that parents should be told that recovery could not be guaranteed. But this was based on the experience of operators and received wisdom rather than on scientific enquiry. A notable feature of the Angiolini Investigation was its commissioning of two reports, one from a combustion engineer with great experience of the operation of cremators (Chamberlain 2013), the other from a forensic anthropologist and archaeologist. By reference to what happens inside a cremator during a cremation and to the skeletal development of babies, they explained why below a certain gestational age the chances of the cremation of a baby producing identifiable human remains are reduced; and from a study of photographs of the remnants of cremations of foetuses they estimated the gestational age at which they might be detected by the untrained eye (Roberts 2013, 2014).

Throughout the period covered by the Investigation Regulation 17 of the Scottish Cremation Regulations (and Regulation 16 of the English and Welsh ones) prescribed what a cremation authority should do with the 'ashes' from the cremation of 'a deceased person'. Primarily they were to be given to the applicant for the cremation or disposed of in accordance with that person's wishes. Although the advice of Institute and Federation was similar, they differed over whether the 'ashes' to which the Regulation referred were the residue of everything with which a cremator had been charged or the residue only of the human tissues. The Institute took the former view, the Federation the latter, despite having had legal advice to the contrary in 2004 in connection with the reclamation of metals from cremations. Which view is correct was one of the two questions about which the Investigation and the Commission obtained a legal opinion. The opinion favoured the Institute's view as well as opining that the 'ashes' included the residue of the cremation of still-births (Woolf and Balfour 2014). The other question, about which the Investigation obtained a separate legal opinion, was: who is the 'applicant' when the application for cremation is signed, not by a parent, but by a funeral director or hospital, as applications for cremation frequently were? Often parents were unaware that a Form A application for cremation of their child had been completed; and the non-statutory part of the form in use at Mortonhall, which allowed applicants to indicate their wishes about the disposal of the ashes, was frequently left blank, received wisdom being that there would be no ashes. In the absence of instructions or an arrangement made with the applicant Regulation 17 obliged the crematorium to bury or scatter the ashes. The opinion given was that the applicant for cremation is the person who signs the application, at least when they are not acting as agent for a parent, which the opinion implies funeral directors would not be when, as in the usual case, they signed that they had been 'appointed in that role' (i.e. to apply for the cremation). The consequence is that crematoria need not enquire whether the intended disposal of the ashes meets a parent's wishes; and, indeed, even if the crematorium knows the parent's wishes it might be difficult for the crematorium lawfully to comply with them (Balfour 2014).

Section 7 of the Cremation Act 1902 empowers the Scottish Government and the Minister of Justice to make regulations about the cases in which and the conditions under which the cremation of 'human remains' may take place. It does not empower them to make regulations about the burning of human tissues that are not human remains. It is an interesting indication of how cultural attitudes to stillbirths have changed that nowhere in either legal opinion or in the report of the Investigation is the question raised of whether a stillborn child is human remains.[31] This, it will be remembered, was a question that exercised the Government's lawyers in the 1920s and 1930s (ch. 5). If a stillborn child is not human remains, any cremation

---

31. Bonomy 2014: 54 does touch on this point.

regulation which seeks expressly to regulate the cremation of the stillborn (such as Regulation 16) would be void, and, equally, a regulation which did not expressly refer to the stillborn (such as Regulation 17) could not properly be interpreted as extending to them. If, however, Regulation 16 is not void, it is difficult to see how any but an arbitrary definition of 'human remains' would not encompass the slightest products of conception; but that Regulation 17 does not extend to all products of conception both legal opinions agree.

Among the many recommendations of the Investigation and the Commission, which reported in June 2014, were: that the cremation of the stillborn and non-viable foetuses should be clearly statutorily regulated; that 'ashes' should be defined as 'all that is left at the end of the cremation and after the removal of any metal'; that, except for cause shown, applicants for the individual cremations of foetuses and the stillborn should be limited to the baby's nearest relative and for the communal cremation of non-viable foetuses to authorised personnel of health institutions, the parents having given their fully informed consent to this; and that applicants should sign the applications personally and their signatures be independently attested. Ever since hospitals had ceased incinerating non-viable foetuses as clinical waste, crematoria had been accepting them for bulk or multiple (or as they are now more sensitively termed 'communal' or 'shared') cremation despite there being no legislation regulating this, and the Institute and Federation had modified their policies to permit this (IBCA 1992, 2001 [not independently published]; McHale 2001; Dunn 2001; ICCM 2004, 2011 [not independently published]). The Commission recommended a complete review of all documents touching on the cremation of babies, the establishment of at least seven working groups to report upon differing aspects of their cremation, and of a standing National Committee on Infant Cremations, chaired by a Government official, to investigate and promulgate good practices throughout the industry. Finally the Commission recommended the appointment of a permanent Inspector of Crematoria with a remit extending to the funeral industry as a whole.

On the day that the Commission's report was published, the Government established a National Cremation Investigation under Dame Angiolini to do for parents who had babies cremated elsewhere than at Mortonhall what she had done for those who had had babies cremated there, i.e. establish whether any ashes had been recovered and what had happened to them; and to report on the processes at, and management of, the crematoria involved and the performance of medical workers and funeral directors in informing parents about the recoverability of ashes and taking and carrying out their instructions (Angiolini 2016). Similar investigations have begun in England and Wales (Jenkins 2015; Ministry of Justice 2016).

The Government quickly accepted all the Bonomy Commission's recommendations (Scottish Government 2014). The National Infant Cremation Committee had its first meeting in October.[32] In the following January a consultation paper about a Burial and Cremation Bill was published (Scottish Government 2015a), and in March 2015 an Inspector of Crematoria was appointed (in ignorance (Scottish Government 2015d: 32, para. 10) of the fact that this was not the first time this had been done (see ch. 6 above)).

Burial and Cremation (Scotland) Act

The Report of the National Cremation Investigation (Angiolini 2016) was published after the Burial and Cremation Bill was enacted (see next section). 202 cases were referred to the Investigation: its Report dealt with the 163 cremations clearly falling within its remit and 14 of the 29 Scottish crematoria where they were carried out. Some crematoria Angiolini praised for their commitment to, and success in, recovering ashes: Maryhill, she was told, had ashes from infant cremations from a hundred years back. At other crematoria Angiolini found practices similar to those at Mortonhall revealed in her first Report. The most startling of her findings concerned Hazlehead crematorium at Aberdeen. Here a belief prevailed that ashes were not recoverable from infants as old as eighteen months, even two years, despite the use of cremators identical to those in, and made by the owner of, Friockheim Crematorium 50 miles way where ashes had always been recovered; and non-viable foetuses and babies had been cremated together with unrelated adults without the consent of the parents of the first two or the next of kin of the third. The ashes from the cremations had been mingled and returned to the adults' next of kin and no record kept of the fate of the babies. Angiolini was able to examine how cremation authorities had responded to the disclosures in her first Report and the recommendations of the Infant Cremation Commission. Not always timeously or appropriately, she discovered. She recommended, among other things, making it an offence to cremate foetuses and babies together with adults without the

32. http://www.gov.scot/Topics/Health/Policy/BurialsCremation/NCIC accessed 19/3/2015.

consent of the next of kin of all, the extension of the remit of the Inspector of Cremation to funeral directors, and the licensing of funeral directors and cremation authorities.

Following the consultation, a Bill was introduced into Parliament and passed. The Burial and Cremation (Scotland) Act replaces the Cremation Acts completely with nineteen sections about cremation, five about the appointment and functions of inspectors (of burial and funeral directors as well as of cremation), and one about the promulgation of a code of practice about the management of crematoriums (the Act prefers this form of the plural to crematoria) but not, apparently, about their operation (BCSA 2016 ss 45–63, 89–93 and 64 respectively). The Bill had far fewer sections than the Act has, almost entirely because of the amount of detail it would have left to subordinate legislation. For this it was criticised by the Delegated Powers and Law Reform Committee (2016). Although local authorities would always have had to provide burial grounds for their areas (BCSB 2105 cl. 2), the Bill had no provision even empowering them to provide crematoriums. The Act does (BCSA 2016 s. 46).

Despite the desire of three-quarters of the respondents to the consultation for the radius clause to be retained (Scottish Government 2015b), it will fall by the wayside without any transitional arrangements or scheme for compensating householders. This was the most controversial of all the Bill's provisions. At Stage 2, in committee where the Government did not have a majority of members, the Bill was amended to prohibit the construction of a crematorium within 200 metres of a 'residential property' and vice versa (Local Government and Regeneration Committee 2016: cols 17–22). At Stage 3, however, the Government mustered its supporters and, with three opposition members, reversed the amendment (Scottish Parliament 2016: cols 8–15). Except for a requirement for cremations to be carried out in buildings, 'crematorium' is defined as 'a building fitted with equipment for the carrying out of cremations' including 'land (other than a burial ground) pertaining to such a building' (BCSA 2016 ss 50, 46(a) and 107(1)), and 'cremation' is 'the burning of human remains' including any processes applied to the burnt remains (BCSA 2016 s. 45(1)): 'grinding' is specifically mentioned. The term 'human remains' is not defined but is extended to include anything put in a cremator with the corpse (BCSA 2016 s. 45(3)). 'Ashes' is defined as 'the material (other than metal) to which human remains are reduced by cremation' (BCSA 2016 s. 45(a) and (3)).

The Act for the first time provides for a scheme of regulating 'private burials' – for example, in private gardens – (BCSA 2016 ss 22–25) but the scheme does not extend to the burial of ashes (BCSA 2016 s. 22(6)(a)). It is not completely clear whether the Act's provisions regulating the exhumation of human remains (BCSA 2016 ss 27–31) extend to ashes. At a time when the public is displaying a penchant for 'porting' ashes the scope of these sections might have to be determined by litigation.

The Act contains elaborate provisions about the fate of ashes, mainly to deal with funeral directors' growing stockpiles of ashes left unclaimed by applicants for cremation (BCSA 2016 ss 51–56). It also has sections regulating the disposal of the products of pregnancy loss (BCSA 2016 ss 69–86) and one allowing its provisions (and the provisions of any other Act) to be applied to other methods of dealing with dead bodies (BCSA 2016 s.99). So it will be possible for innovatory methods such as resomation, promession, sublimation and reverse polymerisation[33] to be regulated should this become prudent (S. White 2011). At present resomation, which has been developed in Scotland, is in use in North America (Sullivan 2005, 2016). These methods are not in themselves unlawful, but, in an echo of the obstacles placed in the way of cremation during the Second World War, an inadvertent consequence of amendments to the Bill may have indirectly made them so.[34] The Bill would have authorised various categories of persons to 'dispose' of human remains. This would have allowed disposal otherwise than by burial or cremation. Because it was felt that the words 'dispose' and 'disposal' were insensitive, they were altered wholescale to the analogous forms of 'bury or cremate' (Scottish Parliament 2016: cols 15–16). One example will show the effect. Under the Bill a local authority would have had to bury or cremate any body for whose 'disposal' arrangements had not been made (BCSB 2015 cl. 56). Under the Act the authority's duty arises if arrangements have not been made for the body's burial or cremation (BCSA 2016 s. 87(1)(b)). Thus

33. Resomation dissolves a body by alkaline hydrolysis leaving ashes (Sullivan 2009), Promession reduces a body to ashes by freezing in liquid nitrogen and vibrating it (Wiigh-Mäsak 2005). Neither release emissions to atmosphere. Sublimation uses hydrogen as a fuel for cremation, Reverse Polymerization is essentially microwaving (Pearson 2007).
34. That this is inadvertent is clear from the Minister's explanation of the amendments which "are technical drafting amendments", having no "effect on the meaning of the sections to which they relate".

an authority learning, for example, that someone proposed to deal with a body by resomation would have to commandeer the body and arrange for its burial or cremation (while, nevertheless, having regard to any wishes expressed by the deceased about the means of 'disposal' (BCSA 2016 s. 87(5)(a)). Only six of the Act's 113 sections are yet in force.

One recent development which the Act singles out for prohibition is a funeral pyre in the open (BCSA 2016 46(2), 50(1)(c) and 107(1)). One, ignited close to the Scottish border in 2006 by Davender Ghai of the Anglo-Asian Friendship Society, was followed by litigation in England which left the status of 'natural' cremation, as its supporters prefer to call it, unclear (S. White 1993, 1997 and 2006). Cranston J., the judge, ruled that the Cremation Act required cremations to take place in crematoria (and thus in buildings), that the consequent prohibition of pyres could infringe rights guaranteed by the Human Rights Act, but that the prohibition was justified. Ghai appealed. By the time the Court of Appeal came to hear his appeal, Ghai had decided, contrary to what he had previously maintained, that his religious requirements could be met by a pyre in a (particular type of) building, so the Court did not have to decide whether the judge had been right to rule that cremations had to be carried out in buildings. Nevertheless it allowed Ghai's appeal and set Cranston J.'s order aside, while remarking that even the flimsiest of structures could be a building and thus a crematorium (Ghai v Newcastle City Council 2009, 2011; Cumper and Lewis 2010; S. White 2010). Since 1994 there has been an officially recognised site on the banks of the Cramond whence ashes can be dispersed on flowing water.

CHAPTER TEN

Scotland's Setting of Cremation

In this final chapter our goal is not to rehearse the descriptions and analyses of the emergence of modern cremation in Scotland already detailed, but to set selected themes emerging from them in a reflection on death and cremation on a wider canvas. One of the challenges of this book was that we had no existing full-length history of burial in Scotland and have had to develop our own chronology of funeral change in modern Scotland. This we have offered not only for positive criticism but also as a guide for the next generation of death scholars who can take up the challenge of portraying how people made their choice between burial and cremation over three generations.

As for this volume, our pragmatic study has shown how modern cremation requires crematoria set within appropriate landscapes, covered by legal permissions and regulation, created through the collaboration of civic and, often, ecclesial institutions, and with a public acceptance and even welcome of this means of treating the dead. This study has offered a remarkably good example of complex and integrated social processes emerging amidst some radically changing social circumstances, including an increased profile of broad secularity. While focused on the Scottish case, the interplaying narrative of previous chapters has revealed in some considerable detail the cultural complexity surrounding this mode of coping with dead bodies. The broad historical frame of change, notably pivoting on the Scottish Reformation, its theological tenets and liturgical practice, has been documented in its move towards the mixed worldviews of today. Our account of cremation in Scotland has, concurrently, pursued the vital dynamics of law and of architecture as key necessities of cultural life where 'society' exists in and through the co-operative participation of both groups and of individuals. Each disciplinary narrative represented in this study, as outlined in the Introduction, has been allowed both to speak for itself and to engage in mutual conversation with the others, helping this study to yield more than the simple sum of its parts. This is not to say that a great deal more could be made of many single elements documented here, nor that a more seamless integration of our disciplinary perspectives might have been achieved, but only that a worthwhile complementarity has emerged that might encourage others in research that lies ahead. In this final chapter our goal is to provide a wider setting still for these disciplinary emphases on death and funerary rites, showing something of their conceptual relatedness as we set the Scottish case in a geographical and theoretical mapping of cremation as a distinctive funerary practice.

Narrative

We begin with narrative, partly because human beings love stories and live within them, and partly because each of our chapters weaves a series of historical, theological, legal, social and architectural narratives into our extensive account of cremation in Scotland. From history as schematised depictions of events driven by distinctive theoretical motivations, and from theological accounts of eras deemed to be influenced by divinely influenced activity, through the creative invention of literature, to the gossip of mundane reality, narratives sustain our worldviews. In Scotland this has involved the remarkable reorientations to the world generated both by the Reformation of religious ideas and practices and by the Enlightenment of thought and its enhancement of individuals and their perception of responsibilities to themselves and to their societies. Amidst these changes we do not forget the emotional dynamics of life, especially those engendered by bereavement, grief and the memorialising of the dead, whether in terms of burial place or within the memories of the living.

In scientific worlds, too, a similar narrative-drive occurs, albeit much more sharply interpreted through theoretical models, while social scientists also deploy theories of change, including those of secularisation, and classify periods such as those of modernity and postmodernity, reckoning these by their distinctive social dynamics. Even some sociological-historical desires to define more recent times not just in terms of secularisation but also of the emergence of a postmodern self are grounded in the dynamics of losing shared ideology and metanarrative. Here, for example, it is highly instructive to pinpoint the radical shift: from the erstwhile Catholic meta-narrative on death, the interim state/purgatory and the afterlife to the Calvinist stance of Knox and the Reformed Presbyterian position on the divine framing of destiny devoid of ecclesial influence. Arguments on the isolated nature of the postmodern self and of 'changing relationships between space and time' would certainly possess an enormous resonance in and through the Scottish Reformation in which the destiny of the self and its potential soteriological bonds with others became radically destabilised (Bauman 2000: 8). It is, quite obviously, not only recent processes of secularisation that have transformed the way people see themselves or, more particularly, have been tutored to see themselves. Whatever may be the case in terms of grand narratives, families and individual networks of association continue to share their own accounts of life, and it is these that often become intensified at times of bereavement and the more explicit dynamism of memory linking us with our recent, and even more distant, dead (Francis, Kelleher and Neophytou 2005).

As for religions, their theological ventures offer their own carefully shaped expression of the way things are, often set within some overarching theory ensuring an appropriately positive outcome for human identities. In the Jewish–Christian flow of thought this account has, for example, been described theologically as 'salvation history' comprised of a series of epochs or dispensations that progressively express the ultimate engagements between humanity and God. Though still found in more conservative Protestant groups this reckoning of time, and of 'time left' before God brings judgement on the world, has largely disappeared in broad denominational Christianity in Great Britain, albeit strongly emphasised by the Free Presbyterian Church of Scotland (Caswell 2009 and 2016). Today, people's concerns tend to reflect more on the earthly life that has gone and on the active memories of the deceased than on post-mortem states. The core cultural value cluster of respect for the dead, dignity in ceremony and care for the bereaved all conduce towards a negotiation of what happens in any funeral, not least at crematoria.

Tonality in Mortality

In terms of tonality, this clustering of concerns is frequently captured in the notion of 'celebration', the celebration of a life, often involving photographic representation of the deceased on service sheets or on display. Requests for people attending to wear special colours or some more 'positive' rather than 'negative' mourning wear are not unusual. This 'life-focus' is reflected in the element of vitality associated with the natural growth evident in landscape design and gardens surrounding crematoria, and extends the notion of tonality from the verbal narratives in eulogies and various readings and music to the physical environment. This extension is frequently taken further still when cremated remains are removed from crematoria for depositing in places associated with the active life of the deceased. Freedom to negotiate the form of ceremony with those participating in it includes the deeply significant fact of choice of 'tone', one that can diverge significantly from some traditionally religious patterns. Religious communities bring their own tonality to narrative and to ritual events framing it and these may either accord entirely with mourners' own outlooks or may generate some degree of dissonance.

Whatever the outlook of people, funerals provide one of life's circumstances when individuals may intuit their own mortality and their place in group memory. And such intuition is all the greater through witnessing the funeral rituals of others. This is precisely where the power of religious institutions has, historically and across cultures, come into its own through accounts of death conquest. Whether in the faith of Abraham with its divine promise of numberless descendants, or in Christianity and Islam, with their hope of resurrection and a destiny of Paradise, or even in Indian-derived traditions of cosmic transmigration under the evaluative force of karma, masses of people have counted on sacred stories as blueprints of their personal destiny. As for Communism it, too, was deeply rooted in a revolutionary narrative of social change and the production of a new type of human being. Even when some contemporary trends speak of highly individualised persons pursuing fulfilment through change, sometimes drawing on notions of spirituality, their existence is, actually, often safeguarded by personal wealth or sustained by a supportive social world. Even solipsism's overly-strong medicine is too much for most, for whom the desire to be true to some most significant-other remains a human constant. There are, of course, persons who, in their time and place, are unable to share their tale of life with others, and for some of these suicide is its own silence, albeit signed off in its own distinctive last message.

Theology

What we have been able to do in this book, notably through Gordon Raeburn's work on post-Reformation funerals in Scotland, is to take up this most crucial phase in Scottish life and thought and show how death rites were worked out in practice at different times and places, and how, for example the 'middling classes' set an example in cremation (ch. 3). Raeburn's doctoral studies, completed as part of the research underlying this book, have been pioneering in identifying theological ideas on death and funerals in post-Reformation Scotland.

Theology is, in itself, a most remarkable human activity that we often take too much for granted. The way that generations learned theology, notably at the old universities, often meant that lecture and library-study were, whether formally or more personally, inextricably bound up with worship. Training for church ministries often took place in this mixed context of thought and liturgical action, which engendered its own form of piety that conduced to a distinctive sense of identity. Indeed, there is strong argument to be made that beliefs which inform a person's identity are, in turn, placed beyond doubt. That belief and identity may cohere in the process of the sacralisation of identity, as the theologically informed sociologist Hans Mol argued, helps explain why individuals and groups are prepared to defend most strongly certain of their theological positions (Mol 1976; Davies and Powell 2015). For, in a real sense, it is one's very identity that is being defended. When beliefs concerning death and one's eternal destiny are the point of debate it is understandable that difference of belief will assume an intensity of its own. This was the case in Scotland's Protestant Reformation and, again, in the post-Disruption generation when the complex interplay of geological studies, biblical higher-criticism and Darwinism challenged theological belief in Scotland, as specifically evidenced in the disputes and 'trial' of William Robertson Smith (Johnstone 1995). Subsequent divisions within Scotland's denominations and yet further shifts in modern worldviews added to the complexity of funerary life because they reflected differently on human identity and its constituting beliefs. Precisely because Christian churches dominated death for millennia, transformations like the Reformation inevitably focused on death, for it is here that every individual and family becomes involved in the ecclesial institution's desire to affirm its belief. Here it is worth recalling that Scotland has its own parallel belief universe of folkloric and fairie beliefs (cf. Henderson 2001).

Truth and salvation

Two aspects of belief that are inextricably bound up with human identity, that bring the remarkable nature of theology to the fore and come into alignment in terms of death, are those of truth and salvation. These foundational concepts touch the very basis of human identity. Philosophical or theological definitions apart, the notion of 'truth' assumes considerable significance due to its attraction for human beings as meaning-making creatures. People possess an affinity with the notion of 'truth' precisely because of their proclivity to make sense of the world, a sense-making that is as much emotional as it is cognitive. It is not surprising, for example, that some ideas – not least those enshrining key scientific discoveries – are described as beautiful. The appreciation of expressions of 'meaning' involves its own form of emotional response. Here we echo the Introduction to this volume and its formulaic expression of the developmental scheme in which emotions transform ideas into values, those values that confer identity then become beliefs, while the beliefs that go further and create a frame for a person's sense of destiny tend to take the form of what we can identify as religious beliefs. The affinity of people with 'beautiful' ideas may well carry its own form of adaptation to both cultural and natural environments, as those ideas provide their own driving force for meaningfulness. Some, perhaps most, religious doctrines fall into this category of beautiful ideas that attract certain individuals and flood their desire for a life that makes sense and, in the process, confer both a sense of joy and of purpose. Moreover, certain individuals either create or come to embody these ideas and, in themselves, become attractive leaders for a wider body of followers. Such are prophets, reformers and charismatic guides for those who catch the 'beauty' at a slightly second-hand level. Nevertheless, the attraction to 'truth' is driven by the similarly significant notion of 'hope'.

Hope, the cultural expression of the biological drive to survive, is 'a fundamental property of social identity' (Davies 2011: 191–8). Hope is experienced as a particular tension of consciousness that gives an individual an intuition that living into the future is worthwhile; good or better things lie ahead. When aligned with religious meaning-making it becomes manifest in ideas of salvation that, in themselves, give a narrative account of identity's destiny. Salvation was the hallmark of earliest Christianity as a sect of Judaism with Jesus as its embodied saviour figure and the new community as its medium. The meaning of Christian 'salvation' took its form in the idea of Jesus not only as a fulfilment of Israel's existence in the world as God's chosen people, but also as the one in whom death itself was conquered and through whom a new world order of a transcendent kind would emerge. Death-conquest, pivoting around the symbolism of the cross and empty tomb as symbols of death and resurrection, provided the bases for many different explanations of divine will, grace and the limited scope of human merit, as well as ultimate victory over evil. Whatever theoretical shade was given to 'salvation' its deeply attractive focus lay both on the individual and the ecclesial community's destiny. It was around these motifs that dying, death, sin, evil, judgement, potential punishment for wickedness and a recreated afterlife took their distinctive Christian shape, in which the dead were not shunned or isolated as impure corpses, but assumed status as the basis for the awaited transformation in God's good time and place.

This religious background was fundamental to the use that Christians came to make of earth burial, despite the fact that Jesus' body had a cave-tomb location. As Christian-influenced culture expanded throughout Europe, for example, people took to earth burial, with the model of Jesus' tomb becoming conflated with earth-burial. The complex symbolism of death–burial–resurrection came to play its own part in fashioning Christian imaginations over death, and dealing with the dead. Just how God would deal with the dead became its own arena of debate, with theology becoming the way and means of pondering these issues, and with liturgical actions furnishing their own ritual means of expressing them. This is precisely where the meaning of the ceremonial of the Mass along with prayers for the dying and the dead, and of potential benefits accorded them through such prayer and more concrete forms of absolution through the ritual-bureaucracy of indulgences, helped foster the theological quandaries and disputes that emerged as the Protestant Reformation. In this process the beauty of ideas in their form as doctrine on the one hand, and the human proclivity for ritual action in liturgical form on the other, came into sharp focus in funeral and memorial rites. In Scotland this very interplay may well have fostered division between Presbyterians and other denominations, and could also be considered in terms of some Irish and Welsh Calvinistic Methodists, Anglicans and Catholics.

Certainly, issues of human identity and of influence or control of that identity, whether in terms of divine predestination, a divinely authorised church authority, social convention or of individual choice, all played and continue to play a part in attitudes to life, death and its entailments. Doubtless, for some, the theological notion that the living can assist the post-mortal state of their kin through prayer or the payment of money for ritual-prayer for the dead would have been an attractive proposition, as the widespread use of indulgences implies: helping the dead through ecclesial means offered its appeal. For others, by sharpest contrast, the doctrine that the destiny of the dead lay entirely in the will and foreknowledge of God was a stream of thought passing biblically from Paul, through Augustine amongst the Church Fathers to Calvin as a key Reformation thinker, and those who followed him in shaping religious change in post-Catholic Scotland. Predestination possessed its own beauty. Theological controversy on death, funeral and destiny offered its own battle of beauties, as intimated perhaps in the Presbyterian heresy trials of the 1870s–1900s briefly alluded to in chapter 2. But times change and so do theological and ideological artistic styles, their peculiar attractions and the feasibility of dogmatic contestation.

Worldview Perspective

Such shifts in style appealing to changing worldviews underlie the period covered in this book, with 'world-view' being a valuable notion that embraces religious, secular and mixed orientations (Droogers and van Hartskamp 2014). From the theological ages of Catholic tradition through Protestant Reform and eighteenth-century Scottish Enlightenment; through nineteenth-century on-going Industrial Revolution and urbanisation; onwards to the twentieth century's transformation through war, social welfare and medical-scientific developments; and into a twenty-first century with its diversity of cultural identities and expectations of life, times have changed. The rise of evolutionary thought in the mid-nineteenth and of modern genetics in the mid-twentieth centuries capture, in themselves, the sense of conceptual shifts underlying what can best be understood as worldviews. The contemporary presence of some, albeit small, radically conservative religious groups that still reflect sixteenth-century theology alongside a majority of diverse groups representing modernised faiths and entirely secular outlooks, makes the topic of funerary rites particularly important. For all die, bodies need disposal, and people retain both their emotional responses to loss and the deep capacity for holding the dead in memory. And, as far as Scotland is concerned, as in most European engagements with death, the cultural resources that lie at hand for use by bereaved people consist not only of 'traditional' patterns of funeral but also of cremation and the diversity of possibilities of the use of cremated remains. These cultural resources have been very well accounted for in this volume through the civic debates and local authority-planning lying behind the rise of modern cremation.

The shift from the Reformation to Chalmers' funeral and to legal considerations of death has offered one example of diverse interests surrounding social change. Men and women of social standing, strong convictions and with diversity of professional, intellectual and commercial concerns, have provided social resources for the population at large, not least at the times of considerable emotional need.

Emotions

These emotional needs are worth highlighting, not only because of the practical occurrence of cases in our previous accounts, but also because the study of emotions has, in recent years, become increasingly prevalent within the Arts-Humanities as well as in social and psychological studies. Previous chapters have covered numerous cases where personal views on cremation were aligned with the emotions, as exemplified in Dr Ebenezer Duncan and his 1887 paper on 'The Reform of our Present Methods of Disposal of the Dead: Earth-to-earth versus Cremation' and his 'first appeal for cremation in Scotland', including cremation as 'the only practical method by which we can avoid the disgusting and dangerous products of putrefaction'. Half a generation later that general statement was so very much more focused and culturally contextualised by our account of journalist Edward Watt in his strong support for a crematorium for Aberdeen in 1921. His thoughts turned on his obviously recent war experience and of demobbed soldiers and their memory of the 'loathsome repulsiveness of decaying humanity' experienced in no-man's-land. Those deeply negative memories he saw as echoed in the notion of earth burial, something that did not apply to cremation, that was so much more desirable given 'the speedy and purifying action of fire'. This very notion of cleansing as a feature of cremation has gained its own academic comment in recent scholars for Britain (Parsons 2005) as for the USA (Prothero 2001); it is an expressive description that, more technically speaking, captures the emotional interplay of the human sense of embodiment and of mortality's decay. As for the 'honest cinder' alluded to in chapter 4, that might not always satisfy more biblically textual believers, for whom the return to dust through the decay of burial more directly expresses the negativity of bodily life as sinful.

As for disgust, it is one of the most fundamental of human emotional responses and the fact of its use in relation to the decay of death reveals a polarity of feeling opposed to a sense of 'respect' accorded to the living and 'dignity' to the newly dead (Darwin 1998: 255–60). Such a spectrum, from disgust to respect and dignity, is highly significant in relation to crematoria as the location in which the corruptible flesh is most rapidly reduced to ashes, a material that never seems to attract the emotion of disgust, but rather of respectful dignity.

A slightly different emotional resonance was encountered, this time at the inaugural meeting of the Edinburgh Cremation Society on 3 February 1910, when the Rev. William Main of that city's Trinity Church commented on his experience of 'a thrill of horror' always associated with witnessing 'the committal of a dead body to the earth'. Was, perhaps, William Main reflecting the interface between human and divine domains pivoting around death, the earth and religious notions of divine destiny? There is, in this sense of 'thrill of horror' something of a motif that would shortly gain much popularity with Rudolph Otto's study of *The Idea of the Holy* and his description of a certain awe or thrill pervading experiences of the divine (1924). Otto identified and Latinised this mode of awareness as the *sensus numinis*, describing its emotional dynamics in terms of being a *mysterium tremendum et fascinans*. This fascinating attraction to a powerful 'unknown' would also seem to be a frequent accompaniment of some deaths and corpses, though perhaps with a stronger negative and repulsive element than that intended by Otto in terms of experiences of the divine. The point between the two is likely to turn on our human emotional sense of engagement with what we intuit as something other than ourselves, whether it be God or a corpse. Each of these might, theologically and philosophically, be said to be both known and unknown, with the potential for dissonance between the two creating a 'thrill'.

The grave differs from the crematorium, not least with the latter reflecting a certain distancing of individuals from the life and earth processes of the natural world, a shift inaugurated through the Industrial Revolution, and enhanced through the architectural creativity sustaining the rise of modern crematoria. There is a sense in which the industrial age influenced the sense of time, speeding up human agency in its transformation of the earth's resources into cultural goods, albeit often to the detriment of wellbeing amongst industrial workers. Nevertheless, modern cremation and crematoria straddled the later nineteenth and twentieth centuries, most especially for towns and cities that had expanded through industrial development and its allied commercial activities. Some would, doubtless, see the post-1950s as a cultural period in the United Kingdom at large when this kind of distancing from death was paralleled by a similar distancing aligned with the emergence of the Welfare State and its hospitals as an increasingly significant location of death. Regarding modern western societies, both hospitals and crematoria can be viewed in terms of sites of competitive architectural status to churches, in the sense that all three have been, and are, in their own way, locations hosting behaviours enshrining core cultural values of human wellbeing, with some evidence even suggesting that people view the crematorium as being in some sense 'sacred' (Davies 1996).

One further emotional dynamic concerns gender issues, death and mode of disposal, and we have already witnessed something of this when noting that, in 1908, approximately a third of the membership in the Scottish Burial Reform and Cremation Society was female, with their 'chief reason for favouring cremation' lying in 'the fear of being buried alive'. The arrival of cremation as a cultural resource has provided individuals with funeral options that were simply not available prior to the late decades of the nineteenth century and, in effect, not until the mid-twentieth century; by which time cremation was a more viable option across the social class spectrum. By 1967–8 cremation had attained roughly 50% of UK incidence of funerals, but it was not until 1977 that Scotland reached that statistic. As for the UK as a whole it attained the low to mid 70% range from roughly 1993 to the present day incidence of 75%.

To give something of a sense of emotional attitudes to such fears as those of being buried alive we can offer some results of a UK-wide survey conducted in 1994 and published the following year (Davies and Shaw 1995). Of the 1,603 individuals sampled in the UK, divided roughly into 400 (200 men and 200 women) in each of Glasgow, Sunderland, Nottingham and London, we can first look at funerary anxieties as they differed between women and men.

Personal anxieties over mode of disposal (UK)

	Burial	Cremation
Women	238 (27%)	154 (18%)
Men	75 (10%)	71 (10%)

(Source: Davies and Shaw 1995, adapted)

This table gives actual numbers of individuals within and not percentages of the total sample. So we have 238 women expressing anxieties over burial and 154 with anxieties over cremation; then there were 75 men with burial and 71 with cremation anxieties. In percentage terms this means, for example, that some 14% of the total UK sample, men and women, had some concern over cremation, while 19.5% of the total UK sample, men and women, had some concern over burial. While these might appear relatively small minorities they would still represent many thousands of individuals if extrapolated to the population at large. For our purposes the significant element is that while roughly twice as many women as men had concerns over cremation (154 to 71) that number rises to roughly three times as many women to men (238 to 75) expressing some concern over burial. Featuring large among burial anxieties were fear of burial and claustrophobia (women 123, men 42), of being eaten by worms (women 72, men 17), and of the body rotting (women 24, men 8). Other concerns expressed by only a few people included being cold in the ground, ideas from horror films, and headstones being vandalised. Only three women and one man were concerned that their graves might be reused. We offer these results only as some possible reflections on the earlier note of the fear of being buried alive amongst some key women in the early cremation movement.

For comparative purposes it is worth adding that the fears expressed in the 1995 UK survey on cremation anxieties were headed by fear of being burnt or burnt alive (women 89, men 35), various family concerns (women 28, men 18), opposition to cremation (women 25, men 11). Some 8 individual women worried about getting back the correct ashes. Here, again, individual women stood out over men in expressing their concerns. We note that it could be argued that men were more reticent in expressing worries than women; we have no direct way of demonstrating that. Again, we also stress the relatively small number of individuals, men and women, expressing their concerns, but these, too, would reflect many thousands if these survey results bear any extrapolation to the public at large. What they do make clear is the evident presence of concerns, and with burial seeming to touch more of them than cremation.

One other set of comparative data from the 1995 survey will be of relevance here, viz., the views of some 211 women in Glasgow compared with 200 London women on afterlife beliefs. People could choose more than one option. So 15% of Glasgow women choosing a 'Life comes to an end' option represents 32 choices as a percentage of 211 individuals, and so on.

Women's expressed afterlife beliefs

	Glasgow	London
Life comes to an end	32 (15%)	49 (25%)
The soul passes on	91 (43%)	90 (45%)
We await a resurrection	23 (11%)	15 (8%)
Return as something/someone else	31 (15%)	27 (14%)
All is in God's hands	82 (39%)	42 (21%)
Other	4 (2%)	5 (3%)
Total	211 (100%)	200 (100%)

(Source: Davies and Shaw 1995)

Of particular note is the marked difference between the 15% of Glasgow women who, at that time, reckoned that life simply came to an end at death, compared with the 25% of London women: inversely, there was a higher 'religious' response in the Glasgow, 39% agreeing that all lies in God's hands compared with London's 21%. The strong agreement on the soul passing on (Glasgow 43% and London 45%) and on the notion that we return as something or someone else (Glasgow 15% and London 14%) is notable in places whose cultural history would normally be regarded as not influenced by Eastern notions of transmigration and reincarnation. By contrast, one might have anticipated that the British cultural history of Christianity might yield a higher inclination to ideas of resurrection, given that formal funeral liturgies and biblical texts used at funerals have long framed burial rites; here we find but 11% of the Glasgow women surveyed, and some 8% of the London women focused on this topic. It might be expected that resurrection motifs would be higher in Glasgow given the strength of Catholicism in that city. As for the idea that everything is in God's hands, as already mentioned above, this would remain an open theme in terms of, for example, the role of religious ideas of predestination that might lie behind that result. So, too, perhaps in relation to the wider role of Spiritualism in Scotland on which we but barely touch in chapter 5 (cf. Church of Scotland 1922; Kollar 2000;

Byrne 2010). In terms of the construction of the questionnaire behind the data we do possess there was nothing to 'test for' predestination, the explicit intention was to mark a religious yet non-doctrinally specific sense of trust. Without adding further detail we can say that men's responses tended much more to non-religious views across these various options.

Secularity, spirituality and mindfulness

Amongst the many issues touched by such attitudes to burial, cremation and an afterlife, is that of grief and of the attitudinal resources brought to bereavement; and just how people cope, grieve and maintain a sense of life as meaningful is as complex now as it probably ever has been. It might even be more difficult in societies often lacking broadly shared worldviews yet sharing experiences of loss (Parkes et al. 2015). As with all institutions, religious denominations evolve with time and adapt to their social environments. One major form of adaptation to the historical-social worlds of recent centuries has been that of modern cremation whose ritual performance is now a matter of negotiation, marketing and networked influence. Churches that were hostile to cremation largely came to accept it, save Orthodoxy. Moreover, people with a this-worldly focus of identity, who might also espouse religious denominational identity or might be avowedly secular, have the option of funerary rites conducted by non-religious agents.

Humanist, secular and civil celebrants all exist as exponents of worldviews that either affirm a non-theistic interpretation of life or who see their ceremonial role as echoing the narrative that a family would wish to tell of their dead kin. Rather in the mode of once-fashionable non-directive counselling, non-assertive leadership of a funeral draws powerfully on the individual, family and networked narrative of the deceased. In one sense, of course, it might be argued that a kind of non-assertive 'leadership' of funerals was precisely what John Knox advocated precisely because of the belief that afterlife destiny lay entirely in God's decisiveness. Through an edited version of a person's life his or her virtues are told, sometimes including a critical point or two if they enhance the overall positivity, with this funerary biography sometimes being accompanied by an appropriate photograph or even photo-collage of the life now past. Favourite music, songs, poems, or readings often replace hymns and scriptural texts. Moreover, family members or friends often speak in reminiscence where once the minister of religion or priest would have spoken of the future life. In terms of worldview thinking such a ritual process is likely to reduce both the conceptual and ideological dissonance to be felt by those who would describe their own framing of their life as secular or as spiritual – where 'spiritual' refers to an awareness of life's significance and of what sources enhance existence and add to its depth – and whose awareness would grate against ecclesially framed language. In terms of the ritual and symbolism of cremation it is certainly the case that crematoria, especially when publicly owned, can be said to privilege secular styles of funeral. In even more general terms, the relatively recent interest in the psychological deployment of notions of mindfulness in relation to life itself (Williams and Penman 2014) and to end of life care has its own part to play in the spectrum of self-resourced worldviews.

As for secularisation, the simple fact of indifference to established religions highlights the significance of the diversity of worldview resources available as signposts for meaning-making, for the human animal is no less a meaning-maker in a hypothetically purely secular age than in some presumed golden age of religious adherence. What changes are the reference points and perhaps the range of meanings with which people are content? That is to say, while some traditionally religious folk may speak of ultimate heavenly destiny, some profoundly secular people may have their horizon of meaningfulness pitched at a more proximate level of family life, intimate relationships, or work and leisure networks. Indeed, it is just such bonds that often make their way into funeral narratives. Moreover, even in groups where religious horizons of eternal destiny are espoused, the more proximate realms of life-experience assume prominence when they die and are remembered.

Ritual-symbolism

To tell familiar tales takes not only time and place but also an acceptable form of expression. Traditional Catholic liturgies provided just such an acceptable form, sanctioned by the grand narrative of Christianity's salvation-history focused in the life, death and resurrection of Jesus and his heavenly abode replete with angelic and other transformed creatures. The dead were transferred to an appropriate afterlife prior to their final beatific vision of God. Liturgical rites and private devotions were activities enabling the imagination and its sustaining emotions that helped people to cope with grief. What is interesting about this book's account of the drives and dissonances associated with the Protestant shift to stark burials devoid of telling narrative is that rites remained. Even if only for a relatively short period of time the advocacy and practice of silent rites is of theoretical interest precisely because of the nature of ritual as repetitive behaviour recognised as a carrier of social values. In this, silence would be as telling as speech if popularly acknowledged.

Funerals carry a plethora of symbolic significance with them, and they have increased rather than decreased over time. Many of these have been covered in previous chapters where we have been keen to ensure discussion of the design of the wider landscape setting through which people approach the crematorium building itself, whether by car – itself a symbol of modernity – or in part on foot. Issues of mood-setting in and through these approaches have not been ignored. The buildings, too, are potentially dense with symbolic significance and have been fully documented in careful detail that draws attention to styles of architecture whether carrying an 'ecclesiastical idiom', a firm move into Modernism, or even symbolic echoes of Freemasonry, itself a significant force in the rise of the cremation movement in Italy and the Netherlands. The Hungarian crematorium at Debrecen is instructive as far as religious and ideological politics are concerned in that it was completed in 1931 in this strongly Protestant part of north-east Hungary, and its architecture includes a large pulpit that stands above the catafalque in a characteristically Protestant position and with the obvious significance that prayers and exhortation would be used. However, Catholic opposition ensured that it did not open for business until 1951 (Mates 2005: 251–6). As an overall mixed Catholic and Protestant country Hungary's subsequent trajectory of cremation reached, for example, some 36% by 2004, a level comparable with Finland's 33%, and the Netherlands of approximately 52%. We return to further statistical profiles later in this chapter.

For the moment we come back to the Masonic theme and to Scotland, where we have seen, for example, how the architect James Chalmers (1858–1927), a member of the Glasgow Philosophical Society and one of the key founding members of the Scottish Burial Reform and Cremation Society, was also Provincial Grand Architect, ensuring that Masonic input would not be absent. Having said that, we have also noted that he was a lay-preacher and could advocate cremation as a practice allied 'with the respectability of the poor'. Amidst such personal and social concern, this architectural and ritual creativity also encountered the negative stance of the Roman Catholic Church albeit that the Catholic Third Marquess of Bute had, as we have seen, been initially supportive of approaching the Vatican on the positive nature of cremation.

So it is that symbols or the specific absence of symbols usually carry hallmarks of particular institutions for Protestant as well as Catholic traditions, but we have also noted how wider aesthetic influences play their part, not least in crematoria that serve a mixed religious and ideological constituency, exemplified in stained-glass windows depicting ashes 'reposing among the angels', where angels expressed a non-sectarian view of the supernatural realm as well as some positive sense of an after-life (Cumming 2005, 2016). Throughout this study we have witnessed the role of particular individuals from numerous professional backgrounds in fostering modern cremation. In retrospect it is particularly important to identify both the fact of such people as they chose particular architects, and then to highlight the role of architects as a professional group who mediate and generate the spirit of their age and transform their grasp of it into concrete form. Just as we now often speak of interdisciplinarity, it might be worth seeing them as inter-aesthetically negotiating ideas and emotions, beliefs, attitudes and doctrines, as they forged funerary environments.

Within Scotland this topic of the intricate interplay of perspectives, notably of belief and rite, had its own resonance because of the innovative nineteenth-century work of the great Scot, William Robertson Smith (1846–1894). Hebrew professor and Arabic scholar, and one seen by some as even the father of British anthropology, he was in the vanguard of later Victorian critical thinking, not least in terms of biblical criticism. Because of this his views were opposed by some conservative churchmen, resulting in bouts of what were, in effect, trials for heresy. Though the young scholar left his Chair at the Free Church College of Aberdeen in 1881 because of this, his subsequent fame as editor of the famed ninth edition of *The Encyclopaedia Britannica* and author of the later lectures on *The Religion of the Semites* (1889) has left an enduring mark in the study of religion. We cannot pursue his arguments here but should at least note the strong emphasis he placed upon ritual as such, though always recalling that he was dealing with ancient Semitic contexts and not with the more recent history of Scotland. Still, it was in a mind redolent of Scotland's theological worlds, as well as of new European ideas of biblical texts and religion in Europe, that he developed his idea that ritual integrated a community and conferred a sense of joy, and that narratives developed to explain the rites rather than narratives existing to create ritual. For him, this expression of rite took precedence over subsequent interpretations given to rites; especially when such interpretations took the form of a myth. His ritual-myth position will remain open for debate yet, in its own way, it is not irrelevant for the 'silent funerals' of Reformation Scotland. For here there was to be behaviour devoid of verbal commentary. Here was ritual without myth, silent action lest inhering tradition, popular ideas or misplaced words contradict the formal theology of predestination. Still, we can hardly argue that Presbyterian funerals fostered 'joy', let alone 'assurance', through their silent respect of God, the divine will and belief in predestination.

One focused issue in which act and interpretation held their own competitive place in cremation concerns the coffin itself and its 'movement' during the ceremony. We have seen this in preferences for a descending mode of removal that, for example, planners at the Maryhill Crematorium deemed the least offensive, given that it would appear to diverge less from the descent of the coffin in traditional earth burial. Here the reference to 'offence' once more pinpoints the role of emotion in the overall consideration of cremation. By contrast, the method of horizontal removal, as at Glasgow's Daldowie Crematorium, has been identified as a 'response to changing preferences in post-war Scotland'. From the later twentieth century, too, opinions over the mode of egress of the coffin have prompted a great variety of opinion, often in terms of final separation of the coffined corpse and relatives (Davies 1995: 20–3). Concern with calming emotion and not triggering this by ritual-symbolic means has been a feature of cremation funerals.

Cremation's symbolic possibilities

The control of funeral ritual for emotional reasons is one thing; control for both theological and political ends is quite another. In practice people are apt to adapt and develop schemes that complement their goals, as when sixteenth- and seventeenth-century Scots constructed 'burial aisles' in their churches to evade the Knox bans (Spicer 2000). We have also seen the complex interplay of theological and aesthetic issues through our accounts of crematorium design in Scotland. On a wider comparative scene it is worth recalling societies under strong political control and their use of cremation for ideological ends. The rise of Communism in what became the USSR, for example, led to the introduction of cremation into a world where the Russian Orthodox Church had, for centuries, been the medium of and for dealing with death. From approximately 1927 key Soviet leaders were cremated with their ashes placed in the Kremlin Wall, a further drive for cremation and the building of more crematoria followed in the 1950s and 1960s, a time of intensified destruction of churches. The first man into space, Yuri Gagarin, was so placed in 1967. Though cremation has hardly won popular applause, even after the demise of the Soviet system in 1991, it has provided a relatively low cost form of funeral for the masses amongst large urban populations.

The Greek Orthodox Church (Nankivell 2008), along with other national Orthodox Churches, not least that of Romania to this day (Rotar, Teodorescu and Rotar 2014), place enormous theological weight upon burial, and in Russia this is now a desirable option amongst those able to afford it in a Russia with its resurgent Orthodoxy. The liturgies surrounding Easter ensured that Christ's Resurrection was paramount and served as the model for burial and for the future resurrection of ordinary Christians. Even though Orthodox Christians might, as in many parts of rural Greece, remove bones from a grave within a relatively short period after burial, once bodily decay had taken place, and locate them in an ossuary, this did not affect the belief in a future resurrection. The close alignment of Orthodoxy with burial and the role of the clergy in its overall process, offered a challenge to Communism and the acceptance of its ideology amongst the people at large. The strong advocacy of cremation was a major attempt at removing this ecclesiastical influence. Within the People's Republic of China it was not, of course, a pre-existing Christian culture that was the challenge, but a variety of regional and local traditions, frequently aligned with respect for ancestors. With the expressed desire to save agricultural land and to reduce the cost of expensive funerals the Republic's leaders announced in April 1956 a 'proposal for cremations' seeking key leaders to advocate this more economical funeral form by example, as was the case when Mr Zhou Enlai was cremated in 1976, with his 'ashes scattered throughout the motherland he deeply loved' (Jinlong et al. 2005: 121).

Ashes, or cremains as in American English, yield one of the most creative symbolic substances to emerge from industrialised processes associated with the human body. Victor Turner's relatively direct account of symbols is valuable when thinking of human ashes (Turner 1969). He saw a double polarity of a single symbol, its ideological pole embracing the more propositional aspect of human meaning, including theological, philosophical and existential statements, while its sensory pole catches the more emotional domains of awareness. While it is useful to think of this double polarity for analytical purposes we find, in practice, that they mutually influence each other. Turner also spoke of symbols as possessing a multivocal or polysemic quality, able to carry numerous messages, with context sometimes emphasising now one and now another. So, for example, while the ideological pole is able to convey the notion of a life once lived as a body that has now ceased, its sensory pole can implement that message when the ashes are cast to the wind. Another example is a purpose-designed urn that reflects something of the deceased's character or hobby carries ashes that can be kept within the home and serve as a focus for the survivor's on-going memory bonds with the dead. Again, if ashes are turned into rings or lockets, for example, then their presence is even more sensory-linked with the bereaved wearer, and become reminiscent of Victorian locks of hair retained in lockets or the like. However, this intimate form of contact with the dead stands at a distance from much in modern cremation, not least in terms of the building within which bodies are burnt (Hallam, Hockey and Howarth 1999; Hallam and Hockey 2001).

Place

'Death', in the abstract, offers something of a distance from the concrete reality of a dead person, but it is the very pragmatic existence of a corpse that makes our account of cremation in Scotland one of detailed immediacy. And this is especially true of crematoria, their settings and ownership. The emergence of modern cremation in Europe was spearheaded by independent thinkers and, notably, by the voluntary societies they established. As this volume has shown for Scotland, their alliance in one-purpose associations led, in key innovations, to the establishment of privately run crematoria. Major civic authorities, serving increasingly large populations in the early and mid-twentieth century, also came to see the practical advantage of cremation over the necessity of creating ever-increasing numbers of grave-spaces. The early opposition and divided opinion of church leaders, probably also in Scotland, tended to mean that ecclesiastical influences of a positive kind were slightly later additions to the emergent ceremonial associated with the symbolic process of bidding farewell to the coffined corpse. And, as in England, the established Church surrendered the initiative. In England both the Provinces of Canterbury and York debated cremation and the appropriate liturgies, though it is not clear whether the Church of Scotland did so. As the twentieth century progressed most Christian denominations – Orthodoxy and some smaller Protestant derived groups apart – participated in services held at crematoria that became the dominant and customary base for cremations. In the new twenty-first century, however, it is often the case that a significant minority of rites are conducted by non-ecclesial agents.

This mixed history not only reveals the interplay of 'the crematorium' as an architected place open to ideological qualification depending upon the mode of rite conducted within it, but also the marked challenge presented to those architects selected for designing it and the influence of Scotland's civic authorities in decisions to appoint particular architects. We have demonstrated this in the cases of Basil Spence and Robert Lorimer, showing how Scotland often chose leading architects unlike England who, in the 1950s and 1960s, made much more use of local authority architectural staff. Their respective decisions (discussions, outcomes, texts and illustrations) show how these new places made their presence felt as symbols of social change. An important contribution of this book has been to highlight the significance of landscape and the physical location of crematoria making a major contribution to studies of design, material culture and the architecture of highly significant social buildings that frame human emotional experience. The interplay of architecture and human emotion not only comes to a distinctive focus in crematoria at the time of a cremation or when the bereaved make return visits to the site, but also goes further through the fact of cremated remains. The instance of the Mortonhall case discussed in chapter 9 would be a case in point. For crematoria certainly do participate in what they represent in terms of a clear social and cultural processing of the dead, but they also generate 'remains' in a way quite distinct from traditional burial practice. Even when remains were actually interred they did not offer the bereaved the same symbolic potency of an imaged body buried at a separate site.

This study's earlier depiction of crematoria as one key 'paradigm of modernity' that embraced motorised transport of the dead and the bereaved along with many other factors pinpointed these buildings as 'neglected' aspects of 'cultural heritage'. It should also be said, however, that from the early nineteenth century the demarcation of sites for the disposal of corpses beyond the aegis of local communities demonstrates another aspect of disposal in industrial society (Rugg 2013). In Great Britain at large, 'cultural heritage' in the form of old buildings, plays an enormously significant, if often unanalysed role in popular imagination and identity. This is as true for key sporting venues in football, rugby and tennis as it is for country houses, castles and cathedrals. Village, then town, and some city churches, as well as town halls and the museums and art galleries created by local and national authorities, all provide a landscape of identity that gives a distinctive feel to localities and nations. This built aspect of identity was radically reinforced by the super-position of war memorials across the length and breadth of

Scotland (J. McDonald 2016), England, Wales and Northern Ireland after the two great wars and other military engagements of the twentieth century. The varied symbolism of sacrifice, heroism, regard for monarchy, and of devotion at large was often conveyed through Christian and sometimes through more classical sculptural motifs.

Dual-sovereignty symbolism

The 'architectural challenge' presented earlier in this book and grounded in the need for both 'utilitarian and symbolic' ends in the design of crematoria can now be taken up again and given a distinctive theoretical interpretation through the notion of dual sovereignty (Davies 2015: 46–8). The theoretical advantage of doing this is that it allows us to relate our extensive legal material to the theological considerations previously presented in more separate discussions. For this concept of dual-sovereignty focuses two major domains of authority in societies at large: the one deals with jural or legal, and the other with mystical or creative-flourishing, aspects of human existence. This perspective works on the assumption that individuals benefit from living in a society where legal aspects of the authority that governs social life are balanced by that 'mystical' authority embodied in and expressed through relationships with other individuals and with agents of certain institutions that may cause us to flourish. Legal authority is easily understood by those of us living in a society framed by the rule of law, and who expect justice to be done and to be seen to be done. In this volume we have covered the legal aspects of cremation in some considerable detail, showing how this cultural innovation was pervaded by legal concerns over the cause of death and any possible illegalities surrounding cremation, notably the Nellfield and Kaimhill cases in Aberdeen (chs 4 and 6). Safety against the cover-up of murder by cremating the deceased has played its role in these accounts. Of analogous significance is the case of assisted dying to which we briefly return below.

What, then, of 'mystical' authority, where 'mystical' refers to life's complex depth and not to esoteric phenomena? Here we touch on succour gained from others, where mystical authority is the opposite of forces that denature a person or engender despair. Many distinctive aspects of life frame such flourishing as in birthday parties, Christmas celebrations, and in Scotland Hogmanay and New Year, when folk wish well for each other, often with gifts and greetings. In more strictly religious terms the theological ideas of grace and of salvation, as already intimated above, serve to enhance a person's sense of self-identity and of a positive sense of destiny with the focused rite of 'blessing' precisely capturing the notion of mystical authority.

The crematorium as a new institution developed within the British Isles can be understood in terms of these dual-sovereignty dynamics. As we have extensively demonstrated throughout this volume in terms of Cremation and Environmental Protection Acts as well as in cases of malpractice exemplified in the 1898 Nellfield burial scandal, cases of human error as in the cremation of the 'wrong body' at Maryhill Crematorium 1911, the Dewar Trial in Aberdeen in 1944 with its stealing and 'reuse' of coffin lids, and cases of serious malpractice over gold teeth and even the reuse of human fat. So, too, with the Mortonhall case discussed in chapter 9. The Maryhill 'wrong-body' account is also, albeit incidentally, interesting because of how it describes the local rabbi as refusing to bury ashes, not on the basis of their being cremated remains but because the ground was not consecrated. This is a telling reminder that, prior to the Nazi use of cremation for extermination, some Jewish opinion was not against cremation as such, an issue open for extensive future research. Within the confines of this study, however, we have seen how the crematorium is a place whose building and location are defined by law to be a crematorium and whose formal processes are controlled by proper legal certification of death and for cremation of a named individual. Its focused technology – behind the scenes – is not only managed in relation to codes of conduct and good practice that a variety of cremation authorities have compiled but is also legally controlled in terms of exhaust gases. This, notably, includes European legislation on emissions and the requisite filtering systems to control them (Wiechmann and Gleis 2012; Vater 2012).

At the same time the crematorium, in terms of its landscape, approach roads, ceremonial and memorial spaces, as well as any areas dedicated to the strewing of remains, sets out to foster the wellbeing of the bereaved as far as is feasible. We saw in earlier chapters how crematoria posed an 'emotional challenge' and that 'sentiment' was deemed problematic for this cultural innovation. We can now set this challenge within the dual-sovereignty scheme of 'mystical' factors aimed at causing people to flourish and not to despair. The background factors supporting such enhancement have, over time, included both familiar religious symbolism and the possibility of not overemphasising such symbolism so as to accommodate people of diverse worldviews. We have seen how some crematorium services have benefited from the use of music, notably organ music, but often with 'favourite tunes' played on sound systems in more recent decades. The use of a descending catafalque has, in its own way, symbolically echoed the lowering of a coffin into an earth-grave. The hearse followed by close family in funeral cars drawing up outside a crematorium marks the solemnity of the event, as does the role of the funeral director and either minister of religion or celebrant of some other worldview, in guiding the family and then leading those present in the funeral service as such.

In terms of the 'mystical' aspect of authority, in the contexts of both the dead and cremation, two words stand as worthy of comment, viz., dignity and respect. Dignity has assumed profound significance in drawing attention to the worth of individuals and to the way they are treated, most especially at times when they are most vulnerable to maltreatment, notably when terminally ill and, finally, dead. Dignity assumes a degree of care rendered to people in end of life care and in the treatment of their body afterwards; its nuanced force lies in the inherent sense of the value of a person as a person. Similarly, 'respect' marks the quality of relationship between persons, not least between the living and the body of a dead individual. It is this double sense of worth and relationship that is reflected in the way cremation staff tend to speak of their work as it involves receiving the coffin, checking the identity of its occupant, marking the ensuing ashes as pertaining to that individual cremation, and returning those remains to an appropriate person after the entire event is completed.

Assisted dying

With both 'respect' and 'dignity', as well as dual sovereignty in mind, it is no accident that the group set up to facilitate assisted dying in Switzerland carries the title Dignitas, and speaks of 'accompanied suicide'. Its point is to stress the will and intention of a terminally sick person to decide for him or herself regarding a doctor- assisted death. The debate on the Assisted Suicide (Scotland) Bill that fell following the first stage of its process in May 2015; followed by Lord Falconer's Bill on assisted dying that met with a very close run of opposition in the House of Lords in July 2015; and a similar private member's Bill debated in September 2015, which met with a significant failure: all these offer material that is wide open to analysis through this dual-sovereignty model. This includes the question of how illegal killing can be avoided or, and this is even more telling, how can it be assured that an old or sick person might not feel some family pressure to desire assisted death. The slippery-slope argument highlights the interface between jural and mystical authority, for the pressure to think of an earlier death than is biologically necessary in order to reduce financial or psychological pressure on kin is not to experience a sense of flourishing. This, of course, is precisely where the hospice movement came in, with its desire to cause the terminally ill to flourish as best as possible until the necessary biological termination of life. This issue of assisted dying is, however, not far removed from early debates and legislation surrounding cremation and the sensed need to ensure, in the terms of the dual-sovereignty model, that all deaths were dignified in the sense of satisfying all legal and mystical proprieties.

The Future

This study has been firmly historical, with this final chapter providing some theoretical guidelines allowing for a more comparative approach to the material presented for Scotland. Just what the future of cremation in Scotland is, and more broadly in the United Kingdom, Europe, and the world at large, remains to be seen for local situations create significant differences. Current trends suggest that the gap in cultural history between traditionally Catholic and Protestant countries is closing, with cremation rates in traditionally Catholic countries beginning to increase. Portugal, for example, moved from a 1992 level of 0.72% to 23% in 2002, and to 51% in 2012. The Netherlands, with something of a mixed religious and secular economy of beliefs went from the 1962 level of 4.7% to a 1982 level of 37%, and by 2012 to 59%. As for Italy its 2002 level of almost 7% moved to nearly 17% by 2012. It may well be that in these contexts cremation serves as its own form of index of secularisation, though it would be a relatively blunt instrument measuring change.

One potentially significant factor in the UK is the emergence of a variety of differently named woodland, natural, ecological, or green burial sites since the mid- 1990s (Davies and Rumble 2012). In England and Wales there are approximately as many such sites as there are crematoria, numbering around 260 or so. It is difficult to be precise in defining such sites for, apart from the areas quite separate from established cemeteries some local authorities, for example, use a portion of land adjoining a long-established cemetery. In Scotland there are, in 2015, a very small number of sites, perhaps only five or six, that are of this type. It is quite likely that the large rural landmass of Scotland with many cemeteries and churchyards will easily accommodate people's funerary needs for a beautiful place with 'fine views' for burial. Time alone will tell.

So, too, with the Scotland-based innovation of resomation, itself a trademark name for the process of dissolving the human body in a chamber of alkaline solution under appropriate pressure (Sullivan, 2006; 2009; 2016). Some American sources even call it green-cremation though no fire is involved. The outcome of this process is a powder-like form that can then be disposed of in any of the ways currently used for cremated remains. If the Government agrees that this should be adopted in the UK it would, technically speaking, not be too difficult for a crematorium to install a resomation chamber alongside modern cremators. Just how people would take to this system, and just what legislative material would need to be put in place remains to be seen. Other ideas concerning body composting, cryogenic freezing of the dead, as well as burial at sea all have their advocates and provide the broad field of death studies with much material for analysis. If and when such practices arise they, too, will doubtless benefit from the strong interdisciplinary and detailed analysis that we have provided in this volume on cremation in Scotland.

Bibliography

ARCHIVES

Aberdeen City Archives, The Town House, Aberdeen
Council minutes
Kaimhill Crematorium file

Aberdeen City and Aberdeenshire Archives, Old Aberdeen House, Aberdeen
Maps of Kaimhill
Kaimhill local histories

Aberdeen Central Library
Council minutes

Aberdeen University Archives Special Collections
MS 3217 Aberdeen coffin trial papers

Cremation Society Archives, Durham University (CSA)
CRE/P/1/B/I 1874–85
CRE/P/1/B/II Minute Book 1887–1903
CRE/P/1/B/VI Minute Book 1935–46
CRE/P/2/F/Box 1 Correspondence with Sir John Mann 1952–3
CRE/P/2/G Correspondence regarding the trial of James Dewar and Alick George Forbes, 12/10/1944, after malpractice at Aberdeen Crematorium, and newspaper cuttings
CRE/P/2/H/Box 1 Public Assistance Authorities: May they lawfully cremate human bodies for the disposal of which they are responsible? 1932
CRE/P/5 Disposition of the dead in wartime 1939–40
CRE/P/5 A Plan for the Disposition of the Dead in a National Emergency through a Scheme to Control and Co-ordinate Cremations and Crematoria and other Available Facilities. Submitted by the Cremation Society and the Federation of British Cremation Authorities, July 1939

CRE/P/5 Cremation of Civilian Dead in Wartime – letter from the Cremation Society to local authorities, September 1939, seeking support for the Society's opposition to a government circular making clear that cremation of civilian dead following air raids would not be permitted, due to wartime difficulties in meeting the requirements of the certification system. With the authorities' replies. With some related cuttings, and 'Civilian deaths through war: arrangements for the disposal of bodies', article in Municipal Review, May 1939, p. 165
CRE/P/6/A Correspondence regarding cremation laws amendments 1946–8
CRE/P/6/A Correspondence and cuttings etc. leading to new regulations 1951–2
CRE/P/6/C/Box 2 Parliamentary papers and official publications 1834–1987

Edinburgh Archives, Edinburgh Central Library

Edinburgh City Council Archives
Council minutes

Edinburgh Crematorium Ltd Archives, Seafield Cemetery Lodge

Edinburgh University Library Special Collections
Resurrectionist activity

Falkirk Archives

Glasgow City Archives, Mitchell Library, Glasgow (GLA)

Imperial College, London, Archives
Lyon Playfair papers

Lanarkshire County Council Archives, Mitchell Library, Glasgow

London Metropolitan Archives (LMA)
PC/COR/1/53 Cremation Regulations 1894–1930

London School of Economics Special Collections

Merchants House, Glasgow, Mitchell Library, Glasgow
Sederunt Book Merchants House from 8 March 1887–7 December 1894 (Volume 11) T-MH1/11.
Printed Minutes of the Merchants House 10 March 1936–March 1940 uncatalogued archive collection from Merchants House
Printed Minutes of the Merchants House 31 May 1944–6 August 1951 uncatalogued archive collection from Merchants House

Printed Minutes of the Merchants House 11 September 1951–7 April 1959 uncatalogued archive collection from Merchants House

Merchants House Necropolis Committee Minute Book No. 4, 6 January 1887–31 May 1900 T-MH 52/1/4

Merchants House: Necropolis Committee Minute Book No. 8, 29 March 1928–30 July 1936 T-MH 52/1/8

Merchants House: Necropolis Committee Minute Book No. 9, 27 August 1936–27 August 1947 T-MH 52/1/9

National Library of Scotland (NLS)

Albert, Edward (ed.) (nd), Edward Theodore Salvesen. Recollecting a Busy Life, typescript (annotated and revised manually) NLS MS 9130. [See Salvesen 1949, below.]

National Records of Scotland (NRS)

AD 14/99/48 Precognition against William Coutts for the crime of violating sepulchres and perjury at Nellfield cemetery, Aberdeen, 1899

AD 63/408/1 Burial and Cremation Bill: Correspondence to Jan. 1953

AD 63/408/2 Burial and Cremation (Scotland) Bill 1954–66

AD 63/408/3 Burial and Cremation Bill: Local Government Law Consolidation Committee SC papers 1951–2

AD 63/408/4 Burial and Cremation Bill: Local Government Law Consolidation Committee: Minutes of meetings 1951–2

AD 64/4 Draft Miscellaneous Parliamentary Bills: Representations, correspondence and reports 1951–79

AD 64/408/5 Cremation Bill (Private Member's Bill) 1952

CH 10/1/43 Records of the Religious Society of Friends (Quakers), records of marriages, births and burials of the Friends' meetings at Aberdeen, Edinburgh and Kelso, 1783–96

CH 10/1/50 Records of the Religious Society of Friends (Quakers), burial notes, 1828–38

CO 1/5/20 Draft Burial and Cremation (Scotland) Bill 1953–66

CS 258/1966/4002 Scottish Burial Reform and Cremation Society Ltd v The Corporation of the City of Glasgow: Declarator 1966

CS 258/1966/4003 Scottish Burial Reform and Cremation Society v Application of House of Lords Judgment: Petition 1966

DD 5/1837 Committee on Scottish Local Government Law Consolidation: Review of work done 1955–64

DD 5/1840 Committee on Scottish Local Government Law Consolidation: Second report 1953–9

DD 5/1847 Scottish Local Government Law Consolidation Committee: Minutes of meetings 1948–57

GD 124/15/192 Order observed at the burial of Charles, Earl of Mar, at Alloa, 4 June 1689

GD 406/1/4006 Correspondence of the Dukes of Hamilton, Hamilton to the Earl of Arran, 28 April 1695
GRO 1/648 Cremation 1907–33
GRO 5/1924 Registration of births and deaths, disposal of newly-born child otherwise than by burial. Pathological purposes etc. 1913–52
HH 60/823 Burial and Cremation Bill 1966 1965–6
HH 61/108 Burial and cremation – legislation – Cremation Bill 1902, 239/54 23 January 1902 – SO Memo – Cremation [HL] Bill – copy of Bill – Lord Monkswell – see memo directing examination of the Bill which it is proposed to apply to Scotland
HH 61/109 Burial and cremation legislation: Cremation, Bills and Act 1952: General 1952
HH 61/111 Burial and Cremation (Scotland) Bill 1951–2
HH 61/112 Burial and Cremation (Scotland) Bill 1953–60
HH 61/113 Burial and cremation legislation: Working party to consider funeral charges: Report 1953–4
HH 61/126/239/64 SO memo – Cremation Act – copy of Act
HH 61/126/239/65 Mr C.E. Troup of Home Office – report of committee appointed to prepare a draft of the regulations to be made under the Cremation Act 1902
HH 61/126/239/67 Registrar-General – cremation – returns draft and reports that so far as they related to the function of the registration department they are quite satisfactory
HH 61/127 Cremation (Scotland) Regulations 1928 (Scottish Office files on 1928 regulations)
HH 61/127/F2/239/92 Cremation Act 1902: Secretary, Edinburgh Cremation Society: Enquires whether s. 4 of the Act applies to crematoria which may be erected by private person or companies; also whether S for S has issued any regulations under s. 7 applicable to Scotland
HH 61/127/F3/239/68 Cremation Act 1902: Local Government Board: Submit observations on the proposed regulations under this Act
HH 61/127/F4 Local Government Board for Scotland LG 38,744: Churchyards and misc: Enclosing two copies of Draft Regulations made under s. 7 of the Cremation Act 1902 for the observations of the Board
HH 61/127/F5 Secretary of State for Scotland 239/104 Cremation Act 1902: Transfer of powers to LGB. under s. 7
HH 61/127/F6 Secretary of State for Scotland 239/104 Cremation Act 1902: Transfer of powers to SBH. under s. 7
HH 61/128/1 Cremation (Scotland) Regulations 1935
HH 61/128/2 Cremation (Scotland) Regulations 1935 (DHS file on the 1935 Regulations) 1931–40
HH 61/129 Cremation 1947–53
HH 61/130 Cremation Regulations: Inter-Departmental Committee appointed in 1947–53

HH 61/131 Cremation Regulations: Inter-Departmental Committee appointed in 1947 to review regulations: Minutes 1947–9
HH 61/132 Cremation Regulations: Inter-Departmental Committee appointed in 1947 to review regulations: Report 1950
HH 61/133 Cremation Regulations: Cremation (Scotland) Regulations 1956–60
HH 61/134 Cremation Regulations: Working party on the Cremation Regulations 1959
HH 61/135 Crematoria – General 1942–55
HH 61/136 Crematoria: Inspectors' reports: General 1944–55
HH 61/138 Cremation procedure: cremation certificates under the 1902 Act 1929–30
HH 61/140 Cremation procedure: certificates under Emergency Powers Defence Regulations (death due to war operations) 1939–53
HH 61/141 Cremation procedure: disposal of remains of newly-born children 1927–43
HH 61/142 Anatomy Acts miscellaneous correspondence 1931–9
HH 61/143 Anatomy Acts miscellaneous correspondence 1939–43
HH 61/144 Cremation and the Anatomy Acts 1945–55
HH 61/687 Burial and Cremation legislation: Burial and Cremation (Scotland) Bill 1953: Scottish LG Law Consolidation Committee: Report 1953
HH 61/704 Crematoria Regulations, 1935: Inspection arrangements 1944
HH 61/906/1 Crematoria: Edinburgh Burgh: Warriston Crematorium 1928–71
HH 61/906/3 Cremation Act 1902: Edinburgh Crematorium Ltd: Site for Crematorium 1928–33
HH 61/906/4 Cremation: Edinburgh Crematorium Ltd: Deputy medical referees 1935–9
HH 61/908/1–3 Mortonhall Crematorium Edinburgh 1954–68
HH 61/994 Cremation Regulations, Cremation (Scotland Regulations, 1928 (DHS file on 1928 Regulations) 1923–31
HH 61/1055 Anatomy, burial and cremation: Human Tissue Act 1961: Legislation drafting of Human Tissue Bill 1961–2
HH 80/865 Merchants House of Glasgow (Crematorium): Petition for a Provisional Order 1949–50
HH 80/899 Edinburgh Burgh: Provisional Order 1954
JC 26/1899/1 Trial papers relating to William Coutts for the crime of violating sepulchres and perjury at Nellfield cemetery, Aberdeen. Tried at High Court, Aberdeen, 1899
JC 36/150 Dewar appeal papers 1944
JC 71/33 Printed indictments 1899
JC 71/77 Printed indictments 1944

New College Library, University of Edinburgh

Church of Scotland annual reports and – especially – Church of Scotland MS CHU 8.1–2 Committee on Public Worship and the Sacraments 1890.
General Assembly Report on 'Supernatural Psychic Phenomena' 1922.

Parliamentary Archives (PA)

HL/PO/JO/10/10/1213/1132 Emergency Powers (Defence) Act 1939: Order in Council dated 25 August 1939 entitled Defence Regulations 1939

HL/PO/JO/10/10/1213/1148 Emergency Powers (Defence) Act 1939: Order in Council dated 1 September 1939 amending Defence Regulations 1939

Royal Commission on the Ancient and Historical Monuments of Scotland (RCAHMS, after 2015 Historic Environment Scotland)

The Basil Spence Archive. MS 2329/SCT

Scottish Burial Reform and Cremation Society Archives

Mann, Sir John (1952) *Extracts from some Drafts of Reminiscences of Sir John Mann, KBE* (August and September)

Mann, Sir John (1954), 'Burning Question', *Funeral Service Journal* (March), 108–10

Scottish Burial Reform and Cremation Society Ltd Minutes of the Board of Directors

DOW 3568/01 Vol. 1, 6 August 1888–3 June 1924

DOW 3568/00 Vol. 2, 22 October 1924–29 March 1961

DOW 3568/02 Vol. 3, 28 April 1961–30 September 1997

The National Archives Kew (TNA)

ASSI 45/105/1 Northern and North Eastern Circuits: Criminal depositions and case papers: Larceny: Bowman and Hirstwood 1945

BD 11/2943 Crematoria: General correspondence and conference papers 1948–69

CAB 75/5/9 War Cabinet Home Policy Committee HPC (40) Series: Minutes meetings Nos 15–53 vol. II: [....] 4. Cremation of war casualties. HPC (40)176 [....] 1940

CAB 134/1976 Cabinet Home Affairs Committee HA(59) meetings F.121

CAB 134/1977 Cabinet Home Affairs Committee HA(59) memoranda vol. I 1–29 F.121

CAB 134/1993 Cabinet Home Affairs Committee HA(59) meetings F.121

CAB 134/1995 Home Affairs Committee HA(63) memoranda vol. II 62–129 F.121

CAB 134/1997 Cabinet Home Affairs Committee HA(65) meetings 1–13 and Index G. 23 1965

CAB 134/2001 Home Affairs Committee HA(65) memoranda 85–144 vol. III 1965

CAB 134/2054 Home Affairs Committee HP(64): Meetings 1–27 Jan.–Sept. 1964

CAB 134/2056 Home Affairs Committee Papers HP(64) vol. II 79–155 May–Sept. 1964

DPP 1/17 Seddon, F.H., and another offence: Murder 1911

DPP 2/2572 Adams, John Bodkin (Doctor): Murder of Joyce Hallett and Edith Morrell, dangerous drugs, forgery 1956

HLG 29/69 Cremation Act 1902

HLG 45/1303 Weymouth and Melcombe Regis Borough: Provision of a crematorium 1936–47
HLG 45/1452 Central Durham Crematorium Joint Committee: Proposed provision of a crematorium 1949–64
HLG 45/1468 Cremation Act 1902: Amendment of section 5: Proximity of dwellings 1931–5
HLG 45/1471 Cremation Regulations 1944–6
HLG 45/1493 Provision of a crematorium and a Garden of Remembrance on cemetery land at Blackshaw Road, Tooting 1947–57
HLG 45/1554 Maidstone and District Joint Crematorium Committee: Provision of crematorium: Boughton Marchelsea CPO 1953–8
HLG 45/1569 Crematorium Act 1902 s. 5: Proposed amendment to section 1957–61
HLG 45/1571 Siting and planning of crematoria: 1957 memorandum 1955–8
HLG 45/1620 Burials and cremation: Committee on the Cremation Act 1902 1947–59
HLG 120/2868 Relaxation of government controls over local authorities: Local Government, Planning and Land Bill; draft notes on clauses and comment 1979
HO 45/6677 Scotch burial licences: Procedure in dealing with applications 1858
HO 45/9474/244 Darlington Burial Board. Erection of crematorium
HO 45/9476/927 Weston-super-Mare: Request for cremated remains to be sown in grave without coffin 1894
HO 45/9531/40582 Cremation: General file showing public sentiment and policy of successive governments: Memos and LOO 546 on legality of cremation 1878–89
HO 45/9541/53096 Removal of body, by licence granted, alleged from one ground to another, but believed sent to Italy. Objections by relatives after removal
HO 45/9807/B633A Paddington Cemetery: Proposed erection of crematorium
HO 45/9887/B17163 Cardiff proposed erection and regulations of a crematorium 1894–1903
HO 45/10113/B11886 Disposal of the Dead Regulation Bill
HO 45/10144 Cremation: Bill 1895–1902
HO 45/10144/B18513/F3 London County Council Clerk: LCC's General Powers Bill: Asks if HO would object to clauses enabling burial authorities in London to provide places for cremation
HO 45/10144/B18513/F5 Mr Henry Cripps: Bill to enable metropolitan burial authorities to make provision for the burning of bodies of dead persons: Encloses draft Bill prepared by him upon which they would be glad of observations: Will attend any appointment HO may make
HO 45/10144/B18513/F6 London County Council (Parliamentary Department): Burial authorities Cremation Bill: Forwards draft of Bill, amended so as to make it applicable to burial authorities generally
HO 45/10144/B18513/F8 Burial Authorities (Cremation Bill) introduced by Lord Monkswell, Burial Authorities (Cremation) Bill [HL] Amendments to be moved in committee by the Lord Belper and the Lord Monkswell

HO 45/10197/B30770 Leicester: Byelaws: Crematorium 1899–1902

HO 45/10249 Cremation: Regulations under s.7 Cremation Act 1902. 1903–8

HO 45/10249/B38626/F12 Return of cases of exhumation of human remains for the purposes of examination during the years 1893–1903

HO 45/10249/B38626/F13 Cremation Committee: Report of Committee signed

HO 45/10249/B38635/F18 Cremation Society of Great Britain: Cremation Act 1902: Draft Regulations: Submits objections and observations and asks to be heard in support of same

HO 45/10249/B38635/F28 Cremation Society: Cremation Act: Suggests need for provision for the cremation of remains brought from abroad

HO 45/10249/B38626/F37 Mr George Danvers Thomas, Coroner for London: Inquests after cremation: Suggests means to preserve coroners' rights to hold an inquest, even when cremation prevents it taking place 'in view of the body'

HO 45/10249/B38626/F42 London Cremation Co. Ltd: Coroners' certificates in 'Form E': Asks what is the duty of a coroner in respect of giving a certificate in Form E, and what fee, if any, may be charged

HO 45/10249/B38626/F44 Mr J. Troutbeck, Coroner, Westminster: Cremation – coroners' fees: forwards letter demanding return of a fee paid to him for a certificate authorising cremation. Thinks it desirable a fee should be fixed

HO 45/10249/B38626/F46 The Coroners' Society, Hon. Sec.: Cremation – coroners' certificates: States that in his opinion it is now the duty of coroners to sign the certificate permitting cremation after inquest, this certificate simply being in substitution for burial order under the Death Registration Act 1874: Suggests HO issue a circular to all coroners

HO 45/10249/B38626/F48 Mr J. Troutbeck, Coroner for London: Coroners' remuneration for cremation certificates: Urges injustice of manner in which coroners are treated

HO 45/11050/152635/F37 Temporary suspension of section 7 of the Cremation Act for cremations of servicemen killed in battle

HO 45/17512 Operation of Cremation Regulations 1930. 1932–5

HO 45/17512/F47 Cremation Regulations – Working of: Memo as to issue of questionnaire for completion by Medical Referees

HO 45/17512/F52 Cremation Regulations: HO circular of 28/5/1935

HO 45/17513/655502/F52A Questionnaires to 1. cremation authorities and (2) Medical Referees under Cremation Regulations

HO 45/18142/F47 Society of Medical Officers of Health: Disposal of the dead: Fd copy scheme drafted by the Federation of British Cremation Authorities

HO 45/20597 Cremation: War casualties

HO 45/20597/F1 Ministry of Health: Civilian deaths due to war operations: Forwards Circular 1779 of 28/2/39

HO 45/20597/F3 Home Office: Deaths occurring in consequence of war operations: Copies of Defence Regulation No. 30: Order of S. of S. authorising clerks to local authorities and CO's to issue certificates of such deaths: Circulars to coroners and clerks to l.a.s.

HO 45/20597/F5 Cremation Society (Lord Horder): Disposal of civilian dead in war times: Forwards copy of circular to l.a.s. suggesting suspension of cremation regulations under Regulation 14.

HO 45/20597/F15 Federation of British Cremation Authorities: Disposal of civilian dead in war time: Request that the cremation regulations may be modified

HO 45/20597/F18 Scottish Home Department: Deaths due to war operations: Disposal of the bodies of civilian dead: Forwards copy of Lord Salvesen's letter

HO 45/20597/F23 Cremation of war casualties: Amendment of Defence Regulation 30: Forwards draft Order in Council

HO 45/20597/F24 The Birmingham Crematorium Secretary: Cremation of air raid victims: Asks for full instructions

HO 45/20597/821700 Cremation: War casualties 1939–46

HO 45/21880 Cremation Regulations 1930: Operation

HO 45/21880/802517/F81 Home Office: Cremation : Doctors' fees: Memo

HO 45/21880/802517/F97 Mr E. Earnshaw: Cremation fees charged by Brighton Medical Officer of Health 1942

HO 45/25619 Report of the Interdepartmental Committee on the Cremation Act 1902 (Cmd 8009, 1952): Minutes of meetings of and evidence submitted to the Committee; reaction of trade associations and other organisations to the report

HO 45/25619/F1 Mr Robert Morgan MP (Stourbridge): Cremation: Setting up of departmental committee to investigate methods so as to secure agreed policy

HO 45/25619/F4a Mr H.J. Squires: Coffin ramp: Operation of profiteering undertakers

HO 45/25619/F5 Scottish Home Department: Crematoria: Inspection and administration: Notify that inspectors have been appointed and administrative responsibility vested in the Department of Health for Scotland

HO 45/25619/F6 Capt. Sir George Elliston, MC, MP (for Blackburn): Cremation: Extension of powers under 1902 Act or revision of regulations: Suggest discussion with HO in the matter

HO 45/25619/F7 Review of the Cremation Act and Regulations: Questions arising

HO 45/25619/F8 Code of cremation practice: News cutting from *Glasgow Herald* 21/9/1945 re preparation by Federation of British Cremation Authorities

HO 45/25619/F9 Lieut. H. Hughes, MP (Wolverhampton): Cremation Act 1902: Amendment to remove legal discriminations hampering cremation practice

HO 45/25619/F15 Home Office: The Cremation Act 1902: Proposals for revision

HO 45/25619/F24 Department of Health for Scotland: National Assistance Bill: Saving in Clause 47 for people opposed to cremation: Forwards copy of letter addressed to Ministry of Health

HO 45/25619/F30 Proprietary Crematoria Association: New Health Act: Doctors' charges for cremation certificates: Completing of Forms B and C: Requests Home Office advice

HO 45/25619/F31 Cremation Committee: Minutes and agenda

HO 45/25619/F32 Cremation Committee: Record of HO/CR papers
HO 45/25619/F33 Cremation Committee: Papers furnished by members of the Committee: Mr R. Howat, Department of Health for Scotland
HO 45/25619/F35 Cremation Committee: Papers furnished by members of the Committee: Mr H.F. Summers, Ministry of Health
HO 45/25619/F37 Cremation Committee: Minutes of first meeting: 24 July 1947: Matters arising: The Cremation Council of Great Britain
HO 45/25619/F58 Cremation Committee: Retention of Form C until appointment of referees can be tightened up: Correspondence from members of the Cremation Committee
HO 45/25620 Report of the Interdepartmental Committee on the Cremation Act 1902 (Cmd 8009, 1952): Minutes of meetings of and evidence submitted to the Committee; reaction of trade associations and other organisations to the report
HO 45/25620/F43 Cremation Committee: Minutes of first meeting: 24 July 1947: Matters arising: The Society of Medical Officers of Health
HO 45/25620/F54 Liverpool Regional Hospital Board: Cremation certificates: Standardisation of fees 1948–50
HO 45/25620/F58 Cremation Committee: Retention of Form C until appointment of referees can be tightened up: Correspondence from members of the Cremation Committee 1948
HO 45/25620/F88 HMSO: Cremation Committee: Final report
HO 45/B24279 Bournemouth: Regulations re interment of cremated remains 1897
HO 45/B32157 Hull Crematorium byelaws: Crematorium 1900
HO 144/1757/425994 Armstrong, Herbert Rowse convicted at Hereford on 13 April 1922 for murder and sentenced to death 1922
HO 144/20185 Criminal cases: Waddingham, Dorothea Nancy convicted at Nottingham on 27 February 1936 for murder and sentenced to death 14–29 April 1936
HO 144/21621/F51 Deaths due to war operations: Copies of circulars to Registrars including a copy of a memorandum for the guidance of doctors which has been circulated to the medical profession by the BMA
HO 186/1225 Burial of persons killed by war operations in United Kingdom 1938–43
HO 282/2 Working party on funeral charges: Working papers and minutes of meeting; report, October 1954 1953–6
HO 282/25 Cremation Regulations: Proposed amendments 1951–8
HO 282/26 Cremation Regulations: Proposed amendments 1955–61
HO 282/27 Working party on Cremation Regulations: Draft Regulations 1958–65
HO 282/40 Cremation legislation: Cremation Bill 1952
HO 299/10 Secretary of State directing inquest (s. 18 of the Coroners (Amendment) Act 1929 in absence of the body – drowning case
HO 347/19/539 Home Office: Printed memoranda and reports: Burial Bill (HC 111) 1888 – Home Office memorandum on (Feb 1889)
PRO 30/72/21 Association of Municipal Corporations report; minutes and reports 1892

PRO 30/72/22 Association of Municipal Corporations report; minutes and reports 1893

RG 48/445 Publicising of procedure where burial is to occur in Scotland or elsewhere outside England and Wales: Poster 1927

RG 48/446 Authority for burials in Scotland: Correspondence with Registrar General Edinburgh re production of certificates to Scottish burial authorities 1927–8

RG 48/458 Removal of bodies out of England: revision of regulations; cremation in England Regulations SI 1930/1016; Cremation in Scotland Regulations SI 1935 /247/S9; Circular GRO No. 3/1954; copy extract from Hansard (House of Commons) 12 March 1975 1930–3 and 1952–4

RG 48/2188 Revision of Cremation Act, 1902, and regulations made thereunder 1947–52

RG 48/3239 Medico-Legal investigation of deaths in the community: BMA recommendations: Setting up of committee on death certification and coroners 1963–5

Tunbridge Wells Archives

Report on the Tunbridge Wells Improvement Bill 1889 2/4/1889

OFFICIAL PAPERS AND REPORTS

Angiolini, Elish (2014), *Mortonhall Investigation: Report* <http://www.edinburgh.gov.uk/info/20242/mortonhall_investigation/957/mortonhall_investigation_-_report/2> accessed 12 November 2015

Angiolini, Elish (2016), *Report of the National Cremation Investigation* <http://www.gov.scot/Resource/0050/00503329.pdf> accessed 26 July 2016

Audit Commission for Local Authorities in England and Wales (1989), *Managing Cemeteries and Crematoria in a Competitive Environment* (Occasional Paper, No. 8, March)

Baker, Richard (2001), *Harold Shipman's Clinical Practice 1974–1998: A Clinical Audit Commissioned by the Chief Medical Officer* (London: The Stationery Office)

Bonomy, Lord (Chair) (2014), *Report of the Infant Cremation Commission* (Edinburgh: Scottish Government) <http://www.gov.scot/Resource/0045/00453055.pdf> accessed 12 November 2014

Brodie, Robert (Chair) (2007), *Burial and Cremation Review Group Report and Recommendations* (Edinburgh: Scottish Government)

Brodrick, Norman (Chair) (1971), *Report of the Committee on Death Certification and Coroners* (London: HMSO [Cmnd 4810])

Carrick, J. and Gairdner, W.T. (1870), *Report to the Board of Police of Glasgow, by the Medical Officer and the Master of Works on Intramural Burying Grounds* (Glasgow: R. Anderson) [Mitchell Library D-TC 14/2/1/No.14]

Corporation of Glasgow (1967), *The Corporation of Glasgow – Parks Department*.

Report to Parks Committee on Cemeteries and Burial Grounds in Glasgow [City Archives (GCA) D-PK 3]

Chadwick, Edwin (1842), *Report on the Sanitary Condition of the Labouring Population of Scotland, in Consequence of an Enquiry Directed to be Made by the Poor Law Commissioners.* Presented to both Houses of Parliament, by Command of Her Majesty, July 1842 (London: W. Clowes and Sons for HMSO [House of Lords 1842, vol. xxviii]

Chadwick, Edwin (1843), *Reports on the Sanitary Conditions of the Labouring Population of Great Britain: A Supplementary Report on the Result of a Special Inquiry into the Practice of Interment in Towns* (London: W. Clowes and Sons for HMSO)

Church of Scotland (1922), *Report of the Committee on 'Supernormal Psychic Phenomena' to the General Assembly of the Church of Scotland 26th May 1922*, Records of the General Assembly of the Church of Scotland, 659–70

Chronicle (1944), *Church of England: Chronicle of the Upper House of Convocation*, 25 May (Lambeth Palace Library)

Clarke, Lord Justice (2001), *Public Inquiry into the Identification of Victims following Major Transport Accidents: Report of Lord Justice Clarke* (London: Stationery Office Ltd [Cmd 5012])

Delegated Powers and Law Reform Committee (2016), *Burial and Cremation (Scotland) Bill at Stage 1* (Scottish Parliament, 2nd Report, SP Paper 864)

Department of Health (2003), *Isaacs Report: The Investigation of Events that Followed the Death of Cyril Mark Isaacs* (London: The Stationery Office)

Department of Health (2007), *Consultation Paper on Improving the Process of Death Certification* (London: Department of Health)

Department of Health (2008), *Summary of Responses to the Consultation on Improving the Process of Death Certification* (London: Department of Health)

Department of Health, Department for Education and Employment, and Home Office (2001), *Report of a Census of Organs and Tissue Retained by Pathology Services in England Conducted in 2000 by the Chief Medical Officer* (London: The Stationery Office)

Fisher, Matthew G. (Chair) (1953a), *First Report of the Scottish Local Government Law Consolidation Committee* (London: HMSO [Cmd 8729])

Fisher, Mathew G. (Chair) (1953b), *Second Report of the Scottish Local Government Law Consolidation (Scotland) Committee* (London: HMSO [Cmd 8751])

Fisher, Matthew G. (Chair) (1953c), *Draft of a Burial and Cremation (Scotland) Bill Prepared by the Scottish Local Government Law Consolidation (Scotland) Committee* (London: HMSO [Cmd 8752])

Home Office (2000a), *Review into Death Certification: Background to the Review* (Feb.) (London: Home Office)

Home Office (2000b), *Review into Death Certification: Questions for Consideration* (March) (London: Home Office)

Home Office (2000c), *Review into Death Certification: Analysis of Responses to Questionnaire* (July) (London: Home Office)

Home Office (2000d), *Review into Death Certification: The Way Forward – Some Options* (Oct.) (London: Home Office)
House of Commons (1893), *First and Second Reports from the Select Committee on Death Certification, together with the Proceedings of the Committee, Minutes of Evidence, Appendix and Index* [373 and 402] (HC Papers 1893–4, 11, 195)
House of Commons (1897), *Report from the Standing Committee on Law, and Courts of Justice, and Legal Procedure, on the Public Health (Scotland) Bill; with the Proceedings of the Committee, 3/6/1897,* 65 [243] (HC Papers 1897, 13, 601)
Jeffrey, John (Chair) (1943), *First Report of the Local Government and Public Health Consolidation (Scotland) Committee* (London: HMSO [Cmd 6476])
Jenkins, David (2015), *Report into Infant Cremations at the Emstrey Crematorium Shrewsbury* <shropshire.gov.uk/independent-inquiry-into-infant-cremations/inquiry-report/ accessed 31 August 2015
Kennedy, Ian, Howard, Rebecca, Jarman, Brian and Maclean, Mavis (2000), *The Inquiry into the Management of Care of Children receiving Complex Heart Surgery at the Bristol Royal Infirmary: Interim Report: Removal and Retention of Human Material: Annex A and Annex B* (London: Central Office of Information)
Local Government and Regeneration Committee (2016), *[Draft] Official Report, 9 March 2016*
Luce, Tom (Chair) (2003), *Death Certification in England, Wales and Northern Ireland: The Report of a Fundamental Review* (London: The Stationery Office [Cmd 5831])
Mackinnon, W.A. (Chair) (1842), *Report from the Select Committee on Improvement of the Health of Towns together with the Minutes of Evidence, Appendix, and Index. Effect of Interment of Bodies in Towns* [Paper 324, HC Papers vol. 10, 349]
Maclean, Sheila (Chair) (2001), *Independent Review Group on Retention of Organs at Post-Mortem: Final Report* (Nov.) (Edinburgh: The Stationery Office)
Maclean, Sheila (Chair) (2002), *Independent Review Group on Retention of Organs at Post-Mortem: Report on Strontium-90 Research* (Mar.) (Edinburgh: The Stationery Office)
MacLeod, Kenneth (1876), *Report of the Burial-Grounds in Glasgow: With Proposals for the Establishment of an Extensive Extramural Cemetery, and the Erection of Public District Mortuaries* (Glasgow: Robert Anderson)
Ministry of Health (1927), 'Cremation of the Remains of Still-born Children', Circular 802b, 15/8/1927
Ministry of Housing and Local Government (1956), *Report for 1956* (Cmnd 193) (London: HMSO)
Ministry of Housing and Local Government (1957–70) and Department of the Environment (1971–8), *The Siting and Planning of Crematoria* (1957–78)
Ministry of Justice (2016), *Consultation on cremation following recent inquiries into infant cremations* <https://consult.justice.gov.uk/digital-communications/consultation-on-cremation> accessed 23 July 2016
Monopolies and Mergers Commission (1987), *Co-operative Wholesale Society Ltd and House of Fraser PLC: A Report on the Acquisition by the Co-operative*

Wholesale Society Ltd of the Scottish Funerals Business of the House of Fraser PLC (London: HMSO, Cmd 229)

O'Hara, J. (Chair) (2002), *The Human Organs Inquiry Report* (Belfast: Department of Health, Social Services and Public Safety, Northern Ireland)

Palmer, Norman (2003), *Report of the Working Group on Human Remains* (London: Department for Culture, Media and Sport)

Redfern, Michael, Keeling, Jean and Powell, Elizabeth (2001), *The Royal Liverpool Children's Inquiry: Report* (London: The Stationery Office [HC12–11])

Registrar General (1882), *Forty-fourth Annual Report of the Registrar-General of Births, Deaths, and Marriages in England (Abstracts of 1881)* [C. 3620] [HC Papers, 1883, 20, I]

Safford, Archibald (Chair) (1949), *Report of Interdepartmental Committee on Medical Certificates* (London: HMSO)

Sanitary Inquiry: Scotland (1842), *Reports on the Sanitary Conditions of the Labouring Population of Scotland* (London: W. Clowes and Sons for HMSO)

Scotland's Population (2007), *The Registrar General's Annual Review of Demographic Trends*. 152nd edn. Laid before the Scottish Parliament pursuant to s.1(4) of the Registration of Births, Deaths and Marriages (Scotland) Act 1965. (Edinburgh: General Register Office for Scotland

Scottish Borders Council (2010), *Response to the Scottish Government Consultation Paper on Death Certification, Burial and Cremation*, 19 October, <http://www.gov.scot/Resource/Doc/313730/0099510.pdf> accessed 17 February 2015

Scottish Government (2010), *Consultation Paper on Death, Certification, Burial and Cremation* <http://www.gov.scot/Publications/2010/01/26131024/0> January 2010 and <http://www.scotland.gov.uk/Resource/0039/00398154.pdf> accessed 12 November 2015

Scottish Government (2014), *Infant Cremation Commission – Scottish Government Response*, June, <http://www.gov.scot/Publications/2014/06/6362/downloads#res453183> accessed 12 February 2016

Scottish Government (2015a), *Consultation on a Proposed Burial and Cremation Bill and Other Related Matters in Scotland*, January, <http://www.gov.scot/Publications/2015/01/2869/downloads#res468846> accessed 12 February 2016

Scottish Government (2015b), *Consultation Analysis Report: Consultation on a Proposed Bill Relating to Burial and Cremation and Other Related Matters in Scotland*, July, <(http://www.gov.scot/Publications/2015/07/9665> accessed 28 October 2015

Scottish Government (2015c), *Burial and Cremation (Scotland) Bill Policy Memorandum*, October, <http://www.scottish.parliament.uk/S4_Bills/Burial%20and%20Cremation%20(Scotland)%20Bill/SPBill80PMS042015.pdf> accessed 4 March 2016

Scottish Government (2015d), *Financial Memorandum in Burial and Cremation (Scotland) Bill: Explanatory Notes (and Other Accompanying Documents)*

Scottish Government (Reid Howie Associates) (2010a), *Death Certification, Burial and Cremation: Analysis of Consultation Findings Phase 1 Report: Questions 1–20*,

51 and 52 <http://www.gov.scot/Resource/Doc/318318/0101513.pdf> accessed 12 November 2015

Scottish Government (Reid Howie Associates) (2010b), *Death Certification, Burial and Cremation: Analysis of Consultation Findings Phase 2 Report: Questions 21–50* <http://www.gov.scot/Resource/Doc/326251/0105109.pdf > accessed 12 November 2015

Scottish Parliament (2016), *[Draft] Official Report, Meeting of the Parliament, 22 March 2016*

Smith, Dame Janet (2002), *The Shipman Inquiry: First Report: Volume One: Death Disguised* (Manchester: Shipman Inquiry)

Smith, Janet (2003), *The Shipman Inquiry: Third Report: Death Certification and the Investigation of Death by Coroners* (London: The Stationery Office [Cmd 5854])

Social Research (2010a), *Death Certification, Burial and Cremation Analysis of Consultation Findings Phase 2: Questions 1–20, 51 and 52*, Research Findings No. 102/2010 <http://www.scotland.gov.uk/Resource/Doc/325789/0101182.pdf> accessed 12 November 2015

Social Research (2010b), *Death Certification, Burial and Cremation Analysis of Consultation Findings Phase 2: Questions 21–50*, Research Findings No. 104/2010 <http://www.scotland.gov.uk/Resource/Doc/325789/0105020.pdf> accessed 12 November 2015

Strutt, Austin (Chair) (1950), *Report by the Interdepartmental Committee Appointed by the Secretary of State for the Home Department* (London: HMSO [Cmd 8009])

Troup, C.E. (Chair) (1903), *Report of the Departmental Committee Appointed by the Secretary of State for the Home Department to Prepare a Draft of Regulations to be made under the Cremation Act, 1902* (London: HMSO [Cd 1452])

LEGISLATION
(in chronological order)

Anatomy Act (AA) 1832
Births and Deaths Registration Act (BDRA) 1836
Births and Deaths Registration Act (BDRA) 1837
Cemeteries Clauses Consolidation Act 1847
Poor Law Amendment Act (PLAA) 1844
Public Health Act (PHA) 1848
Burial Act 1852
Burial Act 1853
Registration of Births Deaths and Marriages (Scotland) Act (RBDMSA) 1854
Burial Grounds (Scotland) Act (BGSA) 1855
Registration of Births Deaths and Marriages (Scotland) Act (RBDMSA) 1855

Registration of Births Deaths and Marriages (Scotland) Act (RBDMSA) 1860
Registration of Burials Act (RBA) 1864
Public Health (Scotland) Act (PHSA) 1867
Anatomy Act (AA) 1871
Births and Deaths Registration Act (BDRA) 1874
Public Health Act (PHA) 1875
Births and Deaths Registration (Ireland) Act 1880
Burial Grounds (Scotland) Act, 1855; Amendment Act 1881
Burial Laws Amendment Act 1880
Disposal of the Dead (Regulations) Bill (DDRB) 1884 [HC Bill 10].
Burial Grounds (Scotland) Amendment Act, 1886
Tunbridge Wells Improvement Bill 1889
Infectious Disease (Prevention) Act (IDPA) 1890
Glasgow Police Amendment Act (GPAA) 1890
Edinburgh Municipal and Police (Amendment) Act 1891
Local Government (Scotland) Act 1894
Edinburgh Improvement and Tramways Act 1896
Public Health (Scotland) Act (PHSA) 1897
Aberdeen Police and Improvement Act (APIA) 1900
Burial Act 1900
Cremation Act (CA) 1902
Cremation Regulations (CR) 1903
Cremation Regulations (CR) 1914 [SR and O, 1915, vol. 1, p. 86, No. 376]
Scottish Board of Health Act 1919
Cremation Regulations (CR) 1920 [SR and O, 1920, vol. 1, p. 434, No. 1286]
Tribunals of Inquiry (Evidence) Act 1921
Church of Scotland (Property and Endowments) Act 1925
Cremation Regulations 1925 [SR and O, 1925, p. 209, No. 761]
Births and Deaths Registration Act (BDRA) 1926
Coroners (Amendment) Act 1926
Registration (Births, Stillbirths, Deaths and Marriages) Consolidated Regulations (RBSDMCR) 1927 reg. 2(3) [SR and O 1927, 1528, No. 485].
Cremation Regulations (CR) 1927 [SR and O, 1927, p. 317, No. 575]
Cremation (Scotland) Regulations (CSR) 1927
Local Government (Scotland) Act 1929
Cremation Regulations (CR) 1930 [SR and O 1930, p. 417. No. 1016]
Church of Scotland (Property and Endowments) Amendment Act 1933
Cremation (Scotland) Regulations (CSR) 1935 reg. 23 [SR and O 1935, p. 281, No. 247 (S.9)]
Public Health Act (PHA) 1936
Registration of Still-Births (Scotland) Act (RSBSA) 1938
Order in Council 1 September 1939 [SR and O 1939, No. 978]
Order in Council 23 November 1939 [SR and O 1939, vol. 1, p. 811, No. 1681]
Order in Council amending Defence Regulations 11, 30 and 47B of, and Adding

Regulations 4A, 15A, 19C, 25A, 25B, 40AB, 60D, 62C, 68A, and 79B to, the Defence (General) Regulations, 1939, 2 July 1940 [SR and O 1940, vol. 2, p. 67, No. 1134]

Defence (Burials, Inquests and Registration of Deaths) Regulations 1942 [SR and O, vol. 2, p. 119, No. 144]

National Assistance Act (NAA) 1948

Merchants House of Glasgow (Crematorium) Order Confirmation Act (MHGCOCA) 1950

Greenock Corporation Order Confirmation Act (GCOCA) 1952

Corneal Grafting Act 1952

Cremation Regulations (CR) 1952 [SI 1569]

Cremation (Scotland) Regulations (CSR) 1952 [SI 1639 (S. 84)]

Valuation and Rating (Scotland) Act 1956

Human Tissue Act (HTA) 1961

Local Government (Financial Provisions etc.) (Scotland) (LGFPSA) Act 1962

Cremation Regulations (CR) 1965 [SI 1965, No. 1146]

Cremation (Scotland) Amendment Regulations (CSAR) 1967 [SI 1967, No. 398 (S. 31)]

Local Government Act 1972

Local Government, Planning and Land Act (LGPLA) 1980

Environmental Protection Act (EPA) 1990

Scotland Act (SA) 1998

Pollution Prevention and Control Act (PPCA) 1999

Cremation (Amendment) Regulations (CAR) 2000 [SI 58 of 2000]

Cremation (Scotland) Amendment Regulations (CSAR) 2003 [SSI 301 of 2003]

Human Tissue Act (HTA) 2004

Human Tissue (Scotland) Act (HTSA) 2006

Government of Wales Act (GWA) 2006

Cremation (Amendment) Regulations (CAR) 2006 [SI 92 of 2006]

Cremation (England and Wales) Regulations (CEWR) 2008 [SI 2841 of 2008]

Coroners and Justice Act (CJA) 2009

Certification of Death (Scotland) Act (CDSA) 2011

Certification of Death (Scotland) Act 2011 (Consequential Provisions Order (CDSACPO)) 2015

Burial and Cremation (Scotland) Bill (BCSB) 2015

Burial and Cremation (Scotland) Act (BCSA) 2016

CASES

Bain v Seafield, *Rettie, Crawford and Melville Session Cases (4th Series)* 12 (1884), 62; *Scottish Law Reports* 22 (1884), 41

Dewar v HM Advocate *Justiciary Cases* 5; *Scots Law Times* 114 (1945)
Fulton v Dunlop, *Dunlop, Bell and Murray's Reports, Second Series, Session Cases* 24 (1862), 1027; *Scottish Jurist* 34 (1862), 512
Ghai v Newcastle City Council (2009) EWHC 978 (Admin)<http://www.bailii.org/ew/cases/EWHC/Admin/2009/978> accessed 28 October 2015
Ghai v Newcastle City Council (2010) EWCA Civ 59 (2011) 1 *Law Reports, Queen's Bench* 591
Gourock Churchyard Case *Poor Law Magazine and Parochial Journal* (1874), 86
In re Kerr [1894] *Law Reports, Probate* 284
Heritors and Kirk-Session of South Leith v Scott 11 *Shaw's Session Cases First Series* 75 (1832), 5; *Scottish Jurist* 110 (1832)
HM Advocate v Coutts (1899) 3 *Adam's Justiciary Reports* 50
Kirk-Session and Heritors of Leith v Friendly Society of Restalrig 3 *Scottish Jurist* 472 (1831)
Kirk-Session of Duddingston v Halyburton 10 *Shaw's Session Cases First Series* 196 (1832), 10 *Shaw's Session Cases First Series* 196, 7 Fac. 161 (1832), 4 *Scottish Jurist* 236 (1832)
Lord Provost of Edinburgh v Kirk Sessions of St Cuthberts, *Poor Law Magazine and Parochial Journal* (1874), 203
McReadie v McBroom, *Poor Law Magazine for Scotland* 1 (1859–60), 301
R v Dudley and Stephens (1884–5) 5 *Times Law Reports*, 29
R v Price (1884) 12 *Law Reports, Queen's Bench Division* 247, 53 *Law Journal Reports, Magistrates Cases New Series* 51, *Weekly Reports* 45, 15 *Cox's Criminal Cases* 389
R v Stephenson [1884] 13 *Law Reports, Queen's Bench Division* 331 and 15 *Cox Criminal Cases* 679
Scottish Burial and Law Reform Society v Glasgow Corporation 1966 *Session Cases* 215
Scottish Burial and Law Reform Society v Glasgow Corporation [1968] *Law Reports Appeal Cases* 138
Swan v Halyburton 8 S 687 (1830), 2 *Scottish Jurist* 307 (1830)
Williams v Williams (1882) 20 *Law Reports, Chancery.* 659, 46 *Law Times* 275, 36 *Justice of the Peace* 726, 15 *Cox's Criminal Cases* 39, 30 *Weekly Reporter* 438, *Times* 9/3/82 and *Reynolds Newspaper* 12/3/82
Wright v Wallasey Local Board (1887) 18 *Law Reports, Queen's Bench Division.* 783; 56 *Law Journal Reports, Queen's Bench New Series.* 259

BOOKS, ARTICLES and ESSAYS

Albert, Edward (ed.), *Edward Theodore Salvesen. Recollecting a Busy Life*, typescript (annotated and revised manually) NLS MS 9130. [See Harold F. Andorsen, below.]
Allighan, G. (1947), 'Burial and the State', *Report of the Conference of the Institute of Burial and Cremation Administration*, 33–42

Bibliography

Anderson, Michael (1996), 'British Population History', in M. Anderson (ed.), *British Population History, from the Black Death until the Present Day* (Cambridge: Cambridge University Press), 361–407

Anderson, W. Pitcairn (1931), *Silences that Speak: Records of Edinburgh's Ancient Churches and Burial Grounds, with Biographical Sketches of the Notables Who Rest There* (Edinburgh: Alexander Brunton)

Andorsen, Harold F. (ed.) (1949), *Memoirs of Lord Salvesen* (London and Edinburgh: W. R. Chambers Ltd

Anon. (1896), 'Up-to-date Heathenism: Cremation', *The Free Presbyterian Magazine* 1(8) (December), 309–10

Anon. (1929), *Freedom Lands and Marches of Aberdeen 1319–1929* (Aberdeen: Henry Munro Ltd)

Anon. (1979), 'Barry, Glamorgan: A Legal Snag', reprinted in *Pharos* 45(1), 29 from *South Wales Echo* (20 March 1979)

Arnott, J.C. (deputising for William R. Watt) (1956), 'An Ideal Crematorium', *Official Report of the Southport Conference of Members and Officers of Burial and Cremation Authorities, 4, 5, 6 September 1956* (London: Federation of British Cremation Authorities and the Institute of Burial and Cremation Administration), 46–53

Bachelard, G. (1957), *The Poetics of Space*, trans. Maria Jolas (New York: Orion Press)

Balfour, Gordon (2014), *Opinion of Counsel: Legislation Governing Cremation of Neonatal Infants, Stillborn Children and Foetal Remains*, 11/1/14, Annex J to Elish Angiolini (2014), *Mortonhall Investigation: Report* <http://www.edinburgh.gov.uk/info/20242/mortonhall_investigation/957/mortonhall_investigation_-_report/2> accessed 12 November 2015

Bauman, Zygmunt (2000), *Liquid Modernity* (Cambridge: Polity Press)

Bennett, Alan (2005), *Untold Stories* (London: Faber and Faber Ltd)

Bennett, Margaret (2004), *Scottish Customs from the Cradle to the Grave*, 2nd edn (Edinburgh: Birlinn)

Bentley, David (1999), 'Death in Nottingham', *New Law Journal* 149, 1094

Bevan, Aneurin (1946), *Cremation* (London: The Cremation Society of Great Britain)

Birnie, W. (1606), *The Blame of Kirk-Buriall* (Edinburgh: Robert Charteris), STC-3089 [Source: *Early English Books Online*. Eebo.chadwyck.com]

Bloch, Maurice (1992), *Prey into Hunter* (Cambridge: Cambridge University Press)

Bonar, Andrew R. (1860), *Presbyterian Liturgies with Specimens of Forms of Prayer for Worship as used in the Continental Reformed, and American Churches; with the Directory for the Public Worship of God Agreed upon by the Assembly of Divines at Westminster; and Forms of Prayer for Ordinary and Communion Sabbaths, and for Other Services of the Church* (Edinburgh: Myles Macphail)

Bourke, Joanna (1999), *Dismembering the Male: Men's Bodies, Britain and the Great War* (London: Reaktion Books)

Bourke, Joanna (2005), 'Death', in *Fear: A Cultural History* (London: Virago), 25–50

Boyle, John (2009), 'The Last Act of the Great Lafayette: Sigmund Neuberger 1872–1911', *Funeral Director*, 92(6) (June), 17–19

British Medical Association (1959), 'The Medical Aspects of Cremation', Appendix VI to the Annual Report of the Council, *Supplement to the British Medical Journal* (11 April), 173–6

British Medical Association (1964), *Deaths in the Community* (London: British Medical Association), a report prepared by the Private Practice Committee 'Medico-Legal Investigation of Deaths in the Community (England and Wales)', Appendix XIV to the Annual Report of the Council, *Supplement to the British Medical Journal* (11 May 1963), as amended and approved by the Annual Representative Meeting, *Supplement to the British Medical Journal* (27 July 1963), 79

Brown, C.G. (1987), *The Social History of Religion in Scotland since 1730* (London: Methuen)

Brown, C.G. (1997), *Religion and Society in Scotland since 1707* (Edinburgh: Edinburgh University Press)

Brown, C.G., (2016), 'Death and Atheism: Narrow Escapes, Bereavement and Funerals as Instigators of Nonbelief and Humanism in Scotland since 1950', paper presented to the conference *Death and Identity in Scotland from the Medieval to the Modern*, New College, University of Edinburgh, 29–31 January

Brown, Peter (1981), *The Cult of the Saints: Its Rise and Function in Latin Christianity* (Chicago, IL: University of Chicago Press)

Brown, Stewart J. (1982), *Thomas Chalmers and the Godly Commonwealth in Scotland* (Oxford: Oxford University Press)

Brown, Stewart J. (2009), 'The Scoto-Catholic Movement in Presbyterian Worship c.1850–1920', in Duncan B. Forrester and Doug Gay (eds), *Worship and Liturgy in Context: Studies and Case Studies in Theology and Practice* (London: SCM Press), 152–63

Brown, Stewart J. (2016), '"Where are our Dead?": Changing Views of Death and the Afterlife in Late Nineteenth- and Early Twentieth-Century Scottish Presbyterianism', in Susan Buckham, Peter C. Jupp and Julie Rugg (eds), *Death in Modern Scotland 1855–1955: Beliefs, Attitudes and Practices* (Oxford and Bern: Peter Lang), 267–86

Brown, Stewart J. and Fry, Michael, eds (1993), *Scotland in the Age of Disruption* (Edinburgh: Edinburgh University Press)

Brown, T. (1878), *Annals of the Disruption*, vol. 2 (Edinburgh: MacLaren & MacNiven)

Bruce, S., Glendinning, T. and Rosie, M. (2004), *Sectarianism in Scotland* (Edinburgh: Edinburgh University Press)

Buckham, Susan (2016), '"Not Architects of Decay": The Influence of Graveyard Management on Scottish Burial Landscapes', in Susan Buckham, Peter C. Jupp and Julie Rugg (eds), *Death in Modern Scotland, 1855–1955: Beliefs, Attitudes and Practices* (Oxford and Bern: Peter Lang), 215–40

Buckham, Susan, Jupp, Peter C. and Rugg, Julie (eds) (2016), *Death in Modern*

Scotland 1855–1955: Beliefs, Attitudes and Practices (Oxford and Bern: Peter Lang)
Burnet, George B and Marwick, William H. (1952), *The Story of Quakerism in Scotland 1650–1850 with an Epilogue on the Period 1850–1950* (London: James Clarke & Co. Ltd)
Byrne, Georgina (2010), *Modern Spiritualism and the Church of England* (Woodbridge: The Boydell Press)
Calvin, J. (1960), *Institutes of the Christian Religion*, ed. F.L. Battles and J.T. McNeill, 2 vols (London: SCM Press; New York: Westminster Press)
Cameron, Anne (2007), 'The Establishment of Civil Registration in Scotland', *Historical Journal* 50(2), 377–95
Cameron, Anne (2008), 'The Fate of the Old Parish Registers under the Registration Act of 1854', *Scottish Archives* 14, 62–72
Cameron, Charles (1887), 'The Modern Cremation Movement', *Scottish Review* 10 (July), 1–38
Cameron, J.K. (ed.) (1972), *The First Book of Discipline* (Edinburgh: The Saint Andrew Press)
Caswell, Glenys (2009), 'A Sociological Exploration of Funeral Practices in Three Scottish Sites: Tradition, Personalisation and the Reflexive Individual' (University of Aberdeen: PhD thesis)
Caswell, Glenys (2016), '"We Can Do Nothing for the Dead": The Free Presbyterian Church of Scotland's Approach to Death and the Funeral', in Susan Buckham, Peter C. Jupp and Julie Rugg (eds), *Death in Modern Scotland 1855–1955: Beliefs, Attitudes and Practices* (Oxford and Bern: Peter Lang), 303–19
Chalmers, J. (1886), 'Planning Sanitary Requirements of Farm Steadings', *Proceedings of the Royal Philosophical Society of Glasgow* 17, 404–39
Chalmers, J. (1889), 'A Scheme of Cremation Suited to the Requirements of Glasgow', *Proceedings of the Royal Philosophical Society of Glasgow* 20, 193–5
Chalmers, J. (1893), 'Some Important Sanitary Problems', *Proceedings of the Royal Philosophical Society of Glasgow* 25, 208–23
Chalmers, James, (c.1927), *Glasgow and its Crematorium* (Glasgow: Scottish Burial Reform and Cremation Society)
Chamberlain, Clive T. (2002), 'Fuels and Furnaces: Changing Fashions', in Peter C. Jupp and Hilary J. Grainger (eds), *Golders Green Crematorium, 1902–2002: A London Centenary in Context* (London: London Cremation Co. PLC), 73–84
Chamberlain, Clive T. (2005), 'European Cremator Development', in D.J. Davies with Lewis H. Mates (eds), *Encyclopedia of Cremation* (Aldershot: Ashgate), 146–8
Chamberlain, C., (2013), *The Cremation of Foetuses, Neonatal and Infant Remains Report*, 30/11/13, Annex B to Elish Angiolini (2014), *Mortonhall Investigation: Report* <http://www.edinburgh.gov.uk/info/20242/mortonhall_investigation/957/mortonhall_investigation_-_report/2> accessed 12 November 2015
Chapman, Guy [1933] (1985), *A Passionate Prodigality. Fragments of Autobiography* (London: Buchan & Enright)

Chapman, W. Dobson and Riley, Charles F. (1952), *Granite City. A Plan for Aberdeen, Published on Behalf of the Corporation of the City and Royal Burgh of Aberdeen* (London: B.T. Batsford Ltd)

Chettle, Lt-Col H.F., representing Major-General Sir Fabian Ware (1941), 'Service Burials and the Duties of the Imperial War Graves Commission as regards Civilian War Dead', paper given at the Annual General Meeting of the National Association of Cemetery and Crematorium Superintendents held at Nottingham, on 28 June, *Journal of the National Association of Cemetery and Crematorium Superintendents* (August), 8–15

Chisholm, John (ed.) (1896), 'Burial', *Green's Encyclopaedia of the Law of Scotland* (Edinburgh: William Green & Sons), vol. 2, 265–6 (1906, vol. 2, 385–6)

Church of Scotland (1922), 'Report of the Committee on "Supernatural Psychic Phenomena" to the General Assembly of the Church of Scotland' 26 May 1922 (Edinburgh: New College Library)

Clarke, J.S. (1944), *Funeral Reform* (London: Social Security League)

Clifford, Robert (2000), 'Home Office: Current Cremation Issues', *Pharos International* 66(1), 6–11

Close, R. and Riches, A. (2012), *The Buildings of Scotland, Ayrshire and Arran* (New Haven, CT and London: Yale University Press)

Clouston, Sir Thomas (1912), 'The Disposal of our Dead', *Life and Work* (November), 342–3

Crawford, A. (2005), 'Introduction', in Hilary J. Grainger, *Death Redesigned: British Crematoria History, Architecture and Landscape* (Reading: Spire Books Ltd), 11–12

Crawshaw, David (1990), 'A Blasted Victorian Cemetery', in Federation of British Cremation Authorities and the Institute of Burial and Cremation Administration (Inc.) *Joint Conference Report Glasgow 1990*, 55–9

Cremation Society (1955), *Official Annual Cremation Conference held in Ayr on Tuesday, Wednesday, Thursday, 28th, 29th and 30th June, 1955: Report of Proceedings* (London: Cremation Society of Great Britain)

Cremation Society of England (1900), *Transactions of the Cremation Society of England* 13

Cremation Society of Great Britain and Federation of Cremation Authorities of Great Britain (1930), *Ninth Annual Conference of Cremation Authorities held at Edinburgh, July 4th–8th, 1930* (London)

Crowther, Anne (2006), 'By Death Divided: Scottish and English Approaches to Death Certification in the Nineteenth Century', paper presented at the Society for the Social History of Medicine Conference, (June) <http://www.gla.ac.uk/media/media_82267_en.pdf> accessed March 2014

Crowther, M. Anne and White, Brenda (1988a), *On Soul and Conscience – the Medical Expert and Crime: 150 Years of Forensic Medicine in Glasgow* (Aberdeen: Aberdeen University Press)

Crowther, M.A. and White, Brenda M. (1988b), 'Medicine, Property and the Law in Britain 1800–1924', *Historical Journal* 31(4), 853–70

Cumming, Elizabeth (2005), *Phoebe Anna Traquair, 1852–1936* (Edinburgh: The National Galleries of Scotland)
Cumming, Elizabeth (2016), 'Phoebe Anna Traquair, Angels and Concepts of the Supernatural in Fin-de-siècle Scotland', in Susan Buckham, Peter C. Jupp and Julie Rugg (eds), *Death in Modern Scotland 1855–1955: Beliefs, Attitudes and Practices* (Oxford and Bern: Peter Lang), 11–29
Cumper, Peter and Lewis, Tom (2010), 'Last Rites and Human Rights', *Ecclesiastical Law Review* 12, 131–51
Curl, James Stevens (1974), 'Scotland's Spectacular Cemeteries', *Country Life* (3 October), 950–4
Curl, James Stevens (nd, c.1975), *The Cemeteries and Burial Grounds of Glasgow*, (Glasgow: Corporation of Glasgow)
Curl, James Stevens (1983), 'John Claudius Loudon and the Garden Cemetery Movement', *Garden History* 11(2) (1983), 133–56
Curl, James Stevens (2002), *Death and Architecture: An Introduction to Funerary and Commemorative Buildings in the Western European Tradition, with some Consideration of their Settings* (Stroud: Sutton Publishing)
Daiches, D. (1977), *Glasgow* (London: Andrew Deutsch)
Dalgleish, T.D. (1944), 'After the Blitz', *Journal of the National Association of Cemetery and Crematorium Superintendents* 10 (1 February), 9–11
Dalgleish, T.D (1949), 'Lawn Cemeteries', *Journal of the National Association of Cemetery and Crematorium Superintendents* 16 (3 August), 69–75
Darwin, Charles [1872] (1998), *The Expression of the Emotions in Man and Animals*, intro. Paul Ekman, 3rd edn (London: HarperCollins)
Davies, Douglas J. (1990), *Cremation Today and Tomorrow* (Nottingham: Grove Books)
Davies, Douglas J. (1995), *British Crematoria in Public Profile* (Maidstone: Cremation Society of Great Britain)
Davies, Douglas J. (1996), 'The Sacred Crematorium', *Mortality* 1(1), 83–94
Davies, Douglas J. (1997), *Death, Ritual and Belief; the Rhetoric of Funeral Rites* (London and Washington, DC: Cassell)
Davies, Douglas J. (2002), *Death, Ritual and Belief: The Rhetoric of Funeral Rites*, 2nd edn (London: Continuum)
Davies, Douglas J. (2011), *Emotion, Identity, and Religion: Hope, Reciprocity and Otherness* (Oxford: Oxford University Press)
Davies, Douglas J. (2015), *Mors Britannica: Lifestyle and Death-style in Britain Today* (Oxford: Oxford University Press)
Davies, Douglas, Kent, Elizabeth and Keizer, Henry (2005), 'International Cremation Federation', in Douglas J. Davies with Lewis H. Mates (eds), *Encyclopedia of Cremation* (Aldershot: Ashgate), xxvi–xxvii
Davies, Douglas J. with Mates, Lewis H. (eds) (2005), *Encyclopedia of Cremation* (Aldershot: Ashgate)
Davies, Douglas J. and Powell, Adam J. (2015), *Sacred Selves, Sacred Settings: Reflecting Hans Mol* (Farnham: Ashgate)

Davies, Douglas and Rumble, Hannah (2012), *Natural Burial: Traditional-secular Spiritualities and Funeral Innovation* (London: Continuum)
Davies, Douglas and Shaw, Alastair (1995), *Re-using Old Graves: A Report on Popular British Attitudes* (Crayford, Kent: Shaw & Sons)
Davies, John (1981), *Cardiff and the Marquesses of Bute* (Cardiff: University of Wales Press)
Davis, Gayle (2009), 'Stillbirth Registration and Perceptions of Infant Death, 1900–60: The Scottish Case in National Context', *Economic History Review* 62(3), 629–54
Dawson, J. (2015), *John Knox* (New Haven, CT and London: Yale University Press)
Deane, F.L. (1938), 'Cremation and Christianity', *Pharos* 4(2), 10–11
DesBrisay, Gordon (1996), Catholics, Quakers and Religious Persecution in Restoration Aberdeen, *The Innes Review* 47(2), 136–68
Devine, T.M., 2012, *The Scottish Nation. A Modern History* (London: Penguin Group)
Directory for the Publique Worship of God Throughout the Three Kingdoms of Scotland, England, and Ireland (1645) (Edinburgh: Evan Tyler), Wing-D1549 [Source: Early English Books Online, eebo.chadwyck.com]
Devlin, W. (1908), 'Cremation', in *The New Catholic Encyclopedia, vol. 4* (New York: Robert Appleton Co.)
Drew, J. (1965), 'Lighting and Landscape for Crematorium Design', *Annual Cremation Society Conference, Report of Proceedings*, 39–49
Droogers, André and Hartskamp, Anton van (eds) (2014), *Methods for the Study of Religious Change: From Religious Studies to Worldview Studies* (Sheffield: Equinox)
Drummond, Andrew L. and Bulloch, James (1975), *The Church in Victorian Scotland (vol. 2) 1843–1874* (Edinburgh: Saint Andrew Press)
Duncan, Eben[ezer] (1887), *The Reform of our Present Methods of Disposal of the Dead: Earth-to-Earth Burial versus Cremation* [read before the Philosophical Society, 27 April 1887; and reprinted from *The Sanitary Journal*, September 1887] (Glasgow: Alex. MacDougall, 1887)
Duncan, John M. (1864), *Treatise on the Parochial Ecclesiastical Law of Scotland* (Edinburgh: Bell & Bradfute)
Duncan, John M. and Johnston, Christopher N. (1903), *The Parochial Ecclesiastical Law of Scotland* (Edinburgh: Bell & Bradfute)
Dunn, Angela (2001), 'The Sensitive Disposal of Foetal Remains', *IBCA Journal* 69(4), 18
Dyer, C. (2004), 'Seven Doctors to Face GMC over Shipman Inquiry Findings', *British Medical Journal* 329 (11 September), 591
Dyer, O. (2005a), 'GMC Drops Charges against Two GPs who Signed Shipman's Forms', *British Medical Journal* 330 (1 January), 10
Dyer, O. (2005b), 'GMC Clears Doctors who Signed Cremation Forms for Shipman', *British Medical Journal* 331 (16 July), 126
Eassie, William (1884), 'Cremation', *Health Exhibition Literature* 8, 280–96

Edwards, Owen Dudley (1980), *Burke & Hare* (London: Polygon Books)
Elias, Norbert (1978), *The Civilising Process: Volume I, The History of Manners* (New York: Horizon Books)
Farquharson, Robert (1899), 'On Cremation. Aberdeen City Lectures' [30 November], *Aberdeen Free Press* (1 December); reprinted in the *Transactions of the Cremation Society of England* 13 (1900), 14–33
Farquharson, Robert (1910), *Dr. Farquharson, M.P., on Cremation. Being a Lecture Given in the Music Hall. Aberdeen, on November 30, 1899, and Forming one of an Annual Series Known as the 'Aberdeen City Lectures', Reprinted from the 'The Aberdeen Free Press' of Dec. 1, 1899* (London: Cremation Society of England)
Farquharson, Robert (1911), *In and Out of Parliament* (London: Williams & Norgate)
Farquharson, Robert (1912), *The House of Commons From Within and Other Memories* (London: Williams & Norgate)
Fellows, Alfred (1940), *The Law of Burial and Generally of the Disposal of the Dead* (London: Hadden Best & Co.)
Fenton, C., and Walker, D. (2012), 'The Modern Church', in L. Campbell, M. Glendinning and J. Thomas, *Basil Spence Buildings and Projects* (London: RIBA Publishing),
Ferenbach, Campbell (1975), *Annals of Liberton* (Edinburgh: Howie & Seath)
Finer, Samuel Edward (1952), *The Life and Times of Sir Edwin Chadwick* (London: Methuen)
Firth, Shirley (1997), *Dying, Death and Bereavement in a British Hindu Community* (Leuvain: Peters)
Fitch, A. (2009), *The Search for Salvation: Lay Faith in Scotland, 1480–1560* (Edinburgh: John Donald)
Fletcher, R. (1974), *The Akenham Burial Case* (London: Wildwood House)
Fletcher, Ronald (1980), 'A National Scandal: The Akenham Burial Case', in Ronald Fletcher, *In a Country Churchyard* (London: Granada Publishing Ltd), 50–71
Francis, D., Kellaher, L. and Neophytou, G. (2005), *The Secret Cemetery* (Oxford: Berg)
Fraser, Donald M. (1996), 'A Tragic Last Illusion: The Empire Theatre in Flames', in *Scottish Disasters* (Edinburgh: Mercat Press), 55–63
Frew, John (1906), '"The Individual Communion Cup" and "Cremation"', *Municipal and County Record* 7 (3 July), 253, 258–60
Geddes, Diana (1972), 'The Scottish Way of Death', *The Scotsman*, 6 March
Gifford, J., McWilliam, C., Walker, D. and Wilson C. (1984), *The Buildings of Scotland: Edinburgh* (Harmondsworth: Penguin Books Ltd)
Gifford, J. and Walker, F.A. (2002), *The Buildings of Scotland. Stirling and Central Scotland* (New Haven, CT and London: Yale University Press)
Glaister, John (1884–5), 'An Enquiry into the Necessity for Legislative Reform in Scotland in Regard to Uncertified Deaths', *Proceedings of the Glasgow Philosophical Society* 16, 305–327
Glaister, John (1893), 'Death Certification and Registration in Scotland: Its Present Defects and a Proposed Remedy', *Glasgow Medical Journal* 40(6), 241–60

Glaister, John (1945), *Medical Jurisprudence and Toxicology*, 8th edn (Edinburgh: E. & S. Livingstone)
Glendinning, M. (ed.) (1997), *Rebuilding Scotland. The Postwar Vision 1945–1975* (East Linton: Tuckwell Press)
Glendinning M. and MacKechnie, A. (2004), *Scottish Architecture* (London: Thames and Hudson)
Gordon, A. (1992), *Candie for the Foundling* (Bishop Auckland: Pentland Press)
Gordon, Anne (1984), *Death is for the Living* (Edinburgh: Paul Harris)
Gore, Bishop Charles (1924), untitled address, *Proceedings of the Third Conference of Cremation Authorities, Wembley*, 3–5
Gorer, G. (1965), *Death, Grief and Mourning in Contemporary Britain* (London: Cresset Press)
Gorini, Paolo (1879), *The First Crematory in England and the Collective Crematories*, translated from the Italian by Geo. L. Larkins (London: Henry Renshaw)
Gorman, Martyn L. (2010), 'Scottish Echoes of the Resurrection Men' (University of Aberdeen: MLitt thesis)
Gosden, P.H.J.H. (1961), *The Friendly Societies in England 1815–1875* (Manchester: Manchester University Press)
Graham, Edward (1905), *The Law Relating to the Poor and to Parish Councils* (Edinburgh: William Green & Sons)
Grainger, Hilary J. (2000), 'Golders Green and the Architectural Expression of Cremation', *Mortality* 5(1) (March), 53–73
Grainger, Hilary J. (2005), *Death Redesigned. British Crematoria: History, Architecture and Landscape* (Reading: Spire Books in association with the Cremation Society of Great Britain)
Grainger, Hilary J. (2008), 'Overcoming "An Architecture of Reluctance": British Crematoria, Past, Present and Future', in Peter C. Jupp (ed.), *Death Our Future: Christian Theology and Pastoral Practice* (Peterborough: Epworth), 116–26
Grainger, Hilary J. (2011), *The Architecture of Sir Ernest George* (Reading: Spire)
Grainger, Hilary J. (2012), 'The Remarkable Rise of Cremation in a Scottish City: Glasgow 1927–1962 (Part 2)', *Pharos International* 78(3), 30–6
Grainger, Hilary J. (2013), 'The Drama of Death: Blackley Crematorium 1957', unpublished paper, Cremation Society of Great Britain Seminar Series no. 2, 'Cremation Matters', 30 October
Grainger, Hilary J (2016), 'Designs on Death: The Architecture of Scottish Crematoria 1895–1955', in Susan Buckham, Peter C. Jupp and Julie Rugg (eds), *Death in Modern Scotland, 1855–1955: Beliefs, Attitudes and Practices* (Oxford and Bern: Peter Lang), 241–64
Hallam, E. and Hockey, J. (2001), *Death, Memory, and Material Culture* (Oxford: Berg)
Hallam, E., Hockey, J. L. and Howarth, G. (1999), *Beyond the Body: Death and Social Identity* (London: Routledge)
Hamilton, L. (1983), 'A Paisley Architect: James Steel Maitland (1887–1982)', *Scottish Georgian Society Bulletin*, 10

Hannah, Rosemary (2012), *The Grand Designer. Third Marquess of Bute* (Edinburgh: Birlinn)

Hannah, Rosemary (2014), 'The Third Marquess of Bute and the Supernatural', unpublished paper given to the conference *Death in Scotland, from the Medieval to the Modern: Beliefs, Attitudes and Practices*, 31 January–2 February (Edinburgh: New College)

Harvie, Christopher (1981), *No Gods and Precious Few Heroes. Scotland 1914–1980* (London: Edwin Arnold)

Havard, J. (2000), 'Existing Safeguards against Secret Homicide are Defective and have been Weakened', *British Medical Journal* 320 (6 May), 1271

Havard, J.D.J. (1960), *The Detection of Secret Homicide: A Study of the Medico-legal System of Investigation of Sudden and Unexplained Deaths*, Cambridge Studies in Criminology vol. XI (London: Macmillan & Co.)

Hellman, L. (1982), 'Ashes to Ashes: Crownhill Crematorium, Milton Keynes', *Architects' Journal* (14 July), 47–61

Henderson, Lizanne (2001), *Scottish Faerie Beliefs* (Toronto: Dundurn)

Hiram, Hilary (2010), 'Morbid Family Pride: Private Memorials and Scots Law', in Elizabeth Anderson, Avrill Maddrell, Kate McGloughlin and Alana Vincent (eds), *Memory, Mourning, Landscape* (Amsterdam: Rodopi), 99–121

Houston, R.A. (2010), *Punishing the Dead? Suicide, Lordship, and Community in Britain, 1500–1830* (Oxford: Oxford University Press)

Howarth, Glennys (1996), *Last Rites. The Work of the Modern Funeral Director* (Amityville, NY: Baywood)

Howarth, Glennys (1997), 'Professionalising the Funeral Industry in England 1700–1960', in Peter C. Jupp and Glennys Howarth (eds), *The Changing Face of Death: Historical Accounts of Death and Disposal* (Basingstoke: Macmillan), 120–34

Hussein, Ian (1997), 'The PFI from a Public Sector Manager's Perspective', *Pharos International* 63(2), 19–21

Hutt, C. (ed.) (1996), *City of the Dead. The Story of Glasgow's Southern Necropolis* (Glasgow: City Library and Archives), reprinted [2007, in shortened form] as *City of the Dead. A Guide to Glasgow's Southern Necropolis*, South Glasgow Heritage Environment Trust (Glasgow: Culture and Sport)

Innes, Alexander Taylor (1867), *The Law of Creeds in Scotland: A Treatise on the Legal Relation of Churches in Scotland Established and Not Established, to their Doctrinal Confessions* (Edinburgh and London: William Blackwood & Sons)

Institute of Burial and Cremation Administration (1992), *The Disposal of Foetal Remains: A Policy Document*

Institute of Burial and Cremation Administration (2001), *Policy Document for the Disposal of Foetal Remains*

Institute of Cemetery and Crematorium Management (2004), *Policy Document for the Disposal of Foetal Remains*

Institute of Cemetery and Crematorium Management (2011), *The Sensitive Disposal of Fetal Remains: Policy and Guidance for Burial and Cremation Authorities and Companies*

Irion, Paul E. (1976), *Cremation* (Philadelphia, PA: Fortress Press)
Jalland, Pat (2010), *Death in War and Peace. A History of Loss & Grief in England, 1914–1970* (Oxford: Oxford University Press)
Johnstone, William (ed.) (1995), *William Robertson Smith: Essays in Reassessment* (Sheffield: Sheffield Academic Press)
Jupp, Peter C. (1990), *From Dust to Ashes: The Replacement of Burial by Cremation in England 1840–1967*, The Congregational Lecture (London: The Congregational Memorial Trust [1978] Ltd)
Jupp, P.C. (1993), 'The Development of Cremation in England, 1820–1990: A Sociological Analysis' (University of London: PhD thesis)
Jupp, P.C. (2002), 'The Critical Years: The Development of Cremation in England, 1918–1952', *Resurgam* 45 (2) (Autumn), 102–9
Jupp, Peter C. (2006a), *From Dust to Ashes: Cremation and the British Way of Death* (Basingstoke: Palgrave Macmillan)
Jupp, P.C. (2006b), 'From Bishop Wordsworth to Dr Major: Cremation and Resurrection, 1872–1922', *Resurgam* 49 (1) (Spring), 33–6
Jupp, P.C. (2008), 'The Council for the Disposition of the Dead', *Funeral Service Journal* 123(7), 103–6
Jupp, P.C. (2009), 'Goodbye to John Knox? G. W. Sprott and the Revival of Liturgy in 19th Century Church of Scotland Funerals', paper given to the Ninth International Conference on *The Social Context of Death Dying and Disposal*, Durham, 9–12 September
Jupp Peter C. and Howarth, Glennys (eds) (1997), *The Changing Face of Death: Historical Accounts of Death and Disposal* (Basingstoke: Macmillan)
Keir, David (1966a), 'Fire and Burial', *The Third Statistical Account of Scotland Vol. XV. The City of Edinburgh* (Glasgow: Collins), 431–41
Keir, David (1966b), 'The People's Homes from 1845 to 1958', *The Third Statistical Account of Scotland Vol. XV. The City of Edinburgh* (Glasgow: Collins), 369–89
Kellas, J. G. (1964), 'The Liberal Party and the Scottish Church Disestablishment Crisis', *English Historical Review* 79, 31–46
Kerr, John (1909), *The Renascence of Worship. The Origins, Aims and Achievements of the Church Service Society*, Lee Lecture (Edinburgh: J. Gardner Hitt)
Kollar, Rene (2000), *Searching for Raymond: Anglicanism, Spiritualism, and Bereavement between the Two World Wars* (Lanham, MD: Lexington Books)
Kyd, James G. (1956), 'Registration', in M.R. McLarty and G. Campbell H. Paton (eds), *A Source Book and History of Administrative Law in Scotland* (London, Edinburgh, Glasgow: William Hodge & Co.), 64–73
Laqueur, Thomas W. (2015), *The Work of the Dead: A Cultural History of Mortal Remains* (Princeton, NJ: Princeton University Press)
Laski KC, Neville (1932), 'Public Assistance Authorities: May They Lawfully Cremate Human Bodies for the Disposal of Which They Are Responsible?' (6 July) (CSA CRE P/2/H/Box 1)
Lawrence, Francis (1889), 'Burial and Cremation', *The Times* (27 April), 13e

Lawrence, Francis (1891), 'Burial and Cremation', *The Times* (19 August), 8d

Laxton, Paul and Rodger, Richard (2014), *Insanitary City: Henry Littlejohn and the Condition of Edinburgh* (Lancaster: Carnegie Publishing)

Leaney, J. (1989), 'Ashes to Ashes: Cremation and the Celebration of Death in Nineteenth-century Britain', in R. Houlbrooke (ed.), *Death, Ritual and Bereavement* (London: Routledge), 118–35

Lewis, Richard Albert (1952), *Edwin Chadwick and the Public Health Movement, 1832–54* (London: Longmans)

Lindsay, Donald P. (1999), 'The Beginning of the Cremation Movement in Scotland', *Resurgam* 42(2), 92–8

Lister, Joseph (1870a), 'On the Effects of the Antiseptic System of Treatment upon the Salubrity of a Surgical Hospital', *The Lancet* 1, 4–6, 42–44; see also (1870b)

Lister, Joseph (1870b), 'Further Evidence Regarding the Effects of the Antiseptic System upon the Salubrity of a Surgical Hospital', *The Lancet* 2 (August 1870), 287–9

Littlejohn, H.D. (1865), 'Intramural Interment', *in Report on the Sanitary Condition of the City of Edinburgh, with Relative Appendices, etc.* (Edinburgh: Colston & Son), 93–9

Longmate, Norman (1966), *King Cholera* (London: Hamish Hamilton)

Loudon, John Claudius [1843] (1981), *On the Laying Out, Planting and Management of Cemeteries and the Improvement of Churchyards* (Redhill: Ivelet Books)

'Mac' (1911), 'Undertaking in Scotland', *Undertakers' Journal* 26(9), 249

MacInnes, R., Gendinning, M. and MacKechnie, A. (1999), *Building a Nation. The Story of Scotland's Architecture* (Edinburgh: Canongate Books Ltd)

Mackenzie, Norman (2006), 'When the Crematorium was a Hotbed of Rumour', *Leopard. The Magazine for North-East Scotland* (August)

MacLean, Norman (1953), *The Years of Fulfilment* (London: Hodder and Stoughton)

MacLeod, James Lachlan (2000), *The Second Disruption. The Free Church in Victorian Scotland and the Origins of the Free Presbyterian Church*, SHR Monograph Series No. 8 (East Linton: Tuckwell Press)

MacLeod, J. L. (2002), '"Greater Love Hath No Man Than This": Scotland's Conflicting Religious Responses to Death in the Great War', *Scottish Historical Review* 81(1), 70–96

McDonald, Juliette (2016), 'Death, Mourning and Memory: Two Apocalypse Windows by Douglas Strachan', in S. Buckham, P. C. Jupp and J. Rugg (eds), *Death in Modern Scotland, 1855–1955: Beliefs, Attitudes and Practices* (Oxford and Bern: Peter Lang), 31–53

McDonald, Stuart W. (2011), *Procurement of Cadavers by Anatomists in Glasgow in the Early Nineteenth Century*, paper given on 23 February 2011 to the Royal Philosophical Society of Glasgow <http://www.royalphil.org/lectures/2011-02-23.xml> accessed 16 November 2015

McFarland, Elaine (1990), *Protestants First: Orangeism in Nineteenth-century Scotland* (Edinburgh: Edinburgh University Press)

McFarland, Elaine (2005), 'Researching Death, Mourning and Commemoration in Modern Scotland', *Scottish Historical Studies Journal* 24(1), 20–44

McFarland, Elaine (2008), 'Working with Death: An Oral History of Funeral Directing in Late Twentieth-century Scotland', *Oral History*, 69–80

McFarland, E. (2010), 'Passing Time: Death in Twentieth-century Scotland', in Lynn Abrams and Callum G. Brown (eds), *Everyday Life in Twentieth-century Scotland* (Edinburgh: Edinburgh University Press), 254–81

McGinnell, Kevin (2006), 'Why Catholics Prefer burial', *Pharos International* 72(2), 3–4

McGinnell, Kevin (2015), 'Celebration of the Catholic Church's 1964 Decision', *Pharos International* 81(1), 16–19

McHale, Bernard (2001), 'Cremation of Foetal Remains', letter to members of the FBCA, 22 July

McKim, John (1944), 'A Survey of Burial and Burial Progress in Paisley: Paisley and the Progress of Burial Reform', *Journal of the National Association of Cemetery and Crematorium Superintendents*, 10(4) (November), 8–9

McLeod, Hugh (2007), *The Religious Crisis of the 1960s* (Oxford: Oxford University Press)

McMillan, R.C. (1951), 'The Birth of a Branch', *Journal of the Institute of Burial and Cremation Administration* 19(2), 68, 76.

McMillan, Robert C. (1946), 'Burial Grounds, Old and New as Lawned Gardens', *Report of the Joint Conference of Federation of British Cremation Authorities and the Institute of Burial and Cremation Administration*, 9–17

McPherson, A. (ed.) (n.d.) [1970], *History of the Free Presbyterian Church of Scotland (1893–1970)* (Inverness: The Publications Committee, Free Presbyterian Church of Scotland)

McQueenie, John (1990), *Presidential Address, Joint Conference of Burial and Cremation Authorities*, 61–70

Maitland, J. Steel (1952), 'Scottish Housing Past and Present', *Royal Institute of British Architects Journal* 59(9), 315–22

Major, H.D.A. (1922), *A Resurrection of Relics: A Modern Churchman's Defence in a Recent Charge of Heresy* (Oxford, Blackwell)

Makepeace, Chris E. (n.d. [1990]), *Manchester Crematorium 1890–1990* (Manchester: Manchester Free Press)

Mann, John (1952), *Extracts from some Drafts of Reminiscences of Sir John Mann, KBE* (Archives of the Scottish Burial Reform and Cremation Society and Cremation Society Archives CRE/P/2/F/Box 1)

Mann, John (1954), 'Burning Question', *Funeral Service Journal*, March, 108–10

Manning, Bernard L. (1952), *The Protestant Dissenting Deputies* (Cambridge: Cambridge University Press)

Marlow, Simon (2008),'Can I Cremate My Own Leg?', *British Medical Journal* 336 (5 April), 774

Mates, Lewis H. (2005), 'Hungary', in Douglas J. Davies with Lewis H. Mates (eds), *Encyclopedia of Cremation* (Aldershot: Ashgate), 251–6

Matthews, S. (2004), *Poetical Remains: Poets' Graves, Bodies, and Books in the Nineteenth Century* (Oxford: Oxford University Press)
Maver, Irene (2000), *Glasgow* (Edinburgh: Edinburgh University Press)
Maxwell, W.D. (1931), *John Knox's Genevan Service Book, 1556. The Liturgical Portions of the Genevan Service Book used by John Knox while a Minister of the English Congregation of Marian Exiles at Geneva, 1556–1559* (Edinburgh and London: Oliver and Boyd)
Meller, Hugh and Parsons, Brian (2008), *London Cemeteries: An Illustrated Gazetteer*, 4th edn (Stroud: History Press)
Mellor, P.A. and Shilling, C. (1993), 'Modernity, Self-Identity and the Sequestration of Death', *Sociology* 27(3) (August), 411–31
Merridale, C. (1999), *Night of Stone: Death and Memory in Russia* (London: Granta)
Metcalf, P. and Huntingdon, R. (1991), *Celebrations of Death: The Anthropology of Mortuary Ritual*, 2nd edn (Cambridge: Cambridge University Press)
Miller, James (2004), 'Another Glass and Concrete Box', in *Inverness* (Edinburgh: Birlinn), 288–303
Mitchell, J.F. (1958), 'A Survey of Pre-1855 Glasgow Burial Grounds', *Scottish Genealogist* 5(1), 2–7
Mitchell, J.F. (1968), 'Graveyards and Development', *Scottish Genealogist* 15(3), 53–5
Mitchell, Peter Chalmers (1937), *My Fill of Days* (London: Faber & Faber)
Mitchison, Rosalind (2000), *The Old Poor Law in Scotland: The Experience of Poverty, 1574–1845* (Edinburgh: Edinburgh University Press)
Mol, Hans (1976), *Identity and the Sacred* (Oxford: Basil Blackwell)
Morgan, Diane (2009), *Lost Aberdeen: The Freedom Lands* (Edinburgh: Birlinn)
Morgan, Lynn M. (2002), '"Properly Disposed of": A History of Embryo Disposal and the Changing Claims of Fetal Remains', *Medical Anthropology* 21, 247–74
Morris, R.J. (1976), *Cholera 1832: The Social Response to an Epidemic* (London: Croom Helm)
Morton, James (2003), 'A Deathly Silence', *Law Gazette* 100(38), 19
Nankivell, John (2008), 'Orthodox Liturgy, Theology and Pastoral Practice', in Peter C. Jupp (ed.), *Death our Future: Christian Theology and Pastoral Practice in Funeral Ministry* (London: Epworth Press), 190–201
Nash, E. (1989), 'Cultural Standards for Crematoria', paper given to the *Institute of Burial and Cremation Administration Conference*, Scarborough, *Journal of the Institute of Burial and Cremation Administration* 56(3), 83–9
National Association of Cemetery and Crematorium Superintendents (1944), *Memorandum on Planning for Post-War Reform in the Disposition of the Dead* (London: National Association of Cemetery and Crematorium Superintendents)
Naughtie, J. (2000), 'Introduction', in Hamish W. Fraser and C.H. Lee, *Aberdeen 1800–2000. A New History* (East Lothian: Tuckwell Press),
Newton, John (2005), 'Cremation, Death and Roman Catholicism', in Douglas J. Davies with Lewis H. Mates (eds), *Encyclopedia of Cremation* (Aldershot: Ashgate), 107–9

Novarino, Marco (2005), 'Freemasonry in Italy', in Douglas J. Davies with Lewis H. Mates (eds), *Encyclopedia of Cremation* (Aldershot: Ashgate), 207–10

O'Brien, Terence H. (1955), *Civil Defence* (London: HMSO)

Otto, Rudolf [1917] (1924), *The Idea of the Holy*, trans. John H. Harvey (Oxford: Oxford University Press)

Parkes, Colin Murray, Laungani, Pittu and Young, Bill (eds) (2015), *Death and Bereavement Across Cultures*, 2nd edition (London: Routledge)

Parry, Jonathan (1994), *Death in Banaras* (Cambridge: Cambridge University Press)

Parsons, Brian (2005), *Committed to the Cleansing Flame: The Development of Cremation in Nineteenth-Century England* (Reading: Spire)

Parsons, Brian (2009), 'Unknown Undertaking: Tracing the Origins of the Co-operative Funeral Service', unpublished paper given to the 9th International Conference on the Social Context of Death, Dying and Disposal, 9–12 September

Parsons, Brian (2012), 'Identifying Key Changes: The Progress of Cremation and its Influence on Music at Funerals in England, 1874–2010', *Mortality* 17(2), 130–144

Parsons, Brian (2013), 'Funeral Directing in 20th-Century Scotland', unpublished paper given at the conference *Death in Modern Scotland, 1855–1955: Beliefs, Attitudes and Practices*, 1–3 February, New College, Edinburgh

Parsons, Brian (2014), *From Undertaker to Funeral Director: The Changing Face of British Funeral Service* (London: Strange Attractor Press)

Parsons, Brian (forthcoming), *From Undertaker to Funeral Director: The Changing Face of the British Funeral Industry in the Twentieth Century*

Pearson, Frederick (2007), 'Flameless Combustion', *Pharos International* 73(3), 26–9

Pearson, William (1951), 'The Institute and the Disposal of the Dead in Relation to the Future', in the 'Notes of proceedings at a meeting of the Scottish Branch of the Institute of Burial and Cremation Administration, held within the Municipal Buildings, Paisley, on Saturday 18th November 1950', *Journal of the Institute of Burial and Cremation Administration*, 20–36

Pettigrew, W.H. (1948), 'War Graves – Scotland', *Journal of the National Association of Cemetery and Crematorium Superintendents* 14(3), 27–9

Piggott, Halvor (1939), 'A Plan for the Disposition of the Dead in a National Emergency through a Scheme to Control and Co-ordinate Cremations and Crematoria' (April) (TNA HO 45/18142/F47)

Playfair, Lyon (1874), 'Address on Health', *Transactions of the National Association for the Promotion of Social Science*, 72–101

Powell, Dean (2012), *Dr William Price: Wales's First Radical* (Stroud: Amberley Publishing)

Prothero, Stephen R. (2001), *Purified by Fire: A History of Cremation in America* (Berkeley: University of California Press)

Raeburn, Gordon D. (2012), 'The Long Reformation of the Dead in Scotland' (University of Durham: PhD thesis)

Raeburn, Gordon D. (2016), 'Death, Superstition and Common Society Following the Scottish Reformation', *Mortality* 21 (1 February), 36–51

Reeves, Joseph (1952), 'The Bill to Amend the Cremation Act of 1902', *Report of Proceedings of Official Annual Cremation Conference in the Winter Gardens, Margate, on Tuesday, Wednesday and Thursday, July 8th, 9th and 10th, 1952,* 6–14

Reid, Harry (2002), *Outside Verdict. An Old Kirk in a New Scotland* (Edinburgh: St Andrew Press)

Reid, Thomas L. (1943), 'Earth Burial or Cremation', *Journal of the National Association of Cemetery and Crematorium Superintendents* 9(4), 11–13

Richardson, Ruth (1987), *Death, Dissection and the Destitute* (London: Routledge & Kegan Paul)

Richardson, Ruth (2008), *The Making of Mr Gray's Anatomy* (Oxford: Oxford University Press)

Roberts, J. (2013), *Anthropology Report*, 16/12/13, Annex C to Elish Angiolini (2014), *Mortonhall Investigation: Report* <http://www.edinburgh.gov.uk/info/20242/mortonhall_investigation/957/mortonhall_investigation_-_report/2> accessed 12 November 2015

Roberts, J. (2014), *Supplementary Anthropology Report*, 21/1/14, Annex D to Elish Angiolini (2014), *Mortonhall Investigation: Report* <http://www.edinburgh.gov.uk/info/20242/mortonhall_investigation/957/mortonhall_investigation_-_report/2> accessed 12 November 2015

Robertson, A.K. (1956), 'The Revival of Church Worship in the Church of Scotland from Dr Robert Lee (1804–1867) to Dr H.J. Wotherspoon (1850–1930)' (University of Edinburgh: unpublished PhD thesis)

Robertson, Edna (1998), *Glasgow's Doctor. James Burn Russell 1837–1904* (East Linton: Tuckwell Press)

Robertson, W.G. Aitchison (1909), 'Cremation', a lecture delivered before the Edinburgh Sanitary Society, on 3 December 1908, reprinted from *The County and Municipal Record* (9 and 16 March)

Robinson, William (1889), Cremation and Urn-Burial (London: Cassell & Co. Ltd)

Rosendale, M. (2014), *Mortonhall Crematorium Investigation: Initial Findings,* 11/1/13, Annex A to Elish Angiolini (2014), *Mortonhall Investigation: Report* <http://www.edinburgh.gov.uk/info/20242/mortonhall_investigation/957/mortonhall_investigation_-_report/2> accessed 12 November 2015

Rotar, Marius, Teodorescu, Adriana and Rotar, Corina (2014*), Dying and Death in 18th–21st Century Europe. Vol. 2.* (Newcastle upon Tyne: Cambridge Scholars Publishing)

Rowell, D. Geoffrey (1974), *Hell and the Victorians* (Oxford: Oxford University Press)

Rowell, D. Geoffrey (1977), *The Liturgy of Christian Burial* (London: Alcuin Club–SPCK)

Royle, Trevor (2007), *The Flowers of the Forest: Scotland and the First World War* (Edinburgh: Birlinn)
Rugg, Julie (1992), 'The Rise of Cemetery Companies in Britain 1820–1853' (University of Stirling: PhD thesis)
Rugg, Julie (1997), 'The Origin and Progress of Cemetery Establishment in Britain', in Peter C. Jupp and Glennys Howarth (eds), *The Changing Face of Death: Historical Accounts of Death and Disposal* (Basingstoke: Macmillan), 105–19
Rugg, Julie (1998), 'A New Burial Form and its Meanings: Cemetery Establishment in the First Half of the Nineteenth Century', in Margaret Cox (ed.), *Grave Concerns: Death and Burial in England* (York: York Council for British Archaeology, CBA Research Report 113), 44–53
Rugg, Julie (1999), 'Nonconformity and the Development of Early Cemeteries in England', *The Journal of the United Reformed Church History Society* 6 (5 November), 309–21
Rugg, Julie (2004), 'Civilian War Deaths in Yorkshire', *Twentieth Century British History* 15(2), 152–73
Rugg, Julie (2006), 'Lawn Cemeteries: A Social History', *Urban History* 33(2), 213–33
Rugg, Julie (2013), *Churchyard and Cemetery: Tradition and Modernity in Rural North Yorkshire* (Manchester: Manchester University Press)
Russell, J.B. (1905), *Public Health Administration in Glasgow. A Memorial Volume of the Writings of James Burn Russell*, ed. A.K. Chalmers (Glasgow: James Maclehose)
Salice, Anna (2005), 'Italy', in Douglas J. Davies with Lewis H. Mates (eds), *Encyclopedia of Cremation* (Aldershot: Ashgate), 111
Salvesen, Edward T. (1949), *Memoirs of Lord Salvesen*, ed. Harold F. Andorsen (London: W. & R. Chambers)
Salvesen, the Rt Hon. Lord (1927), 'The Medico-legal Aspect of Cremation', *Proceedings of the Sixth Annual Conference of Cremation Authorities*, 79–82
Savage, P. (2005), *Lorimer and the Edinburgh Arts and Craft Designers* (London and Edinburgh: Steve Savage Publishers Ltd)
Scott, Ronnie (2006), 'The Cemetery and the City: The Origins and Development of the Glasgow Necropolis, 1825–1857' (University of Glasgow: PhD thesis)
Scottish Burial Reform and Cremation Society (1904), *Ashes to Ashes* (in NRS GRO 1/648)
Scottish Burial Reform and Cremation Society (1912), *Ashes to Ashes* (in NRS GRO 1/648)
Seton, George (1854), *Sketch of the History and Imperfect Condition of the Parochial Records of Births, Deaths and Marriages in Scotland in Illustration of the Important Advantages that would be Derived from the Introduction of a System of Compulsory Registration* (Edinburgh: Thomas Constable & Co.)
Seton, George (1860), *Practical Analysis of the Acts Relating to the Registration of Births, Deaths and Marriages in Scotland* (Edinburgh: Edmonston and Douglas)

Shepherd, John A. (1965), *Spencer Wells. The Life and Work of a Victorian Surgeon* (Edinburgh and London: E. & S. Livingstone)

Shiels, Robert S. (2016), 'The Investigation of Sudden and Accidental Deaths in Mid-Victorian Scotland', in Susan Buckham, Peter C. Jupp and Julie Rugg (eds), *Death in Modern Scotland, 1855–1955: Beliefs, Attitudes and Practices* (Oxford and Bern: Peter Lang), 177–91

Simon, Henry (1896), *A Lecture on Cremation. Also Complete Rules, Regulations, and Scale of Charges for 1896* (Manchester: Manchester Crematorium Company)

Sinclair, Cecil (2000), *Jock Tamson's Bairns: A History of the Records of the General Register Office for Scotland* (Edinburgh: General Register Office for Scotland)

Slevin, John (1956), 'Rural Administration', in M.R. McClarty and G. Campbell H. Paton (eds), *A Source Book and History of Administrative Law in Scotland* (London, Edinburgh, Glasgow: William Hodge & Co.), 13–28

Smith, Fred. J. (1905), *Taylor's Principles and Practice of Medical Jurisprudence, Vol 1* (London: Churchill, 5th edn)

Smith, Michael (2008), 'Death Mourning and Commemoration in Nineteenth-century Edinburgh' (Glasgow Caledonian University: PhD thesis)

Smith, Michael (2009), 'The Church of Scotland and the Funeral Industry in Nineteenth-century Edinburgh', *Scottish Historical Review* 88(1), 108–33

Smith, Michael (2014), *The Secularization of Death in Scotland, 1815–1900: How the Funeral Industry Displaced the Church as Custodian of the Dead (A Study of Private Cemeteries, Public Crematoria, and Bereavement Practices in Edinburgh)* (Lampeter: Edwin Mellen Press)

Smith, Sydney (1928), *Forensic Medicine: A Textbook for Students and Practitioners* 2nd edn (London: J. & A. Churchill)

Smith, Sydney and Cook, W.G.H. (1934), *Taylor's Principles and Practice of Medical Jurisprudence, Vol. 1*, 9th edn (London: J. & A. Churchill)

Smith, Sydney and Smith, Frederick (1955), *Forensic Medicine: A Textbook for Students and Practitioners*, 10th edn (London: J. & A. Churchill)

Smith, Sydney, Cook, W.G.H. and Stewart C.P. (1948), *Taylor's Principles and Practice of Medical Jurisprudence, Vol. 1*, 10th edn (London: J. & A. Churchill)

Smith, W.H. (1969), 'The Future of Cemeteries in a Large City', *Report of the Proceedings of the 28th Joint Conference at Harrogate, 1969* (London: Federation of British Cremation Authorities and the Institute of Burial and Cremation Administration), 44–6

Smith, William Robertson (1889), *The Religion of the Semites* (Edinburgh: A. & C. Black)

Spicer, A. (2000), '"Defyle not Christs Kirk with your carrion": The Development of Burial Aisles in Post-Reformation Scotland', in P. Marshall and B. Gordon (eds), *The Place of the Dead in Late Medieval and Early Modern Europe* (Cambridge: Cambridge University Press), 149–9

Spicer, A. (2007), *Calvinist Churches in Early Modern Europe* (Manchester: Manchester University Press)

Sprott, W.H. (1882), *The Worship and Offices of the Church of Scotland* (Edinburgh: Wm Blackwood & Sons)
Stewart, J. Henderson (1955), 'Education for Cremation in Scotland', *Proceedings of the Cremation Society Conference in Ayr 1954* (London: Cremation Society of Great Britain), 5–7
Stirling, Fiona MacDonald (2009), 'Grave Re-use: A Feasibility Study' (University of Sheffield: PhD thesis)
Strang, J. (1831), *Necropolis Glasguensis, with Osbervations* [sic] *on Ancient and Modern Tombs and Sepulture* (Glasgow: Edward Khull)
Strange, Julie-Marie (2005), *Death, Grief and Poverty in Britain, 1870–1914* (Cambridge: Cambridge University Press)
Sullivan, Sandy (2006), '"Water Resolution": A Mercury Free Alternative to Cremation', *Pharos International* 72(4), 14–17
Sullivan, Sandy (2009), 'Resomation® Update', *Pharos International* 75(3), 4–8
Sullivan, Sandy (2016), 'Resomation has the Least Impact on the Environment', unpublished paper, presented to Cremation and Burial Communication and Education (CBCE), Stratford-upon-Avon, 4 July
Taylor, Lou (1982), *Mourning Dress: A Costume and Social History* (London: George Allen and Unwin)
Thompson, Henry (1874a), 'The Treatment of the Body After Death', *Contemporary Review* 23 (January), 319–28
Thompson, H. (1874b), 'Cremation: A Reply to Critics and an Exposition of the Process', *Contemporary Review* 23 (March), 553–71
Thompson, Henry (1901), *Modern Cremation: Its History and Practice*, 4th edn (London: Smith, Elder & Co.)
Todd, Margaret (2002), *The Culture of Protestantism in Early Modern Scotland* (New Haven, CT: Yale University Press)
Tozer, Basil (1907), 'Premature Burial and the Only True Signs of Death', *The Nineteenth Century* 20 (October), 544–59
Turner, Ernest S. (1988), 'Cremation in Britain', *Resurgam* 31(4), 86–9
Turner, Victor W. (1969), *The Ritual Process: Structure and Anti-Structure* (London: Routledge and Kegan Paul)
Vater, Bruno (2014), 'Emission Control for Cremation Systems', in Rolf Lichtner (ed.), *Handbook on Cremation* (Dusseldorf: Fachverlag des Deutschen Bestattungsgewerbes GmbH.), 179–211
Vaughan, H.A. (1891), 'Cremation and Christianity', *Dublin Review* 23(2), 384–402
Walker, Alan M.G. (1997), *Planning and Listed Building Consent Appeals by Gordon Christie, Christies (Fochabers) Limited: Enzie Church, Broadley, Clochan, Buckie* (Edinburgh: Scottish Office Inquiry Reporters)
Walker, G. A. (1839), *Gatherings from Graveyards particularly those of London; with a concise history of the modes of interment among different nations, from the earliest periods. And a detail of dangerous and fatal results produced by the unwise and revolting custom of inhuming the dead in the midst of the living* (London: Longman)

Warner, W. Lloyd (1959), *The Living and the Dead: A Study of the Symbolic Life of Americans* (New Haven, CT: Yale University Press)

Westland, John Gordon (1958), *The Aberdeen Coffins Case being the Story of the Investigation and a Report of the Trial of James Dewar and Alick George Forbes by John Gordon Westland* (University of Aberdeen: Special Collections MS 3217)

White, Brenda (1983), 'Medical Police. Politics and Police: The Fate of John Robertson', *Medical History* 27, 407–22

White, Brenda (1988), 'Scottish Doctors and the English Public Health', in Derek A. Dow (ed.), *The Influence of Scottish Medicine: An Historical Assessment of its International Impact* (Carnforth: Parthenon Publishing Group), 79–85

White, Brenda (1994), 'Training Medical Policeman: Forensic Medicine and Public Health in Nineteenth-century Scotland', in Michael Clark and Catherine Crawford (eds), *Legal Medicine in History* (Cambridge: Cambridge University Press), 145–63

White, Stephen (1993), 'An End to D-I-Y Cremation?', *Medicine, Science and the Law* 33(2), 151–9

White, Stephen (1997), 'Hindu Cremations in Britain', in Peter C. Jupp and Glennys Howarth (eds), *The Changing Face of Death: Historical Accounts of Death and Disposal* (Basingstoke: Macmillan), 135–48

White, Stephen (1999), 'Founder Members of the Cremation Society', *Pharos International* 65(1), 7–17

White, Stephen (2000a), 'Body Parts', *New Law Journal* 55(5, 12 May), 654–5, 709

White, Stephen (2000b), 'Property in Body Parts and the Cremation Regulations', *Pharos International* 66(3), 12–16

White, Stephen (2001), 'Shipman and Others: Current Inquiries Bearing on Cremation', *Pharos International* 67(4), 15–27

White, Stephen (2002a), 'A Burial Ahead of its Time? The Crookenden Burial Case and the Sanctioning of Cremation in England and Wales', *Mortality* 7(2), 171–90

White, Stephen (2002b), 'Cremation Regulations and Medical Referees: The Past', address to *BMA Conference of Crematorium Medical Referees – Cremation: Which Way Forward?* Friday 26 April 2002, *Pharos International* 68(3), 38–43

White, Stephen (2002c), 'Some Founder Members of the Cremation Society', in Peter C. Jupp and Hilary J. Grainger (eds), *Golders Green Crematorium 1902–2002: A London Cemetery in Context* (London: London Cremation Company), 1–10

White, Stephen (2003), 'The Cremation Act 1902: From Private to Local to General', *Pharos International* 69(1), 14–18

White, Stephen (2006), 'Funeral Pyres and the Law in England and Wales', *Pharos International* 72(3), 19–23

White, Stephen (2010), 'Funeral Pyres in a Legal Limbo', *Pharos International* 76(3), 30–5

White, Stephen (2011), 'The Public Health (Aquifaction) (England and Wales) Regulations?', *Pharos International* 77(1), 10–11

White, Stephen (2013), 'Cremation Act 1902 s. 5 (the 'Distance' or 'Radius' Clause):

The Balloon and String Theory of Statutory Interpretation', *Pharos International* 79(1), 6–11

White, Stephen (2016), 'The Legal Status of Corpses and Cremains: When and Where Can you Steal a Dead Body?', in Susan Buckham, Peter C. Jupp and Julie Rugg (eds), *Death in Scotland 1855–1955: Beliefs, Attitudes and Practices* (Oxford: Peter Lang), 161–76

White, Stephen (forthcoming), *The History of, and Law Relating to, the Churchyards of the Church in Wales: The View from Government Files* (Cardiff: Welsh Legal History Society)

Whitty, Niall R. (2005), 'Rights of Personality, Property Rights and the Human Body in Scots Law', *Edinburgh Law Review* 9, 194–237

Wiechmann, B. and M. Gleis (2014), 'Emissions and Control', in Rolf Lichtner (ed.), *Handbook on Cremation* (Dusseldorf: Fachverlag des Deutschen Bestattungsgewerbes GmbH.), 143–54

Wiigh-Mäsak, Susanne (2005), 'Promession', *Pharos International* 72(1), 3–4

Williams, M. and Penman, D. (2014), *Mindfulness: A Practical Guide in a Frantic World* (London: Piatkus)

Williams, Rory (1990), *A Protestant Legacy: Attitudes to Death and Illness among Older Aberdonians* (Oxford: Clarendon Press)

Williams, Rory (1992), 'Social Movements and Disordered Bodies: The Reform of Birth, Sex, Drink, and Death in Britain since 1850', in C. Crouch and A. Heath (eds), *Social Research and Social Reform: Essays in Honour of A.H. Halsey* (Oxford: Oxford University Press), 97–126

Williamson, E., Riches, A. and Higgs, M. (1990), *Buildings of Scotland. Glasgow* (London: Penguin Group)

Willing, J.A. and Fairie, J. Scott (1997), *Burial Grounds in Glasgow. A Brief Guide for Genealogists*, revd edn (Glasgow: Glasgow and West of Scotland Family History Society)

Willsher, B. (1985), *Understanding Scottish Graveyards. An Interpretative Approach* (Edinburgh: Council for Scottish Archaeology)

Wilson, Harold (1977), *A Prime Minister on Prime Ministers* (London: Weidenfeld & Nicholson)

Wolffe, J. (2000), *Great Deaths; Grieving, Religion, and Nationhood in Victorian and Edwardian Britain* (Oxford: Oxford University Press)

Woolf, James and Balfour, Gordon (2014), *Joint Opinion of Counsel: The Interpretation of Regulation 17 of the Cremation (Scotland) Regulations 1935*, 19/3/14, Annex F to Elish Angiolini (2014), *Mortonhall Investigation: Report* <http://www.edinburgh.gov.uk/info/20242/mortonhall_investigation/957/mortonhall_investigation_-_report/2> accessed 12 November 2015, and Annex D to Lord Bonomy (Chair), *Report of the Infant Cremation Commission* (Edinburgh: Scottish Government) <http://www.gov.scot/Resource/0045/00453055.pdf> accessed 12 November 2014

Yeates, Alfred B. (1924), 'Cremation from the Aesthetic Point of View – The Ideal Crematorium', Third Annual Conference of Cremation Authorities. *Minutes of a Meeting of Delegates of Cremation Authorities*, representatives of the Federation of Cremation Authorities and the Cremation Society of England, held in the Conference Hall at the British Empire Exhibition, Wembley, on Friday, 1 August 1924, at 11.45 am, pp. 20–4 (Durham: Durham University Special Collections. Cremation Society Archive)

Zhu, Jinlong, Fengming, Liu, Yongren, Zuo, Yueling, Gao, Hongchang, Zhang and Jian, Li (2005), 'China: Developments in the Twentieth Century', in Douglas J. Davies with Lewis H. Mates (eds), *Encyclopedia of Cremation* (Aldershot: Ashgate), 121–3

WEBSITES

Dictionary of Scottish Architects. http:/scottisharchitects.org.uk/

NEWSPAPERS and PERIODICALS

Aberdeen Journal
Aberdeen Press and Journal
Aberdeen Weekly Journal
Architect and Building News
Architects' Journal
Borders Telegraph
Bristol Mercury
Daily Free Press (Aberdeen)
Dunfermline Press and West of Fife Advertiser
Edinburgh Evening Dispatch
Edinburgh Gazette
Fife Press
Funeral Service Journal
Glasgow Herald
Inverness Courier
Journal of the National Association of Cemetery and Crematorium Superintendents (to 1947), thereafter the *Journal of the Institute of Burial and Cremation Administration* (IBCA)
Pharos and (from 1980) *Pharos International*
Resurgam
The Express
The Scotsman
The Times
The Undertakers Journal
The Witness

Index of Names

Agnew, Colonel, 114–15, 125
Angiolini, Dame Elish, 239, 242–3
Asplund, Gunnar, 201
Allan, James and Henry, 71, 73, 81, 99,
Allighan MP, Gary, 148
Allison, W.P., 34
Arnott, John, 175–8, 190
Attlee MP, Clement, 148–9
Argyll, Duke of, 84

Bachelard, Gaston, 189
Baldry, Philip, 230
Balfour, Lord, 84
Banks, Dr Cyril, 153n
Bannerman, D.C., 175
Bennett, Alan, 26
Bevan MP, Aneurin, 150
Biggar, John, 111, 113, 133–4, 166–8
Birnie, William, 11
Blair, Graham, 149
Bonar, Andrew, 119
Bonar Law, Andrew, 89
Bonomy, Lord, 240
Boyd, Red Dr Donald, 221–3
Brodie, R.L., 164–5
Brodrick QC, Norman, 212
Brooks, Shirley, 49
Brown, J.T.T., 67–8, 70
Brunetti, Ludovico, 49
Buchan, W.P., 66, 82,
Buchanan, William, 96
Burke, William, 36
Bute, Marquess of, 63, 68–70, 262

Cameron MP, Sir Charles, 18, 52–5, 59–61, 63–5, 74–5, 86, 87, 89, 96, 111
Campbell, George, 55
Carrick, John, 40
Cattell, Cllr James, 221
Chadwick, Edwin, 34
Chalmers, James, 66, 67, 72–3, 76–80, 83, 96, 97, 98, 106–7, 111–12, 234, 261
Chalmers, Thomas, 14, 15–16, 39, 255
Chamberlain, Dr Clive, 240
Childers, Hugh, 57
Christie, Revd George, 102,
Clarke, E.F.C., 74–5
Clarke, Joan S., 148
Clements, Dr R.G., 153
Clink, Stuart, 179
Clouston, Sir Thomas, 96
Cockburn, Bailie, 171
Colville, Lord John, 207–8
Cooper, Lord Thomas Mackay, 123, 144
Cordiner, Thomas S, 170, 172, 181–2
Coutts, William, 85–6
Cranston, Sir Ross Frederick J., 246
Crawford, Alan, 26–7, 32
Critchell, Martin, 229–30
Cross MP, Richard, 57
Curl, James Stevens, 2, 28
Currell, A.J.M., 191

Dalgleish, T.D., 149
David, Bishop T.W., 138
Deane, Bishop Frederick W., 136, 138
Denny, Archibald, 103

Dewar, James, 136n, 141–6
Douglas, Campbell, 67, 73,
Drew, Jane, 190
Dryerne, Dr, 126
Dunvar, Sir John Greig, 200–1
Duncan, Dr Ebenezer, 59–76, 86, 96, 97, 254

Easson, Dan, 101–4, 113, 117–18, 124, 130, 136
Easson, Mrs J.D., 103, 117n, 145
Elliston MP, Sir George, 152,
Enlai, Zhou, 265
Ewing, James, 38
Eyre, Archbishop Charles Petre, 69

Farquharson MP, Robert, 18, 53, 61, 68, 86–90, 102,
Fenton, Dr James, 156
Fitzjames, Stephen, 52, 56

Gairdner, W.T., 40–1,
Garside, G.H., 171
George, Sir Ernest, 118
Ghai, Davendar, 246
Glaister Snr, Dr John, 62, 66, 76, 98, 111, 113, 133–4,
Glaister Jr, Dr John, 144, 157, 209
Glover, J.H., 198–200
Gorer, Geoffrey, 190
Gorini, Paolo, 61
Goven, Horace Arthur Rendel, 184
Gray, R.H., 121
Gray, T. Lindsay, 128

Hamilton, Duke of, 12
Hanham, Thomas, 51–2
Harcourt, Vernon, 53–7
Hardie, D.W., 134
Haden, Francis Seymour, 56, 61
Hardie, Kier, 81
Hardy, Thomas, 116
Hare, William, 36
Harrison, A.T., 193–4
Harrison, Bishop William, 84
Hart, Ernest, 49, 53, 65,

Harvard, Dr John, 210–12, 237
Hay, Dr Matthew, 110
Hay, Douglas RC, 183
Hendry, Mrs Elizabeth Haining, 73–4
Hoey, D.C., 67
Home, Earl of, 84
Hood, Dr W.D., 144, 153
Horder, Lord, 134
Houston, G.L., 71, 98,
Howat, Robert, 151–3, 157–8, 170–1, 203, 207
Howitt, Leonard, 182
Hunter, Revd John, 74–5

Inglis & Carr, 228

Jamieson, E.O.A., 105
John XXIII, Pope, 173
Jones, Cllr Revd Ceiron, 135–6
Jones, P. Herbert, 143, 149, 154

Ker, Miss Margaret, 96
Ker, T. Ripley, 71, 73, 132
Kerr, Dr Douglas, 157, 209,
Key, William, 62, 72–3, 77,
Knox, John, 9–10, 107, 260
Knox, Robert, 36
Kyd, J., 123

Labouchere, Henry, 55
Laming, Lord, 238
Littlejohn, Dr H.D., 41, 43–4, 68, 75, 101–2, 105, 198
Littlejohn, Harvey, 101,
Lorimer, Hew, 181
Lorimer, Sir Robert, 116–20, 125, 129
Lushington, Godfrey, 53–54

McDonald, Father John, 173
MacIntyre, J.G., 143
Mackay, Dr Harry, 142
McKenzie, Leslie, 94–5
McKim, J., 147
McKinnon MP, William, 34

Index of Names

MacLehose, W.J., 170, 170n
McLeod, Revd Dr Donald (Glasgow), 74
MacLeod, Revd Dr Donald (London), 106
MacLeod, K.M., 41–2
MacMillan, R.C., 147–9
Macpherson, Ewan, 94
Main, Revd William, 102
Maitland, James Steel, 129, 178
Mann, Harrington, 62,
Mann Snr, John, 62, 98
Mann Jr, (Sir) John (Edinburgh), 61–2, 68, 67–73, 83, 86, 94, 96–9, 121, 134
Mann, (Sir) John (Lanarkshire), 132–3, 163–6
Mar, Earl of, 12, 51,
Matthew, John Fraser, 117,
Millais, John, 49
Miller, Hugh, 14–15
Mitchell, Sir Peter Chalmers, 111,
Mitchell, Sydney, 99–100, 105
Mitchison MP, Gilbert
Nash, John, 233
Naughtie, James, 225
Noble, George A., 143, 144
Moore, John, 28
Morrison MP, Herbert, 151, 153
Murray, Sir David King, 143

Neuberger, Sigmund (The Great Lafayette), 99–100

Onslow, Earl of, 52
Otto, Rudolf, 256

Pacitto, Cosmo, 226
Parkes, Dr Edmund, 48
Pearce, Mrs J.D., 96
Pearson, Walter, 149
Penman, John, 192, 198–200
Pilkington, Cllr, 112–14
Playfair MP, Sir Lyon, 53, 55, 56, 68,
Potter, Robert, & Partners, 230–1
Price, Iesu Grist, 52

Price, Dr William, 24, 52, 55

Queensbury, Duke of, 12

Rae, Dr Harry, 134
Raithby, Cllr, 114, 116,
Reeves MP, Joseph, 158–9
Reiach, Alan and Robert Hurd, 175
Reid, Lord, 174
Reid, Lord James, 174
Reid, Thomas L, 147
Renshaw MP, Charles, 21, 89, 90
Richards, Charles, 100
Robertson, R.A., 73, 75, 86,
Robertson, Dr William, 101, 115, 125,
Robertson, Dr W.G. Aithchison, 100–1
Robinson, William, 52
Robson, Andrew, 76
Rollo, R. Leslie & Hall, 129
Rottenburg, Paul, 70
Rowell, Bishop Geoffrey, 27
Russell, John Burn, 27, 41, 66, 82, 93
Russell MP, T.W., 90

Salmon, Councillor, 40, 41
Salvesen, Lord Edward T, 104, 114–17, 124, 129, 141
Salvin, Harvey, 227
Sanger & Rothwell, 179, 188, 190, 225
Sergeant, W., 147n
Shaftesbury, Lord, 68
Smail, T.A., 94–5, 121, 144,
Smillie, Robert, 81
Smith, Professor George Adam, 84
Smith, Dame Janet 238
Smith, William Robertson, 251, 263
Spence, Sir Basil, 181, 198–202
Sprott, Revd George W., 47–8,
Steele, Alexander, 197, 199–201
Stenhouse, George Alexander, 224
Stewart, J.K., 192
Stewart MP, J.H., 163, 191
Stotesbury, H.W., 210–11
Strang, John, 38

Stride Treglown, 231–2
Strutt, Austin, 153, 157–8
Sutherland, Dr I.N., 144, 152–3
Swinburne-Hanham, J, 92n

Temple, Archbishop William, 149
Tenniel, John, 49
Thomas, Hugh, 28, 232–3
Thompson, Sir Henry, 49–50, 53, 94, 96
Thomson, W.N., & Co, 129
Tristram, Thomas Hutchison, 50,
Trollope, Anthony, 49
Troup, C.E., 91–2
Turner, Victor, 265–6
Tyler, Superintendent, 82

Vallance, J.M., 122–3
Voysey, C.F.A., 77

Walker, Dr Alexander, 101
Walker, George A., 54
Walker, Stanley, 145
Warburton, William, 37–8
Watson, John, 180
Watson, Sir Renny, 62, 72–3, 83,
Watt, Edward, 110–11, 134–6, 143, 254
Watt, William R., 164–5, 175–7
Watt, Revd T.D., 110
Webster, Professor, 153
Wells, Sir Thomas Spencer, 49, 52, 68, 89n
Westminster, Duke of, 70, 89,
White, Frederick Meadows, 50–51
Williams, Watkin, 51

Yeates, Alfred B., 112

General Index

Aberdeen, 13, 85–7, 95, 109–11, 134–8, 141–6, 219–20, 225–8
Aberdeen Crematorium Ltd, 128–9, 136, 138, 142, 146
Acts of Parliament (individual)
  Anatomy Act 1832, 36–7, 44–5, 88, 155n, 213, 237
  Burial Act, 1900, 90
  Burial and Cremation (Scotland) Act 2016, 244–6
  Burial Grounds (Scotland) Act 1855, 19, 21, 35, 40, 45, 59–60, 89, 90n, 197
  Burial Laws (Amendment) Act 1880, 51
  Cardiff Corporation Act 1894, 86n
  Cemetery Clauses Consolidation Act 1847, 20
  Certification of Death (Scotland) Act 2011, 22, 239

  Church of Scotland (Property and Endowments) Act 1925, 20, 114
  Church of Scotland (Property and Endowments) Amendment Act 1933, 20
  Clean Air Act 1956, 172
  Clean Air Act 1968, 235
  Corneal Grafting Act 1952, 155n
  Coroners and Justice Act 2009
  Cremation Act 1902, 20, 22, 23, 27, 87–91, 115, 121, 127n, 154, 159, 204–6, 208, 236, 241, 246
  Cremation Act 1952, 158–60, 204, 206, 208

  Edinburgh Improvement and Tramways Act 1896, 86
  Environmental Protection Act 1990, 28, 31, 216–17, 221
  Glasgow Police Amendment Act 1890, 88
  Glasgow Public Parks Act 1878, 42
  Government of Wales Act 2006, 22
  Greenock Corporation Order Confirmation Act 1952, 205–6
  Human Tissue Act 1961, 213, 237
  Human Tissue (Scotland) Act 2004, 237
  Infectious Diseases (Prevention) Act 1890, 88,
  Leamington Corporation Act 1896, 86n
  Local Government Act 1972, 208
  Local Government, Planning and Land Act 1980, 235
  Local Government (Scotland) Act 1894, 19–20
  Local Government (Scotland) Act 1929, 20
  Local Government (Financial Provisions etc.) (Scotland) Act 1962, 174
  Merchants House of Glasgow (Crematorium) Order Confirmation Act 1950, 205–6
  National Assistance Act 1948, 155
  National Health Service Act 1977, 238
  Poor Law Amendments Act 1844, 87

Acts of Parliament (*cont.*)
    Pollution Prevention and Control Act 1999, 22, 217, 236
    Public Health Act 1848, 19
    Public Health Act 1867, 20, 88
    Public Health Act 1875, 88
    Public Health (Scotland) Act 1897, 21, 87–8, 140
    Public Health Act 1936, 88
    Public Health (Interments) Act 1879, 207
    Registration of Births, Deaths and Marriages (Scotland) Act 1854, 18, 20–1, 45–6, 54, 130: Schedules H and I, 121
    Registration of Births and Deaths act 1874, 54
    Registration of Burials Act 1864, 54
    Registration of Stillbirths (Scotland) Act 1938, 123
    Scottish Board of Health Act 1919, 121
    Tribunals of Inquiry Evidence Act 1921, 238
Acts of Parliament, administration of, 21–3
Adams, Dr John Bodkin, trial of, 209–10
afterlife, beliefs about, 65, 74–5, 112, 136, 138, 219, 258–9, 260–1
    see also resurrection of the body
air-raids, 138,
altar, 27, 29, 128
angels, 80, 112, 263
architects, crematoria as challenge to, 26–8, 32
architectural traditions, Scottish, 174–5
    and the new social order, 175, 181
architecture, 261, 262–3
    challenges in first designs, 24–5, 35–6, 76–80
    principles of Scottish crematoria, 24–32
    and psychology, 178, 189, 227, 229
    search for a Scottish, 25
Armstrong, Dr Henry Rowse, trial of, 1922, 153

ashes, 53,
    burial of, 97–8, 99–100, 121,
    of children, 23
    cremation of, 23
    definition of, 240–1
    disposal of, 152–3, 240–1
    disposal of stillborn and non-viable foetuses, 239–40
    on River Crammond, 246
    recovery of, 239–40
    from successive cremations, separation of, 153
    of the stillborn, 23: unclaimed, disposal of, 132, 245
    symbolism of, 265–6
assisted dying, 270–1
Association of Crematorium Medical Referees, 209
Association of Municipal Corporations, 88, 158,

Baker Incorporation, 85
Barry Town Council, 235
bereavement, cultural responses to, 254–5, 260–1
Beveridge Report, 147
Biblical Criticism, 47
Bills (individual)
    Disposal of the Dead (Regulations) Bill 1884, 52–7, 64, 87
    Tunbridge Wells Improvement Bill 1889, 88
Board of Health, Scottish, 22
Board of Trade, 68–9, 155
Boards, parochial, 19
bodies, dead: *see* corpses
body, resurrection of, 4–5, 38, 48, 63–5, 74–5, 265
    changing attitudes to 136, 138, 173, 219
    decline of belief in, 136, 138, 259
body parts
    as clinical waste, 237
    cremation of, 237
    unlawful removal and retention of, 237

General Index

Books of Remembrance, 149, 179, 184, 202, 229
British Medical Association, 65, 88, 156–7, 202–3, 211–12
Brodrick Committee on Death Certification and Coroners, 209n, 212, 237, 239
burial, 5–6, 7–8, 9–32
 aisles, 11, 12, 264
 alive, fears of, 257–8
 animal, 100
 in Christian tradition, 26–7, 253
 closure of burial grounds, 40–4
 costs of, 102
 and the Disruption, 13
 documentation of, 20–1
 'earth to earth' system, 56, 61, 67, 89
 grounds, compulsory closure of, 19, 20
 intra-mural 10–11
 liturgy of, 9–16: revival of, 46–8
 meaning of, compared with 'inter', 87
 no previous LGBS responsibility, 90
 Orthodox Churches' support for, 264, 265
 premature, 50, 97–8
 in pre-Reformation Scotland, 9–10
 private regulation of, 245
 provision for, 8, 19–20
 Quaker 12–3
 reform, 12–17: compared with England and Wales, 34
 in Reformation Scotland 9–12, 15–17
 tradition, persistence of in Scotland, 107–8
 in unconsecrated ground, 100
 woodland, 6, 271
 see also churchyards; kirkyards
Burial and Cremation Review Group (Scotland) 2007, 236
Burial and Cremation law consolidation (Scotland) 159, 202–8
burial reform, 10, 12–7, 40–3, 147–8
 in Aberdeen, 109–11,

 comparison between Scotland and England and Wales, 34
 'earth to earth' system, 56, 61, 67, 89
 in Edinburgh, 42–3
 in Glasgow 40–2
 and funeral costs
 and NACCS *Memorandum*, 147–8
 and public health, 33–5, 60, 64, 77–8
 and Roman Catholic Church, 57–8
burial space
 legal provision for, 19–20
 shortage, 40–3
 and urbanisation, ??

Caledonian Cremation Company, 230
Calvinism, 8–9, 24
CAMEO (Crematoria Abatement of Mercury Emissions Organisation), 217
Canada, 47
cannibalism, legality of, 56
Cardiff, 86n
'carrier institutions', 3
Common law, 23
cases (legal)
 Bain v Seafield 1884, 20
 Fulton v Dunlop 1862, 10n
 Ghai v Newcastle City Council 2009, 2011, 245
 Heritors and Kirk-Session of South Leith v Scott 1832, 13: In re Kerr 1894, 87
 Kirk-Session and Heritors of Leith v Friendly Society of Restalrig 1831, 13
 Kirk-Session of Duddingston v Halyburton 1832, 13
 Lord Provost of Edinburgh v Kirk Session of St Cuthbert's 1874, 43
 McCreadie v McBroom, 22
 R v Dudley and Stephens, 56
 R v Price, 24, 52, 55
 R v Stephenson, 52, 55n
 Swan v Halyburton 1830, 13
 Williams v Williams, 51l
 Wright v Wallasey Local Board 1887, 205

catafalques, 28–30, 76–9, 82, 129, 200, 229, 233, 235, 264
   positioning of, 119–20, 125, 128, 129, 177, 181, 184, 190, 199
   see also coffins, committal of
Catholic Church, 4, 9–10, 12, 17, 60, 65, 113, 127, 133, 173–4, 182, 261–2, 271
   and cremation, 65, 68, 69–70, 173–4
   and Vatican ban, 57–8, 173–4
   see also Reformation; body, resurrection of
cemeteries (individual)
   Aberdeen, Allenvale, 109–10
   Aberdeen, Nellfield, 85–7
   Bristol, Arnos Vale, 130
   Edinburgh, Canongate, 42
   Edinburgh, Colinton, 193–4, 197
   Edinburgh, Dalby, 13, 43
   Edinburgh, Dean, 13, 105
   Edinburgh, Grange, 13–4, 16
   Edinburgh, Greyfriars, 42–3
   Edinburgh, Liberton, 193–4
   Edinburgh, Mortonhall, 196–8
   Edinburgh, Seafield, 129–30
   Edinburgh, St Cuthbert's, 43
   Edinburgh, Warriston, 13, 94, 105
   Glasgow, Castlemilk/The Linn, 169, 171
   Glasgow, Cathcart, 72
   Glasgow, Dalbeth, 60
   Glasgow, Eastwood, 96
   Glasgow, Gorbals, 42
   Glasgow Necropolis, 13, 38, 70–1, 166–9
   Glasgow, Piershill, 99–100
   Glasgow, St David's/Ramshorn, 42
   Glasgow, StMary's Cheapside, 42
   Glasgow, Sandymount, 60, 72
   Glasgow, Southern Necropolis, 13, 60, 169
   Glasgow, Western, 72–3, 82–3
   Inverness, Kilvean, 221
   Inverness, Tomnahurich, 221
   Johnston, 97
   Lanark, Murray Memorial Chapel, 164
   Leith, Seafield, 128, 129
   Oldham, Hollinwood, 188, 190
   Paisley, Woodside, 129
   Paris, Pere La Chaise, 38
   Paris, Les Innocents, 80
   Stockholm, Woodland, 201
cemeteries, 13
   'lawn' model, 147–8
   private, 13–17, 34–5, 38–9, 60–2, 68, 72, 82–3, 138
Central Board of Health, 37
Central Price Regulation Committee, 155
Ceylon, 47
chapels 17, 21, 26, 40–1, 42–3, 76–80, 105, 119–20
   of Remembrance, 25, 118–19, 164, 181, 183, 186, 192, 198, 201
China, 265
cholera epidemic 33–5, 37–8, 42–3
   burials, 43
   medical responses to, 48
   riots 37
Church of England
   Convocation debates on cremation 1942–4, 126, 144, 149
   Funeral and Burial Reform Association, 89
Church of Scotland, 12, 109
   ministers willing to preside at crematoria, 83–4
   General Assembly decision on graveside liturgies (1897), 47–8, 83, 107
   and loss of authority in death, 38–9, 44–6, 109
   and registration responsibility, 44–6
Church Service Society, 47–8
churches (individual)
   Coventry Cathedral, 198, 202
   Notre Dame du Haut, Ronchamps, 202
   St Giles' Cathedral, 104
   St Columba's, Pont Street, London, 106
   Westminster Abbey, 104, 116

General Index

churchyards
  and class structure, 11–12
  closure of, 19–20, 40–1, 43
  see also kirkyards
Clements, Dr Robert George, suicide of, 153
clergy, 17
  and funeral reform, 126, 136
  and war-time funerals, 109–10
coffins, 11, 15, 85, 97, 141–6, 152–3, 217, 222
  committal of, 29–30, 78–9, 82, 149, 178, 190, 192, 222, 264
  see also catafalque
coffin cords, 78–9, 193
coffin roads, 38
coffin routes, 30–2
columbaria, 25
Convention of the Protection of the North-East Atlantic (OSPAR), 217
Co-operative Wholesale/Retail societies, 111, 178, 217
coroners, 54, 82, 94
corpses, 9–10, 18–9, 24, 28, 54–5, 110–11, 147
  attitude towards, 49–50, 141–6, 256, 258, 265, 270
  and disgust, 255–6
Council for the Disposal of the Dead (CCD), 134
Coutts, William, trial of, 85–6
cremation, 4–5
  alternatives to: promession, 245; resomation, 245, 272: reverse polymerisation, 245; sublimation, 245
  application for, 91: independent verification of applications, 95, 154, 159–60; meaning of, 241–2
  arguments against, 62–3
  arguments for, 59–61, 63–5, 76–80, 93, 101–2, 110–11, 114–17, 136, 138, 221–3
  of body parts, 237
  certification, *see* cremation certification
  in China, 265

churches' attitudes to, 17, 263, 264, 266–7
  as cleansing, 255–6
  Code of Practice, 151–2, 156: 'Instructions for Funeral Directors', 152
  Council of Great Britain, 150, 154, 158
  deceased's wishes, 91, 155, 213
  definition of, 245
  'dual sovereignty' symbolism of, 268–70
  duration of, 145
  (England and Wales) Regulations 2008, 23
  first in Scotland, 73–4
  and foetal remains, 240
  and forensic issues, 56, 61, 94
  in Hungary, 262
  in India, 4
  Jewish attitudes to, 269
  legal opinions on, 50–2
  legality of, early attempts, 18, 21, 50–1
  medical certificates, false completion of, 237
  of non-viable foetuses, 239–40
  opposition to, 221–3
  as paradigm of modernity, 256–7, 267–8
  of persons in Scotland dying abroad, 132
  pyres, 140, 206, 245
  reform, 146
  Regulations 1903, 23, 91–5, 139–60
  Regulations 1914, 1920, 1925, 1927, 121
  Regulations 1952, 158–60
  Regulations 1965, 209–13
  Regulations (Scotland) 1927, 22
  Regulations (Scotland) 1935: drafts, 92–3, 120–4, 131–2; inspection, 144, 148, 151, 154; reports to Secretaries of State on operation of, 132; Working Party on, 209–13
  Regulations (Scotland) 1967, 209–13: Amendment Regulations 2000, 237; (Scotland) Amendment Regulations 2003, 237

cremation (*cont.*)
   of remains buried for more than one year, 91, 140
   in Russia, 264–5
   and Scottish law, 18
   societies, 95: *see* Cremation Society of Great Britain; Edinburgh Cremation Society; Scottish Burial Reform and Cremation Society
   statistical tables showing progress of, 137, 162, 185, 215
   of stillborn children, 92, 239–43
   symbolism of, 264–6
   unidentified remains, 91, 187–213
   in war time, 139–41: Circular 1779, 139–40; Circular DP2, 139–40; Defence Regulation 30, 140, 144; Memorandum 222, 139
   of the wrong body, 99–100
cremation certification, 74, 78, 91–2, 94
   abolition of, 239
   fees for, 94, 156–8, 202–4, 209
   medical certificates: abolition of, 155, 212, 237–9; false completion of, 142n, 237; fees for, 154–6, 202–4, 212; qualifications of doctors supplying, 91–2, 95, 131; registration, 130–1; Safford Committee on, 155
   right to inspect, 239
Cremation Society of Great Britain (CS) 19, 49–52, 57, 59, 67, 74n, 87–8, 91, 92, 96, 140, 142–3, 150, 155, 158, 165, 205, 209, 227, 239
   founding Declaration of (1874), 49
   split with FBCA, 150
   and Price Trial (1884), 50–7
crematoria (individual)
   Aberdeen, Kaimhill, 31, 128–9, 134–8, 141–6, 154, 219–20
   Aberdeen, Hazelhead, 31, 219–20, 225–8, 243
   Ayr, Masonhill, 31, 163, 183–4
   Blackley, 182–3, 199, 202
   Cardross, 31, 163, 180–1
   Clydebank, 31, 163, 184–6
   Darlington, 143
   Dundee, 31, 128, 135
   Dunfermline, 31, 163, 224–5
   Durham, 235
   Edinburgh, Mortonhall, 31, 163, 198–202, 239–40, 267
   Edinburgh, Seafield, 31, 129–30
   Edinburgh, Warriston, 30, 31, 114–20, 124–7, 141, 144, 153, 171–2
   Falkirk, 31, 163, 191–2
   Friockheim, 32, 222, 228–9, 230
   Glasgow, Craigton, 31, 170, 178
   Glasgow, Daldowie, 31, 132–3, 138, 163–6, 175–8, 180, 264
   Glasgow, The Linn, 31, 42, 169–73, 181–3
   Glasgow, Maryhill, 30, 31, 67, 72–80, 81–3, 95–100, 106–7, 111–12, 113, 125–6, 133–4, 144, 264
   Golders Green, 118, 145
   Greenock, 31, 163, 179–80, 183
   Holytown, 32, 230
   Houndwood, 30, 32, 228, 233–4, 236
   Inverness, 32, 220–3, 229
   Irvine, 32, 229–30
   Kirkcaldy, 29, 31, 163, 179, 187–91
   Livingstone, 32, 231–2
   Manchester, 67, 77
   Melrose, Borders, 32, 233
   Milton Keynes (Crownhill), 232
   Moray, 30, 32, 228
   Northampton, 177
   Oldham, 29
   Paisley, 31, 152
   Perth, 31, 163, 192–3
   Reading, 177
   Rouchan Loch, Dumfries, 32
   Sittingbourne, 28
   South Lanarkshire, Blantyre, 231–2
   Telford, 28
   Woking, 50, 51, 52, 83, 91, 142, 145

General Index

crematoria
  architectural challenge of, 27–30, 266–8
  architectural principles of, 24–32
  building, three Scottish phases of, 31–2
  as new building type, 24, 27
  as paradigm of modernity, 24
  canopies, 182, 183, 226, 227
  chapels, 76–7, 105, 119–20: design of, 175–6, 177, 193
  Chapels of Remembrance, 25, 118–19, 164, 181, 183, 186, 192, 198, 201
  chimneys, 28: design of, 28, 177–9, 225
  columbaria, 72, 75, 112, 125: absence of, 165, 171
  costs, 72–3, 119, 164, 165, 167–8, 170, 172, 174–5, 183, 188, 198–9, 200, 202, 220, 221, 222
  design of, *see* crematorium design
  dedication of, 74–5, 125, 136, 138
  definition of, 123, 91–5, 205, 208, 245
  Gardens of Remembrance, 25, 118–19, 183, 188, 190, 192, 201, 226, 230
  Halls of Remembrance, 193
  inspection of, 144, 242–3
  Investment Company, 230
  as landscape for mourning, 25, 26, 32, 180, 183–4, 189, 191, 192, 230–1, 234–5, 269–70
  legal approval for sites, 22
  materials, local and Scottish, 177, 192, 225–6, 229
  and memorials, 112, 126, 134
  as memorials to the dead, 171, 176
  music, 82, 98–9, 111, 120, 126–7, 166, 222
  opposition to, 221–3, 233
  ownership of, 31–2, 138,
  as paradigm of modernity, 24, 256–7, 267–8
  patronage, 31–2, 128–30, 138, 180: revival of, 224, 228–33; *see also* cemeteries, private
  patterns of Scottish building of, 31–2, 106–7
  porte-cochere: design of, 129, 178
  Room of Remembrance, 182–3
  Scottish development of, 24–32, 224, 228–33: and Scottish identity, 24–32, 174–5, 180, 234–5
  siting of, 71–2, 114–19, 162–3, 166–73, 194–7: approval of sites and plans, 27–8, 154, 158, 162–3, 235; approval transfer from MH to MLGP 1951, 205; in cemetery, 184, 192; separate from cemeteries, 6, 83, 149, 177–8
  as symbol of social change, 25
  windows, 80, 82, 98,120, 126, 134, 188, 190, 193, 200, 227
crematorium design, 24–5, 27, 28, 72–3, 76–80, 106–7, 111–12, 125, 128–30, 134, 164–5, 198–200, 228–235
  as challenge to architects, 266–8
  conversions: cemetery chapel, 119, 188, 233–4; church, 119, 228, 231, 233–4; estate, 118–20, 133, 179, 192–3; house, 118–20, 125
  cremators, design of, 61–2, 73, 76–80, 240
  criticisms of, 26, 30, 98, 198–202, 205, 230, 233
  and emotional challenge, 29–30
  open chapel model, 188, 190, 225
  opposition to, 221–3
  Scotland's attitude to, compared with English, 234–5
  siting, *see under* crematoria
  styles: Art Deco, 129; Beaux-Arts, 175, 180, 182; Classical, 117, 130, 176–7; Domestic, 229–30; Gothic, 72, 78; Lombard Romanesque style, 77, 128; Modernist, 129, 174, 181–2, 224–8; Scandinavian, 179; Vernacular, 228–33
  two-chapel, 164, 171, 175–6, 179, 182, 198, 226, 229
  use of water, 182, 184, 231

death
  in air raids, 139–41
  certificates, 18, 54
  and demographic change, 214, 216, 218

death (*cont.*)
  and emotions, 255–60
  grants, 149, 156
  place of, 214, 216
  place, concept of, 266–8
  registration, *see* registration of death
  theology of, 250–2
Directory for the Publike Worship of God 1645, 12
Delegated Powers and Law Reform Committee (2016), 244
Department of Health for Scotland, 22, 139, 141, 144–6, 148–9, 151, 153, 155, 161–5, 170–3, 180, 186, 194–6, 202–4, 206–7, 210
Departmental Committee on Death registration and Coroners, 212
Dewar, James, trial of, 141–6
Dignity PLC, 230
disgust, 255–6
Dissection, 35–37, 230–1; *see also* Anatomy Act 1832
Disruption, The (1843), 13, 16, 44, 46: and the private cemetery movement, 14–17, 44
'dual sovereignty', symbolism of, 268–70

Edinburgh, 39–40, 42–3, 114–17, 130–1
  as an architectural statement, 117
  Easter Warriston, estate and house, 114–16, 119, 125,
  Scottish National War memorial, 116, 118–19
Edinburgh Cremation Society (ECS), 74n, 94, 100–6, 114–17
Edinburgh Crematorium Company/Ltd, 124–5, 127–8
Edinburgh City Council, 42–3, 114–16, 193–202
Edinburgh Zoo, 117
Encyclopedia of Cremation (2005), 2
environment
  challenge to cremation, 22, 172, 216–17, 231

cost to Local Authorities, 216–17
Environmental Protection Act, *see under* Acts of Parliament (individual)
Episcopal Church, Scottish, 12, 17, 83–4, 127, 127n, 136, 138

Federation of British [afterwards Burial] Cremation Authorities, 111, 146, 149, 151–2, 158, 177, 209, 217, 236
  split with CS, 150
  see also Cremation Council of Great Britain
First Book of Discipline, The (1560), 10, 11, 46
First World War, 96, 106, 109–10, 147
folklore, 5, 38, 251
Forbes, Alick, trial of, 142
forensic concerns, 61
The forme of prayers (1556), 9–10
Free Church of Scotland (FCS) 13, 14–17
Free Presbyterian Church of Scotland (FPCS), 221–3, 249
Freemasonry, 41, 48, 52, 57–8, 79, 106, 262
Friendly Societies, 36–7
funeral directors
  and acquisitions, 217
  and the EPA, 217
  post-WWII developments, 150
  and problems with ashes, 244
  see also National Association of Funeral Directors
funerals
  cholera, 37
  costs, 49, 96, 102, 127, 146, 149, 165–6, 167–8
  Humanist, 6
  reform, 109–11, 146
  secularisation of, 218–19, 223
  sermons, 3, 12
  silent, 5–6, 261–2, 263–4
  and social status, 11–12, 35–8
  superstitious elements of, 9, 16
  traditional Presbyterian, 38–9, 109–11, 221–2

General Index

transport, 27–8, 111, 172–3, 191, 197; *see also* funeral routes
funeral rituals, 3–4, 9–12, 38, 107, 126–7, 147–8, 150, 177–8, 218, 221–2, 251–3, 254–5, 261–3
    and biography, 260–1
    cultural resources for, 254–5, 260–1
    dignity, concept of, 270
    negotiation of, 249–50
    revival of, 17, 46–8
    silent, 5–6, 263–4; *see also* funerals, traditional Presbyterian
    symbolism of, 4–6
funeral routes, 25, 28–9, 82, 107, 109–10, 150, 177–8, 191

Gardens of Remembrance: *see under* crematoria
gender
    and afterlife beliefs, 258–9
    and disposal, 257–8
General Medical Council, 142n, 238
General Register Office (GRO), 121, 130
    functions transferred to SBH, 121n
Glasgow 38, 40–2, 112–14, 127, 169–73, 181–3, 257–9
    Barony Parochial Board, 88
    Kilbowie, 112–14, 134, 135
    Merchants House, 38, 70–1, 167–9, 205–6
    Philosophical Society of, 59–63, 66, 76–8
Glasgow Parish Council, 88
Glasgow Royal Infirmary, 41, 60, 77
Glasgow Herald, 75, 86
Govan Poor House, 88
graves, common 14, 60, 63, 85
    re-use of, 219
Great Southern Group PLC, 221, 230

hearses, 12, 15
heritors, 19
Heriot Trust, 105
Home Department, Secretary of State for, 19, 22
power to suspend or modify the Cremation Regulations, 92, 139–60
Home Office, 50, 51, 89–90, 123, 141, 151, 155, 159, 203, 209–10, 238
    Departmental Committee to draft Cremation Regulations 1903, 91
    Departmental Committee to report on death certification and coroners (Brodrick Committee), 212
'human remains', 23, 57–8
    definition of, 122–4, 241–4
    disposal of, after cremation, 239–43
    see also ashes; corpses
Hungary, 262

Imperial War Graves Commission, 147, 176, 182
incineration, hospital, 122–3
identity
    and belief, 251–3
    and death, 251
    and funeral rituals, 251
    and hope, 252–3
industrial assurance, 37, 147
Infant Cremation Commission, 240
India 4
Institute of Burial and Cremation Administration (IBCA), 146n; *see also* National Association of Cemetery and Crematorium Superintendents (NACCS)
Institute of Cemetery and Crematorium Management (ICCM), 240–1
Interdepartmental Committees on Cremation Regulations, 1945–50, 151–8, 209–10
Interdepartmental Working Party on death certification and authorisation of burials and cremation, 238
International Cremation Federation (ICF), 173
Ireland, 90
Islam, 250

Italy, 4

kirkyards, 12–14, 15–16
  Kirk's loss of control of 12, 16
  see also cemeteries

Labour Government, 148, 187
Labour Party, 109, 114–15, 164
Lambeth Borough Council, 235
Lanarkshire County Council, 132–3, 135, 163–6
landscape, *see* crematoria as landscape for mourning
Leamington, 85n
legal cases, *see* cases (legal)
legal system, Scottish, 17–24
Leith, 129–30
Leith, The Cemetery and Crematorium Co, 129–30
Leverhulme Trust, The, 2, 8
liturgy, *see under* burial
Local Government
  as agent for cremation, 64
  empowerment to provide crematoria (Scottish), 243
  monopoly on crematoria provision, 148, 159
  power to build crematoria, 88, 89, 158
  proposals for its building crematoria, 86, 95–6, 103, 104, 110–11, 112–14, 132–3, 134–5, 147–8, 163–6, 169–73, 176, 194–8, 221–3
  withdrawal from building crematoria, 228–35
Local Government Board for England and Wales, 22
Local Government Board for Scotland (LGBS), 22, 90, 92
  functions transferred to SBH, 121n

Mackay, Dr Harry, trial of, 142n
Medical Officers of Health, 35, 40–1, 42–3, 55, 78, 93, 100–1, 110, 114–16, 125, 155, 211, 211n
  Society of, 157
medical certificates, *see under* cremation certification
medical examiners, 239
Medical Referees, 91–2
  appointment of, 91, 131–2
  functions of, 91, 132, 209
  power to dispense with cremation certificates, 92–3
  qualifications of, 91–2
memorial industry, cremation as a challenge to, 87
memorialisation, 149
Ministry of Health (MH), 139, 144, 150–1, 155
Ministry of Housing and Local Government (MHLG), 212
Ministry of National Insurance, 156–7
Mortonhall Investigation Report, 240
mourning wear, 11–12

narrative, 248–9
National Association of Cemetery and Crematorium Superintendents, *Memorandum on Planning for Post-War Reform in the Disposition of the Dead*, 147–9
  Scottish Branch, 142, 146–9, 147n
National Association of Funeral Directors, 146
  Scottish Branch of, 145, 150
National Association of Parish Councils, 207
National Association for the Promotion of Social sciences, 56
National Health Service (NHS), 154, 187
National Infant Cremation Committee, 242–3
Nellfield burial scandal, 85–7
Noble, George A., 143–4

OSPAR (Oslo-Paris) Convention for the Protection of Marine Environment of the North-East Atlantic, 217

General Index

Orthodox Churches, attitudes to cremation, 263, 264–5

Paisley, 149
Paisley Cemetery Company, 129
Parochial Boards, 19
Perth, 150
Philosophical Society of Glasgow, 59–63, 66, 76–8
Poor Law, 44–5
Pope Leo XIII, 57–8
Pope Pius IX, 57
prayers for the dead, 9–10, 15, 47–8, 107, 109, 253–4
precious metals, recovery and disposal after cremation, 152, 241
predestination, 253–4, 260
Privy Council, 19
procurators fiscal, 92
Proprietary Crematoria Association, 151, 154
Provisional Orders, 167, 179, 205–6
purgatory, 9

Quakers, 12

Radius clause (Cremation Act 1902 s.5), 20, 27, 89, 115, 158–9, 167, 179, 195, 204–8, 235, 244–5
Reformation, Scottish, 2, 5, 9–12, 15, 219, 249, 253–4, 261–2
Registrar General, 21, 123
Registration, campaign to reform, 44–6
registration of death, 18–19, 45–6, 54, 89, 237–9
  England and Wales, 17, 18–19, 139–40
  House of Commons Select Committee on (1893), 18, 89
  and public health, 33–5
  Scotland, 18–19, 45–6, 139–40; not required before burial, 139–40
registration of stillbirths, 122–3
religious symbolism, 79–80
Report on the Sanitary Condition of Edinburgh, 43

Resomation, 272
Resurrection Men, 35–6
Roman law, 23–4
Russia, 5, 264–5

sacred, concept of, 10
Safford Committee on Medical Certificates, 155
Sanitary Commission 1859, 50, 60,
Sanitary Society of Edinburgh, 100–1
Schedule 'H', 20–1
'Scheme of Cremation' for Glasgow, 76–7
Scotland Act 1998, 22
Scottish Board of Health, 22, 121, 144
  Secretary of, 121
Scottish Borders Council, 236
Scottish Burial Reform and Cremation Society (SBRCS) (later Scottish Cremation Society), 4, 18, 44, 65–80, 81, 86, 88, 89, 93, 121, 131, 165, 166–8
  charitable status of, 168n, 174
  founding of, 65–9
  funding issues, 81, 96–7
  name change, 174
  'not for profit' principle, 67–9, 116, 127, 168, 174
Scottish Environmental Protection Agency, 236
Scottish Home Department, 154
Scottish Home and Health Department, 208
Scottish ministers, 22
Secretary for Scotland, 22, 89, 90, 93
Scottish Office, 90, 121, 123, 144
Second World War, 139–41, 150
Secretary of State for Scotland, 22, 55, 89, 90, 164, 167, 169, 195–6, 207, 224
  power to suspend or modify the Cremation Regulations, 141
secularity 189–90, 219, 223, 249–50, 260–1

Seddon, Frederick Henry and Margaret Ann, trial of, 1912, 153
Siemens, 61, 62, 73
Shipman, Dr Harold
   audit of clinical practice, 238
   trial of in 2000, 237–8
Shipman Inquiry, Third Report, Death Certification and the Investigation of Death by Coroners, 238
social class, 10–11, 13, 14, 36–7, 44–5, 57–8, 63–5, 76–7, 127, 250
stillbirths, 22–3, 241–2
   cremation of stillborn children, 92, 122–4
   disposal of, 156
   registration of, 122–3
spiritualism, 5, 109
subordinate legislation, 22

Turkey, 47

undertakers, undertaking, 39–40; *see also* funeral directors
Unitarian Church, 135

Vatican Council, the Second, 57–8, 69; *see also* Catholic Church

Waddington, Nurse Dorothea Nancy, trial of, 1936, 153n
Wandsworth Borough Council, 235
wars
   Crimean, 44, 48
   First World, 96, 106, 109–10, 147
   Second World, 139–41, 150
Westerleigh PLC, 231–2
Weymouth Borough Council, 235
worldviews, 6